THE WILL TO WIN

The Story of Biodun Shobanjo

THE WILL TO WIN

The Story of Biodun Shobanjo

DOTUN ADEKANMBI

Havilah | PRWox

LAGOS. NIGERIA

Cover Design+Photo Layout: Ibeabuchi Ananaba
Page Layout designs: Olumide Femi Ayeni, *(St.Lumize Arts & Ideas) Lagos*
Cover Photo: Aham Ibeleme
Photo Credits: Unless otherwise credited, all photos are from Biodun Shobanjo's collection.
Every effort has been made to identify copyright holders; in case of oversight, and on
notification to the publisher, corrections will be made in the next edition

Published in 2019 by:

Havilah Books
The Villa, 2, Allen Avenue, Akin-Taylor Estate, Ikeja, Lagos
Email: info@havilahgroup.ng
www.havilahgroup.ng
Tel: +234 8037020780

in association with:

Strategic PRWox
Email: info@strategicprwox.com
www.strategicprwox.com
Tel: +234 7034751365

Printed by:
Masar Printing & Publishing LLC
Dubai U.A.E
Ph + 971 50 873 0904
Email: jay.singh@masarprint.com

Visionaries are possessed creatures,
men and women in the thrall of belief so powerful
that they ignore all else – even reason – to ensure that
reality catches up with their dreams.
(*Preface to Time International's* **Man of the Year 1991**: *CNN's Ted Turner*)

Unless people understand the dream,
they cannot act the dream

Biodun Shobanjo

Especially for my brother
Abayomi Adekanmbi,
the amazingly selfless brother who remains my 'father'.

Contents

Acknowledgements

A great number of the people and organisations that helped to make this project possible would probably have forgotten the part they played in it. That is because I spent an incredibly long time to complete it. Whilst I still clearly remember everyone who contributed to the success of this effort, including those who craved anonymity, I plead that I be forgiven if I have unwittingly left anyone out.

Direct quotes are attributed to individuals that I spoke with while gathering materials for the book. As much as possible, too, I have acknowledged all secondary sources – books, newspapers, magazines and the Internet. I take responsibility for the accuracy or otherwise of information whose sources could not readily be identified or whose sources requested anonymity.

Mr Biodun Shobanjo made this book happen. Great life. Undeniable accomplishments. Beautiful story.

'Baale' Jimi Awosika listed four parameters for appraising a book, namely: faithfulness to historical facts; logic/readability; accuracy of names/places and the ultimate intention/reader's take-out. The publication of this book probably meant I did not do too badly on all counts. Sir Richard Ibe, I am sure, can no longer pick me out in a crowd but I enjoyed and still greatly value his contributions.

The matriarch of the Shobanjo family, late Madam Morin Shobanjo, spoke with characteristic candour and motherly affection. Mrs Joyce Shobanjo, Mr. Babatunde Shobanjo, Ms Funke Shobanjo, Mr. Olufemi Shobanjo, Mr. Abimbola Shobanjo and Dr. (Mrs) Dolapo Obuaya (nee Shobanjo) were wonderful in sharing knowledge and experience of the head of their family.

Dolapo twice proof-read the final manuscript, not minding the inconvenience of once doing so at Christmas. Few details escaped her eagle eyes and she quite easily simplified complex thoughts with the precision of her engineering background. Her intervention deeply enriched the quality of the book you now hold. 'Thank You' does not adequately capture my appreciation of her exemplary contribution.

Messrs Festus Akinlade, Victor Johnson, Funmi Onabolu, Osar Emokpae, Steve Omojafor, Dele Adetiba, Chris Doghudje, Allan Ola-Olabode, Babu Akinbobola, Lolu Akinwunmi, Kola Ayanwale and Yakubu Akor (one-time Head, Corporate Affairs, NICON) as well as Chief Oladele Fajemirokun, Mrs. Nike Alabi and Mrs. Biola Ayimonche all helped me to make sense out of the welter of information at my disposal. Mr. Faysal Halabi, Dr. Jide Oluwajuyitan, Mr. Segun Olaleye, Alhaji Garba Kankarofi, Mr. John Momoh, Omooba Sam Ogundogba and Chief Steve Ojo shared very deep personal and professional insights. The late Messrs Sylvester Moemeke (The Source) and Sesan Ogunro made interviewing an absolute delight.

'Mummy O': That's the inimitable Mrs Gloria Omoregie, Personal Assistant to Mr Shobanjo. She asked me a simple but extraordinarily challenging question when I proposed this book: 'are you sure you can do what you are suggesting?' I hope I have creditably answered the question? Thanks for the encouragement and the gentle but firm chiding: 'Dotun, quickly finish this thing now.'

My very wonderful teachers: Prince Bayo Adeniran and Chief (Mrs) Moni Adeniran (my English Language and English Literature teachers at Ekiti Parapo College, Ido Ekiti); Mr Lawrence Oni (one-time Deputy Director of Information in the Ministry of Information of the old Ondo State) and Mr Bayo Onanuga (Editor-in-Chief of TheNEWS magazine) all have one thing in common: a commitment to excellence. Two of them laid the foundation of my communication skill; another taught me that hard/smart work is the only godfather that any true professional needs; yet another demonstrated dissatisfaction with any effort that was less than perfect. The highly cerebral Ms Benedicta Upaa Ayede (former Managing Director of The Quadrant Company) taught me that self-confidence is a by-product of applying knowledge and doing one's best in every circumstance. I am grateful for all the lessons.

Dr. Yemi Ogunbiyi read every page and marked every sentence and paragraph like the very good teacher that he is. The foreword he wrote is a lucid masterpiece by an inimitable essayist. Lanre Idowu skilfully wielded an editor's scalpel to keep the work on track. Ibe Ananaba and Olumide Ayeni added a creative touch of class that is evident in the book's look and feel. Mrs. Olasheni Orimogunje made indexing look easy. Sylvester Atere provided strong support in interviewing sources.

Omolara Oshinuga, Efesa Origbo and Sayo Akinwale gave me excellent perspectives on the Troyka Management Trainee Programme.

My former colleagues at Troyka: Paul Olaleye, Olumide Olayinka, Olakanmi Amoo-Onidundu, Kayode Oluwasona and Ishola Jegede helped to unlock critical group dynamics that helped me to better understand the business and the man.

Senator Babafemi Ojudu, Kunle Ajibade, the late Bayo Oguntuase, Taiwo Obe, Tosin Ajirire, Wale Alabi, Sola Ogunfuwa, Wale Motajo, Yomi Seriki and Tayo Odunlami never gave me rest until the last full stop was in place.

Messrs Tola Lapite, Hafiz Bakare, Adeolu Ogundare, Biodun Fagbohun, Bisi Iyaniwura, Akin Olaniyan, Abayomi Aluko, Isaac Okorafor, Harry Willie Nnanke, Chief Michael Olorunfemi, Air Commodore Kolawole Alimi (rtd), Olutoba Ojo and Kayode Tonade surprised me beyond measure with their generosity and a refreshing ability to listen and share experiences in a world where most people just love to hear their own voices. My big 'Egbon,' Ogbeni Lanre Adesuyi a.k.a. Havilah, never stopped being a 'solution centre.'

Bolaji Aina, Kunle Akintola, Bolaji Okusaga, Yinka Olasusi, Kunle Ogunniran, Soji Tehingbola, Toyin Arogundade, Soji Faboro, Niyi Adeleye, Ojo Sanni, John Kunu, Tive Denedo, Davis Iyasere, Biodun Raufu, Joke Obe, Stephen Dada, Ifeoma Okafor, Steve Ilo, Ajibike Afolami, Segun Babalola, Jonah Iboma and Engr. Dele Agbeyo came through for me at very difficult periods when forward movement became almost impossible.

Mrs Segun Oredugba is a class act: quietly efficient, charming and quite firm. Ebere Keku; Pat Akpederi and Tinu Ajidagba assisted immensely by simply doing their jobs so diligently, especially during Insight's days at Akanbi Onitiri Street, Surulere, Lagos. Mr Shobanjo's personal staff - Humphrey Zikenah, Sina Ogundipe and Adamu Abubakar – always made the task of seeing their principal very pleasant, genuinely warm and sincere.

My wonderful Mum, Abigail Adesipe Adekanmbi (1920 – 2000); loving brother, Dr. Oladipo Ebenezer Adekanmbi (1955 – 2001) and positively unforgettable friends, Olufemi Akinwumi Oludare (1963 – 1992) and Kayode Atere (1961 – 1997) all believed, cared and shared, right until their last breath.

While rounding off work on this book, I had the good luck of meeting and working closely with the former Head of State and Commander-in-Chief of the Armed Forces of the Federal Republic of Nigeria, General Dr. Yakubu Gowon, GCFR. He gave me valuable insight into one of the key policies of his administration, which, incidentally, helped to clear the path for the upward thrust of Shobanjo's extraordinary career.

Special thanks to my wife, Alaba, who endured the torture of my littering the house with audio recording devices, books, magazines and clippings.

My lovely children: Omotola, Oluwafisayomi, Toluwanimi and Oluwaferanmi, often wondered why an 'ordinary' laptop should suddenly become such a forbidden object after my first computer, which contained the original manuscript, crashed. Here is your answer.

I did not start this project with a definite time table for its completion. All I wanted to do was learn. But I believe this is the appointed time for the publication of the book. I, therefore, owe the Almighty God a heavy debt of gratitude for making this possible despite my chronic procrastination; the proverbial writer's block and, when it was least expected, my heartbreaking experience with technology.

Foreword

Biographies in their barest forms are, like histories, subjective constructions of reality. But the finest biographers, again, not unlike historians, constantly strive for a balance in presenting a given reality, a balance between what seems obvious and that which is not easily discernible. That struggle for balance derives essentially from the fact that every given reality is complex and often times, multi-faceted. It is the achievement of such balance in the presentation of facts and details that sets a brilliant biography apart from the others. Dotun Adekanmbi's account of Mr. Biodun Shobanjo's life, *The Will to Win,* belongs, in my view, to the category of well-written biographies.

From the beginning, the author sets out to tell a simple story, that of one man's unusual rise from his early beginnings to the pinnacle of his profession. But as the story unfolds, it soon becomes clear that our subject is not as simple as we thought! Although the son of a modest Weighbridge Superintendent of the old Nigeria Railways Corporation, his grandfather, Chief Moses Towolawi Shobanjo was the Oluwo of Okun-Owa, while his mother is the granddaughter of the first Chief Imam of Aiyepe. Gradually, the author takes us through the journey of Shobanjo's life from his birth in Jebba, through his early education in Jebba, Zaria, and Lagos, to high school at Odogbolu and his earliest jobs, first, briefly at the Department of

Customs, but eventually as a Studio Manager at the old Nigerian Broadcasting Corporation (NBC) in 1964. In the process, the author also traces some of the influences that shaped Shobanjo's eventual rise, but none more than the combined effort of his father and his first high school principal at Odogbolu Grammar School, Mr. Victor George Chinwah, who both gave him a boundless self-confidence and a life-long anchor in Christian religious faith. By the time he left the Nigerian Broadcasting Corporation (NBC), through Grant Advertising, to set up what was to become Insight Communications in 1979, he was only 35!

What comes across, again and again, in Adekanmbi's account is a unique story of an obsessively focused and committed Chief Executive, with a consuming passion for excellence. From the many examples the author provides us with, it is clear that Shobanjo is an unusual manager of people. But more than managing people and inspiring them, Shobanjo also knows how to manage himself. He did not just demand the best of his staff and colleagues; he set standards that inspired them. Whether as the Managing Director of Insight Communications or as Chairman of Troyka Holdings or as the President of the Association of Advertising Practitioners of Nigeria (AAPN), or even as the Chief Executive Officer (CEO) in the famous television series, The Apprentice Africa, he was constantly proactive, driven always by the passion to excel. Being also, forever, knowledge-driven, Shobanjo knew that being a manager was an ongoing experience; for, not only was he always willing to learn new rules and rapidly adapt to change, he was willing to unlearn and discard old precepts that no longer worked. And like all good managers, he also knew when to quit.

And then the author, in his strive for balance and objectivity, provides us with a flip side to the enviable reputation of his subject, reminding us in the process that Shobanjo is not an embodiment of perfection. Quite apart from unearthing some of the controversies that surrounded Shobanjo's business methods, he makes the telling, even if controversial observation of the fact that Shobanjo's failure to groom an obvious successor remains, in the author's own words, "one dark spot in Shobanjo's well-laid out plans for the future" of the empire he had built. It is also to the author's credit that he delved into what he himself described as "perhaps the single most controversial issue in the history of Nigeria's advertising industry," the allegation that Insight 'snatched' the foreign technical partners of another Nigerian advertising agency, Promoserve, at a time when Shobanjo was the serving President of the AAPN. And although it turned out that the idea of a partnership was first mooted by the America-based Grey Advertising Incorporated, (and not by Insight, as was alleged), the subsequent Insight/Grey affiliation that took place barely months after Grey severed its relations with Promoserve, did not go down well with many.

It is not unlikely that what some see, in the words of the author, as Shobanjo's 'sharp practice' by his critics was his creativity, his constant desire to think 'outside the box,' to break out of familiar patterns and come up with new possibilities. Even the most virulent of his critics would concede that as manager, he was a great motivator. He was charismatic, stylish, passionate, even flexible and bold. And being bold meant that he took risks that sometimes paid off.

But a bit of caution. While this is a study of, perhaps, the most outstanding advertising corporate figure in Nigerian business firmament, it is not per se, a book on the Nigerian advertising industry, even if it is fair to suggest that in certain respects, the history of the growth and development of the advertising industry in Nigeria is synonymous with the history of Biodun Shobanjo's life. Because, truly, after the Banjo Solarus and the Sylvester Moemekes blazed the trail in the profession, it was clearly left to the Shobanjos to raise the bar and, this is a vital import of Adekanmbi's story. There are, to be sure, useful tips about the industry, details that members of the industry will find most useful, particularly young entrepreneurs who are either contemplating careers in advertising or even eager to start their own advertising companies. There are even incisive bits on the history of the industry from its inception in 1928, with the establishment of West African Publicity Limited through Lintas, to the founding of Grant Advertising by the late Adeyemi Lawson. It is also instructive that the author was, for six years, a member of staff of Troyka Holdings and was, therefore, able to provide, from that vantage position, a deeper insight into the inner workings of easily the most formidable advertising agency in the country.

In the end, there may not be easy sum-ups about the essential Biodun Shobanjo. Different people are likely to reach different conclusions, which in itself would be an indication of the deep impression that this book is likely to make on all who read and digest it. What, however, will be inescapable is the fascinating image that this book conjures about one of the most successful entrepreneurs in modern Nigerian history.

This is a useful, well-researched and finely balanced book, one that has been written with candour and conviction. It is an important addition to the growing body of biographies of key Nigerian corporate figures and deserves to be widely read. I have no doubt that it will find its way into our Business schools and colleges as an important source book for the study of corporate governance and traditions.

I heartily recommend it.
Yemi Ogunbiyi
Lagos

The Quest

This is an account of my personal journey to understanding. It began about 1990 when I sought private answers to questions that puzzled me regarding Biodun Shobanjo, the founding Managing Director and Chief Executive Officer of Insight Communications and, currently, Chairman of Troyka Holdings, West Africa's largest marketing communications group.

In Corporate Nigeria, he is generally acknowledged as a 'well-focused, hard-playing and fiercely competitive man' who loves to win always. Some other people, however, prefer to see him as a stone cold, I'll-stop-at-nothing-to-get-whatever-I-want son-of-a-gun. Loads of after-dinner anecdotes on his professional accomplishments are gleefully handed down by generations of advertising practitioners.

As a Trainee Copywriter at a Lagos-based advertising agency, I lost count of the number of times that Shobanjo and Insight came up for mention as we prepared to pitch the NICON Insurance account that was then serviced by Insight in the 1990s. Since I lacked the experience with which to reach an independent opinion of him, I could only picture him as some of my senior professional colleagues had described him. The events that shaped our performance, which fetched us a part of the business, and the mental picture of the 'man to beat' fired my imagination and determination to know Shobanjo the more.

Tragedy arranged my first physical meeting with *'Advertising's Billion Naira Man.*[1] I met him on 7 November, 1992 at Atan Cemetery in Mainland Lagos at the funeral of my good friend, Olufemi Oludare, an enterprising young lawyer who died in a ghastly car crash exactly one week after his 29th birthday. This was shortly after he had disengaged from Chris Okunowo & Co, the firm of solicitors retained by Insight Communications.

Before this meeting, we had corresponded. He acknowledged my 'Thank you, Sir, for coming' greetings with a solemn nod. Beyond that, he did not recognise me. Even on that inauspicious occasion I could not shake off the urge to size him up. I saw an urbane, supremely confident person with a strong sense of duty. He looked far too harmless to be the man that proverbially got other agencies weak-kneed whenever his agency was involved in a pitch. I was even more puzzled.

If he was this 'ordinary,' why do other people make him out as 'super-human'? What drives him? Where is he headed? Why would he excitedly blow the Insight trumpet, yet remain disquietingly reticent about exploding the many boogaboos that surround his person and career? I had many questions; yet so few answers, much of which, even at that, were based on heaps of suppositions. I reasoned that he probably found good humour in the stories. But I felt strongly that any man that was as much lionised as he was demonised deserved more than a passing glance. So, I wrote to ask him why he had not deemed it necessary to write his autobiography to unveil the man who inhabits the tales. I never thought he would reply. But he did. He wrote back to say that my proposition had been on his mind but that his schedule was too tight to accommodate an engaging discourse of the scope I had outlined. He totally exploded my stereotype of the attitude of the average Nigerian big shot for whom communication is an obligation with nuisance value.

A year after I received his reply, I met him a second time but in

---

[1] *Headline of Brands & Products magazine cover story on him*

happier circumstances. The meeting lasted approximately five minutes. I later understood this to be the standard length of time for him to decide the direction of his flow with an individual. Whatever impression I made on him at our five-minute meeting gave birth to this book, which is a translation of his commitment to share his experience of over four decades in marketing communications, 25 of which he spent to transform Insight from a start-up to one of Africa's best.

For several reasons, I found his story quite fascinating. It articulates the sense and dividend in challenging conventional wisdom. More importantly, it is a testimonial; one that validates the scriptural and Positive Thinkers' creed that any man can achieve whatever he can conceive and is willing to believe. His story, as best as I could piece it together, is re-told because it holds a universal truth, particularly for every ambitious young professional.

This is the truth: Who Dares Wins![1]

I had the good fortune of experiencing this truth first hand in 2002, which was ten years after my first physical contact with Shobanjo. It was made possible by a phone call from Ms Ben Upaa Ayede, the former Managing Director of The Quadrant Company (TQC), the Public Relations arm of Troyka Holdings. At a follow-up meeting, Ayede talked me into leaving my job as Editor of Business Times, Nigeria's oldest business newspaper, to join TQC. Several of my colleagues in the media described the move as 'crazy.' Yet, it gave me a ringside view of Shobanjo at work and at play. It also considerably turned around my professional worldview.

As I got to know him more over the years, the focus of my initial thirst for knowledge changed. My journalistic instincts saw an opportunity

---

[1] *Motto of the British Special Air Service, SAS*

to tell a great story of leadership and enterprise management. My quest was helped in large part because the questions with which I started out in the early years of my career remained largely unanswered at the time Shobanjo announced his decision to stand down as CEO of Insight Communications in 2004. By this time, too, the dimension of my quest had quietly transformed to a scholarly pursuit of excellence in which the object of my search was exemplified by one man who turned out to be the subject of my story.

But I must say this: you will be mildly disappointed if you had expected this to be the story of Insight Communications. It is not. Admittedly, both Shobanjo and Insight share an intricately inter-woven relationship, one in which he was the arrowhead of the agency's vision and the company, the evidence to sustain his rating as a guru in the industry. Even at this, there is need to separate the man and the institution to avoid falling into the common error of seeing the organisation as a one-man band instead of the orchestra that it truly is. This being so, I have tried as best I could to maintain the same, yet distinct identities of both man and company.

Also, this is not a book on advertising per se. Neither is it an excursion into Shobanjo's private life. It is a career biography, one that attempts to capture his perspective to explain his dream and its realisation. I prefer to describe this book as an extended personality interview conducted in the best tradition of my journalism background. At all times, I recognised the imperative of subjecting claims and counter-claims to strict standards of proof. As such, this book does not pontificate on the practice of the advertising profession neither does it touch on his privacy, except where necessary to illustrate a point or the other. But it does attempt to dispassionately examine critical issues in the industry as they affect the man and his widely acclaimed extraordinary career.

From the outset, Shobanjo made it clear he had no interest in a 'been there, seen it all and done it all' kind of biography. "Apart from my family, I don't see why anyone should be interested in the story of my life," he told me. For him, a good book would be one that serves as an invaluable resource material for aspiring practitioners, academics and anyone seeking access to valuable insights on leadership and success in enterprise management. This book aspires to these.

Before the project got underway, he challenged me to justify the need for it. For this reason, I administered a few hundred questionnaires in a random survey of professionals, including bankers, lawyers, communication experts and students. One of the fields in the questionnaire required respondents who read biographies to rate, in descending order, the top ten Nigerians they would love to read about. Shobanjo was in the 'Top 5' that also included well known professionals like the late Chief Gani Fawehinmi (Senior Advocate of Nigeria) and the late Chief Frederick Rotimi Alade Williams, more popularly known as Rotimi Williams (Senior Advocate of Nigeria). Several respondents based their selection on the fact that some of the listed eminent figures were 'respected professionals', 'controversial figures' and, instructively, had 'good media presence.'

Then, as I later found was common practice with him, he tested for trust. During one of my many meetings with him, he showed me the signed contract between Insight and Grey Advertising, an affiliate relationship that later became a major source of controversy in the advertising industry. At first, I wondered why he readily did that mindful that I easily could have been a suspect if the information had leaked to the media. Much later, I realised he had subjected me to a test of confidence because he became a lot more forthcoming as research on this book progressed.

Time and again, I was asked if he commissioned this book. Time and again, too, I answered and still repeat: 'No'. At any rate, he is the best manager of his image that I know. I embarked on this project for the simple reason that Shobanjo, warts and all, embodies my dream of accomplishment. He long ago agreed to share his experience with me. I was also lucky to have lived a part of his story by working in Troyka Group for six of the best years of my professional life.

One interesting thing about Shobanjo's word is that he treasures it and keeps it. I began to gather materials for this book way back in 1994. The first draft was ready by 1997. But the project was later put on hold for more than a decade. In the intervening period, Shobanjo was bombarded by a deluge of requests from more famous editors, authors and publishers. He never wavered in his commitment to getting me to complete the work I had started. When the pressure got to be nearly unbearable, he referred one of the intending publishers to me. Even after I made a career change and 'shifted loyalty' by exiting Troyka group to work in the insurance industry, he kept faith with 'Oga Dotun' on the project that he liked to describe as a candidate for entry in the Guinness Book of World Records as the longest ever written book. Truth told, every delay along the way was well worth it, the more so as the project needed to be constantly updated to keep pace with his constant motion on the field. Every change affirmed the wise saying that what an elder sees sitting down cannot be seen by a child perched on a pedestal.

What you hold in your hand, therefore, is the result of a collaborative effort. It is Shobanjo's story and my book. It has been made possible in part by the tremendous co-operation I enjoyed from several individuals and corporate bodies that readily shared their experience of him with me. I also enjoyed the candour with which he discussed issues, especially those relating to his widely touted professional "sharp practices."

It is pertinent to mention that occurrences here have been highlighted strictly because of their relevance to understanding Shobanjo. They are not intended as a justification or defence of his person or career. It is, if you will permit, an 'interim' account of the strides of a man who is constantly reinventing himself, just so he could beat his toughest rival and silence his severest critic: himself.

Naturally, one cannot rule out the probability of errors of whatever kind occurring in this work. I accept responsibility for them.

Perhaps, I should add, too, that I am aware that in writing this book I may unwittingly have put a loaded gun in the hands of critics, both of Shobanjo and of my modest contribution to the body of knowledge of him. If I have, I hope such critics will shoot without what boxer Mike Tyson called 'murderous intentions' but, as hard as possible, to show better ways of doing things.

Dotun Adekanmbi
Lagos.
November, 2019

Done With Storyboards...

You divide yourself into a personal life and a corporate life,
And in the personal life you've got friends

Kerry Packer

Biodun Shobanjo, the pioneer Chief Executive Officer of Insight Communications and Chairman of Troyka Holdings, is considered too much of a fighter to stay away from brawls. For that reason, practically no one in Nigeria's business community believed he could ever walk away, 'just like that,' from everyday practice of advertising. But he did.

On 10 December, 2004, he announced his decision to draw the curtain on an illustrious 25-year career as CEO of Insight Communications. Within minutes of the news breaking, it became a major talking point in the nation's highly competitive marketing communications industry. Equally dramatic was the lead up to the shock announcement.

With sprightly steps, he climbed the two flights of stairs that connected his ground floor office to the first floor of the expansive building that housed the administrative headquarters of Troyka. A stickler for time, he walked ramrod straight into the boardroom on the dot of 10.00AM. Clad in a trendy navy-blue suit and a white shirt that glowed with the penetrating intensity of a halogen lamp, complete with his trade mark bow tie, he was every inch a designer's delight. His ensemble was a statement of carefully nurtured cosmopolitan style and his trim figure the envy of youth. Just a few days shy of 60, he looked every inch the story of success that his life had been.

At slightly above 18 degrees Celsius, the room temperature was as he always liked it – freezing. But none of the journalists who occupied the comfortable jet-black executive Italian leather chairs positioned around the large oak-panelled table in the room seemed to mind the cold. They had been told to expect a very important announcement. Thus, their bodies and spirits were kept warm by prospects of the break of a major story by one of Nigeria's most popular newsmakers.

It did not matter that some of the journalists were encountering him one-on-one for the first time. He knew virtually all of them by name and professional reputation just as he was aware of the strengths of their respective organisations. Each one present had been carefully selected to attend the media briefing that was soon to begin.

A step behind him was Jimi Awosika, Insight's Managing Director/Chief Operating Officer and his long-time associate and 'brother'. Both men personify warmth. Their presence instantaneously energized the room and the atmosphere was soon filled with rib-cracking jokes and infectious laughter. As Shobanjo and Awosika began to shake hands with each guest, the journalists rose as one, as though paying obeisance to royalty.

That Friday morning, the 16 specialist writers of brands and marketing and two photojournalists picked from key newspapers and magazines in Nigeria eagerly anticipated news of the addition of another bluechip account to Insight's creative portfolio that was already bursting at the seams. The expectation was not out of place. Over the years, Shobanjo had established a pattern of professional behaviour that begins with him jetting out of Nigeria either late in July or in the early weeks of August for his annual summer vacation in any of the world's capital cities. Insight's former Director of Strategy, Dr. Osar Emokpae, called this 'vision ignition.' News of major account shifts or upcoming pitches often heralded his return home sometime in September or mid-October. This happened with so much regularity that it virtually became a ritual of sorts in the industry. Since the reporters knew he had only recently returned from his yearly retreat before the meeting with them, they made every attempt to second guess the cause of so much pump of adrenalin in the Troyka family. Their best efforts were met by toothy grins from staff of The Quadrant Company, the public relations firm that coordinated the session.

When he eventually sat down at the head of the table, with Awosika to his right and Insight's Director of Finance, Kayode Situ, to his left, the journalists instinctively primed their notebooks and voice recorders to capture the game-changing story he was expected to tell. But there was not much to scribble, as he typically dropped his message without waffle. He glided over every word of his two-page speech with the flourish of an accomplished thespian as he delivered news of his decision to stop "carrying storyboards every day." At first, he did not use those exact words. Out of a heightened sense of drama, he had said something more semantically confounding. He only clarified what he had been doing for about 33 years in an elementary manner because the journalists demanded that they be told in plain English the import of the statement he had just made to them.

"At the end of December 2004, I will stand down as Chief Executive Officer of Insight Communications," he had said.

Tunmise Adekunle[1] of THISDAY newspaper immediately fired his trademark salvo, saying he wanted to be sure of 'what' would happen at the end of December 2004.
"Sir, are you retiring or resigning or what, exactly, do you mean by 'stand down'?"

Shobanjo's face lit up with quiet amusement, for he had long anticipated the question. He knew, too, that it would most likely be raised by any of a formidable trio: Tunmise; Azuka Onwuka (then of Daily Independent newspapers) or Lekan Babatunde (then of Brands & Products, which was later rechristened M2). They were relatively young in journalism but had earned his respect with their deep understanding of contemporary issues in marketing communications and the art of interviewing. These three almost always got him to speak on any subject matter in the world of advertising or, more generally, marketing communications.

"I will stand down means that I will stand down; but if you're not satisfied with that, let me simply say that, from January 2005, you won't find me carrying storyboards every day, which is what I've been doing practically all my life," he intoned with some finality.

The fine points of his response were, however, contained in the press statement that was distributed to the reporters. In it, he clarified his meaning of 'stand down', saying:
"I believe the right thing to do is leave the day-to-day management of the company in the hands of younger, more dynamic, more knowledgeable and extraordinary team of people to create a better company."

---

[1]He died in his sleep in January 2008

He spoke, too, about his 'natural replacement', Awosika:
"(He) is, perhaps, the most knowledgeable and intellectual powerhouse I have ever met in this business; (we) were the principal architects of this company (and) he has, as it were, been my understudy from the day I hired him at Grant Advertising some 27 years ago."

When the reporters looked Awosika's way, he carefully deflected their questions regarding his new role as numero uno at Insight: "My Chairman (of Troyka Holdings) has spoken; he is the man of the moment." But being the ever-so-polite person that he is, he left them with a partially opened window of opportunity: "We can always talk about me later."

Some of the reporters enthusiastically began to dream of exclusive interviews with Insight's new leader. But those who knew him well enough kept their distance because they knew he would not grant any interview in the foreseeable future. Though a great communicator, Awosika liked to deal with the media on his own terms, in his own time and in his own space. Shobanjo long gave up on ever converting him to becoming a very familiar face in the media.

The headlines that captured the essence of Shobanjo's 30-minute meeting with the journalists were loud. His exit from mainstream advertising generated lively interest principally because of the phenomenal growth of Insight Communications, which had always been a hot subject of private and professional discourse. The news, indeed, caught the business community by surprise because few practitioners believed he could cede the daily administration of Insight to anyone else since his name and 'Insight' had always been taken to be the same. Without the agency, what will he do?

He clearly answered the question by highlighting his next professional moves:

"I will continue to serve as Vice Chairman of (Insight's) Board (and) devote my time in strategically partnering with all our clients as well as guiding and counselling those who drive our marketing communications and other service businesses."

His arch-critic, Chris Doghudje, a former Managing Director of Lintas:Lagos, best captured the mood of the time in his newspaper column:

"That Biodun Shobanjo is stepping aside from the day-to-day management of Insight Communications came like a bolt from the blues towards the end of the year." [1]

Much of Doghudje's surprise stemmed from his belief that Shobanjo betrayed his own cause. He especially held the former CEO of Insight to account because of the latter's firm position that advertising practitioners in Nigeria had a penchant for retiring too early in their careers, quite unlike their peers in Europe and America who slugged it out in corporate boardrooms until they were well into their seventies and eighties. As it were, Shobanjo formally bowed out of the business 14 days to his 60th birthday. Justifiably, Doghudje saw this as a contradiction in terms. Like Doghudje, everyone understood 'stand down' to mean 'semi-retirement.'

Even if Shobanjo did not fully clarify the reasons for his voluntary exit during his meeting with the journalists, he provided clues in series of interviews he granted after the event. From these, it easily could be inferred that his decision to opt out of day-to-day administration owed to a combination of age, length of service and the growing dynamism of the market place. In 1976, he was promoted to the board of Grant Advertising, where he cut his teeth in marketing

---

[1] *Advertising by Chris Doghudje, Vanguard, 10 January, 2005, P. 22*

communications. Between that time and 2004 when Awosika succeeded him as CEO of Insight, he had spent nearly three decades in Executive Management positions. He, therefore, felt no need to wait until his ideas became too dated or failed to 'connect with tomorrow's consumers'[1] before he moved on. On a lighter note, he felt he needed to avoid the 'sit tight' affliction of many Africans in leadership positions, especially in government.

Although several distinguished practitioners had played significant roles in the evolution of advertising in Nigeria since it became a recognised professional enterprise in the country in 1928, only a few can be counted ahead of Shobanjo in any unaided industry perception survey. His colourful personality, brilliance and generous dose of controversy have combined to make it impossible not to notice his presence and contribution in any professional or social environment. He, consequently, has had to live much of his professional life under extreme media glare.

No one calls his first name – Abiodun – in full. It is also hardly ever written in full either by himself or by anyone else except, perhaps, in legal documents or by those who are not too familiar with him. In the voicemail box of his phone, he identifies himself simply as 'Biodun Shobanjo.' Although being plain 'Biodun' made him less formal, one needed to know where to draw the line between camaraderie and officialdom because he is quite mindful of the gap between both. This has always been his choice, and it has been adopted by all, even if unconsciously.

Peers see him as 'Biodun Shobanjo' or 'Shobanjo'; close friends and associates all over the world call him 'Biodun' or 'Bibi' while staff and junior professional colleagues know him more affectionately as 'Shobby' or 'Baba', which is a more recent term of endearment in

---

[1] *"Why I stepped Down" (interview with Chidi Nnadi), Daily Sun, 27 December, 2004*

deference to his age. These appelations carry an undertone of admiration or outright dread, either of which is determined by the context of usage or the quality of the speaker's relationship with him.

Amongst practitioners, there is no generally accepted description of the passion that drives his business strategy. However, there is tacit acknowledgement of the fact that he locks to his vision like a homing device and that he dances only to the music that plays in his head. Perhaps, the greatest compliment to his work ethic is the widespread belief in professional circles that whatever he wants, he gets. He calls it the 'will to win'; his critics ascribe it to 'naked ambition'. For a very long time his colleagues perceived him as an 'enfant terrible,'[1] a belief that was fuelled by his characteristic candour. Hear, for example, how he made an important industry announcement on 9 January, 1997 (excerpts):
"...as Insight Communications marks its 17th Anniversary, the Surulere-based agency has formally announced the signing on of Grey Advertising, Inc. as its new affiliates.

Insight's decision to part company with Bates (Worldwide), its former affiliates, was informed by the need to actualise key strategic objectives which include seeing the agency into the next millennium as a major player in Africa and to offer clients unique collaterals which an African focus can engender.

The new partnership, which was consummated on 1st of May, 1996, perfectly fits the desire of Grey **for a strong local partner** (author's emphasis)."

In everyday language, the statement only announced a change in the thrust and tempo of the vision that propelled Insight, which had taken a conscious decision to walk away from Bates Worldwide that billed $4.5 billion at the time. The strategic embrace of another

---

[1] Steve Osuji, 'Enfant Terrible' Mounts the Saddle, The Guardian, October 7, 1995

international partnership, Grey Advertising Inc, which had a bigger billing of $5.2 billion, only helped to demonstrate his belief that business, shorn of sentiments, is all about the size of a man's dream and the perks that go with being bold.

The formal announcement of the Insight/Grey wedlock in 1997 did not take many advertising practitioners by surprise because it had been speculated at great length in the grapevine and thus had lost some of its bite. It was controversial, in part, only because another Surulere-based advertising outfit, the now defunct Promoserve Advertising Ltd, concurrently claimed an 'exclusive affiliate' status with Grey, Inc. At issue were Shobanjo's personality and the force of his vision. This matter will be discussed in greater details later.

Against the backdrop of the Insight/Promoserve face-off over the Grey affiliation and some other controversies, the view has been canvassed that Shobanjo, as an individual, attracts criticisms largely because of his inability to avoid the spotlight. In some way, this is correct because he is essentially a centre court person for whom failure is not an option. More than this, however, is that he is 'over-exposed' in the media simply because his door is hardly ever closed to serious journalists. He is a well-informed news source that reporters increasingly relied upon to offer frank and fresh perspectives either by whatever he said or by his infrequent loud silence on some issues.

The amount of space and airtime he enjoyed in the media in his career and post-retirement make him probably the most talked about practitioner in the history of advertising in Nigeria. Prior to his exit from the everyday grind of advertising in 2004, it was standard joke for some of his long-standing friends to call him up after reading his numerous interviews to poke good-natured fun at the 'guru'. In the few times that his face was missing from the press, even if only to illustrate a story, the question was asked: 'what ails the 'Czar'?'

His compulsive search for news from places near and far and from sources big and small is astounding because he hates to be ill-informed on any subject. At work or at home, he seeks always to be on top of things rather than being behind the news. The landscape of his mind is filled with issues, situations and personalities and he is exacting about details, for he is a compulsive diarist. Each New Year, he transfers entries from an old diary to a new one. Almost every day is accounted for in his big scrawl handwriting, usually in black ink. The unlikeliest of people meet in his diary. Birthdays are never forgotten, anniversaries are neatly compiled and occurrences, good or bad, are well-documented. He probably has an answer to whatever information that anyone required.

In his diary one will get to know that his friends, Sir Steve Omojafor, Chairman of STB-McCann and Victor Johnson, former Chief Executive Officer of MC & A, were both born on 6 January; that his children stayed with former Newswatch CEO, Ray Ekpu, on 3 February, 1992, the day he was released from detention at the Special Investigations & Intelligence Bureau (SIIB) at Panti Street, Lagos after his midnight encounter with hoodlums; that the late political icon, Chief Obafemi Awolowo, was born on 6 March; that the wedding anniversary of his erstwhile associate, the late Yemi Amogbe, is 20 September; that a generation of military personnel (an estimated 150) perished in a Nigeria Air Force Lockheed Hercules C-130 plane crash on Saturday, 26 September, 1992 and were buried 5 October, 1992; that his friend, Dele Giwa, was parcel-bombed 19 October, 1986 and that he became an APCON Fellow 10 December, 1993. Everything is so meticulously recorded he rarely forgets anything. If he does not remember or if he clearly does not know a thing, it just might be that such information was not readily available to him or to anyone at that material time, as it happened on 11 November, 1995.

On that day, the Commonwealth Heads of Government Meeting (CHOGM) announced a two-year suspension of Nigeria's membership of the body. This followed global outcry against the military government's hanging of the Nigerian minority civil rights activist, Ken Saro-Wiwa, and eight others, otherwise called the 'Ogoni 9.' The men were killed on the eve of the meeting of the Commonwealth in Auckland, New Zealand. The net effect of the country's suspension was hard to fathom because it was without precedent in the history of the organisation.

'What do you think will happen?' Shobanjo shot at me as I walked into his awards-littered third floor office then located at 58 Akanbi Onitiri Street in Surulere, Lagos. I had no idea of what he was talking about. As he motioned to me to take a seat, I followed his gaze, which was fixed on the television screen. At the time, I had not even heard the news of the suspension of Nigeria from the Commonwealth, which he had just picked on CNN. Naturally, I drew blank. His other attempts at getting answers to the question he posed to me only yielded a few more educated guesses. As it turned out, much of the international sanctions, which included restriction of visa to members of the military junta and their families as well as reduced military assistance to the country, was targeted at undermining military dictatorship amongst member nations.[1]

Typical of Shobanjo, his outrage at the 'senseless' killings was verbalised only to a limited audience. At heart, he is a naturally cautious person who tends to keep his position on non-professional issues out of public discourse. When he is not on firm ground on any

[1]This conformed substantially with the 1991 Harare Commonwealth Declaration that aimed at promoting the ideals of democracy and good governance

issue, especially in the treacherous terrain of politics, he does not show his hands. Much as he desires social change, he is not attracted to holding public office to achieve that objective; he would rather prefer to change the world from his own little corner of the globe. For this reason, he is not a card-carrying member of any political party. He leads a tightly compartmentalised life; one where personal and corporate values are very well defined and seldom wield undue influence on each other. This fact is better demonstrated in the two subjects that make his eyes to pop out whenever he talks about them: his family and his professional accomplishments. While he is reticent about his person, he is loud about his office.

At a personal level, his hand-pumping, back-slapping warmth commands prompt attention. He is smooth and adept at making people feel comfortable. At any point of his interaction with anyone, that person is likely to feel like the only perfect creature ever to come off God's assembly line. His every sentence is usually punctuated with phrases of optimism; if it is not 'fine' this, it will be 'beautiful' that. In his worldview, things are either black or white with scarcely any grey areas. For that reason, his talk is often laced with absolute terms, 'never', 'first', 'only' and 'ever', all of which tend to heighten views about his purported arrogance.

A porcelain tree placed atop the coffee table in the tastefully furnished ground floor lounge in his former residence in the Government Reservation Area (GRA) Ikeja, Lagos always begged for a closer look. It told his story in small pictures. The top slot on the branches of the tree had Madam Morin, his mother and matriarch of the Shobanjo clan; the baby of the home, Dolapo, occupied the last. In-between the grandmother and her granddaughter were the rest of his nuclear family: himself; wife, Joyce and other children, Babatunde, Olufunke, Olufemi and Abimbola. The family tree, so prominently displayed, served as a constant reminder of his beginning and his future. To one, he owed the gratitude of proper upbringing, especially for inculcating the virtues of boldness, uprightness and godliness. To the other, the future, he owes a responsibility to be a role model, particularly regarding hard work, integrity and, generally, leaving a worthy legacy.

He and his long-time friend, Chief Dele Fajemirokun, are quite vocal in their contribution to the way their church, the Anglican Church of the Ascension near his former Opebi Road residence in Ikeja, Lagos, is administered. But, as Fajemirokun would say, Shobanjo's attitude to matters of religion and faith is 'simply bible-believing', not 'born-again.'

His late father, Joseph, set the tone of his attitude to money and wealth; a fact he is always proud and eager to disclose. The elder Shobanjo told his son that anyone who could not save from a shilling cannot save from a pound. As a practical example, the man erected two buildings out of his meagre earnings as an official of the old Nigeria Railways. His son took a cue from this and, much later in life, used his own lifestyle to teach his children the discipline he inherited from his own father.

Even if his children had easily figured out that waste was alien to him, a casual experience helped one of his sons, Olufemi, to realise the depth of his abhorrence for throwing things away at the least chance. Whilst on holiday in the United Kingdom, Shobanjo requested the young man to get him some stamps at the Post Office. He meticulously addressed the envelopes before he affixed the stamps. Still, he made a mistake on one of the envelopes.

Olufemi was stunned when his father, without minding the time and effort expended, carefully set about detaching the 30 pence stamp affixed to the envelope so he could re-use it:

"I was in awe watching him. If I were in that position, with several stamps to spare, I wouldn't mind doing away with just one. He found a way to remove the stamp; then he explained to me the lesson in life, how you just don't waste things. He is always using every experience, including football to teach life's lessons."

Ordinarily, some measure of his native 'Ijebu' proverbial miserliness could be inferred from this incident, which best illustrates his lifestyle that is characterised by carefully considered spending despite being seen by many as flamboyant. Two years into the life of Insight Communications, he needed to buy a car for which his colleagues encouraged him to buy a Mercedes Benz 200. He listened intently to them and then went ahead to buy a Volvo 244 GLE from Doyin Motors.

The difference between the Mercedes Benz and the Volvo was just about N1,000, a princely sum at the time. Although the purchase was cost-driven there were several other deeper reasons. One was that the N1,000 difference could greatly help him to meet diverse obligations to people who were dependent on him. The management of perception was another. Part of this belief was anchored on the reasoning of his former employer and Chairman at Grant Advertising Ltd, Chief Adeyemi Lawson, who reportedly would allow his managers to ride any car of their choice in so far as it was not a Mercedes Benz. Lawson believed strongly that a Mercedes Benz was the ultimate purchase to announce an individual's 'arrival' in the big league of power players.

In 1982, Shobanjo felt he had not attained the height that required such a luxury. By 1987, however, he believed he had worked 'bloody hard' enough to reward himself with a BMW 730, which raised the room temperature in Nigeria's advertising industry. He subsequently added a Mercedes Benz 230E alias V-Boot and a Jeep Cherokee. Both were expensive at the time of purchase and were intended as status symbols. Up until he disposed of the automobiles after several years of use, they were in excellent shape, which made it unnecessary to heavily invest in new cars year-on-year.

The foresight that he exhibited in his private life also was at play when Insight purchased two 25-seater Toyota Coaster staff buses in the late 1980s. At the time, many thought them to be expensive, if not a wasteful, showy investment but it turned out to be an extremely smart business decision that helped to re-define staff welfare programmes in the advertising industry.

What role is money expected to play in a man's life? This is a question that has been asked across time. For Shobanjo, money is just a lubricant for the good life and a value repository to be handled with a high sense of responsibility. As a result, he has both 'hard' and 'soft' sides to money matters that correspond to his corporate and personal worldviews. At a corporate level, he is especially stringent on the handling of the finances of his organisations, particularly regarding payments for jobs done. He holds the view that, if an enterprise is not to fail prematurely, no service provider should expend its money to run the business of its clients.

Whenever he needed to chase receivables, he did so with vigour, taking advantage of whatever opportunity or venue that was best suited to make his point about getting paid. Some staff of Equitorial Trust Bank (ETB), one-time Insight's client, made this discovery by happenstance during one of their contact meetings at the agency's office in the early 1990s.

"Gentlemen, I hate to interrupt your meeting, but has client paid for the TVC we produced?" he asked the Insight team when he walked business-like into their meeting with the ETB team led by Tunde

Durosinmi-Etti.
"No, Sir"

The ETB team launched a lengthy explanation about having passed Insight's invoice to the office of the Chairman, Otunba Mike Adenuga, who had the sole power to authorise payments for bills with foreign currency components. Whilst Shobanjo did not dispute the bank's right to its peculiar internal processes, he insisted on respect for his own company's trading terms. He went to his office and came back with another signed invoice that he personally handed over to the ETB team leader, asking in earnest:
"When can we now expect payment?"

Unit companies of Troyka Holding do not get preferential treatment in financial control. The fiscal health of each company is subjected to so much scrutiny that it is near impossible for any company to plead intra-group, in-to-in transactions as excuses for high account receivables. Since his rule of prompt payment applied in equal measure to clients of Troyka Holdings and the Group's unit companies, Shobanjo usually did not find it difficult to walk his talk. When the books of a Troyka unit company supervised by Awosika showed piles of unsettled bills with Insight, Shobanjo declined to accede to the company's unspoken plea for sympathetic hearing; neither did he issue a quick payment directive to Awosika: "Please don't tell me Insight owes you so much; Baale (Awosika) is running his own business just like you are running yours. It is your responsibility to ensure that you get paid for your services. And, please, don't come back next time to tell me you still haven't been paid."

But whilst he would guard other people's money, including Troyka's, with his life, practically anyone could have access to his personal money. He often doled out what he liked to call 'owo iyi'[1] to

---

[1] *Yoruba, approximating to gift for random acts of kindness*

subordinates or the personal staff of associates or friends; at times on request, at other times without prompting. Interestingly, though, the people closest to him tend not to benefit from him as quickly as those who are distant from him.

Owing to his strong belief in people, he tries as much as is practicable to avoid situations where disagreements over money could strain otherwise good personal relationships. An incident once caused him considerable anguish that reinforced this position. One of his tenants, who is a popular Pentecostal preacher, shipped out of his apartment in the high brow Ikeja GRA without prior notice despite the mutual respect that he and Shobanjo had for each other. The then young preacher felt the estate agent had his landlord's mandate to increase his rent by nearly 100 per cent. Shobanjo did not become aware of the controversial increment until after the tenant had moved out. He felt highly embarrassed and insisted on a tripartite meeting of himself, the preacher and the estate agent, where the culprit was identified and made to apologise for his misdemeanour. The new tenant on the property was the luckier for the incident, as Shobanjo insisted that the rent only be marginally adjusted above the original level paid by the departing occupant.

'Ruthless' is one frequently used word to describe Shobanjo in a business context. The description does not fit well. If anything, the totality of his being is defined by characteristic bluntness. As an individual or as a boardroom player, he does not nurture undue sentiments. For that reason, it is easy for him to take a friend's phone call and cut it short after a few minutes by letting the caller know that the discussions had taken a while longer than he felt was necessary. Just like that; no offence meant. He readily acknowledged this trait: "People who know me know that I don't bullshit; I'll eyeball you and say I think you are a bullshitter. I always want to call a spade a spade."

Beneath this steel exterior, however, is a very shy disposition that is not quite evident until it is considered against the backdrop of some otherwise mundane decisions as, for instance, where to build his country home. Ordinarily, the patrilineal culture of the Nigerian society should have made the answer to this question obvious. In his case, he chose his mother's homestead, Aiyepe, over his father's at Okun-Owa in keeping with his predisposition to dispassionately analysing issues in his immediate environment before taking a stance. His choice of location was informed, in part, by the close interactions he had with his maternal relations in his early adulthood, particularly in the period after the death of his father. More than this was the fact that his mother lived in Aiyepe. For him, 'life is all about love (and) it is better to care for the living than the dead.'

As it were, Aiyepe offered him some measure of privacy that his larger than life professional image had made virtually impossible in Lagos. It also offered him the kind of privacy that would have been quite difficult to achieve at Okun-Owa because of his family name. Whilst the Shobanjo name in Okun-Owa is quite loud because it is a large, extended family, it is very much subdued at Aiyepe despite his fame in the world of business. The sobering effect of rural life is, indeed, easily evident. Except, maybe, at the Aiyepe Microfinance Bank located at the centre of the town where, say, one or two workers easily recall his name, an enquirer may wander a while seeking direction to his house, which is located at the far end of the street named after him in a secluded part of the town that is a 'reservation area' of some sorts.

Any enquirer who asks after him in this town must be prepared to answer a barrage of questions about his mission, regardless of whether he bears a letter of introduction from him. His mother, for one, never spoke to any stranger concerning him without her son being physically present or having previously briefed her of the visitor's mission. Madam Morin Shobanjo was a strong-willed woman. Her need to protect him was both an expression of a mother's love and a real need to continually watch over him, particularly considering the armed attack on him by hoodlums in 1992.

His house in Aiyepe is a posh bungalow with lush greenery, so beautiful it beckons one to explore its nooks and crannies. The highly fortified building cannot be seen from the outside after one descends the gentle slope that leads to it and it looks distinctly imperial in its rural setting. The peace of its immediate surrounding is only disturbed by the chirping of birds or the barely perceptible drone of split-unit air conditioners or the occasional shrill ring of the telephone. The house has an aura that makes a visitor naturally want to keep his distance. But his mother was unaffected by the luxury around her. Despite his entreaties for her to move into the house, she preferred to reside in her family house at Aba Quarters where her people could step in or out without being intimidated by the beauty or security of her son's residence. The house, a perfect getaway from the madness of the city, has played host to foreign dignitaries and business associates as well as tastefully organised but strictly-by-invitation family events.

Shobanjo's private life could be difficult to read with some degree of certainty. For one thing, he abhors the ego-massaging traditional titles highly favoured by legions of Nigerians. At the opening of Insight's affiliate office in Ghana, he was introduced as, perhaps, the only accomplished Nigerian without a chieftaincy title. This is an apt description because he is, by choice, a non-title holder. Aside his opposition to the proliferation of titles, he has had to turn down countless offers because he feels he is 'too young' and has not achieved 'much' to deserve one. But while he is deprecating the essence of one title, he is busy assuming the eminence of another.

At work where most chief executives go by the rules of officialdom, he prefers the non-gender specific 'Bibi' (derived from Abiodun), which is a more common form of address by colleagues and associates across the globe. He is not averse to his media rating as the 'Czar of Advertising' or, as he was christened by a journalist in the 1980s, the 'Akanbi Onitiri guru.'[1]

By all accounts, he did not mind being unofficially crowned in 1988 as the 'Nigerian Saatchi.'[2] The idea of the 'Nigerian Saatchi' has contextual relevance vis-à-vis his personality. All the informal tales that surround him are indices of corporate success. They also jell with his belief that professional recognition by peers is to be preferred as it is usually hard-won and is hardly ever conferred whimsically. But he is not your typical cultural ambassador, though he speaks of preferring full national dress to his well-cut suits and blazers. But he cannot be missed in a crowd regardless of whether he adorns an 'agbada', a 'buba' or a Canali suit.

If we go by American oil billionaire, Paul Getty's recipe for success, otherwise the 'millionaire mentality', Shobanjo has all the right qualities to attain pre-eminence in his calling. In Getty's calculations, success is hinged on (1) the ability to create luck as well as recognise and utilise whatever opportunity comes one's way; (2) having the right contacts; (3) extreme concentration built on the need to 'show them'; (4) good timing and (5) thinking big, even if out-of-this-world and believing it is achievable.[3]

To these could be added David Ogilvy's admonition that anyone who aspires to reach the top must work hard and be ambitious but not so

---

[1] Akin Adeoya, formerly of Thisday, later publisher of M2
[2] Origin not ascertained
[3] William Davies, The Rich: A study of the Species (Arrow Books, London, 1983)

'nakedly aggressive.'[1] Shobanjo embodies all of these qualities. Considering his personal and professional accomplishments, it, perhaps, is also tempting to situate him within the context of a famous Arab saying that 'the hand you cannot bite, kiss it.'

But to see his life only in terms of the success he had made of it is to miss the point. The more important issue is how he had remained steadfast to his focus on being the best and how he had unmistakably communicated that vision to all around him. That vision has been replicated by virtually all who have worked with him before setting up their individual professional practice. But, as is the case with all perfectionists, he remains palpably dissatisfied with his performance. The motivation to believe in himself and empower others to always do the right thing could have sprung from the fourth stanza of the modified 'School Song' of his alma mater, Odogbolu Grammar School:

> Never shall we relent
> Until our dreams come true
> For generations yet unborn
> To be proud of our work

No surprise here, considering his simple belief that an individual will only be as successful as his vision can possibly take him. This part of him is that which usually does not evoke the outpouring of great emotions. But it is the part of him that was shaped by experience in his early years when he realised that 'life is war' and that each man must learn to rise above his circumstance by fighting to survive.

From early in his life, Shobanjo fought many life-changing battles and manifestly snatched his victory from the jaws of defeat. He fought hard by always remaining one step ahead of competition at every turn. He trumpeted his strengths and masked his weaknesses. In this

---

[1] *David Ogilvy, Confessions of an Advertising Man (Atheneum, 1988)*

way, he truly could be likened to a successful street fighter who, ultimately, is a 'hard' man; one who wins by holding himself up to self-set standards whilst adopting methods and tactics that many may find hard to grapple with but which are easy to replicate when understood.

This is the essence of the story of Abiodun Olusina Shobanjo.

Coming Of Age

Train up a child in the way he should go
and when he is old he will not depart from it.

Proverbs 22: 6

Fear was the first thing Shobanjo conquered in life although he did not consciously work at it. As Christmas rolled by in 1959 he, like everyone else, began to make elaborate plans to celebrate the impending New Year with accompanying pomp and circumstance. He had just attained the age of 15, and with his doting father and dutiful mother at the centre of his universe, he naturally believed he was destined for greater things in adulthood. But the grim reaper called early and made a mess of all plans.

On 29 December, 1959 the bottom dropped off his adolescent existence when his father, Joseph Shobowale Shobanjo, lost the battle for life. That inevitable end of all mortal beings left his son with no choice but to squarely face his destiny. The death of the elder Shobanjo, at age 49, took everyone by surprise, for he had been full of life despite having had to take a voluntary retirement at the Railway Corporation of colonial Nigeria, where he had been a Weighbridge Superintendent. His early exit from work was a protest at having been by-passed for promotion in the office. His expatriate boss, who sought to fill a critical vacancy with a Nigerian, was said to have passed over Joseph, whom he liked, because he thought him a bit too frank; not too diplomatic and, generally, not pliable. He might as well have been describing the younger Shobanjo who grew up to perfectly fit this portrayal of his father.

Joseph Shobanjo's elder brother, Israel, was instrumental to his recruitment into the Technical Department of the Railways Corporation. It was not an unusual choice of employment, considering that Israel himself, was a staff of Nigerian Railway and had invested a sizeable chunk of his life in the education of his younger brother. He had seen him through school at St. Barnabas School in their home town, Okun-Owa, in present day Ogun State and his support did not waver when Joseph was to continue his education in Lagos. It was, therefore, understandable for young Joseph to toe the footsteps of his elder brother by taking up employment with the Railway after school. From that point on, he also started to build his own life and professional career.

About a week before his death, Joseph organised a thanksgiving service at St. Barnabas Church, Okun-Owa as part of activities to dedicate his new building. Midway into the service, he got news that his favourite half-brother, Okanlawon, who was ill, had passed on. He felt as though the world had come to a sudden stop. He turned around and flew out of church, his speed encumbered only by the pockets of air that tugged at his agbada, which billowed in the wind. Other family members dashed after him, with the dust raised by their pounding feet thickening the already dry harmattan air outside the church. As they sprinted down the sandy path that connected the church to the house, they prayed under their laboured breath that their brother should still be alive. Their prayer was answered, for the report of his death was indeed a false alarm.

Everyone returned to church to continue the celebration. The joy in Joseph's heart became a new song in his mouth and his dance steps told the story of a happy, grateful soul. But the laughter and shouts of hallelujah did not last till sundown, as Okanlawon died a few hours later that same day. The loss so badly shook Joseph that he too dramatically took ill. He passed on peacefully after his health condition failed to record any appreciable improvement. In just about one week, the patriarch of the family, Chief Moses Towolawi Shobanjo, the Oluwo of Okun-Owa, lost two sons. But the old man took the occurrences in his stride and lived beyond 100 years.

A pall of darkness enveloped Shobanjo and fear became his companion as he mourned his late father. Lacking the wisdom of age and the stoic disposition of his grandfather, he ruminated over several questions that gnawed at his teenage mind. He found it inconceivable that people should suffer so much pain and misery, especially in the Christmas season of peace and goodwill. But it soon became apparent to him that no one could provide satisfactory answers to the issues that agitated his mind. As he grew older, he quietly accepted the inscrutability of God and His ways because life taught him more about the mystery of God and the ways of the world, especially concerning the complementary nature of good and bad.

But there was one puzzle he did not so readily accept for the simple reason that the pieces failed to fit each time he reflected on the matter. Far too many times he had wondered aloud at the mystery of how his parents got together in the first place. Even in adulthood he could hardly imagine, much less figure out, the unlikely chemistry that gave him life because the backgrounds of his parents were dissimilar in several important ways at the time they took a shot at matrimony.

For one thing, neither Joseph nor his wife, Morinatu (Morin, for short and 'Iye Oyinbo' to many town folks), hailed from the same town as was usually the case in those days. For another, the man subscribed to deep-rooted Christian values, the woman Islamic. She was the granddaughter of the first Chief Imam of Aiyepe, who also was the first person in the community to build a house that had corrugated iron roof that especially commanded attention brought on by the reflection of the sun. Joseph was literate; she was unlettered. He was socially active; she was withdrawn. He spoke forcefully; she, with measured coolness. And he was as light complexioned as she was dark. Yet, Joseph and Morin Shobanjo had a good marriage.

Both had met through third party family intervention, which was the customary way of courtship of their age in the 1940s. As it was the practice of that period, respected members of the larger Shobanjo family took on the task of asking Morin's family for her hand in marriage. This was because the marital norms of the time prevented Joseph from directly propositioning his future wife. A rigorous research was conducted into all aspects of her genealogy, especially in respect of the mental and reproductive health of her family as well as their social standing. Tradition demanded this. She scaled every hurdle.

Accounts of the historical antecedents of the Shobanjos are somewhat sketchy. At a more general level, however, older members of the family were known to have migrated at some point in the distant past from Odogbolu, headquarters of the present Odogbolu Local Government Area, to Okun-Owa, both in today's Ogun State.

Both towns are separated by a mere five kilometres or less. Okun-Owa, at the time was a thinly populated, though somewhat popular backwater in the old Western Region of Nigeria. A good number of latter day Shobanjos regard Okun-Owa as home, but Joseph's son would someday proudly proclaim himself "an Ijebu man from Aiyepe."[1]

Morin, on the other hand, was born in Aiyepe, a rustic settlement that in later years achieved some degree of prominence in the realm of contemporary commerce for the lace fabrics produced by the Austro-Nigerian Embroidery Manufacturing Company. Aiyepe was the home of renowned civil servant, the late Peter T. Odumosu, who was the Head of Service and Secretary to the Government of the old Western Region. It was also the maternal home of the late Chief Sam Shonibare, one of the young, successful financiers of the defunct Action Group founded by the late Chief Obafemi Awolowo.

As a creature of habit, Joseph never left anything to chance. Personal hygiene, order and precision were the tripod of his daily routine. Whenever he set out to do anything, he would clinically check everything to be sure they were as near perfect as possible. He would insist that his food pack be rationed by his wife to the minimum level of waste and yet be enough to share with his colleagues. He would never put up with lateness from junior colleagues who had responsibility for taking his luggage from his home to the railway station.

He had a habit of arriving home each day clutching a copy of neatly folded Daily Times under his arm. Ever so leisurely, he would pull up a chair and immediately begin to read the newspaper while waiting for dinner to be served. He then would pull his slippers off his feet and scour the immediate surrounding with his bare feet to seek out

[1]*Interview in Sunday Times, 21 March, 1995, P.5*

evidence that the floor was dirt-free. If he felt a speck of sand with the sole of his feet, someone's day was ruined. He was such a perfectionist; everyone knew not to mess about with cleanliness in his domain. He loved to meet his house as squeaky clean in the evenings as he had left it in the mornings. Members of his household knew quickly that disorder in whatever form was all that was required to shatter the peace of the home. Today, no one can tell who, between him and his son, had the more obsessions with procedure and cleanliness.

The couple shared some remarkable qualities despite being so different in several respects. Both, especially the husband, could minimally tolerate sloppiness; they shared a single-minded commitment to perfection and they abhorred double-speak. More than her husband, however, Morin tended to take a hard-line stance on these issues. People who knew the couple intimately credited providence with playing a significant role in their union, just as they also acknowledged that Joseph and Morin were quite resourceful in managing their individual differences. Everyone agreed that the husband was a good man and the wife, a virtuous, obedient woman who took commitment to her family as her primary assignment.

Soon after the marriage rites, the groom and his new bride returned to his base in Jebba, an important railway outpost in today's Kwara State, where Morin was converted to Christianity, baptised and confirmed. She was delivered of a son a few hours to Christmas on Sunday, December 24, 1944. The child, in arriving on Christmas Eve instead of Christmas Day, appeared to have chosen to chart what could loosely be regarded as a middle course between a Christian father and a mother who not too long before then professed Islam.

Following the custom of their Yoruba culture, the Shobanjos christened their new infant on the eighth day of his life. He was named Abiodun Olusina; names which, in their ordinary meanings, accorded with the zest for life and expectations of good fortune. The couple had other children: Muyiwa, Dotun (the only female) and Oluwole. Years later, Joseph added another girl, Morenikeji, to his family, though she was not Morin's biological daughter.

As an official of the Nigerian Railway, Joseph enjoyed extensive in-service professional training and was thus easily sold on Western education, which the missionaries had popularised and made quite attractive, particularly in Southern Nigeria. He, therefore, planned for his son to have quality education wherever it was available.

St. Patrick's Catholic School was the mission school that was nearest to the family's abode in Jebba. Shobanjo did not have any difficulty in getting registered at the school in 1950, as he could effortlessly touch his left ear with his right hand when the headmaster requested him to do so. In those days, 'touch your ear' was a major test and criterion for admission into primary school. The test simply required a pre-schooler to demonstrate a certain level of maturity for the rigours of schooling by stretching his right arm over his head, without bending it, to touch his left ear. School authorities relied more on this simple physical exercise than on the production of a birth certificate to ascertain the age of a prospective student. Where the candidate was unable to achieve this readily, he was deemed not to have come of age, with the result that he would be required to repeat the qualifying exercise the following year.

The boy's two-year stay in the school was somewhat uneventful, except, perhaps, for the thorough flogging he once received from one of the teachers for an offence that has now been lost to memory. The beating caused him to lose a fingernail to whitlow. Expectedly, his very protective father felt righteous indignation against both the teacher and the school, which was just as well, for not long after this incident, the student moved further up North with his father who had been transferred to another railway station in Zaria.

A new vista opened for Shobanjo in 1952 when he was enrolled as a pupil at St. George's Anglican School, Zaria. Here, he easily integrated with children from other parts of colonial Nigeria, particularly those of Igbo and Hausa extractions. St. George's taught him two early lessons. First, he began to relate to individuals as equals and, importantly, he started to cultivate relationships based on what each person stood for rather than on the recognition of cultural affinity. This much, Shobanjo himself acknowledged, saying:

"Without being immodest, I am totally detribalised. I made friends from diverse cultures because one just saw people as human beings; it never occurred to me that some were Hausa, Igbo or Yoruba."

In some form, the learning he acquired was in tandem with the refined worldview of his parents, which helped him appreciate, respect and accept individualism as well as remain steadfast in the pursuit of personal aspirations. In his new environment, he also began to grow up to being the kind of young man that his parents had hoped he would be: independent, disciplined, assertive and discerning.

Whereas he acquired formal training at school, he assimilated a culture of smartness from his father and the impeccably groomed military personnel in the neighbourhood. His father's dress sense fascinated him a great deal and it was from him that he cultivated the habit of never wearing an article of clothing picked straight off the rack. The elder Shobanjo was forever happy when the creases of his dress were razor sharp. For that reason, he would always iron his apparel whenever he picked it from the hanger; never minding if it had previously been pressed.

The boy filed several images of the soldiers in his head, for he was instinctively certain that they did all the right things. He learnt to walk ramrod straight and with full magisterial confidence that is today quite easily noticed in his gait regardless of whether he chooses to walk briskly or haltingly. He would readily eyeball anyone, with a gaze so long and probing that the subject of his attention would be tempted, albeit unsuccessfully, to read his innermost feelings through his body language. He perfected the dead-pan gaze as a defence mechanism to mask his shyness. Yet, it is only through a careful study of the narrowing of his furrow or the brief smile that plays on his lips that anyone could be successful at reading his mind. Neither the frown nor the smile lasts for more than a few seconds, except when he is really angry – and the frown becomes more pronounced, with his words coming out in torrents – or when he is in an expansive mood – and the smile becomes a lot broader. In those few seconds, too, he would have made up his mind about whether he wants to keep up the thread of a conversation.

He imbibed more practical lessons about life as he watched his mother at work in her shop. For some years, she was a sub-distributor with the Nigerian Tobacco Company, NTC, which someday in the future would retain the services of her son's marketing communications company. She introduced her son to the art of trading and it did not take too long for faint images of his professional calling in later years to begin to manifest. He was fascinated by the passion with which she ran her business, just as he was mindful of his father's great hope that he would be the family's light bearer, one who would attain academic and career heights that a lot of people could only dream about.

Shobanjo's interest in commerce was soon put to the test by an event that occurred at a time that trust was common currency. As Morin recalled, she had left her two sons at the time in the care of the wife of a close family friend who also had a shop at the Zaria main market. The woman helped Morin mind the shop while she went about some other domestic chores. In her absence, a customer came to pick some stock of cigarettes but claimed he did not readily have the cash at hand because he made the decision to make his purchase on the spur of the moment. The man requested that the little boys be allowed to accompany him to his own shop where he would pay for the goods he had picked up. She obliged.

Biodun and his younger brother, Muyiwa, enthusiastically grabbed the rare opportunity to be out of the sight of their mother as they trundled happily after the man who took them almost half way through the city of Zaria, moving from one street to the other. They did not complain. In truth, they had the fun of their young lives. But the man did not take them to any shop. Instead, he took a comfortable seat at a local eatery, where he invited the boys to join him at table. They declined the invitation to a free lunch because they knew their mother would skin them alive if they yielded to the temptation. The man appreciated their good upbringing yet could not resist the temptation to pull a fast one on the little boys. After a good meal, he simply vanished into thin air.

Both boys were dumbfounded. Neither could fully explain how he lost sight of the man, whose name or address they did not know. What they both knew, however, was that they were in big trouble. They ran back to their mother's shop. Their punishment was reserved for another day by a mother who was only too glad that the man did not try to kidnap the boys. But Morin was not ready to lose her stock of cigarettes just like that. She promptly alerted the police who swiftly apprehended the conman in another part of Zaria while trying to offload the stolen cigarettes.

The incident etched a few lessons in Shobanjo's heart. He observed that, in the workplace, the first rule is to trust people and give them a chance to be true to their word. Or to betray it. He also became wise to the fact that human beings are adept at concealing evil intentions under the guise of being sweet. His mother taught him much more. Whenever he sat with her to keep watch over the wares, she ingrained in him her belief that no individual would get far in life with a wrong attitude. Grit and passion, she told him, ignite the torch of achievement. She let him know that anyone would usually achieve any task, if he sets about it early enough. And she demonstrated that with the right attitude, work could become so much fun.

By chance, he learnt a very important life lesson that people of influence seldom advertised; they live just like the typical next-door neighbour: a little help here, some kind words there and listening ears to other people in good and bad times. Whenever anyone needed help and it was within their power to do something, they just did it without wasting their own or the needy's time with 'come back later' tactics. Because of these random acts of kindness, which they do not rub in people's faces, they easily become the focus of attention and people naturally gravitate towards them. Shobanjo knew that virtually everyone deferred to his father in the tight-knit Ijebu community in Zaria and he knew his dad always carried himself with grace, never riding roughshod over anyone despite the influence he wielded. But he was pleasantly surprised to discover the extent to which his father's kinsmen were ready to show loyalty when sometime in 1952 his father took ill and was hospitalised. They flocked to his sick bed and virtually fell over themselves to offer great moral and material support to his family without counting cost.

Joseph was discharged from hospital only to face his reality of another transfer to Enugu in Eastern Nigeria in the fourth quarter of 1952. While he did not object to his being moved to a new duty post, he was deeply troubled by the nomadic lifestyle that had become disruptive to his son's education. He reflected deeply on the future of his son and concluded that the boy needed a more stable life to give him a fighting chance in an uncertain world. As soon as he received his letter of transfer, he promptly arranged with his elder brother, Israel, to pick up his son and take him down to Lagos where he would begin a new life. The boy did not exactly look forward to going to Lagos, for he could not understand the need for a separation from his family. This, however, did not change his father's decision.

On the contrary, when the rest of the family headed East late in 1952 he left the young Biodun in the care of a friend of the family in Zaria pending the arrival of his uncle. The boy thoroughly enjoyed his stay with his new 'family' in Zaria, though, much later in life, he nursed a major regret as he could not recall, no matter how hard he tried, the identity of his benefactors. In many important interviews, Shobanjo let it be known that he would have loved to show appreciation to the man who, for no price at all, took him under his wings and showed him the kind of love any good father would have showered on his own offspring.

When he arrived Lagos in December, 1952, everything looked strange to him. He had never seen so many magnificent waterfronts and he had never seen as many assortments of lorries and cars. Put simply, Lagos of the 1950s intimidated him, just as it still does every first-time visitor. Although he did not know exactly what he expected of the city, he was certain that he needed to quickly master his new environment and fashion out his own rules of survival.

At the commencement of the 1953 school year, he was enrolled in Standard Three at Ijero Baptist School, Apapa Road on Mainland Lagos, where life was fast-paced. Academics topped the bill; every other thing came second. The new pupil was an above average student who soon found his own level when he made friends. His new, though limited circle of friends included Taiwo and Kehinde Oniwinde; Abayomi Fisher who would later become a Petroleum Engineer and his younger sister, Doyin; Dewunmi Desalu and Femi Oguntoyinbo who later became a Partner at Coopers & Lybrand now PwC. Mike Okonkwo (now the Bishop of The Redeemed Evangelical Mission (TREM), whose elder sister was Shobanjo's classmate, was a year or two his junior at the school.

If life in Zaria was about human relations, in Lagos it entailed taking lessons in personal development. His cousin, Abraham Adegboyega Shobanjo, who was in Standard Six at the same Ijero Baptist School, quickly adopted him as his own blood brother. That early, the slightly older Adegboyega wielded tremendous influence on his cousin's life by playing the role of the elder brother he did not have. He was also the closest figure to a role model that the younger boy had at that stage.

The ground rules in his uncle's home were multifarious, tough and almost punishing, yet they all demanded strict compliance. For one thing, his cousin, Adegboyega, had no patience with children who were academically lazy. In Shobanjo's recollection, "If you dozed off while reading, you would receive a knock on the head."[1] Shobanjo was enrolled for 'lesson'[2] that was administered after official school hours by teachers who organised extra coaching for pupils in the neighbourhood. This was intended to supplement the knowledge acquired while attending regular classes. As the youngest kid around, he had the additional grind of running errands for every other member of the household. Since he had never had to be so far removed from the support of his immediate family prior to his coming to Lagos, he found the personal development training model somewhat too harsh. Adegboyega, however, made him see the positive sides of the 'home training.' He impressed on his

[1] *Interview in Crown Prince, December 1991, P.30*
[2] *The local parlance for private tuition*

younger cousin the virtue of learning, which was continuous and had no worthwhile substitute. He made him believe that there was dignity in labour and that he would always be expected to uphold the twin virtues of honesty and integrity. Everything that Adegboyega told his cousin had the ring of a mantra and they became the bedrock of Shobanjo's personal and professional worldview in adulthood. For these lessons, he remained eternally grateful to Adegboyega for positively impacting his life.

Towards the end of 1957, he wrote and passed the common entrance examination to Methodist Boys High School (MBHS), Lagos. By this time, he had become so confident of his ability to morally and academically hold his ground anywhere. He, however, did not scale through the oral interview conducted by the school. His undoing was his inability to satisfactorily answer the seemingly innocuous question regarding why he did not apply to either an Anglican or a Baptist school. Beyond being influenced by his friends, the Oniwinde twins, who were headed for MBHS, his choice of the school had no deeper personal or academic foundation. Until he got to that 'road block', he had criss-crossed the portals of the major denominations in Christendom. By the circumstances of his birth, he was Anglican. By the itinerant nature of his father's professional calling, he had attended a Catholic school in Jebba and an Anglican institution in Zaria. Because of his father's vision, he had arrived in Lagos to attend a Baptist school. But the Methodist would not have him in their school.

Looking back at the MBHS episode, he recalled: "At the time, it did not ingrain in me any bitterness; but as I grew up, each time I thought about it, I said to myself that religion has unnecessarily divided people. I think it is unfortunate. The missionaries did a good job, no doubt, but I think the element of discrimination is wrong. Children do not bother their heads about religious differences."

With the gates of MBHS shut firmly in his face, he had nowhere else to go. His father who, by then, had arrived Lagos from Enugu, again on transfer, was agitated. Joseph's elder brother, Israel, who himself was an Anglican, brokered an offer of admission for Shobanjo from Ansar-Ud-Deen College (AUD), Isolo also in Lagos. Surprisingly, the very Anglican Joseph swiftly declined the school's offer to his son.

Why would this man, who is married to the daughter of an Islamic cleric, prevent his son from attending a school with an Islamic orientation? Why would he agonise over the rejection of his son by a Christian group and think nothing strange of his own attitude in the present circumstance? He did not explain his action to anyone, not even to his son, close as they were. Many decades after the incident, Shobanjo still cannot rationalise his father's decision. The chance to attend AUD was passed up.

His father returned to his roots at Odogbolu to explore the possibility of getting him admitted to Odogbolu Grammar School, which was founded about a year earlier. Shobanjo sat for a late entrance examination in January 1958. Prior to his writing the examination, he was, strictly speaking, Ijebu in name only. He had never set foot in Odogbolu and he got to know Aiyepe as a child only because his mother had taken him there during one of the many annual vacations that his father loved to spend at Okun-Owa to be close to his own father, Moses. Joseph had lost his mother at a relatively young age, hence the close bond between him and his father. Of the three towns already named in Shobanjo's ancestry, that is, Okun-Owa, Odogbolu and Aiyepe, all of which veer off the present Sagamu/Benin Expressway but are within 50 minutes' drive from Lagos, the commercial capital of the Federal Republic of Nigeria, two of them – Odogbolu and Aiyepe – feature prominently in his later life. From early adulthood, however, he began to be pulled more towards Aiyepe.

On arriving Odogbolu, father and son went to the palace of the traditional ruler, the Oremadegun, the late Oba Fakoya, who was Joseph's cousin. There, the boy met the son of the king, Prince Ade Fakoya, who persuaded him not to accept being placed in the boarding house, should he be admitted into Odogbolu Grammar School. The idea of Shobanjo living in the palace mutually appealed to both boys. When, therefore, he was asked at the interview if he would want to reside in the boarding house or be a day student, he promptly restated the option he had previously agreed with the Prince. The school's Principal, Victor George Chinwah felt the boy was a little rascally and would have been better off in the boarding house. The issue lingered for a little while and it would have stalled the process of admission but for the intervention of the Oremadegun. Chinwah backed down in deference to royalty. He, however, insisted on one condition for admitting the boy as a day student: Shobanjo must live in the palace under the watchful eyes of the Oba. No one disagreed with him. The 'rascal' and his adviser, the Prince, knew too well that whatever regimented lifestyle existed in the palace would be far more tolerable than the hard life of being a boarder in Chinwah's school. They both had a good laugh at the pyrrhic victory of the Principal. But none of the elders was any wiser for the coup that was hatched and executed under their noses.

Shobanjo vividly recalled his first encounter with the Principal: "He probably misunderstood my confidence. I expressed myself freely. It may have been the way I addressed him; it may have been the confidence I exuded. These may have sent some wrong signals to him. But I was young and my father was present; I did not have any cause to be afraid of any Principal."

Stern as Chinwah was, he remained, perhaps, the most important reason that old boys of Odogbolu Grammar School, particularly those of them who passed through him, wear the pride in their alma mater like a fetish. The completely detribalised Easterner had been called upon by the Odogbolu community from his duty post at Eko Boys High School, Lagos to pioneer what he called 'a venture of faith' in a remote part of the Western Region of Nigeria. It was his lot to nurture the school, which was established on 29 January, 1957, to the height where it could rank high among several such community-owned institutions that dotted the educational landscape of the old Western Region.

Chinwah (a.k.a VGC), was a demi-god at Odogbolu Grammar School. He was a strict but fair disciplinarian, a good listener and a sound advisor. When he spoke, his boys trembled. When they talked, he listened. And when he gave advice, the boys took heed. He would say to them that only lazy people used the rains as excuse for non-performance; that nothing ever held back the rain from falling. He encouraged each of his boys to get either a raincoat or an umbrella to be able to beat the rains and work unhindered. In his territory, you were punished for reporting to school a fraction of a second later than 7.30AM. You did not get promoted if you failed the English Language examination. You had your umbrella seized for shading yourself from the sun. You exemplified squalor if you were untidy. You got suspended for unruly behaviour. You got praised for being neat. You got singled out and lavishly praised for academic excellence. And you got special commendation for showing strength of character. Chinwah challenged his boys to aim high and settle for excellence all the time.

Even beyond that, he gave his boys a vision of greatness. He gave them a sense of pride; he taught them to believe in themselves and he did his utmost to promote excellence in academics and extra-curricula activities. These were some of the many reasons the boys also fondly called him 'Very Good Chinwah', derived from his initials 'VGC'. Little wonder he figuratively became a deity that his boys swore by. For these and other reasons too, parents nursed no reservations in totally surrendering their wards for thorough training by the founding Principal of the institution that was and still is affectionately called Odogramms or OGS, for short.

This was the picture of Odogbolu Grammar School and its Principal when Shobanjo was admitted as student number 115 on 28 January, 1958. School records described him as male, Christian, Standard Six certificate holder and a native of Okun-Owa. He was placed in Ogunnaike House, one of four Houses in the school, the other three being Nomuye, Dada and Onalaja. Two more Houses were created in honour of Chinwah and a distinguished old boy, Oladipo Diya, in 1977 and 1997 respectively. In the class of '58 were Bolaji Onanuga, Segun Onayemi, Johnson Ifonlaja, Amos Sotubo, James Omotosho, Michael Afolayan and Emmanuel Adesanya, among others.

Because of Chinwah's love for driving people hard, no one was surprised when he chose a particularly hot day in 1958 to act out a private script. This was at a time that his boys had already become sweaty, nervous and somewhat irritable because the sun had shone a little too brilliantly. The school's tutors and pupils had looked forward to the end of day but the Principal had a different plan. That afternoon, without serving any prior notice, he called an emergency assembly after school. Nobody could fathom the reason behind it except to resignedly conclude that 'God' was about to descend from the 'holy mountains'. Yet, no one dared to blurt out this wisecrack, for Chinwah brooked no nonsense, which was the reason he was also nicknamed 'Terror'.

He said nothing to anyone as he inspected each student from head to toe with the cold intimidating stare of a parade commander at a military drill. He picked 14 boys out of the lot.
Silence.

Everyone longed to get an answer to the unvoiced question: what had these boys done?
Nothing.

The Principal had merely selected the neatest boys who would serve as ushers during the impending inter-house sports competition. He never ceased to amaze his pupils. His timing on the day in question had been deliberate as only the very neat ones could be expected to still remain so after school hours. Everyone heaved a sigh of relief. And the assembly erupted in a loud roar of Up Principal!

Shobanjo, who had been admitted to OGS a few months earlier in 1958, was one of the 14 boys that Chinwah singled out during the unscheduled inspection. But he was no stranger to the ideals that the Principal preached. In many ways, he was a true son of his parents from whom he had inherited traits that Chinwah reinforced at school and which, in adulthood, helped to define him as a man. In school, he could not cloak himself in anonymity. Even if he had tried to do so, he had many things that went against him. His very fair skin, his intellect, his obsession with cleanliness and his showiness all made him easily stand out in a crowd. His knack for rib-cracking jokes, which earned him the appellation 'Aworerin' (a jester) and his diction – he is a Lagos boy, remember – also betrayed him. His pronunciation of local names was especially atrocious and often elicited tear-jerking laughter, as anything would when an Ijebu man pronounced Ijebu-Ode as 'Ij'bodee' or Sagamu as 'Sh'gam'. But his debating skill brought him his first real taste of fame, which, incidentally, also took him to the brinks of disaster.

In 1959, while in Form 2, he accompanied members of the school's debating team to a literary and debating society event. After the major debaters had spoken, the topic was thrown to the floor as the judges tallied scores. He volunteered to speak. His contribution won him applause, honourable mention before Chinwah and a regular place in the school's debating team. But his contribution was not as spontaneous as his schoolmates had thought. Unknown to them, he had thoroughly rehearsed what he would say before they left Odogbolu. Over the years, the habit of making thorough preparation before any major private or professional event remained his trademark.

His new-found fame greatly boosted his level of confidence. He believed he could do just about anything. As proof of his can-do spirit, he chose to explore life in town and was intent on enjoying himself doing this, never minding that the school's promotion examinations were due to start in a couple of weeks. The annual 'Oro' festival, which was just hitting a crescendo at the time in Odogbolu, provided a good avenue for him to act out his dream. In the company of his friends, Shobanjo gave wings to his earnest desire and he was lifted to the peak of excitement by the music and songs of the occasion. Before long, he danced himself to a hospital bed when he fell into a ditch and made light of the abrasion on his foot. The wound festered into a sore that caused him to be admitted in hospital. He prayed that his father would not know the real cause of how he landed in hospital, for if that happened, his goose was cooked.

He was discharged from hospital just in time for him to write his exams. Not surprisingly, his grades were extremely weak but he was very lucky he got promoted 'on trial' to Class Three. His father never saw the results because, unfortunately, he had died by the time they were released. But his uncle, Israel, was greatly infuriated by the poor performance and he expressed his disappointment in very clear terms, just so Shobanjo would sit up and concentrate on his studies. The unsparing reprimand worked; indeed, it brought about a dramatic positive change in the boy. The change, however, did not come about so much by what his uncle said. On the contrary, he was challenged by the resentment he felt regarding how the message was scathingly driven home. Israel's entreaties at this point brought forth a fighting spirit in his nephew, who had now come to terms with the fact that fate had dealt him a bad hand and, as such, he needed to ensure that constructive things emerged from his adversity. He, however, was perceptive enough to realise that the ominous clouds of crises did not gather overnight after the death of his father but long before then. 1959 consequently became the turning point in his life, for he had just been pulled back from the brink of failure.

As he would later admit: "Something in me snapped, which made me realise that once you are on your own, you are on your own and you have got to fight for your own survival. I think it is fair to say that from that moment on I learned to take on life face to face."

He returned to school in 1960 more refined. A stanza of the OGS School Song played over and over in his head with profound clarity:
> What trouble have we seen
> What conflict have we passed
> Fighting without and fears within
> Since we assembled last.

A lot of things changed about him, which everyone immediately noticed. He began to learn how to lead people, how to take charge and how to assume responsibility. In his mind, he ascribed the role of a surrogate father to Chinwah in addition to his position as Principal. From that moment, too, he became one of the front-runners in his class. From that time, he started to carefully nurture an attitude of winning, one that manifested year-on-year in his winning of prizes in Proficiency, Geography, Scripture (Bible Knowledge), Yoruba, English Language and English Literature. He, however, missed the Top 3 slots because of his weakness in Mathematics. In 1962, he was appointed the school's acting Senior Prefect and the substantive Senior Prefect in his final year in 1963, second only to Christopher Ogunlana, in the six-year history of OGS.

Several old boys remembered the Senior Prefect for one thing or the other. Many recalled his neatness; some, his showmanship on the rostrum and others, how he brilliantly played his role as Brutus in the Drama Group's presentation of Shakespeare's Julius Caesar in 1963. But no one ever forgot him as a stickler for rules and regulations. Omoba Oluwole Kehinde (Shobanjo's junior) recalled a brush he had with the Senior Prefect: "As a junior student in Form 3 in 1963, I was not permitted to wear trousers; but being a tall one, a pair of shorts did not go well with me. So, I wore trousers. He called me to order but I explained my situation. He did not buy my argument so we had it out because he threatened to cut my trousers and I knew he could do it. Somehow, he had a re-think and let me be."

During this period, too, Chinwah who was impressed by Shobanjo's moral standing and improved academic performance, gave him a 'half scholarship.' This translated to Chinwah paying half his school fees while his uncle paid the other half. But Shobanjo almost did not sit for the final school certificate examinations because of an argument he had with his uncle who thought that he tried to play smart with the cost of writing each paper. After he wrote his last paper, he had no doubt whatsoever that he had been well groomed to take on life and all that it offered. He felt fulfilled and happy in the knowledge that he could excel at whatever he applied himself. He seldom forgets to thank God for sending the 'Very Good Chinwah' to make a positive impact on his life. As he reminisced: "I had freedom to do things at the appropriate time and, of course, there was Chinwah moulding us to become good and responsible citizens."

The graduating Class of '63 consisted of 16 candidates that OGS presented as its second batch of students who wrote the West African School Certificate Examinations. The school recorded 87.5 per cent success in the examinations in which Shobanjo had one of the best results and two candidates recorded outright failures. Chinwah could barely contain his joy for his venture of faith had succeeded. He continually returned to the theme of success to goad his later in-takes to press home the essence of the school's motto: 'fama facti satis est' (Latin, approximating in English to: 'the fame of the deed is sufficient reward'). Chinwah left OGS in December 1970, after having served for 13 years. Several years after he left OGS, he found 'sufficient reward' in the accomplishments of many of his boys. Student number 17, Oladipo Diya, a one-time Vice-Chairman of the Provisional Ruling Council, PRC, and Nigeria's Number Two citizen between 1993 and 1997, remains the school's most easily recognised alumnus in political Nigeria whilst Shobanjo is the most visible in Corporate Nigeria. In 1997, Diya, then a Lieutenant-General, was roped into a highly contentious military coup said to have been hatched to overthrow then Head of State, General Sani Abacha, who, in 1998, died in circumstances that are still shrouded in mystery. He providentially escaped execution after being controversially found guilty of co-plotting the putsch. Though Diya was one year ahead of Shobanjo at OGS, both men cultivated a friendship that has lasted till date.

Among the many old students, along with Shobanjo, who embodied the sum of Chinwah's achievements at OGS were Emmanuel Adesanya (who became Finance Manager at Mobil Producing); the late Yemi Osindero, popularly called 'Chinwah's Boy' (ex-Commissioner of Trade & Industry, Ogun State); the late Kehinde Ishmael, a.k.a Ishmael K, (a former Deputy Director of the Central Bank of Nigeria); Segun Onayemi alias 'Kano Boy' (who later became a Deputy Director at the Nigerian Accounting Standards Board); Tola Odulaja (former Commissioner of Justice, Ogun State); the late Kayode Okeowo (an insurance broker); Dr Ola Agbaoye (a Real Estate consultant); Matthew Afolayan (former Commissioner of Health, Kwara State and Chief Librarian, Yaba College of Technology); Dolapo Okunuga; Joseph Awolowo; Fatai Adeoye; Olayinka Sadiku and Olu Omotosho (a former Director at the National Clearing and Forwarding Agency of the Federal Ministry of Transport).

For Shobanjo, OGS was a watershed, as it was the place where he got a good perspective of life, power and responsibility: "OGS taught me to believe in people. I also learnt that age had nothing to do with how close you are to people; that if interests aligned, you are likely to see things from the same perspective: you must believe in hard work, honour and integrity and work in the hope of making the world a better place than you met it."

But he had one misgiving about his life in Odogbolu. For the period he lived in the palace of the traditional ruler and in the boarding house at OGS, he did not immerse himself enough in the traditions of his native Ijebu. Perhaps, being young at the time he lived in the palace of the Oremadegun he was too naïve and too pre-occupied with playing away his time to bother about Obaship and other issues of Ijebu culture. Perhaps, too, the shortcoming could be attributed to the Oba's over pampering of his ward.

Shobanjo's stay with the royal household ended, however, on an abrupt note because of a misunderstanding between his grandfather and the Oba. In the circumstance, he had no choice than to live in different quarters of Odogbolu and finally to return to the boarding house at OGS under the watchful eyes of Chinwah. Even after the rift was amicably resolved, his father did not change his stance on withdrawing him from the palace. As Shobanjo bade farewell to Odogbolu Grammar School in 1963, he burnished in his heart the school's creed, which was adapted from Gray's Elegy:

"Far from the madding crowd's ignoble strife
Our sober wishes never learn to stray
Along the cool sequester'd vale of life
We keep noiseless tenor of our way"

If the late educationist, Dr. Tai Solarin, had met him on his way out of OGS, he probably would, as he was wont to, have told the younger man, in a less elegant turn of phrase but more forcefully poignant: 'May your road be rough.' Shobanjo, too, would, perhaps, have been shocked, or maybe even have taken offence, at such direct expression of a curious but bitter truth. But he would have discovered, as he did much later, that life's long winding road is indeed rough.

And oftentimes lonesome.

2

A Place To Stand

But I being poor have only my dreams
I have spread my dreams under your feet;
Tread softly because you tread on my dream

William Butler Yeats (1865-1939)

The premature demise of Joseph Shobanjo shot the master plan for his son's life way off its mark. The father had nursed the idea of his son training to be a barrister, an aspiration he probably got from Bola Shadipe, his very good friend and erstwhile colleague at the Railway. Shadipe later left the world of locomotive engines to earn a degree in law following which he set up a successful legal practice. With the fates of a recently widowed mother and four siblings now inexorably tied to his own destiny, the young school leaver was compelled to consider what appeared to be two choices. He could choose to look out for himself first or place the needs of the family ahead of his own. The reality, however, was that as the first child and first male in the family, he had no choice whatsoever. He just needed to speedily grow into a man to tend the responsibilities of his late father. This called for the first of several personal sacrifices he would have to make at critical points in his life.

To compensate for the loss of his father's moral and financial support, he conceived a plan that required having to work for a while, save up and later pursue higher education. The implication was that he would necessarily have to play catch up with other brilliant members of his class or even his juniors at Odogbolu Grammar School, some of whom had travelled overseas to continue their pursuit of education:

"But what could I have done? There was nobody to sponsor me; I could not sponsor myself; I just could not. I had four siblings I needed to help; there was nobody to help them. If I had chosen to go back to school, what would have happened to them? What would have happened to my mother? Who would have taken care of her?"

Even if his decision to defer the pursuit of higher education was pragmatic, he soon discovered that life hardly conforms to such simple arithmetic permutations. By the time he secured his first job in January 1964, the joy of that initial accomplishment was overshadowed by the heavy price that came with it because formal education ended for him at that point. As a consequence, the elder Shobanjo's dream of a lawyer-son died and the vision was interred with him as another memorial of the shards of broken dreams that often pave the path to success. He felt great pains at the series of events that altered the trajectory of his academic pursuit. But his fighting spirit was significantly revived by the worldly-wise counsel he received from his mother. This encouraged him to set out confidently into the world to chart a new future for himself rather than gripe over what might have been had his father still been alive.

With the help of a certain Mr. Oshikomaiya, an indigene of

Odogbolu, who at the time worked with the Federal Ministry of Finance, Shobanjo was employed as a Clerk in the Valuation Queries Section of the Department of Customs & Excise Service (C & E) in Apapa, Lagos. This was a homecoming of sorts, as some of his former schoolmates like Olu Omotosho and the late Akin Adebanjo, among six others, were already there though they were in different departments as beneficiaries of the goodwill of Oshikomaiya. The well-respected community leader readily used his wide network of contacts to successfully recruit many of his kith and kin from Odogbolu as well as products of Odogbolu Grammar School into the Customs.

Despite the 'home' environment, Shobanjo was not enamoured of life in Customs. In his first few weeks on the job, it became obvious that he could not quite fit into the system. He marvelled at the idleness of his colleagues and seniors who always appeared very busy but, as far as he could see, did precious little aside moving one file or the other from one table to the other at snail's speed. He realised that he could not come to terms with the rigidly codified, bureaucratic, inherently sinecure and sedentary nature of civil service jobs. He felt constrained by the General Orders (G.O) of the civil service, which spelt out the 'dos' and 'don'ts' of every business day. He desired free expression of will, a notion that was diametrically opposed to the letter and spirit of civil service rules, which did not greatly encourage the use of one's initiative but emphasised collective responsibility. Clearly, his go-get-it nature did not sit well with the 'anonymous' living encouraged by the civil service, the more so as he loved to take credit for his work. Worse, he was not comfortable with the rancid air of the corporate environment:

"One thing I saw which did not sit well with me was that there was quite a lot of bribery going on in the place. I knew that in the Long

Room there were many activities going on and I knew that some of my friends were making money illegitimately and I did not see myself working in that kind of place."

By choice, he left the job after six months. The idea of making a career in journalism fleetingly crossed his mind when he began to give serious thought to leaving the Customs & Excise. This was not because he had any messianic calling to radically change the world with his pen. Rather, he was fascinated with journalism because he had been good at the humanities in school. He felt strongly tempted to live out his dream, buoyed by his belief that journalism availed practitioners the opportunity to express some of their innermost feelings in their writings. As the idea gestated, he sought out one of his former teachers for professional counsel. Biodun Oluyemi was quite emphatic when his former pupil, whom he taught Geography at OGS, spoke of a growing interest in journalism:
'You! A journalist? Don't even think about it.'

Oluyemi, who later worked with the defunct Morning Post before he moved on to Lever Brothers, now Unilever Nigeria, was certain that Shobanjo had the talent for a successful career in journalism but did not believe he had the temperament for the job. His reservations stemmed from the general notion that outspoken individuals, like Shobanjo, would usually have a hard time in their practice of journalism, considering that people, especially politicians or government and its functionaries were intolerant of dissent. He advised the younger man against taking up the pen for a living, except he was prepared to make detention, and possibly, imprisonment a way of life. Shobanjo promptly killed the dream, just as he quietly resigned his appointment at the Customs & Excise Department by June 1964 because he had concluded that he was headed for nowhere in the Service.

Shobanjo had all that while also nursed a secret romance with broadcasting or, more precisely, with radio, which he found to be somewhat more appealing than newspapering. Based on his gut feelings rather than facts, he believed that the medium challenged creativity and could give free rein to the kind of creative flair he needed to exhibit. Again, based on intuition, he assumed that the medium taught a few things about developing an individual's spirit of enterprise and personal leadership. He knew for a fact, though, that the ubiquitous reach of radio was a clear route to fame, one that several superstar broadcasters of that age had taken. On-air personalities like Ishola Folorunso and Fola Meadows were among a host of famous broadcasters of the time who had acquired huge cult following owing to the power of radio and their versatility as programme presenters. Shobanjo felt he could become as popular as any of these people; he felt he could take a decent shot at a career in broadcasting and, without a doubt, he believed that radio was the place to be.

To make an in-road into broadcasting, he leveraged the goodwill and political clout of Shadipe, his late father's friend, who put in a few good words on his behalf with then Minister of Information, Chief T.O.S. Benson. The Minister gave him a lead to the Nigerian Broadcasting Corporation (NBC), the precursor of the present Federal Radio Corporation of Nigeria (FRCN). He was invited for an interview and, along with two others – Bukola Asekun (later to become Chief Mrs Ajomo) and Teresa Modupe Ojeh (who later became Mrs Caulcrick) – was employed in 1964 as a Studio Manager (Trainee) on a salary of £16 a month.

The NBC became his second run-in with the civil service. Apart from knowing that he would be required to work shifts, he was not too sure of what else he would be required to do at the station. By his assessment, however, the NBC was different from the Customs &

Excise Department particularly because it dealt with live communication and some form of technology, which made the medium far more exciting than the tedium of pushing files.

But his first day on radio was an anti-climax. Without being told, he quickly found out that the thunder in broadcasting belonged to announcers and presenters with velvety voices behind the microphones, not to operators like him who sweated out the technical details of the job behind the scene. He knew that, as a Studio Manager, public fame might not come at all or, if it did, would not come as early as he had envisaged. He masked his disappointment by turning his emotions inward towards becoming the most competent Studio Manager around.

As it turned out, NBC became a great learning experience for him because discipline was paramount. Studio assignments required that he worked with minimal supervision; everything was time-bound and the only free hand anyone had, if told to produce a programme, was to do it well and do so on time. He did not have any problem with this. Importantly, radio taught responsibility; it stretched an individual's capacity to work long hours to its elastic limit, just as it tested one's temperament as a team player as well as his disposition to working with people from different parts of the country. Radio demanded that everyone operate as a family.

Within a short period, Shobanjo distinguished himself and moved up rapidly in the hierarchy such that in about five years he had completed all the training programmes for a Studio Manager and had become probably the youngest Head of Shift at the time. By his sixth year in 1970, he had become the most senior Studio Manager. Many of the on-air personalities like Bisi Lawrence who presented '15 Minutes with Bizlaw'; the late Banjo Solaru who presented 'Oddities'; Mac Ovbiagele, Kehinde Adeosun, Fela Ransome-Kuti and

Benson Idonije deeply trusted his proficiency and would hardly do their programmes without having him behind the console. By this time, Adeosun and Olu Falomo had left active broadcasting but they came in from time to time to present their programmes.

His friend and former colleague at NBC, Dele Adetiba, who later became Managing Director of Lintas Advertising, recalled: "He (Shobanjo) was an operations person while I was a sports commentator/newscaster. Although we operated in different areas of the business then, by the very nature of our work we had to interact and I think he was a very competent operator, very painstaking. We had quite a lot of operators (but) he was one of a handful of operators that people looked for; you could count on him to get things done most efficiently and properly."

Victor Johnson corroborated: "Clearly, in those early days he distinguished himself in the way he did his things. He excelled within a short period, to the extent that for all major broadcasts, called A-Broadcasts, unless he was there, no one else was allowed to touch them. Then you could see how well organised he was. He was well behaved and punctual. If his shift were to resume at 11.00am, he would be in the office by 9.00AM, taking over gradually from the on-going shift."

Dr Christopher Kolade, who went on to have an illustrious career as Managing Director and later Chairman of Cadbury Nigeria Plc before he became Nigeria's High Commissioner to the United Kingdom, raised the bar of broadcast performance in NBC when he became the Director of Programmes. Shobanjo was a beneficiary of Kolade's exacting quality standard. He produced sports, working alongside the late Ishola Folorunso, more popularly known as 'It's a gooaal,' who was one of his inspirations for getting into broadcasting. He worked with the late Yemi Fadipe, the late Alhaji Tunde Adeleke and

Bisi Lawrence at Outside Broadcast (OB) as well as with Tayo Shofoluwe and Demola Alli, who wrote scripts and presented them in their programmes. His path crossed that of (later to become Afro-Beat legend) Fela Ransome-Kuti (also later to be known globally as Fela Anikulapo-Kuti or simply Fela) when they worked together on 'Just Jazz'. He also teamed up with his friend, Victor Johnson, on 'The Big Beats' presented by ace music critic, Benson Idonije. He also made a lot of friends along the way, even with senior colleagues like the late Marie Irikefe and Fadipe, among others. As he recalled:

"One had wonderful bosses like Kolade, a perfectionist to the core. There were others like Canon Yinka Olumide, Victor Badejo, Ralph Opara, Ishola Folorunso, Yemi Fadipe and Stella Bassey (all deceased). These people, in their own rights, were fantastic broadcasters; they were willing to give one the opportunity to discover oneself and one learned as quickly as one could."

NBC created an opportunity for him to meet several of those that he loved to describe as 'good people'. These include individuals like Emeka Nzewi, Kehinde Okusanya, Fola Meadows, Dele Adetiba, Evelyn Okon, the late Patrick Egbe, Fela, Benson Idonije, Victor Johnson and Segun Ogunbunmi, among others. During this period, too, Foluso Phillips, now Chairman/Head Consultant of Phillips Consulting and Akin Odunsi, former Chairman of Rosabel Advertising and a former Senator, who were both Studio Managers, were his junior colleagues. Over the years, Shobanjo's relationship with some of these individuals waxed stronger and filled him with great measure of pride to recall that some of his best and enduring friendships were cultivated during his days at NBC.

NBC was a good training ground where everyone enjoyed every minute of every day; it was an environment in which the general attitude was one of each person wanting to give his best always and it was a workplace where money was a secondary driver of passion for the job. The fun and camaraderie notwithstanding, working at NBC presented a few anxious moments for Shobanjo as well as every other staff of the Corporation. Nigeria's first military coup, which took place in January 1966, was one of such memorable moments. In the wake of that coup, confusion reigned supreme; no one knew who was who and everyone responded fearfully to a staccato of orders fired by gun-toting soldiers: 'Stop!' 'Who goes there?' 'Advance to be recognised.'

No one, civilian or military, was granted unhindered admittance into NBC until the person's identity was ascertained. Not even a known senior military officer, Olufemi Olutoye, who later retired as a Major General and is now a traditional ruler in Ondo State, was accorded straight access into the premises by sentries at the gate until they were sure of his identity as he drove to drop off his wife, Omotayo (now a retired Professor), who was a Continuity Announcer with NBC. Until the deregulation of broadcasting and the movement of the Federal Capital from Lagos to Abuja in 1991, the studios of NBC continued to be one of the key battle grounds in the first wave of attacks in subsequent coups d'etat in Nigeria, principally because control of the airwaves was one of the early determinants of the success or otherwise of an insurrection. The coup-related incident on the premises of NBC taught Shobanjo the important lesson that one needed to apply the same strict rules to friends and foes in every situation, good or bad, for one never could be too sure when friends would cross the very thin line between friendship and enmity.

But the biggest scare of his life happened in the early days of the Nigerian Civil War that broke out in 1967 when he ran into a military checkpoint. He was returning to Lagos from Aiyepe where he had gone to visit his mother. The vehicle he boarded was flagged down and searched, yet no order was given for the driver to move on.

Everyone wondered why. What happened next took all by surprise: "Hey, you," a soldier bellowed, pointing a gun at one of the passengers, "come here!"
He obeyed.
"Wetin be your name?" the soldier asked, his finger still on the trigger.
"Shobanjo," the passenger answered, as beads of sweat suddenly formed on his brow and began to trickle down his forehead.
"You no be Ibo?"
"Me? No, Sir."

The other passengers quickly came to his rescue. They vouched that he was, indeed, Abiodun Shobanjo, an authentic Ijebu. The soldier walked away, yet wondered aloud how a Yoruba man could have been so fair skinned. Shobanjo exhaled slowly as he suddenly realised that seemingly unimportant issues could become combustible materials that could bring about dire consequences. From that time, he began to exercise more care in whatever situation he found himself having seen that every little thing in life counted for something. The soldiers let him go but his deeply terrified brain had trouble commanding his wobbly feet to board the lorry one more time.

Outside of broadcasting, he lived up to his billing as a 'Fine Boy,' which was his nickname in the early years when he lived with his uncle at Iwaya in Mainland Lagos. Many of his acquaintances then recalled him as the young man who loved the good life, who dreamt a great deal and who wrote 'plenty English'. He did not particularly fall in love with the neighbourhood that had electricity but no television; where there was no pipe-borne water and where he had to walk long distances because there was no vehicle available for his use. But the neighbourhood was pleasant and simple. His motley crowd included his cousin, Adegboyega and friends like Terry

Torlowei and the late Gboyega Ladeinde. He, however, received severe beatings at home because of his friendship with Ganiyu, who was more popularly called 'Omo Baba Eleegun' because his father had several masquerades. His uncle could not fathom how a well brought up Christian boy could get mixed up with the son of a traditionalist. The older Shobanjo did not understand that sports, not traditional ties, held both boys firmly together, as they were good table tennis partners and football team mates.

As was to be expected in such high-density environment, he became deeply influenced by his peers and he, too, soon began to date girls. But, unlike his friends, he did not encounter as much difficulty in his romantic quests because he got a big helping hand from his cousin-in-law, Biola Odejayi, now Chief (Mrs) Ayimonche, a legal practitioner and one-time Education Commissioner in Ekiti State, who supplied him the dossier of the many girls in the neighbourhood. They had a mutually beneficial relationship, for while she was his lookout for his love interests, she also learnt to fend-off testosterone-charged boys just by watching him and his friends play Cassanova.

When he got involved with his first major love everyone believed he was altar-bound. He threw everything into the relationship but, as time passed, it became evident that his best was not enough to sustain the relationship. His spirited attempts to revive the fading union did not sufficiently impress his heartthrob as they headed more resolutely toward a break up. At the point at which it appeared like he might wear down her resistance and win her back in the mid-1960s, his path crossed that of Miss Lanre Folami.

But let us quickly back track in time to some point between 1958 and 1959 when he lived in the palace of the Oremadegun at Odogbolu. He casts his mind back: "One thing that I recall is that, at night, the

Oremadegun used to go to the house of the parents of a girl he wanted to marry as second wife. I would carry a lantern for the Oba as there was no electricity at Odogbolu at the time. I used to get very upset doing this. When I grew up, I found this was a strange way of courting a woman."

When he met Lanre, he did not need a third party or the cover of darkness to play Romeo. Well, not quite. He met her courtesy of his friend, Segun Onayemi, who knew Miss Folami's cousin, Biola. He liked her and she liked him in return, with no one being able to tell who liked the other the more. But the relationship was initially regarded as a 'joke', at least not until it became a long-standing courtship that led the lovey-dovey couple to the altar in November 1971. His friend at NBC, Victor Johnson, was the groom's man at their wedding.

As a bachelor, he hit it off quite well with Fela, who was a music producer at NBC. Inside and outside the studios, a kindred spirit evolved between them and both became friends, though the musician was the much older man. They combed the streets of Lagos night and day. He scarcely missed any of the Sunday 'Jumps'[1] of Fela's Koola-Lobitos Band, which, years later, became Afrika 70. On several occasions, Shobanjo, Victor Johnson and Benson Idonije accompanied Fela to hire loudspeakers at Gbajobi Rhythms on Patey Street, Ebute Metta, Lagos when Fela's band did not have complete public-address systems.

The influence of the late Afro-Beat King in those early years killed off whatever inhibitions Shobanjo might have had about socialising. This became much evident in the things he did in later years when night after night, he began to exhibit his latent talent for singing, or 'focalling' (a corruption of vocalling), as Awosika loved to describe his penchant for grabbing a microphone and belting out his own songs

---

[1] *Music jam sessions*

as the spirit moved him whenever he went nightclubbing with friends and associates. Indeed, the spirit moved freely and frequently. The courage to sing to his heart's content derived largely from his having been a chorister at Odogbolu Grammar School and at St. Francis Anglican Church, Iwaya. To this day, he still prides himself as a good alto singer.

Many believed he usually sang for his own personal amusement, especially when there was need to shake off the monotony of work. Not exactly! For him, singing was a personality-defining matter to act out his conviction that no man deserved to be held down by the opinions of other people in so far as he could convince himself that he is doing what is right; does not exaggerate his strong points and is willing to work at improving his weaknesses. He sang in any form that best expressed how he felt and in whichever way that it lifted his spirit without allowing anyone's judgment of his singing prowess to diminish his self-esteem.

At work, however, he gradually realised that he had begun to find more fun outside work than in the studios and that his job as Head of Shift had become routine and uninspiring. This awareness led him to conclude that he had reached the limit of what NBC could possibly offer him. But he was stuck in a groove because there was nowhere else for him to go in the immediate future. A window of opportunity soon opened for him but it came disguised as two seemingly insignificant incidents that, at first, merely piqued his curiosity. The first of the incidents, which he recalled vividly, occurred in 1969 inside NBC's 'Studio 9', a studio in the external service of the NBC better known as the Voice of Nigeria (VON): "There were two expatriates in the studio (with NBC's Mrs Tomi Oguntayo) and they were armed with two tapes – one containing a jingle, the other an English voice-over (to be mixed and translated into) Hausa, Igbo and Yoruba. Apparently, the expatriates had flown into Nigeria to 'produce' the (St. Louis Cube sugar) commercial."

The wisdom of having two foreigners come to produce an obviously local commercial as well as the economics of the production was beyond his ken. Not long after this, a near-replay of the 1969 episode occurred in 1971. This time, the 'white man' (Allan McClaren-White) was not 'imported'; he was the Deputy General Manager of Grant Advertising Limited, a Lagos-based advertising company. He came in the company of a colleague, the late Yinka Lawson, to record a commercial for Top Beer. Shobanjo was not 'exactly excited' by the quality of work that was done on the commercial and could not understand the basis of the excitement that it generated amongst the Grant team. On both occasions, he was miffed by what he saw as 'wicked waste' and dismal professional competence.

Since his love of radio had begun to wear thin, he began to reflect more on what to make of his professional life. The more he thought about his career, the more he ruminated over those two incidents, thus kickstarting an incipient hunger to explore the world of marketing communications. These incidents eventually set the tone for his entry into advertising and his subsequent determination to re-define the industry's focus with a view to doing things differently and more professionally. Even if broadcasting had brought him relative fame, it was no longer satisfying. For one thing, it did not put enough food on the table; neither did it provide enough answers to his core need for the good life. He knew, though, that he needed to be properly groomed to fit into whatever professional role that might come his way in the not-too-distant future. Being so prepared, he reasoned, would also help him take advantage of whatever future opportunity that could improve his lot financially.

In all the years he worked at NBC, he never let go of the thirst for knowledge because he was conscious of the fine distinction between an enlightened mind and one that was bereft of what it wanted out of life. Besides, having been a brilliant student at Odogbolu Grammar School, it was not logical for him not to have wanted to pursue higher education, which was easily one of several routes by which any individual could self-actualise. He knew that knowledge was the key to fast track the process to success. Having been forced to abandon higher education, he opted to vigorously pursue a new career in public relations. His choice of PR resulted from critical self-appraisal and it was premised on several considerations. These included his strength in the humanities; the aggregate of his informal study of various professional callings in the service industry and his deep love of interacting with people as well as his open-mindedness in looking at developments from a global perspective.

Confident he would excel, he registered to take correspondence courses in Public Relations through the International Correspondence School (ICS). He acquired as much knowledge as he could about his chosen career and worked twice as hard as anyone else to be the leader he believed he could become. The British Council Library on Herbert Macauley Road consequently became his second home. His presence in the library was dependent on the shift he ran at work; he either headed straight for the library from the office if on the morning shift or from the library to work if on the night shift. As he said: "I was conscious that I'd had to make a major personal sacrifice. The best I could do was what I did at the time: seek knowledge by correspondence. If I did not recognise the place of education, I could just have folded my arms and said: that's it. But I always knew who I was. I was a voracious learner, particularly with the baggage I was carrying so I had to double my efforts as far as acquiring knowledge and skills were concerned."

When he wrote the professional examinations of the British Institute of Public Relations (IPR) in 1971, he recorded the Third Best result in the Commonwealth. His performance earned him a cash prize of twenty guineas, which was about twenty-one pounds. This was presented to him by ICS with much pomp and circumstance at the Federal Palace Hotel in Lagos.

Now armed with a certificate in Public Relations, he focused on the yet-to-be-answered question of what he would do with the certificate after he had acquired it. The two incidents at the studios of NBC especially helped to point him in the direction to go and he set out therefrom to re-define his future. In December, 1971, he took the hard decision of ending his seven and half-year romance with broadcasting. If he felt anything at all, it was not regret at leaving broadcasting neither did he experience any paralysing fear of the unknown. Rather, he bubbled with warm anticipation of how he would set about putting a stamp on the future. He was prepared, come what may, to go far. Very far.

3

The Glamour Merchants

In broadcasting, you thought there was glamour (but)
there was nothing to show for it. In advertising,
(the) guys were doing very well and living the good life.
There was glamour.

Biodun Shobanjo

Shobanjo was not pleased with the offer of employment made to him by Grant Advertising Ltd in Lagos. He had been one of twenty-one applicants invited for a written test and an interview by the agency; one of two that made the final shortlist and the one who was offered employment as Assistant Account Executive (Trainee) in November, 1971 on a salary of £720 per annum, which was about £30 short of his pay at NBC. He quickly drew the attention of the agency's management to the disparity in the hope that the offer would be reviewed upward or, at worst, brought at par with his salary at NBC. The agency not only declined to match his NBC emoluments, he was allowed four weeks to consider the offer or forfeit it. He picked the job with reservations.

His decision to join Grant at a lower salary was largely influenced by the plan of NBC to transfer him out of Lagos to Port Harcourt, albeit on promotion, in the last quarter of 1971. For some reason, he considered the new posting to be inimical to the growth of his career. Besides, he felt that radio had lost its allure and he had convinced himself that he had met practically all the 'most fantastic' people anyone could ever hope to meet in the medium. He never had the chance to contemplate what his future at NBC would have been like because the offer from Grant helped to get him off the horn of dilemma that he would have had to contend with at the station were he to disobey the transfer order.

But it was an accident of history that he began his advertising career at Grant. He had wanted to work with Lintas Advertising, which he felt would have been a good ground to launch a new career since it was the leading advertising agency of its time. Lintas was also the nearest place he could call 'home' because it was the agency where he knew more people than anywhere else. These were people he had known at NBC and had come to respect; they were people he had come to regard as kindred. Among them were the late Banjo Solaru, Segun Ogunbunmi and Mac Ovbiagele, who later founded Macsell Associates. These men, alongside Olu Falomo, had provided the impetus for him to explore the possibility of a career in advertising. They had all made smooth transitions from broadcasting to advertising and they now lived the kind of good life he had always desired. They drove nice cars, lived in nice houses and obviously had glamorous jobs. Best of all, they had enough money to spare.

Whereas he perceived advertising as Goshen, the land of plenty, his uncle, Israel, was not similarly persuaded; understandably because of his background as a retiree of the Nigerian Railway Corporation. For him, any non-pensionable job and any profession that did not command a considerable degree of 'clout' in society could only be regarded, charitably, as one of the many careers for dropouts. At best, he regarded advertising as just being a shade better than journalism which, at the time, too, did not parade as many graduates as other popular professions like medicine, engineering or law. Shobanjo would encounter similar perception challenge in the 1980s at a meeting with former President Olusegun Obasanjo who was then a private citizen after his first run as Nigeria's military Head of State. During a chat at a private party organised in honour of Obasanjo in London, the retired General earnestly 'advised' Shobanjo to engage himself in more 'fulfilling' professions such as agriculture or banking instead of this what-did-you-call-it-again? vocation. As Shobanjo recalled, Obasanjo promised to give him a parcel of land at Ota, Ogun State where he (Obasanjo) had a vast tract of land on which his then Temperance Farms (later to become known as Obasanjo Farms) was sited so that Shobanjo could try his hands on farming.

Much of the poor perception of advertising as an economic activity derives, as it were, from the stereotyping of practitioners as street-wise, hip dressing, smooth-talking and incredibly loud but vain glamour merchants. In popular view, advertising is a profession in which frippery is oftentimes mistaken, even by practitioners, for substance. In part, this accounts for much of the confusion in the business in which people are unable to distinguish an 'advertisement' from core 'advertising' or, for that matter, tell an 'advertiser' apart from a 'practitioner'. But misconception or no, Shobanjo saw advertising as the vocation that held the key to his future as he contemplated leaving broadcasting in the early 1970s.

'Big brother' Solaru gave him a lead that he diligently followed to the offices of Lintas, which was located at Tinubu Street, on Lagos Island. After he spoke with some officers in the company's hierarchy, he sat back to await a reply that never came. The fruitless wait availed him the opportunity to recce the advertising agency environment before he focused his gaze on the one-year old Grant Advertising, which was at the time shopping for talent, though it did not advertise vacancies to be filled.

By the time he began his new career at Grant, advertising practice in Nigeria was 43 years old. As documented by the former Chairman/Chief Executive of Lintas, the late Sylvester Moemeke,[1] the business took off on 31 August, 1928 with the incorporation of West African Publicity Limited, WAP, at Africa House, Kingsway, London. WAP was established at the instance of Welshman G. I. Lloyd, then an employee of African & Eastern Trade Corporation based in Ghana (then Gold Coast), a company under the aegis of the octopoidal United African Company, UAC. In 1965, WAP metamorphosed into Lintas:London before becoming Lintas:Lagos, after the indigenisation decree was promulgated in 1972. Late in 2003, the agency again changed its name to LOWE LINTAS.

For a long time, Lintas (acronym for Lever International Advertising Service) completely ruled the nation's marketing communications business. However, noticeable erosion of the agency's market share began to occur in the wake of Nigeria's independence in 1960. The period witnessed the advent of a few more agencies that were owned mainly by expatriates, although there was also a measure of local participation. Graham & Gillies and D.J. Keymer & Company were two of the early major players in the industry, though neither of them was recorded in the annals of advertising in Nigeria as having posed any serious threat to the market leadership of Lintas. Among the new entrants were Horniblow Cox Freeman (HCF), S.H Benson (which later became Ogilvy Benson & Mather before becoming extinct in the early 2000s), Melican Publicity, Odularu News & Publicity and Olu Adekoya Press Agency. Grant joined the league in 1970.

---

[1]*The Development and Future of Advertising in Nigeria, APCON 'Advertising Day' Lecture, (1996) P.2*

Grant, it might be said, was a 'child of circumstance,' conceived primarily to answer a crying need in the corporate life of its founder, the late Adeyemi Lawson, businessman and Chief Executive of West African Breweries Limited (WABL). Long before the birth of Grant, Lawson had reached the independent conclusion that WABL and its brands, Top Lager Beer and Vitamalt, a non-alcoholic drink, were under-performing in the market, in part, because of less-than-professional handling of their marketing communication. Lawson's conclusion was rational, particularly when viewed against the backdrop of the sparkling performance of competition, notably that of the market leaders, Nigerian Breweries Limited (now NB PLC), brewers of the immensely popular Star Lager beer. Nigerian Breweries, it need be mentioned, enjoyed the advantage of having its brands promoted by the more experienced and astute Lintas, which, incidentally, holds the record of having had the longest hold on an advertising account in Nigeria. In 1948, the agency began to service Star Lager beer, which, until 2016 did not know a second home. The realignment of agency roster by Nigerian Breweries that year saw Lintas lose its prestigious and high billing 68-year Star Beer account to DDB South Africa. In January 2018, the Star Lager account berthed at Insight.

Based on the nature of the problem that he had identified, Lawson concluded that he had to establish an advertising agency. On 18 August, 1969, he incorporated Grant Advertising International (Nigeria) Limited with an authorised share capital of £10,000 (N20,000).[1] This resulted from an agreement with Grant Advertising International Limited of Chicago, USA, which took 51 per cent of the new company's equity against the local partners' 49 per cent.

Grant (Nigeria) opened for business on 20 April, 1970 with a staff of six that comprised Ian R. Warne (Australian/Managing Director); Allan McClaren-White (Account Supervisor); Yinka Lawson (Client

[1] *Grant's 10th Anniversary Supplement, Daily Times, July 11, 1980, P.14*

Service Executive); David Akinyemi (Creative); Aliu (Finance Executive) and Nike Fadaka (now Mrs Alabi), Secretary and Administration Officer. Nike later became Managing Director of Universal McCann, a media independent company. The agency, which was the 43rd worldwide office of Grant International, operated temporarily from the suites of Bristol Hotel on Martins Street, Lagos before it moved to the fifth floor on the African Continental Bank (ACB) Building at 148 Broad Street, both offices in the then heart of Lagos Island business district.

The company's Board of Directors comprised Chief Lawson; Chief Chris O. Ogunbanjo, a leading commercial practice lawyer; Bob Runtz (American); Morgan Shrader (American) and the CEO, Ian R. Warne.

Grant had the effervescence of an American agency. The office environment was generally warm although the tone of the agency's creativity was set in Nairobi, from where Shrader supervised the Lagos office. Within a year, the agency became 'the place to be'. It was young. It had verve. It was truly exciting. And it was creatively on a rampage. By year's end in 1970, more than 20 clients had signed-on Grant as their agency of record. Among these were Coca-Cola, CSS Bookshop, Doyin Investments, West African Breweries, Bank of America, Air India, R.T. Briscoe, Taylor Woodrow, EMI Records, Johnson & Johnson and Merck Sharpe & Dohme (MSD). The company quickly leap-frogged to the third position on the billing table behind leaders Lintas and S.H. Benson, which placed first and second respectively. By the end of that year, Grant billed £84,871 (N169,742). Lawson was immensely pleased that within a short time his business hunch had become a huge story of success in enterprise management.

The pace of success naturally created a compelling need to boost the company's staff strength to match the quantum of its growth. In November, 1970, Grant recruited Festus Akinlade as Client Service

Executive. Prior to his joining the organisation, he had worked for about five years in a similar position at S.H. Benson, where he had abandoned his earlier dream of training to be an engineer. A year later, 27-year old Biodun Shobanjo, who was just a month-old in matrimony, assumed duty at Grant as Assistant Account Executive in December, 1971.

Whether by design or coincidence, providence brought Akinlade and Shobanjo together at Grant Advertising, which became the proving ground for two ambitious young men who were intent on making good in their professional calling. At the time, no one could have divined the great impact that they both would have on the rise and eventual fall of the agency. Neither could anyone have predicted the dizzying height to which one of them would take the advertising profession in years to come.

When Shobanjo came on board, he was assigned to handle public relations functions, his first love. But in two weeks he dumped PR like a bad habit. By his reckoning, his first major outing was an utter disappointment. Here was what happened: an itinerant Indian cyclist, Nawab, made a stopover in Lagos during his cross-country tour of Africa. For five consecutive days, he rode and perched on his bicycle at the Race Course on Lagos Island, sustained only by the non-alcoholic Vitamalt that he drank intermittently. WABL, makers of the malt drink, set about exploiting the PR fall-out of the cyclist's feat and it became Shobanjo's lot to co-ordinate publicity for the event. The press was invited to meet the cyclist and cover his subsequent courtesy call on the Oba of Lagos, the late Adeyinka Oyekan, at the Iga Idungaran palace.

Somehow, the expected PR mileage almost fell flat. Shobanjo believed that the journalists who covered the event took all that happened at face value and did not probe enough to understand its significance vis-à-vis the energy-giving Vitamalt hence, the perfunctory treatment of its news value. His romance with PR as a career subsequently came to an early end because he saw no bright future ahead of him. His apprehension was based on fears that his productivity would be determined largely by the outcome of his relationship with a third party, the media, which, in his most recent experience, had not performed above par. The Vitamalt/Nawab episode consequently altered the course of his career, as he switched over to mainstream account management at the end of his second week in the agency. Discovering and making a lateral shift to core advertising was a clear case of divine intervention that Shobanjo himself recognised as icing on the cake. Until he got to this point, he had virtually committed himself to the pursuit of a career in public relations, understandably, because of his professional PR certification. His primary objective when he gunned for a job with Lintas was to pick the PR-oriented ticket in the agency. Ironically, the job was given to someone who eventually declined to accept the offer.

His change of job function at Grant was made easy by the proximity of Public Relations to Advertising as professional disciplines. It was also helped by the fact that the agency adopted a traditional model of operation that made client service personnel the centrepiece of business. Shobanjo's inherent people management skill; his ability to deliver on time; his knowledge of the media and the deep intuition that undergirded his PR functions made him an ideal candidate for the role of an account management executive - primarily a 'go-between' in client/agency relationship. The 'fit' meant he could quickly and properly grasp the essence of the client service function in a typical advertising agency. This entailed the ability to properly distil a client's brief to colleagues across other departments in the agency, notably: Account Planning, where consumer research was primary; Media Planning, which determined the best channel to effectively reach consumers at the least cost; Creative, which conceptualised how best to communicate with the consumer and Production, which technically executed creative solutions. The 'fit' also required that the Client Service personnel should convincingly sell the agency's creative solution to the client at the most economic cost whilst achieving payment within the shortest possible time. Best fit was, however, generally achieved by matching a staff's professional background with his temperament and the agency's need.

Depending on the size of an agency, these job functions were oftentimes not too finely distinguished; they easily overlapped. Owing to the overlap of job functions, it was not an uncommon experience of the time for a Client Service Executive to write scripts, produce commercials as well as perform so many other ancillary functions in the process of managing an account. In this respect, Grant was a 'doing' workplace where experience was basically hands-on. Everyone was expected to learn as fast as was possible. The basic idea though was not to make an account handler a Jack of all trades, but a well-rounded professional and a true brand builder who could be trusted to fully understand where a brand was coming from and the direction in which it was headed. With such understanding, it was believed, the executive could properly communicate the brand essence at the drop of a hat. In Shobanjo's case, his public relations skill aptly complemented the demands of account management and the need to keep both client and agency interfaces happy.

His first assignment in his new role as an account handler turned out to be another Vitamalt assignment. It was as though fate had set out to help him redeem the disappointment he felt during his first major outing in the business. In writing his first advertising proposal, he drew heavily from his experience at Odogbolu Grammar School under Chinwah because he needed discipline and single-minded focus. He also leaned on his NBC experience from where he dug up the twin needs of promptitude and painstaking attention to detail. He thus cut his professional teeth with the Vitamalt job with practically no supervision by his bosses who made a presentation of the proposal to WABL's management that included the Chairman, Lawson, and Managing Director, Chris Haythorne. The client approved an estimated N250,000 to run the national campaign.

The confidence he gained from the experience fledged as he handled other accounts, notably: Nigerian Paper Mills; Merck, Sharp & Dohme (makers of Mintezol); R.T Briscoe, Wellcome and EMI Records where, coincidentally, his old friend, Fela, had become a recording artiste on the label. Perhaps the biggest confidence booster at work was the fantastic camaraderie that ran through the rank of Grant staff. Everyone flowed naturally within the structure. Colleagues quickly became friends and everyone became a part of a small, happy family. 148 Broad Street, where Shobanjo shared office with Richard Shittu, literally became a home away from home. Among his first few friends were Festus Akinlade, Robert Akinowa and Tunde Fatile. Akinlade's first impression of Shobanjo was quite positive: "He was willing to learn and he did learn very fast. He had a likeable personality; he had charisma (and) he was easy-going."

Professionalism thrived in the agency because of the quality of support that staff got from the company's top management. Shobanjo experienced this first hand whilst working on the EMI account, during which time he once had cause to leave the client's office when a scheduled meeting failed to commence on time. He had left the Broad Street office of Grant in good time for the meeting with his client interface, Mr Mike Wells, an Englishman and Managing Director of EMI Nigeria Ltd, at Apapa, both locations being then almost at extremes of metropolitan Lagos. For more than two hours, he waited to see the client, who, he was told, was 'very busy.' Upset, he left EMI. By the time he returned to the office, the client had called to report the young Account Executive to Grant's General Manager/CEO, Jim Cochran, an American. Cochran asked Shobanjo why he unceremoniously left the client's office. He responded by restating his two-hour wait to see the client who appeared not to have seen anything wrong with not honouring a properly scheduled appointment. This information caused the General Manager to call the client to tell him in no uncertain terms that his action was unacceptable. The client apologised to the agency as well as to Shobanjo who promptly filed the valuable lesson that any good employee would always display courage to do the right thing once he is convinced that his establishment would back him up.

As a professional and as a private citizen, he continually demonstrated his impatience with sloppy time-keeping. In the 1990s, he, as Chief Executive of his own enterprise, was caught in a web that was like what he experienced at EMI in the 1970s when he and his team had a scheduled mid-day meeting with Equitorial Trust Bank's Chairman, Mike Adenuga. As was to be expected, Shobanjo arrived for the meeting well ahead of time. Adenuga was busy. Tired of waiting at the ETB Chairman's visitor's lounge, he dropped his call card with the desk officer a few minutes past noon, with a terse message: "Please tell him I was here but I've had to leave." The young agency personnel who went with him caught the clear message: respect yourself so you can demand professional courtesy from your client.

1972 was a momentous year for business in Nigeria, of which the advertising industry was a major beneficiary. In that year, the Federal Military Government under the leadership of General Yakubu Gowon promulgated the Nigerian Enterprises Promotion Decree, popularly cited as 'Indigenisation Decree, 1972' as part of concerted efforts to grapple with the challenge of economic dislocation occasioned by the prosecution of the 30-month Nigerian Civil War, 1967 – 1970. Prior to the promulgation of the Decree, the government had enunciated a post-war programme of socio-economic recovery built on the platform of 3-Rs: Rehabilitation, Reconciliation and Reconstruction. The decree manifestly provided official protection for enterprises that were deemed to be cottage in orientation to position Nigerians to begin to take charge of the 'commanding heights' of the economy.

The decree stopped the injection of foreign capital into 40 broad groups of enterprises that in Schedule I were 'exclusively reserved' for Nigerians. Section 4 (2) of the decree declared an enterprise as 'alien' if it did not have 'Nigerian citizens or associations' in control of its entire capital or proprietary interest. Top on the list was the 'advertising and public relations business.' The implementation of the Indigenisation Decree necessitated the divestment of alien equity in the listed businesses. Nigerian investors acquired the divested equity and the new ownerships were reflected in the structure and, in some cases, the names of the affected organisations. This period marked a turning point in the history of advertising in Nigeria because it heralded the second stage of growth in the industry.

Grant's first response to indigenisation in 1972 was to raise its share capital from the initial N20,000 to N40,000. This enabled the local partners to buy lock, stock and barrel the shares divested by the offshore technical partners, Grant International. The deal also permitted continued use of the 'Grant' trade name in the West African sub-region. The agency thereafter moved to a more spacious office complex at 48, Bode Thomas Street, Surulere, Lagos.

The physical relocation was also a manifestation of the creative dynamism of several exciting hands and minds that included David Akinyemi, the late Tunde Fatile, Gabriel Adeyola, and the late Joe Akeredolu. The quantum of great advertising campaigns that Grant produced and executed notwithstanding, the ranking of agencies according to billing did not record any change. The pack was still led by Lintas, OBM and Grant in that order. The indigenous agencies remained too far behind to be considered as threats to the leadership of the industry by the 'Top Three.'

At an individual level, 1972 was a good year for Shobanjo whose hard work was recognised and rewarded by Grant's management. He was confirmed as a substantive Account Executive with 100 per cent pay rise. His new annual salary of £1,440 opened the gateway for him to begin to live the dream he had of the good life.

Industry-wide, Nigerians began to fill vacant senior management positions as expatriate staff of advertising agencies began to depart the country in the wake of the implementation of the Indigenisation Decree, 1972. With time, too, clients who had hitherto preferred expatriate interfaces on the agency side began to accept the reality of change as they were left with little choice than to accept and respect competent Nigerian professionals. The new order of things paved the way for the accelerated ascent of Akinlade and Shobanjo within the Grant hierarchy, the former being the senior. They were the bright boys in the eyes of management and they were systematically groomed to take over from the expatriates whenever they left. By 1974, both had risen to become Account Supervisor and Senior Account Executive respectively.

As Senior Account Executive, Shobanjo experienced first-hand how corruption oiled the wheel of some of the glamour in the business.

He saw real money in a brown envelope that was packaged as a gift for him by the chief executive of an outdoor contracting agency. It was obvious the money was intended as bribe for him to gloss over his repeated complaints over several decrepit sites that the company maintained for a Grant client. The outdoor agency owner felt the 'young man' proved 'difficult' in their previous discussions on the subject because he wanted 'something' that he probably did not want to ask for upfront. Shobanjo rejected the money and gave a four-week ultimatum for the contractor to fix the defective billboards or risk getting the media placement order cancelled. The titled traditional chief was rattled and he immediately reported Shobanjo to one of his tenants who also happened to be a Grant client. Whatever it was they discussed resulted in urgent repair of the hoardings and a new-found respect for Shobanjo. Incidentally, the same degree of dissatisfaction that caused Shobanjo to professionally threaten the outdoor agency owner with cancellation of his media order also prompted his foray into the outdoor business several years after this incident.

Administratively, Grant experienced rapid changes by the mid-1970s. The pioneer Managing Director, Warne, moved on and was succeeded by Jim Cochran who also moved soon after. In 1975, Ian Johnston assumed office as General Manager of the agency. The company's power structure changed soon after the agency signed a Technical Services Agreement with McCann Erickson Advertising, London on 20 July, 1976. This was a direct consequence of McCann buying over the offices of Grant International in Africa. Although the signing of the agreement expedited the departure of Johnston, there was no vacuum in the corporate hierarchy. Based on the advice of the departing Johnston, the owners of Grant assigned higher responsibilities to Shobanjo and Akinlade who were seen to have manifestly earned their pips. The time, indeed, was right to hand them bigger canvas on which they were expected to paint their own pictures.

The board announced Shobanjo as Grant's Managing Director, which made him the first Nigerian to hold the position in the agency. Akinlade was appointed Vice-Chairman of the Board while McCann's David Hemsley was appointed as Resident Professional Consultant. All three made up Grant's Executive Committee. Shobanjo and Akinlade, at ages 32 and 33 respectively, set a record of some sort because, in those days, top-level agency operatives did not quite come that young. There are suggestions that both men must have benefited immensely from a barely perceptible mentoring programme within the system for them to have recorded such quantum leaps in their short careers at that point. Both men discounted any 'godfather' theory in relation to their fast rise to the top. For Shobanjo, especially, the promotions were very well earned: "It was more of hard work, commitment and dedication as well as the quality and application of knowledge. It also had to do with the ability of the boss to see through innate qualities."

On the job, Akinlade and Shobanjo both exuded great confidence required of knowledgeable and well-trained advertising practitioners who aimed to get as high as was possible in the company's chain of command. Both were helped along the way to the top by diverse circumstances of the time, notably their diligence, hard work and loyalty in the service of the company; government's promulgation of the indigenisation decree and the resultant departure of senior expatriate agency employees. They also reaped bountifully from the global realignment of international agency affiliations and subsequent change in the ownership structure of Grant. Above all, they owed their success to the bold decision of the agency's board to look inwards and bet on in-house talents rather than opt for external recruitments to draw from the ready pool of senior management staff of other agencies. The sum of these decisions was the rare opportunity they both had to excel in management despite their relative young ages.

It is important to understand that up to this point of his life, Shobanjo had had no other higher formal education beyond the secondary school certificate he obtained at Odogbolu Grammar School and the Certificate in Public Relations he got by correspondence from ICS. In the intervening years, he had become a Full Member of the British Institute of Public Relations and a Full Member of the British Institute of Marketing, having attended the Institute's college in the UK in 1977. Shobanjo's career exposure to various training programmes in different parts of the world, however, makes him one of the best trained practitioners in the history of advertising in Nigeria. He served Grant just as he advanced his dream of the good life.

Even without university education, he resolutely refused to allow popular belief to cast him in the mould of an under-achiever who would have needed a convenient crutch to prop up under-performance in whatever form. Whereas popular belief tended to put university certification as the bridge to the good life, he always saw open-mindedness as well as willingness and continuous quest to learn from principles and practice as the key to success in any endeavour. With a sharp mind that many doctorate degree holders cannot contend with, he has always lived by a simple philosophy that no one should ever feel incomplete before anyone else. Time and again he has commended this philosophy to ambitious young people who may find themselves hemmed in by modest academic attainments or any other form of personal or professional complex. In his worldview, paper certification, though desirable particularly in the fiercely competitive 21st Century, is the least of the prerequisites needed to reach the top. For him, anyone that aspires to be successful must have a vision that is locked to a goal like a military homing device. And the vision must be backed by character and sustained by consistent stoking of the fire in the belly without which no individual or corporate organisation can hope to reach higher grounds.

When Shobanjo walked into the labour market in 1964, his only goal was to succeed at whatever he applied himself. He knew he would get far. But he did not know it would be this far or that it would be so fast. Indeed, by the time he assumed office as Managing Director, it could be said that he had truly succeeded beyond his wildest imagination.

The mood of success recorded by Grant under the leadership of Shobanjo, Akinlade and Hemsley is, perhaps, best captured by an ex-staff, Foluso Babu Akinbobola (now Chairman of Medialink, an outdoor advertising company): "At that time, in terms of billing, (Grant) was Number Three, after Lintas and OBM. But it had what the others did not have – aggressive young professionals being trained by a combination of Shobanjo, Akinlade and Hemsley. These three were forward-looking. They were not alike but the combination made the place interesting."

Shobanjo's rapid rise to the top in 1976 received a major boost when his five-year old marriage was blessed with a baby boy christened Babatunde. His joy knew no bounds. But his joy was also short-lived. For reasons that were not too clear, the Board of Grant, early in 1977, reshuffled the agency's top management and reversed itself on the appointments that were made in the previous year. Whilst Hemsley remained as Technical Consultant, Akinlade was moved away from the Vice Chairmanship of the Board to become Managing Director while Shobanjo was moved one notch down to become Deputy Managing Director.

Various arguments have been advanced for the board's reversal of its initial decision on the appointments of Akinlade and Shobanjo.

According to a school of thought, the re-designation of both men occurred because some of the founding owners of Grant were no longer comfortable with the idea of designating Akinlade, an 'outsider', as Vice-Chairman because it was considered an aberration for a nominal shareholder to be conferred with a high social status of an 'owner'. It, therefore, was believed that a re-designation was necessary to change the equation to keep the 'employee' out of the power loop.

Another strand of argument postulated that Akinlade initiated the process of change, for he was said to have actively angled for the managing directorship. This stance was hinged on the premise that he probably perceived the Managing Director's position to be more visible, more prestigious and, by extension, more powerful in the everyday running of the organisation than the Vice Chairmanship position that he occupied. Akinlade vehemently denied this, admitting, though, that it was not out of place for him, as the most senior Nigerian staff of the agency, to have expected to clinch the Chief Executive Officer's (CEO) slot in the first instance. Whilst he was emphatic that he had nothing to do with the restructuring and that he did not know the reasons for it, he did not rule out other possibilities. As far as he knew, the board "must have got some report" or "something probably went wrong." He insisted that when the changes were made he was 'not excited.'

Another school of thought described the board's decision simply as the result of a not-too-keen appreciation of human nature and how to handle it. This was because neither Akinlade nor Shobanjo appeared to have been availed sufficient justifications, if any, for the action. Or if they were, as it turned out, little was done far too late in the day to be understood or appreciated by all concerned because it was clear that the board shifted the goal post after a goal had been scored. It, therefore, was no surprise that the action cast a slur on whatever good intention that may have informed the change.

To be sure, none of these arguments can be said with a high degree of certainty to reflect the principal reason(s) for the administrative policy somersault at Grant in 1977. What is known for a fact is that the board of Grant put a firm wedge between two talents that could have been tapped to maximally lift the agency higher than the height it attained. In the process, the fate of the company was sealed.

At the outset and as far as the eyes could see, the management reshuffle did not affect the rhythm of the agency's performance. At the level of inter-personal relationships, however, the re-designations eroded the basis of trust between two erstwhile good friends and it entrenched a degree of mutual suspicion. Outwardly, the agency's boat enjoyed a smooth sail. In reality, it was adrift and needed just a little rocking for it to capsize. Akinlade and Shobanjo scoffed at these suggestions, arguing that the owners of the business reserved the right to run their establishment howsoever they deemed fit.

There was no doubt that both men had disagreements on several critical issues. Shobanjo was not happy with certain policies of the Board; he believed that Grant no longer had the capacity to dream big and bold and he was convinced that the agency's leadership had become too ensconced in a comfort zone to even aspire to leadership in the advertising business. He strongly believed that the agency had become all motion without movement and there was no longer a clear-cut direction of where it was headed. Akinlade disagreed with him on all scores.

By the end of 1978, the fire in Shobanjo's belly had begun to dim, for which reason it became increasingly difficult for him, in 'spirit', to remain in the agency. At every turn, he continued to reach into the innermost recesses of his soul to put his fighting spirit to the test. For him, it was sufficient to recognise adversity or whatever other challenge life may have thrown at him but to back down or run away was the ultimate crime, for he loved to frontally confront life. And win. By the time all these feelings began to percolate, it was clear to all who could read between the lines that the differences between Shobanjo and the agency's establishment, as represented by Akinlade, had become 'irreconcilable'. He, too, had seen the need to move on to end his summer of discontent

In October 1979, he resigned from Grant.

4

GRANT:
Sorry, I've got to Go!

My only regret was that there was so much to do
but little was done.

Biodun Shobanjo

The cause of Shobanjo's inevitable departure from Grant
Advertising is not as straightforward as its course. For that
reason, some of the issues that precipitated or hastened it call
for more clarifications, as doing this will create further understanding
of much of his career decisions after he left the agency. Several years
after the series of incidents that climaxed in Shobanjo's departure,
most ex-staff of Grant of the 1970s still cannot explain what triggered
the rumble at the top echelon of the company. For different reasons,
neither Akinlade nor Shobanjo was keen on re-visiting the issue.
Akinlade did not think anything extraordinary took place, saying: "the
things that happened to us are things that normally happen in any
organisation." Besides, he argued that his love of Jesus Christ did not
encourage dwelling on past events or nursing a grudge against

anyone. Shobanjo did not think that re-opening the chapter would serve any useful purpose, the more so as he believed that the present has vindicated the position he took in the past.

Whilst both men dismissed the notion that the restructuring of the company disrupted the easy flow between them, there is no argument that, at the corporate level, what happened between 1977 and 1979 generated unintended consequences. These, paradoxically, negatively impacted the once-vibrant agency yet had positive after-effects on the history of advertising in Nigeria.

Recrimination appeared to have set in after the board restructured the agency's organogram. But its embers were not fanned by typical office power play because neither officer was invested with executive decision-making power when both were first elevated to the board of the company. That power still did not devolve to them when Akinlade and Shobanjo were designated as Vice Chairman and Managing Director respectively. Executive authority, strictly speaking, resided with the Chairman, Lawson. People who knew the men well enough shared the opinion that Akinlade, despite being introverted, was a jolly good fellow while Shobanjo, an extrovert, was projected as a 'reasonably nice' yet 'hard as nail' professional. Until things began to fall apart between them, this combination helped to point Grant in the direction of corporate success because they complemented each other by maintaining a proper balance of each other's strengths and weaknesses. Whilst the description of both men might appear somewhat simplistic, a graphic illustration of their corporate persona provides better illumination.

An ex-staff of Grant cited a hypothetical example of a messy front office to demonstrate how both men would react to situations that required management decision. Akinlade, it was said, would set about clearing the mess himself but only after having openly complained about staff wanting him to do their jobs for them. Shobanjo, on the other hand, would walk right past the same mess, pretend not to have noticed it and immediately fire a sizzling hot query to whoever had the responsibility for keeping the place neat in the first instance. But the case of how both men handled David Akinyemi, who was one of the founding staff of Grant, provides a live illustration of the differing personality and corporate management styles of the new Managing Director and his deputy.

Akinlade and Shobanjo both acknowledged that Akinyemi, a highly talented yet extremely whimsical artist, resigned his job as many times as he was persuaded to keep it. Whilst Akinlade tolerated the eccentricities of the artist, Shobanjo could not condone them. Indeed, Shobanjo called Akinyemi's bluff by accepting one of his many resignations at a time Akinlade was away on official assignment. With the shoe now on the other foot, the artist pleaded to have his job back. It was the last time he would ever resign his appointment until Shobanjo left Grant.

The former 'Top Two' men at Grant had very simple explanations for the way they handled Akinyemi.

Akinlade:
"He (Akinyemi) was one of the founding members of Grant. I met him there; he had his whims and caprices (but) he was very good (and) my objective was setting professional standards. At a point when he was becoming and unbecoming, we split the Creative Department, (and) made him a figurehead. That was the best I could do. There was no way I could ask him to go into the cold; he was very good, we met him there (at Grant). You do not throw such a person out. I will not do that anywhere."

Shobanjo:

"Akinyemi consistently took it upon himself to hold the agency to ransom. You had to do his bidding or else he would not do a job when you needed it. Luckily for me, (he resigned) when the Managing Director was out of town. I quickly accepted his resignation, telling him not to serve out his notice period. He could not believe it. Of course, I was dead serious, too. For three days, he kept begging to be re-employed and I refused. When I eventually agreed, I laid down conditions, which he needed to follow to the letter and which he followed scrupulously until I left Grant."

Both viewpoints, placed side by side, tend to validate the argument that Akinlade is the better man and Shobanjo the better manager. But there is a major problem with this characterisation, for it heightened the perception of the MD as 'too soft' to be effective and his Deputy as 'ruthless' and, perhaps, 'overly ambitious'. Until the restructuring of the top management of Grant, Shobanjo was never regarded as being 'too ambitious.' On the contrary, he was, according to Akinlade, 'very loyal' to the agency. Shobanjo, too, affirmed that his loyalty to the organisation was informed by his initial plan to begin and end his advertising career in Grant. He, however, began to review his career plan the moment he started to doubt the focus and effectiveness of the leadership of the company.

On the surface and considering all that later happened, it might appear as though Shobanjo had a major problem with Akinlade at Grant. This will not be correct. His problem was Grant itself, which he felt was gratuitous in its handling of Nigerian staff and, importantly, had begun to divest itself of the creative challenger's mentality that shot it to prominence in the industry not long after it commenced operation. Indeed, his grouse with the agency could best be summed up in his words in an interview he granted a now-defunct celebrity news magazine[1]: "The company (Grant,) had seen the need to... call people like us to clear up the mess created by the expats who earned thrice as much as we did and who enjoyed four times as much benefits as we enjoyed."

There is need to put the interview in context. Long before the promulgation of the Nigerian Enterprises Promotion Decree of 1972, expatriates occupied the driver's seat in the practice of advertising in the country. Unlike in the present time, they also were unchallenged as leaders in the manufacturing and productive sectors of the economy, where indigenous initiatives were few and far between. Not surprisingly, advertising service providers and users of the service had mainly one thing in common: the colour of their skin, white. This had larger implications for advertising practice, as agencies tended to recruit expatriates to lead client service functions to take advantage of the white-on-white syndrome. At the time, this made a lot of business sense. The path to change was beaten by Nigeria's first graduate Client Service Executive, Moemeke, whose exemplary performance in holding down the client service function at Lintas went a long way to demonstrate that skin pigmentation was immaterial to professional excellence. In Shobanjo's recollection, the white-on-white syndrome took on a ridiculous dimension when, sometime in 1975 or thereabout, Grant, then headed by Johnston, hired an expatriate mechanic as an Account Supervisor:

"At the time he was hired, he had come to attend the Ba'hai (Faith) Conference. He came wanting to see the Managing Director... he was offered a job. But the man had never seen the inside of an agency (and) he had no clue as to what he was to do. He was given a car and a house at Apapa. Out of curiosity, I had asked him about his background. He said he was a professional mechanic and that his

---

[1]*Crown Prince, Op.cit p.25*

wife (a journalist) had filled him in on agency practice. The saving grace was that (his employment) was only for a short period as we were to discover that the Immigration Service at the time would not grant him a re-entry visa on scrutinising his papers and finding that he was most unqualified for the job that he wanted."

Grant, under the leadership of Akinlade and Shobanjo, also had McCann's Hemsley, a highly experienced advertising practitioner, as Resident Professional Consultant. The tripodal arrangement, on the face of it, had the two Nigerians as the most senior agency personnel. In real terms, however, Hemsley had a better contract in terms of remuneration and other perquisites attached to his office. In terms of accommodation, he initially resided in the high brow Marine Road, Apapa whereas the MD resided on Iwaya Road, Yaba and his Deputy in Surulere, both of which were in somewhat more densely populated areas that were not the best for the perceived 'big' positions they held in the agency. Much later, Hemsley moved to the exclusive Victoria Island while Akinlade moved to Ilupeju, a semi-exclusive part of Mainland Lagos. Shobanjo remained in Surulere. For the MD, the relocation was a relative improvement on his former habitation. Shobanjo felt this was not quite right, as it did not help them with exposure to the key people they were supposed to be interacting with for success on the job. His position was hinged on the fact that advertising is a people-based enterprise in which business outcomes are often determined by the quality of personal relationships that exists between clients and agency personnel.

Akinlade did not share Shobanjo's perspective on this issue. For him, the issue of the quality of their housing was irrelevant. He felt that 'personal comfort' was not as important on the job as proving to the owners of the business that they had chosen fit and proper Nigerians to oversee their interests.

Another sore point was that Shobanjo wondered aloud why Grant, which could afford to pay the school fees of Hemsley's children in Europe, could not extend the same gesture at a local level to its Nigerian management staff, even if only to the Managing Director. In his reckoning, doing this would not have negatively impacted the foreign exchange components of the agency's operation since payments to the Nigerians would have been denominated in the local currency, Naira, not in dollars. At the point of making this argument, Shobanjo's only child was barely one-year old whilst Akinlade had two of his children at K. Kotun Nursery and Primary School, a Surulere-based private school that was a favourite of the upper middle class.

Again, Akinlade did not subscribe to Shobanjo's line of thinking. His reason was that it was none of their business because they were not party to the agreement between Grant and McCann. More to the point, he did not want to risk incurring the ire of other Nigerian staff, who, he argued, might "kick against their colleagues" if they noticed too much disparity in their emoluments. Some other members of the board, too, were emphatic that the disbursement of the company's money was none of Shobanjo's business. He did not contest the fact. But he believed it was patently unfair not to be rewarded in a manner that was commensurate with his input.

The plank of Shobanjo's argument for leaving Grant was that the agency had become creatively blunt; missed its business bearing and, consequently, stagnated.

By 1972 or thereabout, a semblance of official ranking had long been established in the advertising industry in Nigeria. The indices of leadership were not simply limited to billing or staff count. Several other inter-twined business fundamentals were also taken into consideration. These required, for instance, that the leadership be indubitably seen as a solution centre, one that fully understood the business of its clients and could anticipate their changing needs as well as be well-positioned to offer creative solutions. Again, the leadership was expected to be able to attract and maintain quality manpower, just as it was expected that the company would be profitable, with staff genuinely projecting themselves as the organisation's brand ambassadors. Whereas reliable data was hard to come by to clearly establish these parameters, the degree of visibility of the brands handled by each agency in the market place became a vital, even if unofficial, index for the ranking of agencies. On all scores, the leadership of Lintas could not be controverted. OBM was next, with Grant placing third.

In real terms, the position of Lintas was practically guaranteed by its corporate parentage since the agency handled the very many market category leaders produced by the UAC/Lever Brothers group. OBM did well, too, managing various client portfolios from different sectors of the economy. Grant did not fare badly with its hotchpotch brands from such diverse sources as Food Specialities, Coca-Cola, Briscoe and Nasco.

Proponents of the stagnation theory posited that other agencies seemingly conceded automatic leadership of the industry to Lintas in part because they did not see any way by which they could claw their way into the agency's pie or develop the market to grow their business. They, therefore, were content with playing second fiddle. For some other people, Grant stagnated because of 'lost' business opportunities in the handling of various accounts. They claimed, for example, that the agency's creative platform lost its sharp edge and that rigour was missing in the interpretation of briefs with the result that brand building solutions were no longer as robust as they used to be. Worse, they claimed that the agency's creative solutions took longer than was necessary to articulate and execute. The result was that Grant was stuck in its Number 3 groove and it did not seem to be in any position to make a dramatic showing that could upstage either OBM or Lintas, then or in the nearest future. Shobanjo, who subscribed to these positions, strongly argued that the dynamism of the advertising business was a compelling reason for a serious industry player to successfully challenge the supremacy of Lintas despite its corporate parentage. In countless interviews after he left, he, without mentioning names, consistently described the lethargic management of Grant as one major reason it was difficult to aggregate the business imperatives that would have made the agency imbibe the mentality of a serious challenger. Doing this would have lifted it out of its perennial also-ran position.

Akinlade disputed the stagnation theory, arguing: "I think we were aspiring to be Number One. We had a strong team, we had very good accounts... he (Shobanjo) was a part of the decision – taking process, the executive. He knew what was going on within the organisation. There was no decision I took without consulting them (Shobanjo and Hemsley)."

He, however, believed that his former deputy may not have been too pleased with him for a far more serious reason. He disclosed that Shobanjo had propositioned him about breaking ranks with Grant but not necessarily as partners. When he sought to understand the need for this intended course of action, he recalled his deputy as having told him that he believed the two of them had reached the apogee of their respective careers within the establishment and, therefore, should seriously consider casting their nets far afield to make good for themselves in their new endeavours. Akinlade said he was not receptive to the idea mainly because he reasoned that the owners of the business, particularly Lawson and Ogunbanjo, would be highly disappointed and would probably have described their younger compatriots as 'ingrates'. He believed that if they defected from Grant, it would have adverse effects on the careers of other Nigerians employed by either Lawson or Ogunbanjo in their other companies. He did not think it was right to break away. Or, if they needed to, he felt the timing was not auspicious.

Shobanjo did not remember ever having discussed a breakaway with Akinlade. Thoughts of going solo at that point, he maintained, had not crossed his mind so there could not have been any basis for such a discussion or any suggestion of one with Akinlade: 'I was too much of a loyalist to have contemplated this, much less suggested it to Festus.'

Even at that, it is not difficult to understand his impatience with the establishment, for he is a quintessential stand-up-and-fight personality. His desire to see Grant as nulli secundus in the industry would probably qualify as one of the few things that he earnestly desired but was unable to achieve. It was obvious that his thinking was at variance with the Managing Director's. Although he tried his best to mask his disappointment later events would show he was not too successful at doing this. It only took a casual remark early in 1979 by a friend, who was also a valuable client of Grant, to awaken him to the reality that his corporate life had almost lost its sizzle. The client said, 'leave Grant', but not exactly in those words.

He initially thought the idea heretic. But when he saw beyond his doubts, he realised that the bell had begun to toll for him in the agency. He harboured no illusion that something needed to give, both for his own sake and in the interest of the organisation. He gingerly nursed the idea of an exit and soon found sufficient justification for it, but he was not exactly sure of how early this would have to be. In October 1979, circumstances took the situation out of his control following which he dropped his notice of voluntary resignation with the Chairman, Chief Lawson.

The 'sudden' resignation of the Deputy Managing Director caught several people unawares. Staff asked themselves: why would Mr. Shobanjo resign just like that? They knew there had been a restructuring of the administrative system but they, like most other people, could not fathom the need for it. The surprise expressed by the staff was understandable. Between 1976 and 1979 Shobanjo had supervised the recruitment of a corps of bright young people to join the move to push Grant into the thick of breakthrough advertising. Among the eager beavers were Foluso 'Babu' Akinbobola (who later became a President of the Outdoor Advertising Agencies of Nigeria, OAAN); Jimi Awosika (currently Group Managing Director of Troyka Holdings) and the late Sesan Ogunro (former Chairman/Chief Executive Officer of Eminent Communications). The latter two crossed over from Radio Nigeria, Shobanjo's former constituency. Another, Richard Ibe, a graphic artist, who had a short stint as an insurance clerk with Royal Exchange Assurance of Nigeria (REAN), was recruited in 1976. Yemi Amogbe (now deceased), an accountant, also came aboard during Shobanjo's tenure as Deputy Managing Director.

Many of these young professionals saw Shobanjo as the livewire of Grant, first, because his presence was hard to ignore but, more importantly, because of his can-do spirit. He made them believe that nothing was impossible. He made them believe that with breakthrough thinking, disciplined creativity and strong persuasive presentations an agency could do no wrong with clients. He rewarded their hard work with more audacious targets. He became something of a folk hero and they tended to align him more with Grant than they did Akinlade. Some of these young people would later become active participants in the revolution that shook (and is still shaking) the marketing communications industry in Nigeria.

Speaking generally, the effect of the organisational change on the operations of the agency was 'not too noticeable' because the contending forces did their utmost to mask their disagreements and did not allow their differences to seep out uncontrollably to the lower crust of the company's hierarchy or cause any sharp division amongst staff. Outwardly, everything seemed all right because the Managing Director and his deputy put out a front that proclaimed 'business as usual.' Inwardly, the cauldron boiled at the top and, with Shobanjo's resignation, spilled its content. Everyone had reasons to be surprised at the turn of events.

On receipt of Shobanjo's resignation notice, Chief Lawson summoned the younger man to a meeting to discuss his planned exit. The seasoned entrepreneur wanted to know the real reasons behind his action but he only got explanations that were short on details. The Chairman painted a rosy picture of the future in which Shobanjo had a significant role to play in the business. The Deputy Managing Director, however, stood by his decision to leave the agency when the Chairman requested he withdrew his letter of resignation. He thanked the Chairman and the company's board for the years of support and encouragement that culminated in his rise to the position of Deputy Managing Director, which, at his age, was unexpected and overwhelming in a competitive business environment. He re-affirmed his decision to quit, arguing that doing otherwise because of the Chairman's intervention would create the impression that he desperately wanted the Managing Director's job. The meeting with Lawson ended on that note.

Like a typical Yoruba elder, Lawson calmly accepted the younger man's resignation. If he was unhappy about it, he did not let it show, perhaps, because he appeared to have developed a soft spot for Shobanjo whose professional competence and business acumen he had noted over the years. Two incidents lend credence to this position. Soon after the business mogul established a combined residential and industrial estate that is today known as Agbara Estates, the first by any Nigerian, he carefully handpicked a crop of young men to join him in 1978 on the supervisory board of the new company. The board comprised Lawson; his son, Kolapo; Alex Thomopoulous, now Vice Chairman of The Guardian newspapers; the late Abdulai Taiwo and Shobanjo. The board was headed by Lawson's friend, the late Mr. Henry Etim Duke, father of the former Governor of Cross River State, Donald Duke. The elder Duke was at the time Chairman of the Nigeria Customs & Excise Service. It did not matter to Lawson that Shobanjo had confessed not having a clue as to what real estate management was all about. He was just confident that the rookies he had assembled were very smart, fast learners who would begin to contribute to the success of the enterprise in the shortest possible time. Unfortunately, however, Shobanjo had to relinquish this appointment less than one year after due to his resignation from Grant advertising.

Shobanjo's business-like disposition was also not lost on Lawson. This was reinforced in 1977 when the Deputy Managing Director of Grant refused to accept a request for advertisement placement from the Grail Movement, of which Lawson was the founder in Nigeria. Ever before Shobanjo joined Grant, the Movement had always placed all its advertisements through the agency, which was understandable considering Lawson's involvement with both organisations. What riled Shobanjo was the backlog of payments that the Movement had not offset. For this reason, he declined to entertain a full-page placement request brought by Mrs Ayonmagbemi, the Advert Manager of Modern Publications, owned by the late Chief Bisi Onabanjo, a former Governor of Ogun State. He walked on very thin ice here. He was an employee of Grant; Ayonmagbemi was a member of the Grail Movement; her husband was a member of the Board of Grant and Lawson connected all the dots. Shobanjo was not fazed when she issued a subtle threat that Lawson had instructed that the ad be run. He told her it was not to his understanding that Grant was established to run ads on credit for anybody, the Grail Movement included, irrespective of its founder and his links with Grant. Ayonmagbemi was shocked. She reported the incident to Lawson but was twice shocked when the Chairman wrote his cheque in full settlement of all outstanding debts and pre-paid the new ad so it could run as scheduled. Lawson commended Shobanjo's action but was roundly displeased with those who serviced the account from the Grail Movement organisation. His displeasure stemmed from not being made aware of debts owed Grant; for him, business was business. A subdued Ayonmagbemi returned to Grant the next day to apologise to Shobanjo for her needless insistence that the ad be run on credit.

In the wake of the happenings in the company, the Grant board convened an extraordinary meeting to discuss, among other issues, Shobanjo's recent resignation. The meeting failed to persuade Shobanjo to withdraw his notice of resignation. Whilst other board members wondered at Shobanjo's determination to leave, Akinlade was not in any way surprised. He quietly told the board all he knew. Shobanjo, too, was not surprised by Akinlade's disclosures. There and then the board knew that any attempt to prevail on the Deputy Managing Director to rescind his decision would be an exercise in futility. His resignation was accepted.

Not long after the board meeting, a furious Akinlade stormed the agency, flexing his biceps. By then, all the prime targets of his fit of anger at the 48 Bode Thomas Street offices of Grant had bolted from the barn. Shobanjo calmly ended his eight-year career in the agency on 31 December, 1979 at the expiration of the mandatory three-month period of disengagement stipulated in his terms of employment.

Two days after he formally signed off from the agency, he opened a new chapter in the history of advertising practice in Nigeria. That chapter also made him one of the most successful and most talked about enterprise managers in Nigeria. In his new role as the evangelist of a new order in the advertising business, he became a dominant force, a well-cultivated and carefully nurtured brand. It did not matter whether one loved his personality or approved of his hold-no-prisoner approach to doing business; what mattered was that he walked his talk and he, without apologies, exuded the confidence of a thoroughbred professional. He knew it; competition acknowledged it and the market responded positively to his dream. This made him so happy and, perhaps, a trifle immodest, as he declared to a journalist[1]:

"I am the guy they love to hate."

Of his experience at Grant, he would later say:

"It was a great learning period for me, I received tremendous amount of training. There was easy followership. I was able to carry the staff along with me because a lot of them believed there was something to learn from me. I learnt from them, too. If only we had moved along the lines I advocated at the time, Grant Advertising could have been one of the best advertising agencies in the country today."

Perhaps.

---

[1] *Crown Prince, P.30.*

Team Shobanjo 2018: with Joyce, sons, daughters, in-laws and grandchildren

Dad, Joseph Shobowale Shobanjo died in
December 1959 at age 49

Mum, Madam Morinat Alaba Shobanjo aka
'Iye Oyinbo' died in September 2018 at age 100

Biodun and Joyce Shobanjo with sons, daughters and in-laws

Generation 3...Biodun Shobanjo's grandchildren

Biodun Shobanjo with wife, Joyce, at grandfather in-law's funeral in Asaba, Delta State

Super Dad! with Olufemi (left), Funke, Dolapo, Abimbola and Babatunde (L)

With Mum and Joyce at Dolapo's engagement

Celebrating Joyce at 40

Wedding bell...with Joyce at son, Femi's wedding to Elaine

Stepping out...With Joyce

Family ties:
From left: Nephew, Kunle Anipole; daughter in-law, Elaine; daughter, Funke;
Biodun Shobanjo; son, Babatunde; daughter in-law, Abimbola and sons, Abimbola, Olufemi at the surprise party
held to celebrate Troyka Holdings/Publicis Groupe's equity partnership

Strengthening the bond of friendship: with Engr. Leke Dina and Chief Oladele Fajemirokun at a family event

At work and at play with long time buddy, Chief Akin Odunsi, at an AAPN function and a social engagement

With Chief Oladele Fajemirokun and Prof. Oye Ibidapo-Obe (c)

Friend…Dele Giwa, Editor-in-Chief of Newswatch Magazine
who was parcel-bombed on 19th October, 1986

Former Governor of Ekiti State, Otunba Niyi Adebayo;
Former Governor of Ogun State, Aremo Olusegun Osoba and
Oba Sikiru Adetona, the Awujale of Ijebuland

Former Governor of Ogun State, Aremo Olusegun Osoba (l),
Olori Dayo Onagoruwa and Oba Sikiru Adetona, the Awujale of Ijebuland

Out sailing...with Joyce and David Neil and wife

Aloha! Enjoying Hawaiian hospitality
in the company of Dr. Kayode Ojutiku;
Dr. Mrs. Doyin Ojutiku and Joyce

Sharing quality time with friends in Hawaii
Front row: Dr Yemi Ogunbiyi; Chief Mrs Sade Ogunbiyi;
Joyce and Biodun Shobanjo; **Middle:** Dr. Mrs Doyin Ojutiku;
Mrs Yinka Ayanlaja and Mrs Elaine Ogunbiyi;
Back row: Dr. Kayode Ojutiku; Mr Tunji Ayanlaja, SAN
and Dr. Layi Ogunbiyi.

Time-out in Hawaii with Joyce, Mrs Yinka Ayanlaja;
Mr. Tunji Ayanlaja, SAN; Mrs Elaine Ogunbiyi;
Chief Mrs Sade Ogunbiyi and Dr. Layi Ogunbiyi

At a social function with late insurance magnate, Prince Yemo Adeyera (l)
and the former Chairman of Punch newspapers, Chief Ajibola Ogunsola

88

In-laws: Biodun Shobanjo, Mrs. Shirley Obuaya, Mrs. Joyce Shobanjo, Dr. Tony Obuaya

Gen. Theophilus and Mrs Daisy Danjuma

Self-financed construction of a community road at Aiyepe

Shobanjo's country home in Aiyepe

5

Have You Considered Working Anywhere Else?

"I'll end the tyranny of the status quo.
I'm a pathfinder"

(Wharton Executive Education advertisement)

J imi Awosika, the young Client Service Executive that Shobanjo recruited into Grant Advertising in January, 1978, watered the seed of the idea that changed the advertising landscape in Nigeria. It all started when they both travelled to Jos, the capital of the former Benue-Plateau State in 1978 for a meeting with their interface at the headquarters of Nasco Group of companies, a multi-faceted business enterprise founded by the Nasreddin family of Eritrea. The Group, which had considerable interests in manufacturing and food processing, among others, was one of Grant's major clients supervised by Shobanjo who, over time, had developed very strong business and personal ties with its Group General Manager at the time, Saleh Nasreddin. The long-standing relationship of the duo was built on the twin-pillars of professionalism and mutual respect. By unspoken consent, neither man allowed friendship to stand in the way of business, as they worked in earnest to ensure that both remained mutually exclusive.

When Shobanjo was ushered into Nasreddin's office for their scheduled client/agency meeting, he was ice-cool on the outside but, inside, he nursed a big measure of positive discontent. The contact meeting progressed as usual but after it ended, Nasreddin let slip his observation about the widening gap between Grant's creative work and its non-passionate presentation by the account management team. He had been perceptive enough to spot Shobanjo's frustrations, which was not a surprise considering that any experienced business person who has had any respectable interaction with agency personnel could always tell when an account handler had lost the power of conviction. In not so many words, the business executive advised the adman to go open his own shop, if he felt caught in a gridlock at Grant. Shobanjo's razor-sharp antenna caught the remark that Nasreddin made so casually.

As a frequent visitor to Jos, he had fallen in love with the city that was devoid of the characteristic chaos associated with urban dwelling. Jos, at the time, had a magnetic pull and cool weather that many agree was conducive for dislodging cobwebs from any man's head. This contrasted with Jos of the present time that has become the hotbed of religious and political upheavals. Shobanjo often fell under the spell of the city and was always eager to leave the hustle and bustle of Lagos behind to luxuriate in the cool embrace of the hilly and windy environment. He arrived Jos in the company of Awosika and the late Taiwo Odunewu, then a Senior Account Executive, not knowing that the trip would mark the beginning of the end of his career in Grant. By the time they left the city, he and Awosika were preoccupied with thoughts of the discussions that took place in the client's office. Speech was unnecessary as they individually weighed the implications of Nasreddin's suggestion, for he had hinted at executing a coup from within the Grant hierarchy.

Awosika searched his boss' face for clues, any clue whatsoever, as to what was running at the back of his mind. Shobanjo's face was inscrutable. Soon enough, his brow twitched, as it is wont to do anytime he found something to crow about. Awosika got his cue and began to push the merits of the idea of founding a new creative outfit, not minding what his boss thought.
Sir," he began tentatively, "Don't you think Saleh is right?"
"About what?" Shobanjo shot back.

The sharp retort momentarily threw Awosika off balance. He was not sure if his boss was fishing for information or that he glowered at him to convey his irritation. But he was beyond care as he forged on with his arguments: "I don't think it's a bad idea, Sir, for you to set up a new agency as Saleh had suggested. You have the experience, the contacts and the will to change the face of this business. And if you set your mind to it, you can do it; we both know this."

"Hm!" Shobanjo grunted. Awkward silence followed, as his head began to simultaneously process the weighty challenge from Nasreddin as well as its reinforcement by Awosika, who had expected to be reprimanded for preaching the 'heresy' of floating a new agency. Both men did not seem to have been bothered by Odunewu's presence.

When Shobanjo eventually spoke, it was to warn his subordinate never again to bring up the matter. He felt he could wish it away because he had always pictured himself not as an entrepreneur but as an employee hoping to retire someday from Grant. Yet, given his unease with the situation in the office, the idea of an exit from the agency held some appeal. They dropped the subject and bantered on other mundane issues on the flight back to Lagos. But they both knew that the subject would crop up somehow, someday in the nearest future.

In the end, the prodding by Awosika won the day. With time, Shobanjo became convinced he had heard the call, though its form had not fully crystallised in his mind. There were grey areas needing illumination for him to tell where to lay the first bricks. On subsequent trips to Jos, he cleverly evaded questions posed by Nasreddin concerning the extent of consideration given to his earlier suggestion. He similarly kept Awosika at bay until a clearer perspective of the project emerged.

About the time this was happening, Steve Omojafor and his colleagues, Akin Odunsi and Tunde Adelaja, also came quite close to re-writing the script of Shobanjo's career. The trio had been classmates and friends since their days in the Department of Mass Communication at the University of Lagos between 1969 and 1972. In the labour market, however, they all headed in different directions. While Omojafor and Adelaja pitched their tents with Lintas a few years apart, Odunsi joined Grant in 1974 and for the second time in his career, his professional life crossed path with Shobanjo's whereupon they developed a close-knit relationship. Odunsi later introduced Shobanjo to his old schoolmates. All four got along quite fine and built a social and professional relationship that, over the years, survived the twists and turns of competitive pitches in adworld. As the trio began to fine-tune the proposal for the establishment of Rosabel Advertising in the late 1970s, the idea of bringing Shobanjo on board came up for consideration. He then was in the UK attending a training programme. The idea gestated amongst the Rosabel musketeers but, in the end, did not take root, as Shobanjo declined an invitation extended to him through Odunsi who met with him in London. He could not consider a move out of Grant at the time because he felt the agency was treating him fairly. More than this, he held back mainly because of his deep respect and admiration for its Chairman, Chief Lawson.

Ironically, Adelaja, one of the Rosabel trio, was the first person to whom Shobanjo breathed a word about his plans to explore the possibility of setting up an agency. They spoke when Adelaja visited him at the Churchill Hotel, London, during a trip to the UK in 1979. The discussion cropped up because Shobanjo kept faith with his firm rule of always getting information first hand from knowledgeable and reliable sources. As they both strolled on Oxford Street, London, he stopped Adelaja to enquire about the cost of floating a new advertising agency. They discussed various possibilities but did not arrive at any specific figure for the start up. It was no-brainer that any agency, existing or proposed, that intended to take on the leading agencies had an uphill task in terms of the availability of tested personnel, financial muscle, physical infrastructure and general goodwill in the market. In strict financial terms, the 'Big Three' advertising agencies of the time: Lintas, OBM and Grant firmly controlled the market.

Year-on-year, each had consistently recorded a minimum annual billing of N6 million. In his heart, Shobanjo knew that only a King's ransom would breathe life into his dream communications company. He was mindful of the odds stacked against him but he was not deterred because his goal was to re-create the Saatchi & Saatchi magic on the local scene. The Saatchi brothers, Charles and Maurice, were world-renowned for founding the famous Saatchi & Saatchi agency that stunned Europe and, indeed, the global advertising world, within a decade of being in business.

Beyond finance, Shobanjo knew he would also need to grapple with the challenge of staffing the proposed agency. Though the advertising industry in 1979 employed several good hands, these were not as adventurous as their modern-day cousins. For most of them, the grass was greener where they stood and they felt safer under the shade provided by their employers. After a deep reflection on his objectives vis-à-vis the manpower needed to succeed, he mentally summed up the qualities of the professional colleagues he would need to make the crossing to the Promised Land: "I looked basically for people who shared the kind of vision that I had... young people who were dynamic, who were knowledgeable, who could be developed, who had innate talents that would blossom over a period of time, who I thought would be committed, who would be honest and who had integrity."

The emphasis on the intertwining of youth, knowledge, passion and integrity in the human resource blueprint immediately made it evident that greenhorns had little or no place in his scheme of things. Since the realisation of his ambition was contingent on speed and elements of surprise, it also immediately became evident that he would have to look a lot more inwards for solutions. In the circumstance, the most viable option was to headhunt from Grant. He thus began to pencil down members of his 'dream team', a task he knew would be easier to accomplish than pooling financial resources for take-off. When he felt the time was right, he summoned his confidant, Awosika, to apprise him of the new development. The younger man promptly aligned with the plan of his boss, fully convinced that the move was long overdue.

Feyijimi (Jimi, for short), the first child of Mr. and Mrs. Samuel Kokumo Awosika, was born in 1953 in Owo although he is an indigene of Ondo in Ondo State. He attended St. Joseph's College, Ondo and Government College, Ibadan before he gained admission to the University of Lagos, where he read Mass Communication and graduated in 1976 as one of the best in his class. Like Shobanjo, he, too, had a very short stint on his first job. He worked for just three months with the United African Company, UAC, before he, again like Shobanjo, dropped anchor at the studios of the Nigerian Broadcasting Corporation, NBC, which he left as a Senior Sub-Editor in 1978. While at NBC, he had confided in a few people that he would very much love to make a career change, from broadcasting to advertising. The moment he declared his interest in advertising practice, fate took charge, steering him to Grant and inexorably to Shobanjo. Two of the people he spoke with were his boss at NBC, Abiodun Adeniyi and his old teacher at Unilag, the late Professor Alfred Opubor. Both virtually dropped him on Shobanjo's lap.

When the applicant met his prospective employer, each instantly took to the other, particularly because they shared a common trait of incurable optimism. In truth, the six-foot one-inch Awosika is a likeable fellow, especially when he speaks. Highly cerebral, he is mightily expansive – the laughter in his voice is wildly infectious and he is not given to being slow. Often, Awosika's words merely amplify the vivid picture he effortlessly creates in a listener's mind with his gestures. He is every client's dream of what an agency staff should be: highly knowledgeable; amazingly proactive, very passionate about the business and, socially, the life of the party.

It turned out that Awosika was never formally interviewed for the job at Grant, though he confessed he knew little of advertising. Indeed, he did not have much to say about the reason he desired employment with the agency except that everyone he had spoken with described Grant as the place to work. While Awosika was struck by the neat profile and relative youth of the Number Two man in the agency who then was only 33, Shobanjo saw a 'very brilliant young man who had tremendous opportunities ahead of him.' The nine-year difference in age and the gap in their official status did not stop them from building a strong relationship that was based on mutually earned respect. By mutual adoption both became 'brothers.' The crossing of paths between them was remarkable because it took almost one year for Shobanjo to hire Awosika who, by this time, had become fairly close to the Deputy Managing Director and a regular visitor to his home. The degree of their closeness was such that Shobanjo knew Awosika's girlfriend at the time and he had become his surrogate brother. One week after Awosika was hired, something unusual happened. His mother drove herself to Grant in her Datsun 180K to specifically thank Shobanjo for hiring her son. She exacted a promise from the Deputy Managing Director to take Jimi under his wings, not just as his boss but as his mentor and big brother. Shobanjo has kept the bargain to this day. About two weeks after Awosika joined Grant, Shobanjo's second child, a girl, Funke, was born. The happiness of the occasion further helped to cement the relationship between them. Today, Awosika sees Funke as his first daughter.

Together, Awosika and Shobanjo constituted the think-tank that honed strategies to birth the new agency. The more they mulled over their secret project, the more they came to the realisation that they had five key challenges to meet. First, they needed to define the vision of the company. Next, they needed to agree on the corporate identity of the proposed entity without losing sight of the environment as well as infrastructure with which it would operate. They also needed to resolve the issues of funding, staffing and take-off date. At work and at play, occasionally in the office but frequently at home, they began to take the problems apart one after the other, leaving no stone unturned, yet mindful of the need to maintain absolute secrecy without which the project might be stillborn. It was just as well that few people knew that the tango in Grant was headed for a denouement by the time the idea of the new agency was mooted early in 1979. The relative stability in the work environment, therefore, worked to Shobanjo's advantage, as he enjoyed relative peace that enabled him to sharpen his strategies with minimal distractions. Whatever pressure he felt was more in his mind and of his own making, not the creation of external forces.

Shobanjo truly dreamt big concerning the company, knowing that the degree of confidence that a buyer has in what is being sold as well as in the pedigree of the seller were critical elements of successful advertising. He envisioned an agency that would be the most creative business communication partner to any client in the country; one that would deeply understand the dynamics of the marketplace as a platform to craft persuasive messages that clearly, creatively and consistently impel action. In his calculations, no local agency of the time measured up to these expectations and aspirations, so none could serve as a model for his start-up. His benchmark was international. As we shall soon see, his determination to raise the bar of performance, even at the conceptual level, would someday become a source of constant irritation to other players in the industry.

In terms of the market need, Shobanjo and Awosika easily agreed the core corporate values of the business. Quality was a key element that was clearly spelt out in the company's blueprint. This took various forms. One was that the agency's services must help clients to realise their business goals. Another was that the agency's employee welfare programme must guarantee a better life for the workforce and their dependants. The long-term focus on both exernal and internal stakeholders was deliberate; it was to ensure that the proposed agency was judged by its own self-set high standard. That way, it was envisaged that the commitment to excellence would easily mark out the company in the industry. They also put in place a series of other non-negotiable issues that would undergird the operations of the company. As an enterprise, the new company must be profitable through fair returns on investments; it must operate within the economic laws of Nigeria and, most important, it must be people-centred, with all workers being properly groomed to reach the peak of their careers. This was captured in the belief that top talents make the difference and that the application of these top talents, if well managed, would lead to consistent production of outstanding work, with fame and fortune assumed. Almost four decades after, this is still the guiding principle of Troyka Group. In general terms, the outfit was conceived to be the preferred agency in the communications industry. No deadline was set for attaining this goal.

If conceptualising the corporate philosophy of the company was easy, funding the dream was next to a nightmare. In matters of finance, the modern-day Moses and his Aaron reached the 'Red Sea' a lot faster than anyone could say 'Exodus'. At the bank of the sea of lucre, they badly needed help to cross over to the 'other side'. On a conventional scale, his dream was a very tall one to which none of the existing local champions could hold a candle. As he saw it, particularly after his discussions in London with Adelaja and subsequent personal research, even if he adopted the best cost-cutting measures necessary for a start up enterprise, his proposed best-in-class creative agency would gulp no less than N100,000 to get off ground. His bank statement could not support that kind of dream and he was mindful that efforts to come by that tidy sum of money in 1979 would nearly be equivalent to physically moving a mountain. But he believed too much in the dream to be deterred.

He and Awosika spoke discreetly with a few people whom they thought could give wings to their dream. They got tonnes of promises but the potential financiers were all short on delivery. In desperation, they opted to invite affluent citizens to take up equity in the proposed company for which they were willing to concede as much as 60 per cent stake, if only to ensure that their plan saw the light of day.

Awosika's uncle-in-law, the late Chief Abiola Oshodi, entered the picture when he introduced the duo to prominent lawyer/politician, Chief Hilario Babs-Akerele, who later became the State Chairman of the National Party of Nigeria, NPN, in Lagos in the Second Republic. Babs-Akerele quickly let them know he already was a shareholder in Akrel Advertising that was owned by his cousin, Kofoworola Bucknor-Akerele, who later became a Senator and, in 1999, the Deputy Governor of Lagos State in the Third Republic. But he also let them know he could be interested in the new project because of the enthusiasm of the promoters and especially because of the introduction from Chief Oshodi. He, however, told them straightaway that he was sceptical of advertising as a profitable business venture. He did not think the return on investment could compare with what could realistically be made on the sale of, say, rice, which, at the time, was a fast-moving commodity in Nigeria. He requested for cash-flow projections and allied information on the company, just so he could arrive at a decision on whether to stake his money on their dream. From that point, the business promoters began to soft-pedal on discussions with Babs-Akerele because of their reading of his disposition. Intuition told them that their potential backer did not believe in the project, perhaps, because of whatever experience he might have had at Akrel advertising. They never went back to him.

Nasreddin came to the rescue. He graciously gave a lifeline of N25,000 to Shobanjo despite not having been apprised of developments on his earlier suggestion until the need to raise funds arose. The money was not a loan but an expression of goodwill. But he made it clear that an automatic movement of the Nasco account out of Grant to the proposed agency was out of the question. If the new agency needed the business, it must, like everyone else, fight for it.

Awosika arrived Jos early one Thursday morning in September, 1979 to pick the money from Nasreddin. It was a hefty sum both in terms of value and physical weight, as it consisted of different denominations of bank notes and some coins at a time that N20 was the highest denomination of the Naira. He immediately raced to Kano Airport to catch the Lagos-bound evening flight of Nigeria Airways, the nation's flag carrier. He could not secure a boarding pass. The hard airport bench became his bed for the night and the bag of money served as his pillow. Every so often he woke up and gave the bag a vigorous shake to be sure the money in it was safe. Friday came and it went, yet there was no space on board any departing flight from Kano. He was nearly paralysed by the fear of losing the money. In the wee hours of Saturday morning, he was virtually smuggled aboard a flight from Jeddah. From the airport, he made straight for Shobanjo's residence in Surulere and was only able to relax after he handed over the money intact. The 48-hour stress test convinced Awosika he was on the right path though they were unable to raise the remainder of the take-off fund from several other sources they had contacted. Until they got the fresh fund from Nasreddin, the only other contributor, apart from Shobanjo, was Goddy Amadi who was Shobanjo's very close friend and client at Unipetrol.

The search for a suitable name for the outfit proved elusive for a while. They discarded as many names as they considered. Much earlier, they had agreed that whatever name they came up with would not represent any person's names, initials or his idiosyncrasies; rather, it must communicate the essence of what the agency would offer. They pored over BRAD Advertising Media, a standard reference published in the United Kingdom. The publication was a major resource because everyone knew it to be Shobanjo's 'bible' while Advertising Age and Campaign magazines were his daily guide. BRAD failed to throw up any name that could match their ambition to float an enterprise that would be self-starting and record-setting. Still, Shobanjo refused to settle for any other 'good' name that could easily pass. Instead, he counselled that the issue be re-visited later to avail more time to generate more ideas and increase the chances of success in the search for the right name. As he is wont to say whenever he mulled over a serious issue that appeared to defy quick solution, he lapsed into his native Yoruba language and told Awosika: 'je ki a fi oju inu wo,' which, in its ordinary meaning, approximates to considering the matter with the inner eyes. The casual remark had a nice ring to it, for it assumed a high degree of introspection, maturity and patience to achieve an expected end. 'Oju inu' became the nugget of an idea that they bounced against the length and breadth of Shobanjo's living room until it came out refined as Insight. The name survived the '24-hour test', which is a rule of thumb in advertising to determine if an idea truly is the idea. Its application is simple: any idea that failed to generate as much excitement the day after it was conceived cannot be said to be the idea.

Insight generated a lot of excitement because it suggested being propelled to success by internal momentum. Over time and across cultures, it has been proved that the success or otherwise of any enterprise is intricately intertwined with the twin principles of proactivity and the propensity to channel thoughts in the right direction. Insight embodied both notions and its chic appeal was a bonus. Thus, was Insight Communications born. As events in the growth of the agency would show much later, the choice of 'Communications' over 'Advertising' was also a masterstroke.

Convinced that Insight's human resource base would come from a selective headhunt of some hands from Grant, Shobanjo zeroed in on a few candidates with Awosika topping the list. Apart from bonding perfectly from the first day they met, Shobanjo felt Awosika deserved a shirt because he had distinguished himself as an account handler. Within a very short period of his employment as a trainee Account Executive, Awosika had been assigned to work on two of Grant's biggest accounts, namely Food Specialities (on which he worked alongside the late Mosun Oyenuga and David Hemsley – who was the Account Director) and Nasco (with Shobanjo). He also worked with Shobanjo on the Nicholas Laboratories account. Awosika is fussy about getting things done properly and he tends to have them done his own way. His client servicing creed, which has survived till date, requires that agency personnel be ambassadors of the brands in their care and, as such, do whatever was necessary to build the brands of clients. His philosophy is built on the simple premise that value is always from the point of view of the receiver, not the giver. 'Take an investment approach' is his popular refrain when he counsels agency personnel who do not feel appreciated by clients.

From very early in his career, he exhibited Shobanjo's belief that a good agency staff must always stick to his client like a tick and, figuratively, become the client's third arm. Over the years, Awosika had been this and more to all his client interfaces. In and out of office, Awosika is very much persuasive and few can resist him when he turns on the charm, as his one-time client, Piyush Nair, then Marketing Director of De-United Food Industries, makers of the popular Indomie Noodles, would readily testify. During one of their numerous social engagements, Awosika persuaded Piyush to 'share a beer' with him. In the thick of enlightened discussions on several subject matters that were laced with intermittent jokes, throaty laughter across table and a few more shared bottles, it dawned on Piyush that he might go well past his threshold. He playfully but firmly pulled the reins and stopped. "Come on, Jimi, you're going to kill me!" he exclaimed in mock seriousness.

Having worked together for about two years, Shobanjo and Awosika had become physically and mentally attuned to each other. For the subordinate, Shobanjo became 'Egbs', which is Awosika's anglicism of the Yoruba word, 'Egbon' or 'Big Brother while the leader referred to his lieutenant as 'Wosh(ie)', derived from Awosika, or simply by his first name, Jimi. Years later, Awosika got to be called 'Baale' by everyone in the Group of companies that emerged out of the success of Insight because of his position as the indisputable No. 2 citizen in the Group. The uncompromising professionalism of the younger man weighed heavily in his favour with Shobanjo. The warm personal chemistry between them was a huge dividend. Shobanjo knew and believed that Insight's client service department would be in very good hands.

Shobanjo was tentative in his approach to other members of his proposed team because he needed to be sure they could sing with him from the same page of the hymn book. He approached Richard Ibe in a roundabout manner. He began to fish for information to ascertain if the Art Director, who worked with him on the Eternit account, was ready and willing to hop aboard a new boat, should an opportunity present itself. He had reasons to zero in on Ibe whom he had persuaded to make a career in advertising instead of teaching. The two had first met in 1974 when Ibe, then an undergraduate at the Ahmadu Bello University, ABU, Zaria, picked a vacation job at Grant. Shobanjo, then, was a Senior Account Executive. Ibe again worked briefly at Grant in between completing his bachelor's degree in Graphic Design and getting called up for the compulsory one-year National Youth Service Corps, NYSC, programme. Twice, the Lagos-born artist of Igbo extraction had attempted to enlist in the Nigerian Army; twice, he was unlucky. He was on the verge of taking up a teaching appointment in Kano in 1976 when he once more met Shobanjo who talked him into joining Grant as a Studio Manager in August, 1976. By 1979, he had risen to the position of Art Director winning awards for high productivity for two consecutive years. This, for Shobanjo, was enough to qualify him for a place in the proposed outfit.

During one of their many trips to Eternit's offices in Sapele in then Bendel State, Shobanjo and Ibe discussed everything and nothing. In-between, Shobanjo casually asked: "Richard, have you ever considered working anywhere else apart from Grant?" Unknown to him, Ibe had previously turned down about three of such surreptitious offers. Though Shobanjo did not come at him frontally, the artist knew what his boss was driving at. He tactfully played along.
"Not really; but it might be an interesting move if I find a good idea promoted by someone I deeply respect, like you, Sir."
End of discussions.

For Copy, Sesan Ogunro was an obvious choice. The young man from Ise-Ekiti, whom Shobanjo had employed in 1977 from NBC where he was a Sub-Editor, had a knack for consistently churning out good headlines, among them was 'Have a gooood time on Top', which was one of the most memorable copylines of the time that was developed for Top lager beer. Ogunro, like his boss, had a lively, sunshine disposition. They ate lunch together from time to time and evolved their own interesting glossary of culinary terms among which was the high falutin 'lugbson temerity', which was their saucy nickname for bushmeat. Each man understood the other's code and temperament and, as a result, bonded well. His place was assured.

Johnson Adebayo also made the list due to his expertise in print production. Thereafter, Shobanjo looked no further as he felt he now had his complete team. Awosika did not think so. He pointed out a gaping hole in the selection: no one had been pencilled down to manage Insight's finances, a function that he argued strongly would play a significant role in the success or otherwise of the company. Awosika suggested Grant's bean counter, Ibiyemi Amogbe, for the job. For personal reasons, Shobanjo objected. The argument went forth and back for a time. As with the debate on the need to pull out of Grant, Awosika successfully convinced his boss on the merits of his position. Shobanjo backed down on his objection to Amogbe's nomination. The accountant thus became the sixth and final member of the founding Insight team.

Though each member of the group had been carefully sounded out and selected, none of them, except Awosika, knew that anything serious was afoot. The form and content of Insight, including the list of its founders remained a closely guarded secret for about nine months because Shobanjo and Awosika did not intend to tip their hands until the structures were fully on ground.

Insight, it was agreed, would take off sometime in the first quarter of 1980 or thereabout. The 'civil' war atop the Grant hierarchy was only beginning to rage by the time the theoretical framework for the establishment of Insight Communications was firmly in place. By then, too, both Shobanjo and Awosika had resolutely committed to leaving their employers. Like Shobanjo, Awosika felt that Grant no longer pulled in the same direction. More than this, he believed that the intellectual capacity of the agency had become somewhat pedestrian and Grant that existed in 1979 had become very much different from the 'electric' organisation he joined in 1978. Both men resolved it was time to get out. They ventured a bit into the open in September, 1979 by co-opting Shobanjo's Secretary, Iyabo Fadojutimi into their camp. She provided secretarial assistance in the preparation of the documents of the proposed agency. When push came to shove at Grant, she pitched her tent with Insight.

Shobanjo was quite dramatic when the time came to put the young guns in the picture. He chose a setting that bore striking resemblance with the biblical 'Last Supper'. Late in September, he invited the members of his new team to lunch at Benhop Restaurant, the celebrity hangout located off Bode Thomas Street, a few metres away from Grant's head office. Characteristically, they traded banter as they ate. Without skipping a beat, he casually informed them of his resolve to quit Grant. The surprise that registered on their faces was palpable; they stopped eating and looked at one another to be sure they heard right. A flurry of questions followed: Why? When would he leave? Where was he headed? What would he do? Questions. And many more questions. Shobanjo smiled ever so lightly, for he had them precisely where he wanted. Surely and slowly he unfolded the plan.

He explained his dream to the minutiae. He sought their commitment to the objective. Anyone who was not fully sold on the idea was given a chance to quit at that stage. No one moved. One after the other the men agreed to sign up with Insight. Ogunro summed up reactions to the 'Benhop Declaration' thus: "He [Shobanjo] told us the dream: to practise advertising the proper way. He had picked the 'Dream Team'. We did not think twice about (joining Insight). We were all young, still bubbling with ideas and had a quest for zero-defect. We just wanted to forge ahead." Ibe's attitude was no less instructive: "I felt it was time to take a risk; there was little to lose. I did not see anything terrible ahead of me. I believed in the kind of things I had been told."

On 16 October, 1979 the agency was incorporated as a limited liability company with its full name officially registered as Insight Communications Limited.

There are suggestions that Shobanjo handpicked the men on the strength of their personal allegiance to him. This is not correct. True, he had a hand in the employment of each of them, but this was because the recruitment function fell under his management portfolio. More important than this was the fact that each of the selected men was a rising star on the payroll of Grant at the time. The careful selection of people with varied skills and outlook pretty much aligned with Shobanjo's management philosophy that a good leader must support himself with smart people; the better if they are smarter than he is. Plus, they were all young men in search of adventure, even if the picture of the future was hazy. With Insight, he matched his own charisma, forcefulness and inner strength with the belief, energy and sense of purpose of his subordinates to create a highly-motivated team of game-changers. As it were, the young men voluntarily bartered their individual career prospects for Shobanjo's offer of excitement and leadership.

In picking his team, he was careful to marry the quality of the vision with the determination to ensure that he and his followers pulled in the same direction to achieve a common goal. Many enterprises in history are recorded to have failed because of the inability to achieve this match. To that extent, he was true to his belief about working with ambitious, young and knowledgeable individuals, for it made the job of the leader much easier. Each of the talents that he picked had leadership potentials that could be developed. In his estimation, the primary role of any leader is to understand his people and motivate them; for which purpose, "intellectual prowess is no prerequisite."

The vote of confidence that he received at the lunch time meeting helped because it provided the impetus to accelerate plans to have Insight on its feet as early as was practicable. At Benhop, each man was assigned a key responsibility that corresponded with his specialisation. The men, however, could not keep a simple secret. Long before Shobanjo and his men put in their letters of resignation, Akinlade had caught a whiff of their plan, including being in possession of a list of the people involved. He stayed pre-emptive action only because, according to him, he had been 'warned not to act'. He waited for events to unfold before he made his move. When he did, it was too late in the day to arrest the situation.

Awosika was the first to get the hint of trouble. He was his usual voluble self when his colleague and Akinlade's Secretary, Kate Ekwuonu, strolled into his office one morning late in October, as she had done so many times before. But he almost had a seizure when Ekwuonu, after making small talks and with mischief as bright as crimson on her face, spoke of knowing what 'you Insight people' were up to. With all sweetness, he denied the existence of Insight or what-did-Kate-darling-call-it-again? He could not wait for her to leave his presence before he shot like lightning to Shobanjo's office to apprise him of what he had just heard. It made sense that if Ekwuonu knew of the plan, then her boss knew as much, too. But who leaked the plan? At what point was its cloak of secrecy lifted? No one was sure of the 'who?' and the 'when?' Although there were speculations that Johnson Adebayo inadvertently compromised the plan, no serious effort was put into resolving the mysteries. The matter was quickly allowed to rest because there were far more important and urgent issues to deal with.

With this development, Shobanjo promptly drafted his letter of resignation and delivered it to the office of the Chairman. He did not avail Akinlade, who then was in the United Kingdom, the benefit of advance notification of his decision to leave the agency. His five junior colleagues resigned swiftly, too. Akinlade returned to the country to meet a rash of resignations awaiting him. By his own admission, he had no objection to Shobanjo's decision to quit but he 'felt bad' about his deputy's 'lack of courtesy' to him. Events at the extra-ordinary board meeting that was summoned in the wake of Shobanjo's resignation compelled Akinlade to spill the bean on the hitherto carefully concealed incorporation of Insight.

Akinlade tried unsuccessfully to persuade the boys to remain. He was particularly not pleased with Awosika whom he had thought would have a re-think, if for nothing else than that they both hailed from Ondo town. When persuasion failed, Akinlade talked tough. He called a general meeting of staff during which he gave everyone who wanted to leave 'just two hours' to think things over. None had second thoughts. When he began to flex his executive muscles, the rebels had run for cover. Their severance package scarcely could cover their indebtedness to the agency; they left Grant virtually penniless.

The 'small boys' were not the only ones that saw Akinlade's 'red' eye. He also took a few tough actions against Shobanjo, first, by declining to authorise the payment of his severance entitlements, which, till date, are unpaid. Shobanjo's request to purchase one of the two official vehicles attached to his office was also denied; indeed, the Managing Director impounded the official vehicle of his former deputy when the latter sent his driver to the office to collect his mails. Shobanjo's request to take over the payment of rent on his official quarters at 8 Chilaka Close, Surulere was similarly turned down although he had found the property and negotiated a three-year rent that was paid in advance. He had only lived in the apartment for one year by the time he resigned from the agency. When he offered to refund the two-year balance of the rent to Grant, Akinlade declined, claiming there was a plan to accommodate an expatriate staff in the building. No one lived in the house after Shobanjo moved out, as it was under lock and key for nearly two years. Odunsi, Omojafor and Adelaja intervened in the face-off between Akinlade and his deputy. This helped to soften the MD's stance, following which he allowed Shobanjo to enjoy the perks of his office as Deputy Managing Director until the expiration of his notice of resignation on 31 December, 1979.

The Insight team was high and dry in the last quarter of 1979. The team had no office; the company had no business and everyone was flat broke. But they pulled through, motivated, as it were, by the need to stave off hunger as well as by their burning desire to 'prove a point' to the Grant establishment.

It will be recalled that in September 1979, the embryonic Insight received a cash gift of N25,000 from Nasco's Nasreddin. This amount represented half of the N50,000 support that he had initially promised Shobanjo. The shortfall in cash contribution made it imperative that the promoters explored every possibility to inject further capital into the project. To this end, the promoters of the business took two simultaneous steps, the first of which required all six founding members of Insight to monetise their stakes in the company to heighten the commitment of everyone to the destiny of the outfit. Shobanjo put down N19,000, which he beefed up to N24,000 in February, 1980 with a N5,000 loan from his cousin, Adegboyega. Awosika paid N1,000 plus a further N7,500 paid on his behalf by his mother. Ibe, Adebayo and Ogunro paid N1,000 each while Amogbe contributed N500. This way, all became shareholders/employees of the agency.

Next, Shobanjo invited his friend, Goddy Amadi, then a staff of Unipetrol, an oil-marketing firm, to take up equity in the organisation as an external director. Some years earlier, Amadi, not minding stiff opposition from his colleagues, had facilitated the approval of a petrol dealership in Ibadan for Shobanjo. His invitation to the board of Insight, therefore, was both a gesture of goodwill and a reflection of his financial contribution to the take-off of the agency. Amadi took up N15,000 equity that he raised to N17,000 in December, 1979 with additional N2,000 subscription. Much later, Shobanjo approached Mr. Ayo Idowu whom he affectionately called 'Bros'. The businessman was not looking for investment opportunities. Still, he staked his money on Shobanjo's capability. Idowu chipped in N50,000. About one year into the life of the new agency, however, his subscription would test the ability of Insight to survive in the tough business terrain.

In all, Insight began its life as a corporate entity with a capitalisation of N128,000; a debt profile of N104,000 for various hire purchase obligations and Shobanjo's belief that God had a special purpose for the agency.

The agency's temporary operations headquarters was Shobanjo's official residence in Surulere, which he later vacated and was let out to emerging billionaire businessman, Aliko Dangote. That was until his good friend, Dipo Onabanjo, an Estate Manager (now Chairman of Stop Centre) who also was then just setting up his own practice, secured office accommodation for them at No. 1 Calabar Street in Surulere, not very far from their former agency. Ironically, the property, owned by Chief Bayo Alamutu who, at that time, worked with the Nigerian Hotels Ltd, was at a road fork that, perhaps, was symbolic of the crossroads the associates had suddenly reached. Paradoxically, the house number tallied with the aspiration of the new agency, which hoped to be the best in the advertising industry in the not-too-distant future. Equally interesting was the fact that the house was built in a flood-prone neighbourhood that, on the face of it, made it easy for the men to either quickly swim or sink together.

They rented the entire building, for which they paid a princely

N18,000 for one year before they renovated it to taste. They leased air conditioners from Leventis Technical for the offices and Shobanjo's new official residence at Femi Ayantuga Street in Surulere, which was a stone throw from his new office. They paid the sum of N3,000 as lease advance for six months. They also bought some items of furniture from Leventis Stores. This was the first sign the adworld got that Insight would be a serious agency. Erstwhile boss of Promoserve Advertising Ltd, Allan Ola Olabode, recalled that Shobanjo said to him when he (Olabode) visited Calabar Street not long after the birth of Insight: "Look, Allan, everything you see in this building is all that has been there since Day One."

When Insight began to prospect clients, it had a very tough beginning. Its team furiously banged on many doors. Insight did not get the Nasco account just for the asking. Its Chief Executive, Saleh Nasreddin, kept his word that the new agency despite the enormous goodwill that its principal enjoyed with him, must fight for it and prove its capability to handle Nasco's business. The agency similarly approached a couple of Grant's other clients who spurned the new agency's offer of corporate service not because Insight's principals were unknown but because of their official loyalty to Grant. This, perhaps, made the new company hungrier for business than it would otherwise have been. A small measure of success was still recorded at the outset. First, the agency won the International Correspondence School's account. The ICS business turned full cycle for Shobanjo who, it will be recalled, took tutorial instructions in public relations by correspondence from the school in his days at NBC. As an advertising practitioner, he handled the account at Grant. When he resigned from Grant, he cabled the company's London office to intimate it of his move. He received a curt reply at home that ICS would work with Insight. This lifted his spirit enormously. Next, he called up Tony Drake, then Marketing Director of Wellcome, a pharmaceuticals production company. Drake was emphatic that Wellcome would do business with Insight. Account Number 2 was in the kitty. Thereafter, everything dried up.

By December, 1979, a more definite date in the New Year was set for Insight Communications Limited to commence business. The unanticipated leak of the plan made the rush imperative because there was need to address the dire financial position of the company's founders. Since they were stampeded into resigning from Grant, they had received no salaries subsequently. They all shared about N6,000 given by Shobanjo and Amadi to tide them over during the Christmas season.

For Shobanjo, especially, the signs of what was to come manifested at Christmas. Quite unlike before when, as Grant's Deputy Managing Director, he usually received about 40 season's hampers from friends and business associates to demonstrate goodwill during the yuletide, he received a laughable four after serving notice of his resignation from the agency. Not one of these came from media owners or, for that matter, from clients. Two each came from suppliers and relations. The message was loud and clear: the only currency people know and respect is 'now', for which reason they find it more convenient and beneficial to deal with chairs rather than with the man or woman that sits on them. No one, it would appear, was ever too interested in the promise of a 'better tomorrow'; everyone wanted things to happen 'here and now'. Shobanjo took the message in his strides and dismissed the fear of failure.

None of the men holed up at No.1, Calabar Street voiced the fear of failure, though it loomed large in their subconscious. None blinked, too, as they stared their collective destiny in the face. They were primed to take on all-comers and fulfil their goal of making Insight the Mecca of advertising in Nigeria. The mood of the house was upbeat as they waited for the dawn of the New Year. Nothing, it seemed, could dampen their shared enthusiasm and hope.

6

Insight:
Firing On All Cylinders

Those who desire to reach and keep their places
at the top in any calling must be prepared to do so the hard way.

Chief Obafemi Awolowo (1909-1987)

nsight was registered simply as a limited liability 'communications' enterprise. Outwardly, this seemed just like a rose by another name, considering that, at the time, it was customary to tag an 'advertising' label on every agency. But the thoughtfulness that gave rise to the name only became apparent nearly a decade after the founding of the company. This was when the pattern of the agency's approach to client's businesses; its growth and, much later, the birth of a holding company with several business units validated the conception strategy of the founders of the company. For marketing purposes, the agency created an outstanding corporate advertisement that was illustrated with an animal model, a giraffe. Connotatively, the full-page advert left no one in any doubt that Insight meant to stand out in an environment that was crowded, yet open to any serious-minded taker. Even if there was any doubt that Insight meant business, it was cleared up by the unpretentious and declarative tagline: 'We see farther.'

Seeing farther, in part, was a declaration of the agency owners' long, near-clairvoyant peep into the future. They had an idea of how the market might evolve and how they would key into it; they had foreseen probable explosion in the number of advertising agencies; they had clearly defined the kind of clients they would work for and they were uncompromising in defining the company's operating environment in terms of people, infrastructure and knowledge base. They opted to take position as a different agency that would service its clients so well they would be most reluctant to go anywhere else. Insight, thus, needed to seize advantage of speed and capacity to handle large volumes of briefs in the deadline-infested business of advertising. The implication was that a full complement of motivated staff was required for takeoff despite its larger implications on the wage bill.

Insight entered the market on Wednesday, January 2, 1980 in the thick of a severe downturn in the nation's economy. Whereas older competitors already billed several millions of Naira and had cornered practically all the high-spending, advertising-savvy clients, Insight was launched with lean capital and limited institutional support that was represented by its primary client, the International Correspondence School, ICS, which billed just N15,000. It thus remained to be seen what spectacular thing the new agency would bring to the table.

On Day One, Insight shocked the industry with its 18-member workforce. Excluding the six founders, the agency had on its register: Iyabo Fadojutimi (Secretary to the Executive Chairman); Sola

Akande (Senior Finance Executive); Sola Oyedipe (Finance Executive); Dan Usonwu (Media Executive); Hector Macaulay (Media Manager); Demola Adeduro (Junior Artist); Anna Balogun (Tea Girl) and J. Owoeye (Dispatch Clerk/Rider). Others were Sam O. Akintaju (Senior Finished Artist); Y. Kehinde (Secretary); E. Sode and T. Allen (Receptionist). The crowd, as it were, was geared to reflect the absolute confidence that the agency's promoters had in their dream.

Hitherto, most agencies opened as one-man outfits that operated from small apartments that seemed to match the vision of their founders. This model usually relied more on luck and pluck for physical and financial growth. The founders of Insight chose to travel a different route by conceptualising the agency as big from inception, both in terms of its physical structure and the quality of its creative offering. The decision to start out big despite the odds stacked against them reflected Shobanjo's view that the size and strength of an agency are complementary, not mutually exclusive, for with size comes strength.

With hindsight, Shobanjo counselled new entrants into the corporate world against seeing the founding of Insight as an ideal model for business start-ups. The picture he saw was grim in terms of manpower, which, he admitted, was probably "second division but with a potential and determination to move to the first division in not more than two seasons." In his estimation, the Client Service Department of Insight at inception comprised 'mainly rookies;' Creative was a 'mishmash of brilliant individuals;' there was 'nothing fantastic' about Media while the Finance department consisted of 'veterans of Grant's Finance Department' who made up for their limited academic knowledge with tested and trusted cognate experience. If the dream had faltered, Insight would probably have become one of several interesting case studies of grand business collapse. But failure was not an option for the team.

Before the agency opened for business, the strategies for winning in the marketplace were clearly spelt out. Though Shobanjo was very well known in the industry, he was mindful that virtually all the key businesses that Insight had in view had been spoken for in terms of their working with existing agencies. It, therefore, was inevitable that the concept of canalisation be adopted for client solicitations. In its basic form, canalisation involved putting in best endeavours to get a foot in the door of a client prospect by introduction, referrals, person-to-person contacts and submitting unsolicited proposals. These efforts were often preceded by putting target clients under a microscope and dissecting their innards to discover opportunities that prospects may not have spotted but which Insight was ready to proffer as solutions. 'Performance' was emphasised as a critical element of tactics that would be used to put Insight in the minds of prospects, should the agency get a chance to make a presentation. This was hinged on Shobanjo's belief in the maxim that "you only have an opportunity to make a good impression once." For this reason, premium was on 'effects' as defined by the content of presentations; the comportment and dress sense of presenters as well as the quality of equipment that they took to presentations. Combined, these made canalisation expensive, time consuming, oftentimes frustrating and an avenue to potential conflict if the target organisations had other agencies on retainer.

The optimism with which Insight launched out was watered down by the challenges posed by the market at a difficult time in the economic history of the nation. At a professional level, many clients still subscribed to the thinking that advertising was a 'favour' to be dispensed out of magnanimity. The mindset derived mainly from the global challenge of how to effectively measure the contribution of advertising to the bottom-line of enterprises. This challenge had been envisaged at the stage of conception. Shobanjo envisioned Insight as a business partner that would offer creative brand building partnerships, of which core advertising would be an input. At formal take-off, therefore, the team was primed to engage all clients in never-ending dialogues towards evolving workable business solutions that would be timely and flexible. To this was added the need to consistently scan the environment for opportunities and threats that might impact the client, who then would be better placed to execute proactive response.

If Insight was to succeed, it was obvious it would need to create a reorientation of values that, in the first instance, would require that advertising be seen from the perspective of a multi-dimensional partnership. The key dimension was that the agency and its clients must respect each other whilst recognising the limits of what advertising can or cannot do. This, as Shobanjo has vigorously argued, required that an agency must be fully cognisant of the fact that advertising is a 'support' endeavour with 'product performance' being 'king'. In similar vein, it meant that clients must accept, as he likes to counsel, that "advertising (primarily) helps a rolling ball roll faster but cannot get a ball to roll uphill'. The key goal is to ensure there was no miscommunication between an agency and its client in terms of deliverables. This way, the agency would not be under undue pressure to overpromise whilst the client would have clearly defined and easily measurable parameters with which to appraise the performance of its agency.

The defining qualities of Insight, as previously highlighted, rested on having a firm grip on the imperatives of the operating environment as a necessary step to accelerate the process of making the company virtually indispensable to its clients. However, something more fundamental was required to set the company apart from competition. This was a culture that would survive the inevitable dilution of the original dream in later years. It was agreed that a leading strategy, not a reactive philosophy, was critical to anticipating and evolving fresh solutions to the needs of clients in the face of Nigeria's consistently inconsistent economic policies.

After much brainstorming, Shobanjo evolved a simple, Greek-sounding idea with the acronym SOQNOP, which was primarily a flexible strategy of differentiation. It recognized the need to give every business the best thinking that could go into making it prosperous; it took into consideration the fact that, often, the best communication was neither the most expensive nor the cheapest. In full, SOQNOP means Selling On Quality, Not On Price. In practice, it meant using the platform of creativity, honesty and consistency to deliver target-driven superior solutions. The strategy assumed that discerning clients would always adequately remunerate an agency for the quality of work done, even if it meant paying a bit more for such services. At the heart of the strategy was the belief that good things do not come cheap. From the outset, Insight chose to be a premium niche player. Nearly four decades after its founding, Insight is still a premium niche player.

For these plans to succeed, much premium was placed on flawless internal processes to engender consistency in the quality of the agency's output. Each staff was required to take responsibility for the quality of their work and be committed to the agency's corporate culture of all-round excellence. All agency personnel were expected to be abreast of their staff and line functions in terms of administration and client interface respectively. They closely monitored competition, just so Insight was not blind-sided in the race for the consumer's naira. For the sake of the future, a multi-disciplinary approach that would be reinforced with first class hands-on training was kept in view for staff recruitments. The agency also took the unbeaten path of submitting itself to annual performance appraisal by clients to track the degree of customer satisfaction.

The foregoing, however, required strict discipline, for which Shobanjo was business-like in quickly setting the tone. He cautioned his team members against seeing Insight as a vehicle to exact 'vengeance' on Grant. The agency's driving force, he told them, derived from them knowing that they opted out of Grant by choice to do things differently, not for the zeal of wanting to be their own bosses. He argued that the eventual success of Insight should be great tribute to the trust and opportunity that were provided but not optimised by Lawson and Ogunbanjo, whom God had used, one way or the other, as impetus for the realisation of the new vision. He told everyone that every business day began at 7.30AM; dress code was official, prim and proper and all were to work as if their lives depended on it. His men understood and complied accordingly.

Since the hierarchical structure of Insight was also bit of a carry-over of the chain of command from the days at Grant, with Shobanjo being the most senior, his younger colleagues had no issues with the new agency's organic structure, which was very clear. He was the only one out of the company's six co-founders that sat on the board alongside two external directors. The other principals, regardless of their status as shareholders, understood the need to earn their wings, if they ever hoped to become directors in the company. Again, this model ran contrary to existing corporate practice whereby virtually all 'founders' of a business were automatically accorded the status of directors, regardless of their equity holding.

More instructive, however, was the fact that the arrangement reflected the levels of equity participation of each promoter as well as the letter and spirit of the company's Memorandum and Article of Association. The open and frank clarification of who would or would not sit on the agency's board at that material time helped to pre-empt any possible threat to the stability of the company. This way, each man completely understood his position within the set up. The strong belief in Shobanjo's leadership and his keen sense of fairness contributed significantly to the smooth-running of the agency, especially in the resolution of conflicts. But it need be said, too, that the 'boys' were too pre-occupied with the excitement of raising hell in the industry to care about the niceties of corporate power play.

When the agency opened for business, it behaved typically like every organisation in a growth mode: it was in a hurry; it was bullish and it yielded no quarter to the old order in its march to capture new territories. The behaviour was consistent with the imperatives of corporate survival since the agency needed to gain traction in the industry. Much to the chagrin of the Association of Advertising Practitioners of Nigeria, AAPN (now Association of Advertising Agencies of Nigeria, AAAN), Insight knocked on every corporate door regardless of whether the agency was invited or not. This was in breach of practically every known rule on client solicitation contained in the Association's Code of Standards and Practice. Insight's liberty to close in on its target enterprises because it was not encumbered by the AAAN's Code made a lot of members of the sectoral body quite unhappy. In their eyes, Insight and its leadership, operated like a band of outlaws in the industry.

Perhaps, more damning than the actual breach of the Code was the agency's bravura. Insight eyeballed everyone in a manner that said: 'so-we-stepped-on-your-toes-what-can-you-do?' But no one could call it to order since it did not subscribe to AAAN rules. The grandstanding naturally riled fellow practitioners and it, paradoxically, marked the birth of the Shobanjo mystique as a hardball player. Insight pressed this to maximum advantage because it caused many practitioners to begin to surrender to the company's firepower, even when it had not fired or contemplated firing a shot.

The agency's corporate arrogance at that point was mere hype to gain attention. It arose out of the need to gain visibility and increase the company's chances of success. The strategy worked. With time, real pride, arising from accomplishments, took the place of irreverence but the industry hardly noticed the difference in the way the agency carried itself. The perception of Insight as an unrepentantly 'aggressive' agency and its leadership as unsportmanly did not abate considerably until the agency re-wrote the industry form books with years of consistent high-octane performance. The paradigm shift was also helped by the excellence displayed by several ex-Insighters when they formed their own partnerships whilst still following the guidelines that marked out Insight as a different kind of agency.

Insight's creative and business development teams brainstormed the more and sourced ideas from anywhere that they could gain inspiration. At that stage, Shobanjo crafted two of the most persuasive letters of introduction he ever wrote in his career. One went to the Chief of Defence Staff, the other to the Inspector-General of Police. Both contained proposals on how to recruit some of Nigeria's most brilliant talents into the armed forces and the Police. Both proposals were prompted by his extensive study of trends and activities within and outside the advertising industry as well as the distillation of ideas from reputable local and foreign publications. The ideas that he tried to sell were stillborn; his efforts were not dignified with any response from either the military or Police hierarchy.

The agency's search for something to hold on to in the market place yielded result nine days after it opened for business. On 11 January, 1980, Insight placed an 8" x 2 column press material in Daily Times on behalf of its client, ICS. The headline: "Your fast way to success..." was a paradox that was laced with great humour. Here was an agency that was badly in need of a 'fast way' to make headway in the market selling the idea of a fast way to success! But they plodded on. Several weeks later, the business drought began to ebb just as it appeared that Insight was set to arm its critics who felt its people were all 'mouth.' Wellcome, one of the two accounts acquired in January, 1980, began to send in briefs for execution. Then Nasco Foods signed on. But the arrival of the food company came with a load of trouble because the berthing of the account nearly brought Insight in direct conflict with Grant.

When Shobanjo resigned from Grant, the decision makers at Nasco merely asked him to confirm what, to them, were mere speculations. He formally informed the company's management that he had indeed tendered his notice of resignation to the management of Grant. He did not hear again from the company until the Vice-Chairman, Abdu Nasreddin, requested to meet and size up the Insight team. A shrewd businessman, Nasreddin, who also doubled as Nasco's Group Managing Director, headed the conglomerate's worldwide operations from the Group's Head Office in Milan, Italy where he reported to the Group's Chairman and founder, Ahmed Nasreddin, fondly called Baba. News of Shobanjo's exit from Grant caused him to fly to Nigeria to appraise first hand the strengths of both Grant Advertising and Insight. He made it clear that Nasco had no plan to jeopardise its interest by sentimentally placing its business, which was the biggest fast-moving commodity goods company in Northern Nigeria, in the hands of a weak marketing communications company. His assessment of both agencies, therefore, was dispassionate.

Not long after Abdu Nasreddin's visit, Nasco wrote to Grant to withdraw its account from the agency whilst it appointed Insight as its advertising agency of record. Akinlade fought hard to retain the client but he could not persuade Nasco to stay. Even at this, Insight could not immediately bed the new account because Grant did not let go of Nasco, which owed the agency about N600,000. The client settled the debt and resolved other sundry issues regarding its terms of business with Grant, which still was not happy.

Days after Nasco's formal disengagement from the agency, Grant added a new twist to the drama with the publication of a half-page public notice in Daily Times of 20 February, 1980 to dispel 'rumours' that it had gone under. The advertisement fingered a 'former top executive' of the agency as the source of the bad mouthing. It went further (excerpts): "The said executive took advantage of the two other Executive Directors' absence from the country in October, 1979 to execute his plans to disrupt, albeit unsuccessfully, our company's operations in order to ensure the successful launching of his own agency... The said executive, having been found guilty of misconduct, breach of trust and divided loyalty by a committee of shareholders set up by the Board of Directors was asked to withdraw his services to the company. Thereafter, (the) resignation of four (sic) other disloyal members were accepted..."

The publication only fell short of publicly identifying Shobanjo, Awosika, Ibe, Ogunro, Johnson and Amogbe as the culprits. Yet, anyone remotely connected with the advertising industry and the development at Grant would easily have connected the dots. Although the departures from Grant happened less than six months earlier, the agency's management got its basic arithmetic wrong: Shobanjo and five, not four, others as published, resigned in the first wave of exits. In terms of explaining the course and circumstance of the migration of the Insight team from Grant, the public notice was not fair.

The Insight team was initially disturbed by the tone of the publication, which they considered to be libellous. But they chose not to react immediately to it, in part, because Shobanjo, by nature, is not given to impulsive reaction to issues except when a pattern had been established. He likes to firmly control the content and timing of his utterances, especially when there is a high probability that a third party might be negatively impacted. He also is not favourably disposed to criticising people and institutions in public to allow room for concerned parties to make amends. Usually, he would resort to writing personal letters to the individuals concerned to put things in perspective. If the matter was already in the public domain, he still would ensure that the other party received his letter before his formal response is released to the media.

That Insight did not formally respond to the Grant advertorial yielded an unintended positive result. It encouraged the business community to pay a bit more attention to the irreverent 'boys' of Calabar Street, who now had an added mission to 'turn sneers into cheers.'

Whilst Grant was throwing spanners in the works, Shobanjo was pre-occupied with seeking solutions to overcome Insight's financial difficulty. Part of the problem was that the agency had not cut its teeth with media owners because it was new and, as such, needed to make largely cash transactions. Besides, clients were hard to come by for the same reason of Insight being new on the block and untested as a body. It thus became imperative that fresh funds be injected to keep the venture afloat. For this reason, he invited businessman and 'big brother', Ayo Idowu, onto the board. As earlier stated, Idowu put down N50,000. This development necessitated an enlarging of the board, which, in turn, caused Shobanjo to relinquish his position as the agency's 'Executive Chairman' whilst adopting the nomenclature of Managing Director. The revitalised company now had a three-member board made up of Amadi who was Chairman; Shobanjo, Managing Director and Idowu, a board director.

Help also came from the two-year old Rosabel Advertising, which made significant contributions to easing Insight's headache with media owners. Rosabel graciously agreed to place Insight's advertisements. This way, the agency's commission from placements in the media were secured to buoy the health of the books, for which Insight gladly split the commissions earned.

Gradually, the rank of clients began to fledge. The register that initially had ICS and Wellcome now had Nasco, Rokana Industries, Coates (West Africa) Threads, Anglo-West African Bottlers (bottlers of Gold Spot and Limca), Askar Paints, Senn-Sound, Brian Munro and Cheseborough Ponds.

The Bristol-Myers account presented a unique case study because the company's Regional Director was not enthusiastic about placing the business of the pharmaceutical concern in the hands of an 'untested' agency. Consequently, he instructed the General Manager, Les Bothright, who then ran the company's offices at Coker Road in Ilupeju, Lagos, not to work with Insight. Bothright defied his boss and did exactly what he was told not to do. He gave Insight the brief to produce a campaign for Angiers junior aspirin. The agency returned with a 60-second television commercial as well as radio jingles and print advertisements. The outcome stunned the Regional Director who clapped spontaneously to register his satisfaction with the creative solutions that were proposed. But he also felt some degree of embarrassment for reaching a hasty conclusion by underestimating the creative ability of the young agency. When the campaign, 'Angiers Junior Aspirin – The Name Mothers Trust', broke, it received warm and positive acclaim that generated high awareness and patronage of Angiers junior aspirin in the market. Several mothers of that age recall the campaign with nostalgia. From a marketing communications point of view, the success of the Angiers campaign helped to prove that strategic decisions are better left in the hands of local managers who are more in tune with the nuances of their markets.

Insight gradually began to enjoy a bit more relief from media owners as the accounts began to roll in. Rallying the media was altogether neither too difficult nor too easy to achieve. This, in part, was because Shobanjo's resignation from Grant had aroused the curiosity of media establishments. Why would a Deputy Managing Director suddenly leave a bubbly agency? News of the number of staff that left with him also made the story more captivating. Media marketers kept Insight under close observation but chose to remain on the sidelines waiting to see how the revolution would unravel. The first to show any real understanding was then President of the Newspaper Proprietors Association of Nigeria, NPAN, the late Chief Olu Aboderin, the founder and Chairman of The Punch group of newspapers, who, incidentally, was the old boss of Shobanjo's wife. The newspaper magnate saw Shobanjo as an enterprising young man who needed to be encouraged.

The publication's Executive Director, Sam Amuka (a.k.a Sad Sam), now the publisher of Vanguard newspapers, and the newspaper's Advertisement Manager agreed no less with Aboderin. Insight subsequently began to enjoy some credit facilities from The Punch group, a gesture that greatly helped the agency's cash flow. Not long after this, the newly established Concord Group of newspapers owned by billionaire publisher, the late Bashorun M.K.O. Abiola queued behind Insight. The Concord Group of newspapers, unfortunately, folded up in the wake of the famous June 12 struggle to validate Abiola's 1993 presidential election victory that was annulled by former military President, General Ibrahim Babangida. Abiola himself died in controversial circumstances in 1998 while still in detention.

From this point, a bandwagon effect became noticeable. Media owners in Northern Nigeria, especially in the broadcast sector, gave Insight tremendous support that paved the way for the agency's soar-away success. Some of the early help resulted from the good word put in with Northern media owners on behalf of the agency by Alhaji Garba Kankarofi, the former Director of Commercial Services of Kano Broadcasting Corporation who later retired as Managing Director of Radio Kano: "I was shocked to discover that the first Local Purchase Order (LPO) we got from Insight was in care of Rosabel. I asked Shobanjo why he had to do this, and he told me it was because Insight was new and wanted to be credible. I told him he was sufficiently credible in the industry and we had no reason to doubt him. I thereafter told my colleagues in other Northern stations that Insight had a great future. One could see the signs of greatness because Shobanjo was a serious-minded person. We all resolved to help him and help Insight. I did not know he was going to be this great; I only felt within me that he would achieve greatness."

The goodwill that the owners of Insight had long established with some of their clients also helped considerably to ease the agency's cash flow. Tony Drake, the Marketing Director of Wellcome, was one of those who stood out in this regard. Aside from moving the Welcome account to Insight at its start up, he sought the co-operation of the company's Finance Manager, Mr. Kushimo, to pre-pay on presentation of the agency's invoices. He also got the concurrence of his own supervisor in the UK, John Martin, who had been Shobanjo's friend from the days at Grant. The arrangement, however, stopped abruptly because the Indian Managing Director, Mr. Khwaja, made so much fuss that compelled the company's management to have a re-think.

Mindful of the agency's less-than-complimentary image among its peers, Shobanjo spearheaded the move to put a lot of shine on Insight and enhance its standing within the industry. In record eight months from its inception, the agency fulfilled stringent registration conditions to become the 51st Corporate Member of AAAN on 6 August, 1980. This automatically put paid to the 'fly-by-night' label pinned on the agency by AAAN members. Clients, too, quickly acknowledged Insight's new elite corps status. However, membership of AAAN had its downside for Insight, which, from the time of its acceptance to the fold, had its wings clipped. This made it impossible for it to play outside the rules of the Association without being sanctioned. Not everyone forgave the agency for its past 'transgressions;' many practitioners still viewed Insight with suspicion. They cried foul when the profile of the agency began to rise, for they did not quite seem to understand its rapid growth. Insight, on its part, continued to thump its chest as its portfolio of clients and creative works continued to enlarge.

For an agency that started out with a paltry billing of N15,000, Insight had a good run in 1980. By year's end, the agency billed N1.5 million. In terms of creativity, Insight produced some of the most talked about advertisements of the time. These ranged from the visually striking 'with Sparkle toothpaste, you've got nothing to hide' to the cost-driven, typography-dependent 'when you've tried

Excedrin... you'll know why it's more expensive.' On the down side, however, the marriage between board member, Idowu, and Insight did not survive the first 365 days. Idowu left the board following disagreements on how best to run the agency.

Even at that early stage, it was clear that Shobanjo had brought his personality to bear on Insight. The company's profile showed at least three of his primary traits. First, none could deny that here, at least, was a very elegant agency that did things in grand style. It had big, showy offices; it had fine, young, even if somewhat brash, talents and it had very tall ambitions – to be the biggest in billing, the best in creativity and be a haven of the most competent hands in the business. Again, the agency's capacity for hard work manifested quite early. Every brief was the brief. Neither distance nor the nature of a prospect's business was a barrier and staffers often worked ungodly hours to meet deadlines. In addition, Insight loved (and still loves) to win, not just for the money but for the prestige and not just to boost professional confidence but also to prove a point about being the ultimate solutions centre. To the extent that Shobanjo's worldview significantly rubbed off on the organisation, any attempt to separate both could potentially do harm to either or both. Even, today, this perspective has changed only slightly.

1981 rode in on the wings of a thick harmattan haze. Like the weather, the economic climate in Nigeria was inclement, as the civilian Federal Government headed by President Shehu Shagari continued to grapple with the indices of economic decay. The Fourth National Development Plan (1981 – 85) also did not look near anything that would take off, neither did it look realistic. The gloom was exacerbated by the shortfall in national revenue because of the fall in oil production. The prospects of real growth in the economy in the New Year were bleak, but typical of Nigerians, hope stubbornly filled the air.

At Calabar Street, expectations were high that business would boom in 1981. However, no one could hazard a guess as to how well or how fast this would come to be. At least, not before Rosabel's Odunsi introduced Shobanjo to the late Kunle Fatona, a non-executive member of the board of Cocoa Industries Limited (CIL), a Lagos-based commodities marketing company. CIL, it so happened, was in the process of a vertical-forward integration that meant diversifying from full-scale cocoa processing to the production of malted cocoa beverage. The company had then just formulated a malt drink brand that needed to be introduced into the market. The big challenge was how to hit the market and attract significant consumer attention to be able to upstage its two major competitors, Nestle Foods, makers of Milo and Cadbury, makers of Bournvita and Pronto. Both had virtually cornered the market.

Although CIL had closed the list of agencies to be invited to pitch its account, Fatona graciously introduced Shobanjo to the CIL management who agreed to include Insight in the pitch list. With that, Insight became agency number 13 that was invited by CIL's Managing Director, Mr. Ayo Iyowu, to pitch the business to market the new product, Vitalo. With eyes on the N1.5 million budget, Insight threw itself into the contest in the hope that it could help make a way in the market for CIL's food drink as well as break the dominance of the market leaders, Milo, Bournvita and Pronto. The agency saw an opportunity to double its 1980 billing, which was a gamble of some sort for which it hoped that the figure 13, widely regarded as jinxed by the superstitious, would prove to be a lucky number. In their calculation, a Vitalo account in the kitty would sharpen the skills of the creative team as well as enrich the agency's portfolio in consumer marketing.

All the invited agencies made presentations to a short-listing committee that included Mrs. Titi Ajanaku, now a leading female politician, and the Rt. Rev E.O.I. Ogundana, who later became Bishop of Remo Anglican Diocese. Insight presented about three proposals at different stages of the pitch. None was limited to conventional advertising thinking. All the presentations went beyond providing the expected core communications solutions. The agency adopted complete integrated marketing communications as its platform to manage and, indeed, chart the direction of the dialogue between brand Vitalo and its consumers. As such, its presentations touched on other critical areas as sales, distribution and marketing.

When, however, the final presentation before CIL's board hit the home stretch, the Insight team stumbled, as an unanticipated technical glitch ensured that the well-produced radio jingle did not play. The presenters did not panic; instead, they mimed the jingle with an infectious enthusiasm that killed off their mountain of worries. The legendary grandmaster of presentations, Peter Marsh of the British firm of Allen Brady & Marsh (ABM), would have been proud of their performance. The surge of inspiration came because the team was aware that the presentation of business solutions was clearly as important as the content of the solutions being sold. They also knew that a good presentation often demonstrated a team's knowledge, capacity and enthusiasm to do the job at hand. The CIL chieftains were sufficiently impressed by the spectacle in the boardroom, just as they they felt refreshed by the passion that was exhibited by the presenters from the agency. They had no second thoughts about their first choice of agency to push Vitalo: Insight.

The 'Ides of March' brought Insight its first 'Big Break'. The agency won the Vitalo account in March 1981. From that moment, too, Shobanjo became a lot closer to CIL's Managing Director, Iyowu. This development helped to demonstrate his cardinal belief in getting personal with his business interface to have a better appreciation of a client's position.

Vitalo attained instant celebrity status when the advertising campaign broke. 'It's marvellous what Vitalo can do for you' soon became a colloquial expression used to encourage flagging spirits. It sometimes was also used irreverently to rebuke friends who were deemed not to be keeping up with the times. The popularity of the product became manifest when it began to get unsolicited mention everywhere. Such was the power of Insight's creativity on the brand. The execution of the Vitalo brief firmly established Insight's creative and marketing-oriented reputation. From that point, the agency began to get the kind of attention it thought it deserved.

From the stage of conception, Insight had been programmed not to fit the mould of any existing local agency. The template was 'international' because Shobanjo had a global perspective to doing business. From his days at Grant, he had religiously taken to keeping tabs on the course of the invasion of Europe by Saatchi & Saatchi, the creatively brash UK agency that was established in the 1970s by the Saatchi brothers, Charles and Maurice. On a closer look, the founding of Insight exactly 10 years after the birth of the British firm appeared to have resulted from his pre-occupation with re-enacting the feat of the Saatchis in Nigeria. Today, he feels a lot comfortable with not being drawn into responding to speculations regarding whether the birth of Insight vis-à-vis the story of Saatchi & Saatchi was coincidental or deliberate. The course of Insight's history, however, makes it seem probable that the agency's birth was more deliberate than coincidental.

Shobanjo's global business outlook did not arise from a flight of fancy. Rather, it was grounded in the knowledge that the world, even without the advantage of the Internet and today's advanced interactive technology, had become a small village, one that held prospects of further shrinkage. His wide exposure to global best practice in advertising naturally had an impact on his professional worldview. He knew that any local company that intended to remain relevant in business must avail itself of the advantages of offshore technical cooperation.

This, however, was not popular in the industry in the early 1980s, though the 'Top 3' agencies of the time had one form of biological relationship with one foreign agency or the other. Lintas:Lagos had a genetic relationship with Lintas Overseas; Ogilvy Benson & Mather (OBM) enjoyed a partnership with Ogilvy & Mather (O&M) while Grant (Nigeria) became an automatic affiliate of McCann-Erickson after the latter bought over Grant International of Chicago. With his experience of international agency collaboration and focus on manpower development, Shobanjo committed himself to getting Insight affiliated to any of the many reputable networks of worldwide advertising agencies because it held the key to qualitative development of the agency's workforce.

As he and Awosika tinkered with the shape of Insight in 1979, they also compiled a list of leading international agencies that they intended to court for possible technical co-operation. For obvious reasons, Saatchi & Saatchi topped the list of their prospective brides. Shobanjo mandated Awosika to make initial contacts with the London agency but the Saatchis were not interested, perhaps, because they then had a Eurocentric business focus. The negative response did not deter the team, which promptly approached a host of other international agencies in quick succession.

Young & Rubicam (Y&R) declined. Leo Burnett said 'No'. Batten Barton Durstine & Osborn (BBDO) was not interested. J. Walter

Thompson (JWT) was not sold on the idea either. Fatigue began to creep in when another round of approach to eight other international agencies did not yield any positive response. Foot Cone & Belding (FCB) held out a ray of hope. Shobanjo's presentations to FCB in London and Germany did not yield dividends. But this was for a different reason. In FCB's rating, Insight was cool but Nigeria was not hot for investment in advertising. The country's history of political instability did not particularly help Insight's case. Years later, the real reasons for the negative or lukewarm response from international agencies became much clearer: the African market, at the time, was too undeveloped, too unstructured and too unstable to command priority attention from clients who, through their choice of the markets they entered, subtly dictated the direction in which an agency headed.

Ted Bates, however, proved to be a lucky exception. The agency, which was founded in 1940 by Theodore Bates, is, perhaps, best known for bestowing on adworld the concept of Unique Selling Proposition (USP) that was propounded by Rosser Reeves. Insight contacted the Managing Director of Bates London, Michael English, who advised on the need to stick to protocol in accordance with the structure of the agency's operation. This meant that only the President of International Operations, Stephen Rose, was competent to consider Insight's request. He was based in New York. Rather than head for the US, Shobanjo booked a flight to Sao Paulo, Brazil. This was no accident but the result of careful planning to capitalise on the 1982 Congress of the International Advertising Association (IAA), which presented a good opportunity for serious professional networking. He met Rose 'by chance.' They both spoke and found a common ground that, in itself, did not present much surprise, considering that the reason for being of Insight bore close affinity with the six-point 'Guiding Principles' of Bates[1], which the

---

[1] *Philip Kleinman, The Saatchi & Saatchi Story (Weidenfeld & Nicolson, London, 1987 pp.73-74).*

international agency had enunciated thus:

• Be Competitive
To identify, develop and strengthen unique competitive advantages in everything we do: strategic thinking, advertising execution, media planning and buying.

• Build Brand Assets
Our clients manufacture products,
Ted Bates manufactures brands.

• Think Global, Act Local
Optimise all global competitive advantages;
Recognise that ultimately every sale is a local sale.

• Challenge the Status Quo
We must have new thoughts.
We must be curious.
We must be courageous.

• Be Honest
We must be honest with ourselves and with our clients.
Mutual trust is a powerful resource

.• Aim High
How you rank is everything.
We must be Number One in quality, in size and in scope.

Based on the Sao Paulo meeting between Shobanjo and Rose, a two-man team from Bates, comprising John Hoyne (who later assumed the position of President/Chief Operating Officer of Bates Worldwide after a management coup) and Christian Sinding, visited

Nigeria on a fact-finding mission. Their report favoured doing business with Insight.

In September 1982, Shobanjo, accompanied by Insight's Finance Controller, Yemi Amogbe, flew to New York to initial the technical agreement between the two agencies. Bates' CEO, Bob Eakin Jacoby, signed for his agency. From the preliminary contact to the formal signing of the agreement at the 1515 Broadway, New York headquarters of Ted Bates, the process of affiliation took about 11 months and cost Insight two trips to the United Kingdom, one to Brazil and one to the United States. By the agreement, Insight became a member of the Bates family, which then had 140 offices in 46 countries and a worldwide billing in excess of $2.5 billion.

The first five years of Insight, that is, 1980 - 1985, clearly brought to the fore a very significant hallmark of the man and the agency, which the competition continually ignored at great risk. Shobanjo is a phenomenal optimist who has a knack for creating his own luck. He amply demonstrated this trait in the selection of the agency's original human resource team. Each person that made the team clearly had bright career prospects ahead of him. No less stringent parameter was used to recruit staff at the first opportunity; prospective Insighters were expected to have the instincts of a barracuda preferably underneath the mien of a dove. Each employee was also required to demonstrate acute capacity for independent thoughts and an ability to initiate and implement damage control measures in a crisis.

Often, Shobanjo chose well. Perhaps, nothing best illustrates his knack for spotting and nurturing his kind of people than the list of those who passed through the portals of the company, especially in its first two decades. They all made their mark. Notable among them were: Funmi Onabolu, who later became the agency's first General Manager before he established Bates Cosse, of which he is the CEO; Nuru Adeleye who rose to become the Head, Print Production; Tunde Ogunlaiye, who became Creative Director before moving on to be Vice Chairman of the Peapco Group; Vincent Oyo, the former General Manager of Insight and later Managing Director of The Quadrant Company before he left the group; Jimi Bankole, who was acknowledged as one of the most prolific copywriters in practice before he relocated abroad and Osarenren Emokpae, who became Executive Director, Client Service/Strategic Planning before he left to set up the Peapco Group. Others include Enyi Odigbo, the founder of DDB Lagos; Udeme Ufot, now CEO of SO & U; Georgie Umunna, now a marketing consultant; Julia Oku, also now a consultant; Gbemi Sagay, a co-founder of S.H.O.P.S; Longley Evru, now CEO of Angels Communication; Gabriel Abah; Phil Osagie, now Head Consultant, JSP Communications; Lere Awokoya, now CEO of TBWA Concept; George Noah, who became the Chief Executive of the Lagos State Advertising and Signage Agency, LASAA; Paris Agaro of Franchise Advertising; Yomi Sonuga, now owner and Chairman of Bras Motors; Demola Fowler, CEO of TMC Ltd; Dapo Olugbodi, now a Property Development Consultant in Europe; Lanre Adisa, now CEO of Noah's Ark and Foluke Ayuba, to mention a few.

Since Insight was conceived to operate as a knowledge-driven organisation, the management of the agency did not spare expense to train different categories of staff either locally or overseas. In part, the agency's heavy investment in human resource was premised on Shobanjo's belief in the power of knowledge. He further believes that the worth of a service provider could easily be discerned from the quality of the last training received by its people. This position is understandable considering his appreciation of the wide hands-on experience he got at Grant. His belief in training was also deeply influenced by his personal recollections of the frequency of training programmes that his father underwent as a staff of the Railway Corporation. In his calculations, an employer can only bet on good return on investment when employees are well trained and well paid. On the flip side, he believes that only maladjusted employers would fret at making huge investment on training because of fears of inevitable voluntary or forced disengagement of staff. The measure of his confidence in people empowerment programmes is embedded in the motivational can-do licences that he routinely issued to staff:

"Any rank that I give you, you can proudly wear anywhere in the world. If you belong in Troyka Group, you must excel; you must display knowledge when you talk with a client. When you step out of the room and another person from elsewhere comes in, the client must know that you're clearly better. Anywhere you go, people must know you're different."

Even with motivational licence, a member of staff still must be found worthy of trust. Shobanjo makes no exception to the rule of accountability set out for agency executives because of his firm belief that financial discipline and personal integrity were inviolable if an individual or an organisation must command respect. Awosika explained this worldview matter of factly: "We are not in the business of catching thieves; but don't fiddle with money because there is no second chance if you are caught." In this respect, Shobanjo led his staff by example. Early in the life of Insight in 1980 he urgently needed a N3,000 personal loan for which he forwarded his request to the Finance/Admin Controller vide a two-paragraph memo in which he advised on the tenor of the loan as well as the modalities of deductions in six monthly instalments of N500 per month. At the time, he was Insight's 'Executive Chairman'. About the same period, Jimi Awosika needed a loan of N1,500 to sort out urgent domestic issues at the Town Planning office in Lagos. Shobanjo's minute on his subordinate's memo spoke glowingly of Insight's 'willingness to render assistance to members of staff, especially on their domestic problems,' yet, he approved only N1,000 to be liquidated within four months by Awosika. Since he operated from a high moral ground, it was not difficult for him to apply the same parameter of approval to Awosika's request despite their closeness.

Years after Insight had stabilised, Shobanjo never let go of his personal conviction that leaders must be willing to sacrifice and make themselves examples by not abusing their privileged positions. He exemplified this in the manner he led Troyka. He often insisted on paying for personal services rendered to him by any of the group's unit companies. Occasionally, though he would plead that he be allowed to enjoy a 'Chairman's discount.' Where such services are rendered to his family members or friends, the same principle is applied. His transparent display of fiscal responsibility not only helped to greatly stabilise the business of the flagship from its inception, it became sacrosanct in Troyka Group.

Much of the emphasis on financial discipline bordered on the need to protect the integrity of staff against blackmail by external parties. Insight's former Credit Control Officer, Segun Olaleye clearly understood the basis of this policy sometime in the late 1980s after a Lagos magazine publisher complained to Shobanjo that he had demanded money from his staff to facilitate the payment of outstanding debt owed by Insight. Olaleye was immediately summoned to defend himself. He quickly produced records that showed, without any prior contacts with the magazine's representatives, his consistent recommendations to the Head of Finance to pay the publication. After listening to Olaleye, Shobanjo took three immediate and decisive steps. He instructed the Finance Department to work out the total debt owed the magazine, which he authorised for immediate payment. He instructed then Head of Media, Vincent Oyo, to cancel all media orders issued to the magazine, which he followed up with a memo to make the instruction formal and final. He thereafter told the publisher never again to solicit advert placement from Insight because he had lied against his staff when all he needed to do was make a request for payment of outstanding debt.

Whereas he was more inclined to giving heads of department the free hand to pick their staff, he liked to critically appraise the quality of his personal staff as well as the company's front office executive. Since these categories of employees constituted the first point of contact between clients and the agency, the responsibilities that they discharged often allowed little room for errors because their action or inaction could cause an agency to win or lose businesses. In this respect, he never compromised standards. He demonstrated his seriousness by deliberately positioning the office 'reception' area as space for marketing, one in which any visitor would see time spent waiting to be attended as time very well spent. Current copies of periodicals and daily newspapers were always neatly arranged as many times as visitors came and left the room.

The television set was always on a news channel and some of Insight's executed campaigns were well set out against very neat backgrounds. At intervals, messages from intended hosts were relayed to visitors so they do not feel in any way neglected or unappreciated. The transformation of the physical orientation of the reception and the mental attitude of the desk officers short-circuited any feeling that the space was a mere holding area for visitors or a less supervised office space for staff to engage in idle gossips. The setting of the lounge was an admixture of excitement and serious business and it had an aura of success. For these reasons, Insight and Troyka companies have over the years paraded some of the best receptions and front office staff not just in the marketing communications industry but in Corporate Nigeria.

By 1983, Shobanjo's tenacity of purpose had become much evident as he led Insight to stamp its authority as a pathfinder. That year, the General Elections in Nigeria provided a platform for him to demonstrate his uncommon ability to spot and maximise opportunity to stay ahead of competition. Before this time, the power of the mass media in politics was not quite evident. Instead, politicians in the country conducted their electioneering campaigns on the strength of powerful rhetorics delivered from rostrums mounted at several locations across the length and breadth of the country.

Newspapers and broadcast stations merely reported news from campaign venues. All that changed with the election of former British Prime Minister, Margaret Thatcher, in 1979 when excellent and effective communication conceived by Saatchi & Saatchi helped the Conservative Party back to power after a long sojourn in the political wilderness. The Saatchi agency sandbagged the Labour Party with a razor-sharp 'Labour Isn't Working' creative advertising campaign that confounded the opposition and caused the electorate to deliver the keys to the 10 Downing Street official residence of British Prime Ministers to the late 'Iron Lady'. The lessons of that achievement were not lost on politicians in Nigeria.
Even if the leaders of the six registered political parties in the Second Republic saw good sense in the need to creatively package their campaign messages to the electorate, most of them preferred to work with foreign advertising agencies than with their Nigerian

counterparts who they believed were less experienced in these matters. The party in power, the National Party of Nigeria (NPN) – whose flag bearer was the incumbent President, Alhaji Shehu Shagari – signed on Saatchi & Saatchi preparatory to the flag-off of electioneering campaigns. With NPN unavailable, Insight actively pursued prospects of getting to work with any of the remaining five parties.

Ordinarily, Shobanjo would have preferred that Insight worked for the Unity Party of Nigeria (UPN), which was the leading opposition party. From an ideological perspective, UPN, led by the late Chief Obafemi Awolowo, best articulated Shobanjo's latent people-oriented conviction of equal opportunity for all. The party, however, did not oblige Insight the campaign. The other political parties, namely: Nigeria Peoples Party (NPP); Peoples Redemption Party (PRP); Great Nigeria Peoples Party (GNPP) and the newly registered Nigerian Advanced Party (NAP), were not considered to be in serious contention for the Presidency.

NAP, however, signed on Insight. This was a huge challenge because the party was new on the political terrain and there was glaring absence of strong political structure from which it could launch an effective campaign to put its presidential candidate, Dr. Tunji Braithwaite, a top flight, Lagos-based lawyer of Leftist political persuasion, in the State House. NAP gave Insight a simple brief to develop a campaign that would creatively communicate the party's key message: 'Change'. With that assignment, Insight became the first local agency in Nigeria to handle a full-blown political campaign. For Shobanjo and his team, the NAP assignment was just another brief in a full day's job; it did not require them to subscribe to the party's worldview. But the job required strict professionalism, just in the same way that a barrister would take on a case and passionately pursue it to its logical conclusion, not minding if the client was right or wrong. The campaign cost NAP about a million naira.

Insight plunged head-long into the assignment. The agency developed several intensive messages for the print medium and created strong audio and visual concepts for prime-time broadcasts on radio and television. Braithwaite was also 'packaged' in a manner that fitted his personality as a 'rebel' with a cause. His refrain that 'things have just got to change,' generated a lot of buzz anywhere he or his party campaigned. However, whilst the advertising campaign dramatically shot up awareness of NAP and its manifesto among the electorate, it did not necessarily increase the party's public approval rating. On campaign trails, Braithwaite spoke way above the head of the average voter, both in terms of the content and the presentation of his manifesto. Regardless of whether he addressed gatherings of university dons or communities of road transport workers, butchers and market women or groups of artisans, Braithwaite's language was elevated and it had the unapologetic flavour of a committed Marxist. He freely used words and phrases like 'revolution', 'lumpen elements', 'compradour bourgeoisie' and 'proletariat', ad infinitum. Majority of the people just did not understand him and, owing to other considerations, the few that did were not too persuaded. Naira and rice were the key vote swingers but neither Braithwaite nor his party doled them out as the ruling party did.

Predictably, neither NAP nor any of the other four opposition parties matched the NPN, which controversially recorded a 'landslide' victory by winning majority of the elections at the State and Federal levels. The opposition parties derided NPN's victory as a 'moonslide' and an affirmation of the party's unbridled determination to win from the Sahara Desert to the Atlantic Ocean. NPN apologists, on the other hand, ascribed the party's victory to a 'bandwagon' effect that resulted from the switch of allegiance by voters who chose to align with the NPN owing to its streak of nationwide victory at the legislative, gubernatorial and presidential elections that were held in quick succession. The party's Chairman, Chief Adisa Akinloye, was emphatic that the electorate voted NPN so they could have 'rosy cheeks' like members of the ruling party.

The election results heated up the polity. In one of the Eastern States, a newscaster with the public broadcast station, Nigerian Television Authority (NTA), walked out while on air, expressing disgust at the 'pack of lies' that he was being made to read on the news. In Imo State, the incumbent Governor, Samuel Mbakwe (1929-2004), sensed that he would be rigged out of office and quickly made a state-wide broadcast to announce his re-election ahead of whatever results that were declared by the Federal Electoral Commission (FEDECO). In Oyo State, the incumbent Governor, Chief Bola Ige (1930-2001), screamed that citizens of the State should resist his 'defeat' by NPN's Dr. Omololu Olunloyo. In Ondo State, the 'spontaneous reaction' of the people to news of the defeat of the incumbent Governor, Adekunle Ajasin (1908-1987), by his former deputy, Akin Omoboriowo (1932-2012), who defected to NPN, gave rise to widespread arson and murder of political opponents. Not surprisingly, the upheavals set the tone for the overthrow of democracy and the return of the military on 31 December, 1983, under the leadership of the tough talking, never smiling duo of Generals Muhammadu Buhari, who was Head of State and Tunde Idiagbon, now deceased, who, as Chief of Staff, Supreme Headquarters was Buhari's deputy in the Supreme Military Council (SMC). Things, indeed, changed, but not in the way NAP had envisaged.

This, notwithstanding, Shobanjo rated Insight's creative campaign for NAP as highly successful and he deemed Braithwaite's unique dressing as one of the high points of the campaign. He conceded, though, that there could have been a probable misreading of the sophistication of the Nigerian electorate of the time, particularly in terms of their understanding of the candidate's ideological bent. On his part, Braithwaite believed that Insight did a 'wonderful job' so much so that his relationship with Insight and its leadership remained until he passed on in 2016.

Many people, including advertising practitioners, however, hold contrary views. For some, the campaign was below par, especially because Braithwaite, in his 'dansiki' and 'neckerchief' appeared "too 'unserious' to be taken seriously."[1] Some other critics believed that it was incurable optimism to have expected wholesale public communication to generate a different outcome to NAP's critical political challenge when it was apparent that Braithwaite was too militant for 1983 Nigeria. However, the critics were also quick to concede that his get up, "overtly militant in outlook and voice, may have been NAP's translation of the revolutionary spirit."[2] This latter position somewhat coheres with Shobanjo's stance on the impracticability of using advertising to make a ball to roll uphill.

The NAP campaign experience, however, gave Shobanjo and Insight a head start in political advertising in the 1990s when the agency handled the campaigns of the National Republican Convention, NRC, in the life of the botched Third Republic. During that assignment, Shobanjo also struck enduring relationships with NRC's Publicity Secretary, Dr. Doyin Okupe, and then National Chairman, Chief Tom Ikimi, who later became Nigeria's Foreign Affairs Minister under Military President, General Sani Abacha and Senator Ben Obi.

The spectacular rise in the profile of Insight in the mid-1980s gave rise to widespread allegations of ethical and professional

[1] Steve Omojafor, *The Media, Advertising and '83 Elections* published in *Advertising in Nigeria*, Feb/April, 1984, p.6
[2] May Nzeribe, *The Media in Politics*, ibid.

misconduct against the agency in adworld. Critics charged that the agency's briefs were executed abroad by Bates with practically no local input. They also alleged that Insight had by that time perfected the modern-day art of 'settlement,' that is, bribing client interfaces to secure business. The colourful lifestyle of the agency's leadership was cited as ample proof that Shobanjo and his men were fiddling with money that belonged to clients. Some of the charges, it would seem, were part of aggression that was transferred from the early days of Insight when it breached AAAN's rule that forbade direct solicitation of member agency's clients. Some others appeared to be offshoots of insufficient understanding of Shobanjo's business outlook and his lifestyle.

Perhaps, it is necessary to counterpoint Insight's fast growth with the complaints of some other local operators of that era to put the issue in perspective. Whereas Insight confidently took the fight to the 'Big Boys' on their own turf, some other agency owners sulked over what they saw as the inequality of business distribution. For the latter group, business was skewed in favour of "three agencies which were formerly owned by foreigners and still retain erstwhile foreign names."[1] This was a veiled reference to Lintas, OBM and Grant. While others agonised over the frustration of the 'spirit of the indigenisation decree' because the three agencies controlled about 90 per cent of total advertising billing, Insight and a couple of others like Rosabel, Promoserve and PAL skilfully plotted how to wrest control from the older agencies. The difference in orientation is significant because at no time have agency owners in Nigeria appeared to agree on how best to do business. Whereas there was noticeable bellyaching about the trajectory of Insight's rise in the industry, the path of the agency's flight is, perhaps, better articulated by two highly respected voices whose perspectives span about two generations of advertising practice.

---

[1] *10th Anniversary Supplement of ROD Publicity, Daily Times, 12 May, 1981*

For the doyen of advertising, Moemeke: "[Insight] then and now has one thing in common: the single-mindedness of producing advertising that would make a difference. In doing so, it came across many feet on which it stepped. Also, because [it started] in what might amount then to a jungle, [Shobanjo's] agency did a number of things that the like of our own agency [Lintas] would never have dreamt of doing. That is because the rules by which we operated would not allow us to do so [like not handling competing accounts and staying away from politics and politicians]. All these rules bound us but this new agency [Insight] had no such rules and had every room to manoeuvre. So, all he did was what one might call 'tax avoidance', not 'tax evasion'."

Lolu Akinwunmi of Prima Garnet saw the birth of Insight as being in keeping with change in a continuum: "There is always a minor revolution in every industry about every five years. Previously, the first-generation agencies [Lintas, OBM and Grant] did things in specific ways. By then, quite a few agencies were like accounting firms, dull and routine. Insight made a big splash; it brought something new – creative media buying, exciting campaigns and flamboyance – that was not necessarily negative. It [Insight] was avant-garde; it dared to be different and broke out in a different way."

By 1986, the Insight 'revolution' had translated to a turnover of a little less than N10 million and 35 clients, 75 per cent of which were multinationals. Journalist Jimi Disu quoted an excited Shobanjo as boasting that 'now, we do not touch business of less than N100,000.'[1] Shobanjo, however, later disclaimed this quote that was attributed to him, saying the briefs that were declined were those in which the agency and client had fundamental disagreements on the quality and execution of creative solutions. By this performance,

---

[1] *Vanguard, 15 May, 1986*

Insight served notice to adworld that it seriously aimed at being Number One in the industry not just in terms of the numbers but also in terms of offering the best creative solutions to all their clients. Considering the agency's success, Shobanjo highlighted two things that Insight would not do. First, it would not deal with unsophisticated clients and it would reject any new brief that conflicted with that of an existing client. The latter pledge soon gave rise to a revolution in Nigeria's advertising industry.

Ironically, the more Insight soared, the more Grant Advertising Ltd struggled to stay afloat. The mixed fortunes of both agencies did not escape Shobanjo who, though saddened by the plight of his former agency, could not help but anticipate the imminent and seemingly inevitable disintegration of Grant: "The difference is clear between both agencies (Insight and Grant) – while one is alive and kicking, the other is dead, ready to be buried."

Grant proved him right by going under many years later despite spirited efforts to keep it afloat by its directors ably led by Otunba J.K Randle, a renowned chartered accountant, who became the agency's Chairman.

Although Insight had brushed aside strong challenge from other agencies to place second to Lintas on the billings table by 1986, industry watchers had begun to give the younger agency the creative edge based on some spectacular campaigns that it ran during the period. Notable among these were the campaigns for Angiers junior aspirin and Nasco cornflakes as well as the Gold beer dancing bottle – 'Oh My Gold' – television commercials. Dulux Paint's 'the only way to paint a masterpiece' campaign was also exceptional.

In 1987, the agency moved from its Calabar Street offices to a more spacious location at Plot 58, Akanbi Onitiri Close, also in Mainland Lagos. The movement was both symbolic and strategic, as Insight had come of age and needed more room for its creativity to fledge. Thoughts of how Insight survived the anxiety of the early days at Calabar Street often elicit wry smile from Shobanjo. Awosika's laughter, on the other hand, often rolled like thunder whenever he remembered some fun moments in the heat of the difficult days. Like the day Dogo, the security guard, shut everyone out of the office having locked the gate and was nowhere to be found. The early birds simply scaled the low fence of the building to gain entrance. Dogo was assailed with a thousand and one questions when he eventually showed up several hours later. "Oga, no vex. Ya son fall for contractor," he explained as he apologised for his unavoidable absence from his duty post. All questions dried up instantaneously. "Ya son fall for contractor." Meaning what? All planned disciplinary measures were discarded after it dawned on all that Dogo meant that his son, a casual labourer, fell off the scaffold at a construction site!

By 1989, the nine-year old company proved it was no longer content with being a challenger; it wanted the ultimate prize of being acknowledged as the industry leader. It gave the 61-year old Lintas a good run for its money. By this time, Insight had 97 staff on its payroll, a billing target of N35 million, which was achieved and a client portfolio of 32 'solid' accounts (see below):

1. Abbott Laboratories
2. Access Bank
3. African Petroleum
4. Afprint/Aflon/Afcott
5. Atlas Nigeria Ltd.
6. Brian Munro

7. British Airways
8. CAPL
9. Central Bank
10. Cheseborough Products
11. Chrislieb
12. DHL
13. Dunlop
14. Femina Hygienicals
15. Femstar/Warri Bottlers
16. Food Specialities
17 Haco Products
18. Household Products
19. Lever Brothers
20. Nasco Foods
21. Nestle World Trade
22. NICON
23. NICON-NOGA Hilton
24. Nig. Bag. Mfg Co. (BAGCO)
25. Nigerian Catering Co.
26. Reckitt & Coleman
27. SCOA
28. Sona Breweries
29. Superbru
30. Tate & Lyle
31. Wellcome
32. West African Threads Co.

By the mid-1980s, the fast and furious pace of growth recorded by Insight Communications as well as some unanticipated challenges compelled the founders of the agency to revisit the company's conception blueprint. The feasibility document had recognised the need to "diversify into other areas of communication like public relations and marketing consultancy as and when these fields dictate a very cost-efficient operation." The idea of diversification was borne out of the need to maintain a multiple stream of income to be derived from seizing professional opportunities. Before these opportunities came, Insight faced the threat of losing some of its valuable clients owing to the poor performance of outdoor contractors. This forced the agency to embark on the diversification of its service portfolio through the establishment of Klinsite Outdoor Services in 1984. Klinsite's goal was to take charge of the outdoor advertising needs of the agency's clients to pre-empt imminent loss of crucial businesses. By late 2007, Klinsite, which metamorphosed into Optimum Exposures Ltd in 1988, had become Nigeria's most innovative outdoor advertising company.

Prior to 1989, public relations service came as standard business offering by most advertising agencies. Insight changed all that when The Quadrant Company (TQC) was registered as Nigeria's first structured public relations consultancy. The promulgation of the Nigerian Institute of Public Relations (NIPR) Decree No. 16 of 1990 confirmed that the dream of Shobanjo and his team was spot on regarding global best practice in marketing communications. Specialisation was the name of the game. TQC opened for business in 1990 and has consistently maintained its position as Nigeria's No. 1 public relations company.

Again, in 1990, another 'baby' was born in the Insight family. Four years earlier, Shobanjo had said that the agency would not touch any new business that conflicted with existing in-house accounts. Insight missed a lot of good business opportunities in the bid to keep faith with this pledge. The succession of losses also constrained the growth of the agency, which had reached a point where it could not afford to be too top heavy. It was not in any position to maintain about six Executive Directors. This contrasted with Shobanjo's experience at Grant, where the agency, which billed less than N2 million, hired about six expatriates. He, however, was unwilling to contemplate the flipside of the agency being unable to keep its army of well-trained personnel who now needed to break the agency's self-imposed glass ceiling. He knew well enough that empowering people was a cardinal pillar for the founding of Insight. The search for quick answers led to the idea of floating a second line agency, MC & A (Marketing Communications and Advertising) Ltd, which became Nigeria's first second line advertising agency.

All at once, MC & A solved two major problems for the managers of Insight. It became home for some of Insight's best hands who might have been forced to float their own outfits or move to rival agencies to advance their careers once the top became too choked up at Insight. MC & A also ended the spate of missed business opportunities. The new agency, which was affiliated to Saatchi & Saatchi, gave Insight a run for its money in all departments. It was creative, it was a client's delight and it was profitable. The dividend of diversification was instantaneous in various economic sectors. In the foods and beverages sector, for example, Insight handled Nestle whilst MC & A pitched its tent with Cadbury; in oil and gas, Total berthed at Insight but Texaco found a home at MC & A. Both agencies beat each other silly in pitches, as though they did not have a common paternity. The advertising industry was not particularly thrilled because many practitioners felt strongly that it was wrong for an individual to own two rival agencies. They believed that the idea of operating a second line agency still did not sufficiently address the problem of managing account conflicts in the business. Worse, they believed strongly that staff of Insight and MC & A shared confidential client information.

At an individual level, Shobanjo felt a high degree of personal pain in the way some media owners received the news of the birth of MC & A: "(They) felt that our plan was to 'kill' Insight and thereby get whatever debts they were owed written off."

The viewpoint, which began as whispers soon gained ground in the industry. The rumour mill, it turned out, was fuelled by a well regarded professional in the broadcast media sector, where he was a top gun in a national television station. Ironically, the same man did not see any moral contradiction in currying favour from Shobanjo whom he entreated to help facilitate the recruitment of his daughter by the same MC & A!

It was not too difficult for Insight to float two major companies in quick succession because it made a lot of money during this period. By 1989, the agency controlled an estimated 10% share of the advertising market in Nigeria. Rather than declare dividend, shareholders ploughed back the money into the diversification programme. By the end of 1990, Insight's industry market share increased to 13%. Whilst the figures looked impressive, it did not immediately dawn on the management of Insight that the agency had begun to haemorrhage, as almost all its best hands had either been seconded to sister companies or had moved on to new things to advance their careers.

In continuation of its diversification programme, the leadership of Insight in 1990 created Troyka Holdings that had Shobanjo and two other Insight pioneers, Awosika and Ibe, as Chairman and directors respectively. Troyka was born primarily to preserve the leadership of Insight in the industry by means of promoting a 'concentric array of businesses' that would absorb the heat from competition, leaving the core, Insight, unscathed. Aside from Halogen, which is an assets protection company, all the unit companies were in the core business of marketing communications. Each had a Managing Director or General Manager who reported to the board of the holding company. In the main, the Group adopted a model that was somewhat like the Japanese horizontal 'Keiretsu' that encouraged 'in-house' arms-length transactions amongst sister companies.

The Insight story was, however, not all bliss in the 1980s. At different points, the agency went through difficult patches for which the management did several 'crazy' things to keep the agency afloat. One of these involved floating a trading company to do everything to help cashflow especially after a first-generation bank turned down the agency's request for a N10,000 loan to stabilise its operation. 'Everything' included importing newsprint and stockfish. Put simply, it meant going into businesses that the agency's owners did not understand. Among other things, Shobanjo and his colleagues bought boats and headed for the South-South of Nigeria where they partnered with some fishermen at Ibeno in Akwa Ibom State. The business was an epic failure, as they got far more stress than the improved cashflow for which they had hoped. With burnt fingers, they quickly shut down the operation and imbibed a key lesson to stick to communications, which was their area of primary competence.

At age 10 in 1990, Insight had become something of an institution within and outside the advertising industry in Nigeria. Consumers of advertising arrogated top-of-mind creativity to the agency. Everyone tended to brand every good advertisement as an Insight creation even when the agency had no association with the brand in question. The large chunk of memorable creative work produced by Insight made it nearly impossible not to think of the agency as the engine room of creativity in the business. The measure of confidence that the agency enjoyed from its clients translated to a control of 13 per cent of total industry billing in 1990. The agency truly did well and it had become clear to all that it would only be a matter of time before it overtook Lintas on the billing table. At every point, Shobanjo advertised Insight as the best agency in the land and its staff, as the most properly groomed for business. In his reckoning, the sheer numerical strength of the agency, which at some point was more than 128 employees, gave the company a "solid and, perhaps, unfair advantage" in adworld. Suffused with joy at the phenomenal success of the agency but tempered by a need to have his vision better understood, Shobanjo proudly told the glitterati that graced Insight's 10th anniversary gala: "Unless people understand the dream, they cannot act the dream."

The dream was to be the best on all indices of corporate performance. It had scriptural basis that said simply that anyone, with faith the size of a mustard seed, could move mountains. The strong desire and amazing hard work put into actualising the dream became the ghost of an ideal that pursued the Insighters until the agency edged Lintas off the Number One spot in 1991. (see table next page)

Insight would have compounded issues for Lintas:Lagos, if Shobanjo had jumped at an offer of affiliation dangled by Lintas International which invited him for discussions in its London offices. He only shared details of the information with few of his associates at Insight. At the time of his invitation to London, Insight was the love of the life of Lever Brothers in Lagos, working on such brands as Lux toilet soap, Rin soap and detergent, Blue Band margarine and Oroyo vegetable oil, which were all brands that had been taken away from Lintas:Lagos. Insight was later to lose these accounts because of global agency alignments. Shobanjo declined the Lintas International offer, which, if he had been as unscrupulous as he had been tagged, he easily could have accepted, especially considering that the clients of Bates, Insight's affiliate at the time, were not present in Nigeria.

	1986 (N)	1987 (N)	1988 (N)	1989 (N)	1990 (N)	1991 (N)	1992 (N)	1993 (N)
Total Market N'000	200	240	300	345	400	520	720	930
% Industry Growth	10	20	25	15	16	30	38	29
AGENCY								
Insight	9.9	16	26.4	35	53.9	88	135	185
Billing/ Share of Market	5%	7%	9%	10%	13%	17%	19%	20%
Lintas	16.9	20	40.41	66.67	78	85	100	120
Rosabel	6.8	10.9	15	25	40	45	60	107
Grant	9.6	10.5	12.5	15	21	10	20	25
OBM	8.0	9.5	13.5	16	20	22	25	35
Promoserve	3.3	4.4	5	6	7	10	40	74
STB	-	-	-	-	3	20	45	89
LTC	-	2	5	9	12	15	18	42
MC & A	-	-	-	-	8	25	35	52
SO & U	-	-	-	-	2	5	20	35
Others	145.7	166.7	182.49	172.33	159.1	190	215	138

Source: Osar Emokpae, Stemming the Incidence of high Labour Turnover in Insight Communications Ltd (Unpublished Ph.D. dissertation, 1994)

As Insight and the new unit companies in Troyka prospered, other 'children of business decision' were born to the group. They included Link Studios, which was established in 1991 to meet the pre-press needs of Insight and MC & A. In 1992, Halogen Security, an assets protection company was born. It was the first non-core communications company in the group. Its birth was fortuitous yet inevitable after the midnight armed attack on Shobanjo on January 31, 1992. A rash of other companies came on board in 1997, notably: All Season's Media Company (Mediacom), a media independent; African Barter Company (ABC), a broadcast programme content provider; MIT Healthcare Ltd, a specialist healthcare marketing communications company and Optistal, a steel fabrication outfit that specialised in the erection of outdoor advertising structures.

Some of these companies later went under, in part, because they seemed to have been ahead of their time. Some others failed because, at the time, the expansion programme did not have built-in early warning signals that could have staved off their demise. But the majority that survived remained, without argument, Number One in their specialist areas. Combined with Insight, they generated annual revenue in excess of N17 billion for the Shobanjo-led group of companies before his exit from day-to-day administration of the business in 2004.

In 1993, Shobanjo's dream received a massive international boost when Advertising Age, a globally respected marketing publication, listed two of his organisations, Insight and MC & A, alongside Promoserve Advertising Ltd in the 50th Annual Agency Survey. The survey ranked the Nigerian outfits among top non-US agencies by country, judged by global billing of gross income and turnover. Advertising Age reported that Insight billed $8,405,000, Promoserve $3,347,000 and MC & A $2,000,000. It was the first time, since 1989 when the survey began to include non-US agencies, that any Nigerian agency was listed. Unofficial figures put Insight's billings in 1995 and 1996 at N240 million and N380 million respectively. MC & A, on the other hand, recorded N65 million and N90.5 million respectively during the same period.

How did Shobanjo and his team pull off this feat in less than two decades? A reading of the seminal text: *In Search of Excellence: Lessons from America's Best Run Companies*[1] by Thomas J. Peters and Robert H. Waterman (Jr.) provides some answers. In the book, Peters and Waterman posited that excellent companies almost

---

[1] *Warner Books, New York, 1982 pp. 13 – 15*

always manifest eight attributes, to wit: (1) a bias for action, (2) managing close to the customer, (3) autonomy and entrepreneurship, (4) productivity through people, (5) hand-on, value-driven, (6) sticking to the knitting, (7) simple form, lean staff and (8) simultaneous loose-tight properties. All eight attributes abound in sufficient quantities in the broad operation of Troyka or, specifically, in the running of Insight. Simplified, these eight characteristics manifested Shobanjo's belief that creative forests do not exist. In his view, any agency or business that perpetually showed 'flashes of creativity' would also perpetually remain an 'also-ran'. For him, therefore, any organisation that aims at being the best must 'lead, manage and perform; not follow, respond and conform.'

Insight's forward-looking strides received acclamation from the business world. Under Shobanjo, the agency won more creative awards and honourable mentions for excellent professional practice than any other agency in Nigeria (see list in Appendix II), its nearest rivals being Rosabel, Prima Garnet, TBWA-Concept Unit and DDB Lagos. The agency's winning streak continued with Awosika at the helms. In 2012, eight years after Shobanjo left the saddle, Insight led the league of agencies that were adjudged to be the most creative in Nigeria at the seventh edition of the Lagos Advertising and Ideas Festival (LAIF) with a haul of 25 awards comprising four Gold, 10 Silver and 11 Bronze medals.

This notwithstanding, it remained a matter of surprise that Insight, under the leadership of Shobanjo, did not win any international advertising-based award despite the breadth of its showing on the local scene. This is against the backdrop of the mistaken belief that Lintas won advertising's biggest award, a Clio, in 1989 for the 'Turn to Star, the ideal brew' commercial. Lintas, in fact, got a special commendation which, nonetheless, was a first for any Nigerian agency. Shobanjo had a simple response: "International awards do not come easy. We had put in for awards twice or thrice in the last couple of years... for me, it is either Cannes or Clio. They do not come easy, but we shall keep on trying."

He was satisfied, though, that within the Bates Network, some of Insight's creative works were considered worthy of commendation. These included the BAGCO Super Sack, Pepsi Big Blue and Naira Lottery commercials. Under his watch, Insight reeled out some of the most exciting campaigns ever to come out of Nigeria's advertising industry in the last three decades. In the agency's show reel were campaigns for the BAGCO Super Sack series, Vaseline Petroleum Jelly, Vaseline Perfume Baby Jelly, Vaseline Herbal Cream, Askar Paints, Vitalo, Gold Beer, Maltonic, Angiers Junior Aspirin, Chevalier, Calypso coconut drink, Natusan Baby Cream, Jumbo Cubes, Rin, Equitorial Trust Bank's partnership ad, Indomie Noodles commercials, Milo, 7-Up Hi-Life promo, Mirinda 'Orangemen', Peak Milk, Sona Breweries' inflatable balloons, Nasco Foods, Pepsi Big Blue, the introductory press advertisement for SIO Motors and Nigeria's first TV Reality Show, Gulder Ultimate Search, which ran for ten seasons. Often, however, the strength of these campaigns was felt more in the electronic media – which, unwittingly, may have reflected Shobanjo's bias given his early experience in broadcasting. A cursory look at the agency's profile of awards, however, showed impressive performance across all media.

There is need to say, however, that the immense popularity of some of Insight campaigns also made them prone to deep controversy. The National Family Planning logo, for instance, raised a lot of dust. The campaign, a project of the Federal Ministry of Health, which was sponsored by the US Agency for International Development (USAID) and the John Hopkins University Centre for Communication

Services, came under severe criticisms for "violently disregarding public sensibilities'.[1] It was seen as promoting an 'unNigerian' idea of the ideal family: a man, a woman and a child. Reactions to the campaign spanned the length and breadth of the country and they cut across diverse socio-economic and cultural groupings. Shobanjo was quick to admit that the campaign was a major landmark in his career because it generated the most 'deep-seated attitudinal biases' he had ever encountered.

The BAGCO Super Sack commercials also came under scrutiny after their first release. They were variously described, among others, as 'aggressive' and 'violent'. The commercials were withdrawn and repackaged. They won awards.

The 7-Up Hi-Life promo, which re-defined consumer promotions in the 1990s, was grounded by the National Agency for Food, Drug Administration and Control (NAFDAC) for containing 'compulsive elements' capable of encouraging excessive consumption of soft drinks. This was because the star prizes were sleek Daewoo Espero saloon cars that were, at the time, symbols of social and economic status. NAFDAC felt that the dream of consumers to win these much sought-after automobiles could escalate the incidence of diabetes, as recorded in 'clinical evidence' of past promotions that were presented by the Diabetic Association of Nigeria. Shobanjo felt that NAFDAC was not a disinterested umpire. The General Manager (Corporate Affairs) of Seven-Up Bottling Company at the time, Faysal Halabi, was similarly inclined, especially because a similar promo by a rival beverages producer about the same time did not come under the regulatory agency's hammer.

The innovative three-man Mirinda 'Orangemen' teaser, which received public relations support from The Quadrant Company, did

[1] *Emevwo Biakolo, An Advertiser's Ambush, The Guardian, 30 April, 1994*

not escape close examination. The Lagos Command of the Nigerian Police stopped the campaign that took Lagos by storm, arguing that it took the action for security reasons. Indeed, the Police questioned Amuzie Akpaka, an Executive Director of The Quadrant, about the sudden appearance of 'aliens' that walked the streets of Lagos and got attracted to anything in sight that had an orange colour. The campaign generated an admixture of fear and fascination that did not escape attention, as no one had seen anything of the sort in the country.

In these, no one disputed the fact that Insight's exceptional performance was the result of tight bonding of the company and its vision driver, Shobanjo. Both were extremely focused, thoroughly committed to professionalism, extremely hungry for business and fiercely competitive. It was not unheard of, at this stage of the agency's life, for Insight's staff to move straight to a presentation from the office, having worked overnight. It was common sight to see Shobanjo holding klieg lights for camera operators on location. He drove himself hard. He expected no less from his subordinates. For these reasons, every big win usually called for big celebrations in the house, much in the same way that a big sulk greeted every loss, though this was rare. In the early days, the team held informal post-pitch analyses at the car park at Calabar Street. Much later, everyone would just huddle in any available office.

Shobanjo often felt very bad whenever he lost a business. If he had cause to believe that the result of a pitch had been predetermined, his sense of disgust was twice multiplied. When, however, he believed that Insight was beaten fair and square, he was also quick to concede defeat. He would, at such times, as he is wont to, lapse into his native Yoruba language and say to his men: '*Baba ise ni awon people yen gbe wa.*'[1] Or, if he felt that his or any other senior

---
[1] *Competition put up a superb performance*

executive's insistence on a particular strategy had cost Insight an account, he usually would walk into the office, hold somebody's hand or playfully punch another on the shoulder and confess: *Omo boy, awa la gbe awon omo yen si koto.*[1] When, therefore, he sensed that preparations for subsequent presentations were headed towards another debacle, he would scream: 'hey, you've started again o!'

Whether Insight won or lost, Shobanjo had an article of faith: he would religiously compose nicely worded and personally signed 'Thank You' letters to prospective and current clients after every major contact. This was usually done within 24 hours of a meeting. For him, this was an important part of canalisation or making in-roads to new businesses or growing existing ones. Almost always, this guaranteed Insight another shot at a lost business opportunity at a future date or empathic listening to progress an existing account. This fact was well illustrated in the 1980s when Insight sought affiliation with FCB. Though the proposed technical co-operation did not work out, the staff of the international agency did not forget the thoughtful Nigerian whose agency did things in grand style. FCB helped Insight to win both the British Caledonian (now British Airways) and ICI (CAPL) accounts in the 1980s. The gesture of never forgetting to thank someone or everyone for every 'little' thing seems so ordinary; yet almost everyone takes it for granted. Oftentimes, the opportunity cost of such forgetfulness is great.

The success of Insight, however, did not preclude occasional moments of anxiety like, for instance, when the agency experienced high labour turnover. At some point, Shobanjo subscribed to the notion that there are probably fewer than '50 quality advertising professionals' in the nearly 90-year old profession in Nigeria. This, in part, stemmed from the fact that he had long noticed that clients

---

[1]*We misled the boys*

usually agonised over moving their accounts from one agency to the other because of the dearth of truly professional shops. He was also mindful that industry records rated Insight among the few agencies that enjoyed long tenure on their accounts, some of which were won in the early years of the founding of the agency. Whilst he could readily attribute Insight's long hold on its businesses to the founding principle that the agency would consistently and impeccably serve its clients to make any planned movement of an account unnecessary, he could not so scientifically rationalise the spate of staff exits from the agency in the mid-1990s. The search for answers prompted him and Troyka's Director of Strategic Planning, Dr. Osar Emokpae, to conduct a comparative study of agency operations. The results were both shocking and obvious: agency operators had grown complacent on many fronts and left their barn doors too badly protected from raiders and dreamers within and outside the industry.

The study faulted agency operators on five grounds that ranged from faulty personnel policies to combative justification of avoidable mistakes. Broadly, the results showed that agencies (1) recruited staff believing they would have a short tenure, (2) failed to train their employees, (3) failed to remunerate employees equitably, (4) lost such staff eventually and (5) justified the labour turnover by concluding that such staff were, at any rate, under-qualified. These findings led Troyka management to reconfigure the dynamics of its human resource policies. Resultantly, it became mandatory for all unit companies in Troyka Holdings to pay equitable salaries, usually above industry standard and to allocate a significant percentage of their budgets to staff training in their annual operating plan (AOP). The overriding principle was that any agency would retain valuable clients if it could retain professional associates.

Whereas it is easy to dismiss charges of unethical conduct against Insight and Shobanjo, it is a lot more challenging to knock the argument that, for a long time, Insight was a one-man band. Critics often cited Shobanjo's dominant personality to reinforce this argument. The perception is wrong. What we see is a strong personality with a carefully nurtured media image that is sustained by a followership that has absolute confidence in the quality of his leadership and the well-devolved power structure of the establishment. To the extent that it is necessary to put a name, a colourful one, too, to the organisation, Shobanjo equals Insight and vice-versa. To the extent that his personality is inextricably woven to the fabrics of the company, he did well as the joy-bearer of Insight. To the extent that all three remaining owners of the business and their subordinates shared a common vision of professionalism and total quality, Insight is an orchestra.

Way back in 1986, Shobanjo predicted that "the economy and the pressure we get from our clients will dictate how far we will go."[1] Truly so. Insight, and indeed, Troyka Holdings, has pushed the Shobanjo name beyond frontiers he imagined. He is, today, the most visible and most accomplished advertising practitioner in Nigeria. The organisations he co-founded had lived up to his expectations, though he is still reaching out for more.

But success came at a very high price.

---

[1] *Vanguard, 15 May, 1986*

7

Haemorrhage

The higher up the flagpole you climb,
The more your underwear is exposed

John Madden

Ordinarily, the men at Number 1 Calabar Street were not given to superstition; yet when adversity hit the Insight team exactly thirteen days into the life of the agency, they could not help but wonder if it forbode anything ominous. Awosika recollects vividly: "My mother was a great support for the agency; she would come around to see how we were faring. I remember talking to her on the morning of January 15, 1980. I told her we needed about N6,000 to pay staff salaries and she asked me to come for the money by 6.00 p.m. that day. When I got home, the money was there but my mother was dead."

The demise of 'Mama Jimi', as the Insighters fondly called Mrs. Esther Adetoun Awosika, shook them all. She had gladly suffered the dream and contagious high spirits of her son and his colleagues, advising them as any good mother would, chiding when the need arose and providing moral and material support without counting cost each time they knocked on her doors. Her 'children' reciprocated her labour of love by pulling all stops to accord her a befitting burial.

Within a week of her interment, the Insighters pulled themselves by the bootstrap and plunged headlong into the business of everyday living. There were bills to pay. But the trauma brought on by the loss of Mrs Awosika was just the beginning of a series of internal bleeding that Shobanjo, as an individual, and Insight, as an organisation, would suffer in the days ahead. The critical few that threatened to shatter the man and blow apart his establishment shall be examined in near-chronological order.

Boardroom Conflict

Shobanjo holds the view that no professional is prepared for executive assignments until he has experienced oftentimes vicious corporate power play that could either make or shatter his career. He should know, having traversed the minefields of boardroom intrigues at Grant. Trouble in Insight's boardroom brewed within 12 months of the company's inception. Whilst the board members – Goddy Amadi, Ayo Idowu and himself – had no disagreements on the need to build a profitable enterprise, they had divergent views on how to reach their goal and they did not have a common opinion on how best to run the agency.

As Insight's only executive Director, Shobanjo believed that the company's management ought to enjoy a high degree of free hand in the day-to-day operation of the agency, not run to investors to seek approval for every need. The kernel of his position on the application of executive initiative was that it engendered swift decision-making.

The other directors, on the other hand, preferred the minimalist approach of the Civil Service that based career advancement on a codified one-grade-one-step system that had built-in checks and balances to help guard against potential abuse of power by a CEO.

The administration of staff emoluments embodied the differing perspectives of the board. At the end of Insight's first financial year in 1980, the agency recorded an operational loss. Yet Shobanjo recommended increased emoluments across the board for staff, with the exception of himself, against the 1981 fiscal year. Both Idowu and Amadi preferred that staff advanced by grade, with increase in salaries not being more than, say, 15 percent. Shobanjo disagreed with this position, arguing that management ought to be trusted to exercise discretion in the reward of talents. He contended that advertising agencies should not be subject to civil service-like structures and guidelines, if the creative juice of staff was to be stirred towards achieving better results in the New Year. The underlying argument was the need to keep faith with staff empowerment, which was one of the pillars of the agency's vision at its start up.

Idowu, it would appear, strongly did not share this viewpoint. Shobanjo, too, was not enthusiastic about what he saw as attempts by external directors to tinker with agency operations. Neither shifted ground. An exchange of correspondence between both men followed as they drifted apart the more. In no time, Idowu convinced himself that his membership of the Insight board would no longer serve any useful purpose. He offered to leave, but not without demanding that he be paid the full value of his N50,000 equity participation in a lump sum within three months.

Insight was in a quandary, as it was financially too lean to meet

Idowu's demand. This was at a time that the agency's operation was severely constrained by low cashflow. The Chairman, Amadi, was determined that the company must survive. His pride as a friend was on the line, as was his financial stake in the agency. He could ill-afford to have both go down the drain. As his contribution to rescuing the situation, he surrendered his country home in Egbu, Imo State as collateral for a N60,000 loan from the British American Insurance Company (BAICO). Ibe collected the papers of the property. Several years after, it became a private joke that Imo State showed its good and 'bad' sides to the Insight family. Amadi's support came from the State, just as Awosika had a close shave with death in the State when the team travelled to the East in the 1990s to attend the funeral of Ibe's father. Whilst others chose to use the staircase of the hotel where they lodged, Awosika opted to take the lift. He was trapped in the lift for some 20 minutes because of a sudden, though not unusual, power outage. His colleagues were agitated when he could not be found at the meeting point in the hotel's lobby. The intercom in his room rang out as many times as it was called and there was no alternative means to reach him. The lift operator was out of sight. When he eventually showed up, the visiting Lagosians rushed at him and pelted him with a barrage of questions that bordered on how to rescue their trapped colleague. The lift was eventually forced open, whereupon a sweaty Awosika stepped out casually and strolled past his colleagues whilst whistling as though he was used to that kind of situation every waking moment!

Idowu's deadline significantly agitated the minds of his co-directors. No one wanted a face-off with him in the event of a default so as not to send obviously wrong signals to all who had closely followed the fortunes of the new company, not least of whom were their former colleagues at Grant and the prospective clients on their 'hit' list. Though the team was ill-prepared for this first experience in corporate crisis, Lady Luck appeared to have gone to bed without thoughts of their predicament in mind. Providence, however, saved the day for Insight. The agency received a kiss of life from Anglo-West Africa Ltd, later known as Femstar Ltd, bottlers of Limca and Gold Spot brands of soft drinks. Awosika got the company to pre-pay N70,000 for some jobs that the agency had proposed. Idowu was paid his N50,000 in the nick of time in June 1981 and in a lump sum, as he had demanded.

Shobanjo was on a business trip to London when the money was paid but his sigh of relief could have been heard in Lagos. The edge-of-the-precipice experience convinced him and others that the young agency would not die.

But the tempest still raged.

Split in the 'Dream Team' and Other Departures
As far as partnerships go, Insight's A-Team' of six ex-staffers of Grant Advertising – Shobanjo, Ibe, Awosika, Ogunro, Adebayo and Amogbe was unwieldy. But it hung together for more than twelve months before noticeable cracks began to appear in the structure. Ogunro and Adebayo were the first to leave the agency. They both resigned after about 18 months. The duo, Ogunro said, left because they felt that, like Shobanjo, their spirit of enterprise needed ample freedom to bloom. They, therefore, chose to strike out early to run their own 'show' so that they could cast their net far afield, even in uncharted waters. Perhaps, they would have stayed a while longer within the fold but for some incidents that occurred during their stay at Calabar Street.

At inception, as had been shown, Shobanjo, alone, was on the company's board with Amadi and Idowu who were external directors. All others were shareholders/employees. All six subscribers to the company's Article of Association had agreed to swim or sink together in view of their stakes in the destiny of the company. By common consent, everyone was expected to pour his heart and soul into the business. This tunnel vision disallowed any form of professional distraction, meaning that moonlighting in whatever form, by anyone, amounted to 'high treason'. At some point, however, Ogunro and Adebayo began to get involved in 'private practice' in professionally related and unrelated fields. In one instance, they were involved in the execution of a drainage construction contract whilst their colleagues sweated it out at the new Insight, whose future they could not tell. Shobanjo was totally disappointed at this development, especially because Ogunro, whom he liked very much, was involved. But the disciplinarian in him would not allow them to go scot-free. Ogunro and Adebayo were consequently cited for disloyalty to the company in demonstration of Shobanjo's intolerance of people who were not committed to the common cause.

He promptly changed the administrative line of reporting within the agency to accommodate the punishment that was meted out to the duo. Hitherto, all who left Grant headed their various departments and each reported directly to the Executive Chairman, as Shobanjo was then designated. For breaching the collective gentleman's agreement, both Ogunro who was a Senior Copywriter and Adebayo who was the Print Production Manager lost their right to report to the Chief Executive. Instead, they were made to report to the Art Director, Ibe, who was also instructed to keep watch over their movements. Shobanjo suspected that for reasons of professional pride, Ogunro and Adebayo would not accept the new arrangement. He was right. Both resigned by the end of 1981 to start their own partnership, Eminent Communications Ltd, which also became a highly successful advertising agency. This, notwithstanding, Ogunro held his erstwhile boss in high esteem. Sadly, though, Adebayo committed suicide in 1992, months after he parted ways with Ogunro. Sadder still was that the gentlemanly Ogunro, at age 61, was himself shot dead at Christmas in 2013 shortly after attending a carol service in his church in Ikeja, Lagos.

The departure of the two men, especially that of Ogunro, who had matured greatly as a copywriter, created a void in the operation of the company but Shobanjo was determined to make up for the losses. Before this occurrence, he had, through his long-time friend, David Neale, met Hamish Gibson, a writer in London who also knew several people in the advertising industry. Among Gibson's friends was John Hegarty, one of the owners of the world-renowned Bartle Bogle Hegarty agency, who then worked for TBWA, a small agency at the time. Shobanjo reasoned that if Hegarty could help train Ibe in the art of copywriting, then the latter would make up for Ogunro's exit. This was precisely what happened. For four intensive weeks, Ibe understudied Hegarty. On his return to Nigeria, his writing skill had developed dramatically. He was to be Insight's Chief Writer and Art Director until Lere Awokoya was hired to join him as Writer. Years later, Awokoya, on leaving Insight, set up the high-flying Concept Unit, now TBWA/Concept.

Either by design or coincidence, neither Insight nor Ogunro's Eminent Communications pitched a common account from the time of the breakaway. However, in the campaigns for the botched Third Republic presidential elections in 1993, the two agencies locked horns conducting the creative communications warfare of the National Republican Convention (NRC) and the Social Democratic Party (SDP) respectively. Industry watchers believed that the combined Rosabel & Eminent/SDP outflanked Insight/NRC, especially in the broadcast category, where the SDP radio/TV commercial, 'On the March Again', produced by Rosabel practically replaced the National Anthem. Although the communications campaign of the presidential race was brilliant, the political outcome was disastrous for Nigeria, which has not known real peace since the results of the 1993 election of billionaire M.K.O Abiola as President were annulled by his friend and Military President, General Ibrahim Badamasi Babangida.

The falling out among friends continued in 1987. This time, it was the turn of the Finance Controller, Amogbe, to depart. The cause and course of the rift are, at best, hazy. A bit of history is needed here for the sake of clarity. Shobanjo had met Amogbe in the United Kingdom sometime in 1977 or thereabout. Again, Rosabel's Odunsi played a crucial role in their meeting, as he introduced the two to each other. Both Odunsi and Amogbe had been classmates at CMS Grammar School, Bariga, Lagos. Odunsi sought Shobanjo's assistance in the relocation of Amogbe who was reluctant to return to Nigeria. Shobanjo obliged by offering him the Number Two position in Grant's Finance Department. By 1979, Amogbe had become the Head of the Finance Department. In this period, too, it had become clear that the personal chemistry between him and Shobanjo did not exactly work right. This explained Shobanjo's initial objection to having the Head of Finance in his original line up until Awosika made a strong case for his inclusion.

The core causes of Shobanjo's grouse with Amogbe could be summed up two ways in order of severity. He believed that Amogbe had no respect for constituted authority and that he was not faithful to the ideal of corporate survival. Amogbe was accused of operating a fleet of taxi cabs whose drivers reportedly often came to bicker in his office. On the other hand, Amogbe's exit seemed to have been largely influenced by his inability to endure what he perceived to be Shobanjo's autocratic management style and lack of empathy. Matters got to a head when Amogbe showed up late for a management meeting because, as he claimed, he had been involved in a highway accident. Shobanjo, in a fit of quiet storm, demanded to know if the accident occurred in the line of duty or whilst he was engaged in extra-agency activities. Amogbe was incensed. He blew a fuse, stormed out of Shobanjo's office then at Calabar Street and went back to his own office at Insight's annexe on Adelabu Street. The force of his angry departure left Shobanjo's usually tidy office in a mess, with broken china here, some memorabilia put out of joint there and puff of dust everywhere.

Shobanjo picked his phone and called to request Amogbe kindly take his seat because the meeting was not yet over. Amogbe declined to re-join the meeting. Each man refused to back down. The possibility of an amicable settlement was foreclosed after Shobanjo insisted that the Finance Director should report to anyone but him. Amogbe left the agency much later after the showdown. His stake in Insight was bought out. He ran his own business until he died in 2003.

What was not so obvious to some of Shobanjo's young colleagues at this stage was that he, too, had had to make a few personal sacrifices to ensure that Insight did not flounder. One of these involved an opportunity to pursue an advanced management course at the globally-renowned Harvard Business School. Much as he was inclined to accept the Harvard offer, its timing conflicted with the Insight founding team's aspiration to build a world-class company. The agency, at the time, was too young to leave in the hands of younger colleagues who looked up to him for professional guidance. He reluctantly let the offer lapse to avoid meeting a dead company at the end of his pursuit of personal self-development agenda. Many years later, the resultant success of Insight justified his decision to sacrifice self for others.

Up to this point, the story of Insight read like a children's nursery rhyme. Six men originally stood on the wall. Three 'fell': Ogunro, Adebayo and Amogbe. Three – Shobanjo, Awosika and Ibe remained standing until 2000, when Ibe took an early retirement. At the end of 2004, Shobanjo relinquished the last vestige of executive power when he chose to 'stand down' as CEO of Insight after 25 years in the saddle. It was, perhaps, fitting that Awosika remained the last man standing, considering his hard-to-ignore role in the founding of the company; considering his industry rating as an intellectual powerhouse and considering his close relationship with Shobanjo. They have enjoyed a personal and professional relationship that has spanned more than three decades. By Awosika's own admission, he has spent more time of his life with Shobanjo than with anyone else.

Not surprisingly, questions have been asked regarding what went wrong with the team. Perhaps, nothing unusual happened, as the falling out was only a part of the teething problems associated with the coming together of people of diverse orientations in a new enterprise. Admittedly, an admixture of business and personal considerations was a key element in the breakaways.

With hindsight, Shobanjo said of the team: "The sixth person (Amogbe, that is), even if he was my friend, was not part of the team I originally conceptualised. So if there was a five-man team including myself and there are two left, we can be said to have scored about 60 per cent which is not bad because when you pool people together to form a company the rate of failure is always high."

Both Insight and Troyka were fortunate that, generally, the personal chemistry between Shobanjo and his men have tended to be right. For this reason, both organisations have survived and prospered in the intervening years because they are ideas driven, not people-dependent. This derived from the helmsman's fundamental belief that the exit of people, no matter how highly placed, must never be allowed to negatively affect the fortunes of any organisation.

The split in the original Insight team, notwithstanding, Shobanjo has remained an apostle of partnerships in enterprise management, especially in creative fields such as advertising or the service industry in general because no individual possesses all the skills required to succeed. His passionate belief in the convergence of diverse sets of skills in a business venture was buttressed by the superlative performance of each carefully selected member of the original Insight team. The success of his vision also validated his position that aspiring entrepreneuers should be a lot more circumspect about starting up business on the sole criterion of friendship. He would rather that friendship developed out of business: "Business with friends? I will try not to do it. I will rather keep my friends. I am not advocating this as a universal rule, as I can only draw from my experience. There are exceptions but avoid it if you can."

He also spelt out some other critical elements that undergird successful partnerships. For him, every enterprise must have a clear leader, who need not be the oldest, but must be the one with tested leadership and technical skills as well as the best understanding of the common vision. He easily filled this position at Insight because, apart from being the oldest, he was by far the most professionally qualified member of the team.

He is convinced that a partnership cannot and should not be taken seriously if the partners cannot clearly spell out the attitude of each person to money. This is because of his strong belief that an enterprise cannot go far when individuals place undue premium on money and its role in the business. Awosika and Ibe shared this viewpoint. He is also strongly persuaded that God plays a great role in holding together the fabrics of any partnership, just as He directs the course of any business. The implication is that the place of the Supreme Being must never be taken for granted in any partnership.

Whilst he recognised that careful planning and realistic appraisal of facts on ground could help prevent avoidable problems in any partnership, he also acknowledged that the best laid out plans could still be derailed by unanticipated occurrences. Should this happen, he counselled that the partners-in-breach should be cut loose at the first opportunity before their conduct becomes cancerous to the organisation. The manner of exit would, however, be critical to how all parties feel after the separation. He demonstrated a possible exit strategy by changing the order of reporting when Ogunro and Adebayo needed to be disciplined. By making both men to report to Ibe, he knew full well that their bruised professional egos would make the parting of ways inevitable but it also would be easier to manage. Where, however, a tougher approach was required, he believed that no one should fight shy of calling a spade by its proper name. In the circumstance, a formal meeting of all partners should be called to discuss the breach and mete out appropriate sanctions, even if it meant demanding the immediate exit of the offending partner. All options must be carefully considered without malice to anyone.

Without argument, Insight and Troyka Holdings, like any other organisation, lost a good number of thoroughbred professionals over time, either through breakaways in the early days of Insight or the exit of senior level professionals from the Group in contemporary times. Yet, the culture of excellence in the delivery of service, which was entrenched in the founders' blueprint, has remained the mark of distinction that binds current and former members of Insight and the Troyka family. This culture is made more evident by the continuing brilliant performance of Insight after Shobanjo's departure as CEO as well as the aggregate of positive results shown by the two groups that make up the alumni 'association' of Troyka Group.

The first group comprised members of the original team and some contemporary joiners who left the group to establish their own agencies. Over time, most of them have recorded remarkable degrees of professional success and have continued to be relevant to defining the course of the marketing communications business in Nigeria. At one time or the other, each member of this group, as earlier recognised for their contribution to the growth of Insight across time, was a 'favoured child' of Shobanjo. Of the lot, however, the departure of Funmi Onabolu, as we shall see later, had the most profound personal effect on him.

The second Group consisted of former staff of Insight/Troyka Holdings who left at junior, middle or senior management levels to pick employment elsewhere and have shone brilliantly in the corporate establishments where they pitched their tents. In this category are, amongst several others, Mike Meze, who joined Promoserve before veering off to core PR practice; Kayode Oluwasona, who became Managing Director of Rosabel Leo Burnett, Busola Williams, who joined TBWA Concept; Akin Adesola, who became Creative Director of SO & U before joining Lowe:Lintas and Boye Adefila, who joined Globacom before moving on to TBWA Concept.

The circumstances of staff departures from the Group were generally based on the need for self-actualisation rather than by a clash of egos or acrimony except in one or two instances where certain individuals were thought to have 'drifted away from the dream and needed to be so reminded. Regardless of the manner of their exit, members of the Insight/Troyka alumni association still hold Shobanjo in high esteem and are proud to be recognised as 'graduates' of his various institutions. Emokpae, the former Director of Strategic Planning, affirmed this viewpoint in his book in which he asserted that Shobanjo shared the same 'visioning paradigm' with Prophet Nehemiah in the Scriptures in the sense that he knows 'how to focus on the major (whilst) delegating the minors.' Emokpae also held himself out as a living example of Shobanjo's leadership gift of conceiving visions whilst leaving others to run with them, without any fear of being outshone by any subordinate: "It was under Biodun Shobanjo that my planning credentials blossomed, for which I am eternally grateful."[1]

Shobanjo was deeply philosophical in his reflections on the departures from Troyka across time: "I found that when you look at great multinationals, they are started either by one person or two. They would usually put their mission statement in one corner of the office in the hope that employees will try and understand where the founder(s) is (are) coming from. If you can retain people who could internalise the mission, you then hope they are able to pass (the culture) down from generation to generation...I regret to say that there was no way the drift could have been arrested because in terms of providing the infrastructure for (staff) to stay and grow with the company I believe we did the best we could. When you look at the matrix that would make an individual stay, you will find that on a scale of 10, Insight had provided about 6.5 or 7. The remainder, for me, is mainly economic. There really is little we can do about that."

The quality of achievements recorded by former employees of Troyka Holdings profoundly supports Shobanjo's oft stated

---

[1] *Osar Philips Emokpae, The Great Expectations: The Secret to Abundant Life (The Book Company, Lagos, 2004, P.88)*

admonition: "Strike, if you are the hammer; do not slip, if you are the handle."

Coping with Divorce

Shobanjo's marriage to Lanre Folami, which was contracted on 21 November, 1971, ended about the time Insight was getting its bearings in 1982. The marriage had produced three children – Babatunde, Olufunke and Abimbola – before the couple separated. The timing of their divorce was most inauspicious, though a few of their friends believed that a bit more patience probably could have saved the marriage. She, sadly, passed on in February, 2018.

With three kids in tow and a business that was yet to stabilise, Shobanjo knew he had a problem on his hands, as he needed to achieve a proper balance of fatherhood and a career that was being re-defined at a blistering pace. Both were serious matters and neither left any room for failure. But the immediate and greater challenge was to ensure that the house was in order so that the children did not feel any lack. He also needed to create room for them to accomplish whatever they were destined to achieve in their lives. The foundation for the unique bond that exists between him and his children was laid during this period. "I gave those kids all the support a father could give his children. In fact, nobody would have known there was not a woman at home and I was not reckless enough to make my house a place where every woman came in and out, which most relatively young (men) would have been tempted to do."

The distraction in the home front ended in 1983 when he married Joyce (nee Onwuka), whom he had met whilst he was Deputy Managing Director at Grant. His wedding to the woman he fondly loves to call 'Aunty Joyce' or 'Iyawo Ijebu' was the culmination of what could best be regarded as 'reversed consolation', for she married him when his emotions had not long before then taken a battering; just as he had met her when she was grieving over her dead fiancé.

Practically every good thing that happened to Shobanjo occurred in Surulere on mainland Lagos. His career in advertising got its proper bearing at Grant Advertising Ltd in Surulere; he nurtured Insight to good health in Surulere and he met his future wife in Surulere as well. Perhaps, rightly so, because the Yoruba word, Surulere, approximates in the English language to 'patience is rewarding'. But Shobanjo is not an exceptionally patient person; he loves to satisfy his curiosity as quickly as possible. Indeed, it was curiosity that got the better of him when he first saw the tall, very elegant and fair-complexioned Asaba-born Joyce. He had seen her a couple of times in a restaurant at Itolo Street in Surulere where he usually had his lunch. Each time, she was elegantly dressed. He walked up to her the next time he stepped into the eatery in the company of Odunsi and Akinlade. A few advertising principles hit him with profound clarity when he tested them in relation to the real-life situation that he faced when he saw Joyce. In advertising parlance, he needed both to properly 'interrogate' and 'romance' a brand just so he could gain valuable 'consumer insights' that would enable him to make a hard-to-resist 'sales pitch'. He did all that and he left the restaurant that day with a firm foot in the door to her heart.

From thence, they began to exchange pleasantries. But when, later, the receptionist at the Nigerian Breweries Ltd where Joyce then worked buzzed her in the office to say 'this guy from Grant' wanted to talk to her about modelling for a product, she did not think twice about it. She turned him down flat. He persisted; she resisted. He eventually broke down her resistance; not with the lure of a modelling contract but with sweet, good-natured humour. Joyce admitted she 'went along with that.' They got married in 1983 and are blessed with two children – a son, Olufemi and a daughter, Dolapo, who is more fondly regarded as daddy's second wife because of her splitting resemblance to her father.

As he built Insight and the Troyka companies, he never lost sight of the need to also build the home front. Joyce and the five children mean the world to him, as did his mother. He showered love and affection on all of them. He was especially determined to reward his children with the best education he could afford. For him, no sacrifice was ever too much. In this regard, he received a lot of encouragement from his friend, Odunsi, who once counselled that they both cut down on their collection of made-to-order suits, so they could effortlessly bear the cost of their children's education abroad. Shobanjo never forgot that piece of advice. He was extremely successful at giving his children proper education, as all of them are graduates of very good institutions across the world. Babatunde, who was formerly based in the United States, currently works as a Business Director with Leo Burnett; his first daughter, Funke, an economist, was Vice-President in a global finance institution before she joined FBN Capital where she is an Assistant General Manager (AGM); Abimbola worked for a television station in Lagos before he moved over to Halogen Security; Olufemi, a lawyer, works at the Nigerian Stock Exchange (NSE) as an Assistant General Manager (AGM) while Dolapo, a doctoral graduate of Chemical Engineering of Imperial College, London; Birmingham University and a Rolls Royce Scholar, worked initially with an international oil company in the United Kingdom and currently runs her own online clothing company in the UK. Four of his children are married and he is a proud grandfather of eight grandchildren.

His closeness to his children, especially the girls, is the butt of several jokes in the household. Joyce would often tell the girls that they cannot marry their father whereupon Dolapo would tell her mother never to rule out the possibility because they could run away to some far-flung places where no law frowned at such relationships. In his corporate life as well as on the home front, Shobanjo ferrets for information always because he does not fancy being in the dark on any subject matter. He is always on top of every domestic 'gossip': who had a new girlfriend; who had what nicknames; what is in vogue; what had gone out of fashion and all the sorts. Dolapo considers him 'hip'; the others agree. Ever the doting father, Shobanjo is never too far away from his children and in-laws as well as prospective in-laws. Wherever they may be in the world, he constantly gets in touch with them by phone or by email.

Funke sums up her father: "(He is) a friend you will want; a brother you will want; a husband you will want and a father you will want. For all his kids, he is our role model." For Dolapo: "There is not one word that can sum up Biodun Shobanjo, except one invents one."

The family's natural bond plays out in so many ways. The children, acting in concert with their mother, never ran out of ideas for practical jokes that they played on him from time to time.

'Aunty Joyce,' he once thought out aloud to his wife during a trip to the UK, 'Can you imagine: these children don't know how to show simple appreciation to their dad on a Father's Day.'

His surprise arose from the fact that none of the children had said anything to him on Father's Day. Each had woken up and gone about doing things as they would have on any other day. Femi who was in Cardiff, Wales at the time did not call; Dolapo said she was going to see a movie in company of her friends and his other sons did not even acknowledge his presence. Funke was the only child that offered to take him out in the spirit of Father's Day. When they stepped out of the house, she walked him straight into a restaurant where his wife, children, cousins, nephews and nieces and other people numbering about fifteen welcomed him with a loud chorus: 'Happy Father's Day'. He was pleasantly surprised by his fast thinking children and a wife who all lovingly showed that a guru at work is an ordinary gentleman at home.

They again got the better of him a few days to Christmas in 2008 when they playfully took advantage of his well-known soft spot. He had never hidden the fact that Folakemi Olubukola, Funke's daughter and his first grandchild, is dear to him. He looked forward to seeing mother and child in Nigeria at Christmas. Brimming with excitement, he called Funke to remind her to expeditiously process her baby's application for a Nigerian passport so that their trip would not be jeopardised. She casually replied that she was due at the Nigerian High Commission in London the following week to finalise the process. As she spoke, she prayed desperately under her breath that no announcements be made because she was already on board a plane to Nigeria. She had previously agreed with Joyce that a driver be sent to pick her up at the airport and that the driver be instructed not to blast his horn to get the security personnel at the house to open the gate. She wanted her arrival to catch her father by surprise. One part of the plan however, became difficult to implement because Shobanjo was somewhat puzzled when he was unusually egged on to sleep early. Mercifully, he was in the dream world by the time Funke and her daughter got home. Joyce quickly took the baby and carefully placed her on the bed by her sleeping grandfather who woke up with a start and was truly surprised by the hearty laughter all around his bed.

Shobanjo's labour of love is not lost on the children. He was amazed when Babatunde took him on a historical excursion of the good time they had in the early 1980s at the National Stadium, Lagos where they had gone to watch some wrestling bouts that featured many popular international and local stars in a line up that included Mighty Igor and Nigeria's Power Uti. Though lifted shoulder high by his dad to enjoy the slams, Babatunde, then about five years old, was fast asleep. The boy also never knew that the only N500 in his father's pocket had been picked by some rascals in the scramble to gain admittance into the venue.

However, for all the love that he showers on his children, 'indulgence' never featured as one of the primary words that characterise their relationship. His children did not grow up the way many people would have expected, considering his accomplishments and economic status. Indeed, they spent a lot of time in Aiyepe with their grandmother so that they could keep touch with his humble beginning and realise that life, for him, had not always been as easy as it seemed. He never withheld discipline when he needed to instil one. He set rules that no one could break without satisfactory explanation and the children knew very well, too, that disobedience would always draw swift repercussions. Even at that, it was inevitable that the exuberance of youth would occasionally brush the wisdom of age. His children managed to breach a few rules because they knew he religiously followed time and routines that were predictable from the break of dawn to nightfall; they knew what to do or avoid at what time of day. The girls knew there was a problem whenever he prefaced his statements with 'Young Lady' or 'I am very upset with you.' They usually found ways to escape punishment by launching their explanations with loving 'Oh...but daddy' arguments. The boys, on the other hand, almost always made punishment inevitable and incremental because they tended to be argumentative whilst rationalising their actions whenever he needed to make them realise how and where they had badly 'messed up.'

Babatunde aptly captured the scenario: "Ordinarily, he calls me 'Mr. T.' The moment I hear my full name 'Babatunde', I know trouble is at hand and there is no getting out of it. At that stage, the only sensible thing one can do is to bite the bullet and move on."

Regardless of the scolding, his children never felt he was less than fair whenever he administered discipline. They knew he wanted the best for them and that he wanted them to climb peaks higher than he had. He sees himself more as a guardian angel, one with a charge to give each child an opportunity to self-actualise. He helps each child to figure out various options towards attaining his or her individual goals. When, for instance, his son, Olufemi, spoke of his ambition to be a 'very successful and very wealthy' business person, he did not dissuade the youngman from nurturing his dream, which he jocularly remarked was a genetic trait he had picked from his Delta State-born Mum whose Igbo ancestry was noted for 'business'. As he was wont to do, he carefully explained to his son the need to have a 'profession' upon which he could build his entrepreneurial ambition. He and his wife encouraged Olufemi to study law, which was considered to be a 'versatile' profession. He thereafter introduced him to several tested legal practitioners who had made waves in the world of business, so he could tap into their experience. The boy needed no further convincing before he bought into his 'refined' dream. But he had to be further persuaded to study for a master's degree in commercial law and attend the Nigerian Law School to be well-rounded for the challenge ahead. For every door that Shobanjo held open for his children, he always added that it was the business of each child to determine how best to make use of the resultant relationship.

He emboldened each of them to know their rights and to stand for what is right to earn respect. Abimbola knew this first hand when he was involved in a late-night accident on his way from the gym not too far away from the house. A trailer that was conveying goods to the house of a Senator who lived in the neighbourhood reversed into his car and damaged it. When the matter was brought to the attention of the politician, he promised to fix the damage. He thereafter gave Abimbola his telephone number.

"Call me," the Senator said.

The young man called his father, instead. But he was not prepared for the 'inquisition' that followed. His dad wanted to know why he drove too close to the trailer in the first place; he wanted to know if he put on his hazard lights to warn the other driver and he wanted to know if, as a last resort, he tried to catch the trailer driver's attention by tooting his horn.

"Yes, dad," Abimbola responded.

"Sort it out. If I wasn't in Nigeria, would you be calling me to act on your behalf in this matter?"

Abimbola still did not call the Senator. The politician, too, did not call him; neither did he fix the damaged car. Shobanjo repaired his son's car and advised him to be more circumspect when people gave him their word. He admonished him to learn how to look out for himself because the people he would be tempted to call up in times of difficulty were not supernaturally talented to solve all problems.

Whilst parents naturally pray and expect their children to outperform them, Shobanjo's constant re-invention of himself has meant that he has unwittingly continued to raise the bar of performance that his children would be expected to surpass. Although they are doing quite well in their individual callings, his children are also acutely aware that society would always compare them with their father to determine if, indeed, they are the 'true' children of their father.

Olufemi readily acknowledged this challenge: "For bearing 'Shobanjo', people already expect certain standards. They expect you have been properly trained and they expect to see that you have the right thinking, the right traits and the right focus. He has done so much in his life and there is more credibility and respect for how he has been able to build himself up. We, too, have personal ambitions to match or exceed what he has done. So one has a very large shoe to fill. But being a 'Shobanjo' has its upside because the name helps to break some ice and it helps one to begin a conversation in difficult situations."

For Babatunde, the pressure to excel would have been overwhelming but for the fact that his father had helped to put issues in proper context so that each child knew objectively that parents simply set benchmarks and thereafter passed the torch: "Growing up as Biodun Shobanjo's first child made one quickly realise the kind of shoes one needed to fill. The problem is that the shoes kept getting bigger as one grew up. The good thing is that he quickly helped me establish that life is not about filling anyone's shoes but about creating one's own path. I have stopped thinking along the line of 'there's this huge guy that I have to follow' because, at the end of the day, it is for me to go out there and chart my own path."

Shobanjo's expectations of his children, though high, are grounded in the reality that they had not travelled the same route as he did and so could not be expected to be exactly like him. "I am driven by the challenges of the past. I was a young man who had prospects but suddenly had his supporter cut off. My children have always had me. I did not go to public school by public transport; I trekked. They never went to their private schools by public transport; they had a driver take them. We had two different settings; the motivations were different; they were more privileged than I was, so life has been much easier for them."

Whilst his children could fall back on him if all else failed; he had only God, his uncle and his mother to look up to as he developed himself and took care of his siblings. He used the lessons of his past to teach them to understand and appreciate the importance of integrity, hard work and other positive virtues. He constantly encouraged them to aim high and not allow his own achievements to appear too unattainable as to discourage them from reaching their individual goals. His scorecard on each child reflects the joy of a satisfied father: "Tunde has his head well-screwed on; his bosses say very nice things about him; he is not carried away by his circumstance. People tell me Femi at the Nigerian Stock Exchange is really very good. Funke is doing very well at FBN Capital. Abimbola is doing well at Halogen where he is contributing and adding value. Dolapo is also doing exceptionally well in her chosen field."

Whereas Shobanjo is used to living his life under intense media scrutiny, he maintains a near rigid personal policy of keeping his family away from public glare to allow each of them live the kind of lifestyle of their choice. He did not relax the rule when Funke got married. Her wedding was held in the United Kingdom with just his family members and close friends in attendance. He did the same thing when his son, Olufemi, got married and repeated it in 2012 when his last child, Dolapo, got married.

'Mummy, Oga don Die!'

For some reason, there were fears that Shobanjo might die young, like his father with whom he shared a lot in common. But for Lady Luck, an early evening accident would have brought the 'prophecy' to pass during an events-laden weekend.

On Sunday, 29 June, 1986, he barely escaped with his life in a lone accident as death lurked less than a hundred metres away from his house. The day had dawned like any other before it. The only difference, perhaps, was that it was filled with expectancy throughout the world as the FIFA World Cup tournament climaxed in Mexico City. Football fans could not wait to see which of the contending finalists, Argentina or Germany, would lift the coveted soccer trophy. Professional and amateur bookmakers came up with various permutations of victory. Shobanjo and Joyce hedged their bet on Argentina though they were both pre-occupied with diverse thoughts before the game commenced.

Whilst he had a party to attend before the match, his wife had a heavy weight on her chest. She, however, did not tell him. Instead, she told her mother that she felt unsettled because of a bad dream she had the previous night. The older woman counselled her daughter to read the Bible and allow God to handle the rest. Man and wife agreed he should get home on time from the party so that, together, they could both catch the excitement of the grand finale of the global soccer fiesta. He was yet to return from his outing when the match started. His wife, too, had forgotten to read the book of Psalms, Chapter 91 that her mother recommended for spiritual uplift. When she remembered, she hurriedly got off her chair, knelt and rushed quick prayers to God. Thereafter, she returned to her seat by the television and resigned herself to watching the game with the children. No sooner had the match got underway than the house-help and 'mai-guard' (security staff) barged into the living room.

'Mummy, oga don die,' they announced without ceremony. Joyce was too engrossed in the match to catch what they said. It took the wailing of the children for the message to register. She bolted out into the street from their 31 Opebi Road, Ikeja, Lagos residence only to see her husband laid out on the ground 'exactly' as she had seen him in her dream. What happened?

Shobanjo had dozed off behind the wheel and his car veered off the road by the Talabi Towers residence of the late top-flight medical practitioner, Victor Awosika. The vehicle ran over a mound of sand at a construction site and upended close to his (Shobanjo's) house. Help came instantly but rescue was made difficult because the car's doors had been firmly secured from the inside. The broad Opebi Road became chaotic as other motorists parked to lend a helping hand to the trapped occupant of the car. Inside the car, the stereo blared and the minutes ticked by, just as the engine purred under the hood of the car in its upturned state. Soon, a side window was smashed and he was dragged out, unconscious. He was thrice lucky. The engine idled but did not ignite, else he probably would have been roasted alive. The accident occurred near his home and the scene was a stone throw from his friend and personal physician at the time, Dr Tosin Ajayi. A long plank served as a stretcher with which he was rushed to Ajayi's First Foundation Hospital across the road. When he came to, his eardrums were splitting from screams whose source he knew too well. He motioned a nurse to 'tell that woman (Joyce) to stop shouting... she is always shouting; why is she shouting?' That was the message Joyce received and knew instantly that God had worked in her favour by answering her prayers and sparing the life of her husband. When she was later informed that

Argentina had won the Mexico '86 mundial by beating Germany 3-2, she really could not be bothered. Her sweetest victory lay traumatised on a hospital bed.

He was on admission for about 10 days. Among the first few callers to his hospital bed were then Deputy Editor-in-Chief of Newswatch magazine, Ray Ekpu and the magazine's flamboyant Editor-in-Chief, Dele Giwa, who four months later, would be killed by a parcel bomb on October 19, 1986.

Bloodbath in Adland

1991 was a 'bloody good' year in Shobanjo's life. Good, because it brought with it some juicy accounts, notably Equitorial Trust Bank, Devcom Merchant Bank and 7-Up Bottling Company that helped Insight to push Lintas to the deep end on the billing table. Bloody, because it was the year of incidents he feels 'very unhappy' to remember or discuss in any detail. The year, to borrow an adage from his native Yoruba language, broke wind in his mouth and spiced it with honey; he neither could gulp the offensive air nor spit out the honey. 1991 was a hard-to-describe year that packed a bit of history.

When the board of Troyka Holdings established Klinsite Ltd, an outdoor advertising company, it was to press the competitive advantage of the Insight family in the industry. No one knew it would someday transform into a killing field. When the company engaged the services of Dr. Nwogu Okere, an international finance expert, as its General Manager, Shobanjo and his colleagues believed they had the best brain for the job. They turned the company over to him and he did very well by turning it around from relative obscurity to being an industry leader. This was until he fell victim of a dastardly extra-judicial killing on Wednesday, 15 May, 1991.

The circumstances of his death, to this day, remain controversial.

According to Police account, Okere was shot by officers on patrol who took him for an armed robber because the car that conveyed him refused to stop after it was flagged down at a checkpoint. The Police also maintained that Okere's car looked like the one that had earlier been reported stolen from Insight's fleet.

Newspaper accounts, however, controverted the Police version of what transpired. Okere, it was reported, had taken refuge at the Mobil filling station along the Gbagada/Oworonshoki Expressway, having been hotly pursued by two vehicles whose occupants had earlier shot at him. He was shot at point blank range at the filling station in a 'three-minute action',[1] even with his hands raised in a gesture of surrender. His assailants, thereafter, took his body away, all in the full glare of his wife, May, who was with him in the car.

The management of Insight also offered concrete proofs to rebut the Police claim:
Fiction: Okere's vehicle seemed like the one that Insight's accountant, Kola Ogunde, had reported stolen.
Fact: Okere's official car was a cream colour Peugeot 504 saloon; Ogunde's a red Peugeot 505 ST saloon.
Fiction: The Police was on alert for Ogunde's car.
Fact: Okere was killed sometime about 1.00 pm; Ogunde reported the loss of his car about 2.00 p.m at the Pedro Police Station, Shomolu, Lagos just about the same time as Okere's car was brought to the same station.
Conclusion: The loss of Ogunde's car could not have prompted Okere's killing.

The killing generated countrywide furore but full disclosure of what transpired did not see the light of day from the Police, which merely 'regretted' what The Guardian newspaper, in an editorial, described

---

[1] *The Guardian May 17 & 18, 1991*

as an 'unprovoked, inexcusable killing'. Till date, the Police has declined to admit culpability; rather preferring to blame Okere's driver for failing to stop when told to do so.

Klinsite's woes did not end with the killing of Okere whose successor in office, Courage Ogbebor, a lawyer, suffered a similar fate seven months later. Ogbebor was shot on 2 December, 1991 by suspected 'armed robbers.' He died a week later at the Lagos University Teaching Hospital (LUTH), Idi-Araba, Lagos. The culprits were never apprehended. The trail of the back-to-back murders has gone awfully cold yet the mystery of the motive for the killings has not been unravelled. Similarly, there has not been any clue to the identity of the perpetrators.

In 1992, Klinsite metamorphosed into Optimum Exposures, perhaps to break the jinx that had begun to trail its operations.

Seventeen years later, the Troyka family would once more be enveloped by a pall of sadness when Insight lost Funmi Lufadeju, a promising professional, in June 2008. She was one of the most senior graduates of the Group's Management Trainee Programme left in the employ of the agency. Her young life was terminated by armed robbers on a Saturday night as she headed home after finishing preparations for an upcoming major pitch. The target of the robbers was her car, a Honda CR-V sports utility vehicle, which was one of the several eye-popping vehicles that Insight bought for senior managers to reward their hard work.

Her loss was especially painful to Shobanjo because she had just been promoted to the position of a Senior Account Director a few months before her demise. He had insisted on her elevation when, as Chairman of Troyka Holdings, his approval was sought for the promotion of key staff of Insight. The occurrence made him wonder if things would have turned out differently if he had acted otherwise.

1992 Opebi Shoot-Out

Shobanjo may not be a Bible-thumping Christian but he knows by rote the story of Jacob's epic battle with God in the dead of night. Jacob, the Scriptures say, wrestled with God and held his ground until the early hours of the morning when the Lord eventually prevailed by knocking his hipbones out of their joints. The Almighty blessed Jacob for putting up a gallant fight. Jacob, too, easily admitted that he had undergone an uncommon experience for which he was thankful to have had his life preserved.

About midnight on Thursday, 30 January, 1992, Shobanjo began a similar life or death battle; not with God but with hoodlums and, later, the men of the anti-crime squad of the Nigerian Police. Everything that could possibly have gone wrong almost went wrong that night. Unlike Jacob's, Shobanjo's fight was not a hand-to-hand combat; rather, it was a more sophisticated encounter in which guns were fired at will.

The incident began harmlessly enough when a shrill ring of the telephone early in the morning of that day had Shobanjo reaching to take the call, thinking it was Joyce who was en-route Lagos from New York. The caller did not identify himself. Instead, he made a simple, mafia-style demand: Shobanjo should get N100,000 ready for collection by midnight; else, he would have his 'arse blown off.' The idea rankled. He did not ascribe the call to the antics of a prankster or a crank, for the spate of killings at Klinsite, with the last just a little over a month before the phone call, had put him on his guard. It crossed his mind to think that a 'grand plan' was afoot to hit at the heart of Troyka Holdings. There was no other way he could explain the call for him to swiftly raise and pay such a large amount of money to an unknown person when the caller probably knew that he, an Ijebu man, was unlikely to have that kind of money at home at that time of day. He called the Police which sent a team to his home about 12.50AM. His plea that a roadblock be mounted near his Opebi Road residence was turned down, but he was given every assurance that officers would 'keep an eye' on the neighbourhood during their regular patrol.

He did the next best thing he could think of in the circumstance. He took stock of all he stood to lose if the threat became real. Even if he had the cash at home, he was not about to avail any rascal a free lunch. His wife, mercifully, was yet to return from her business trip to New York. Joyce was originally not scheduled to return until another week or two but she had called the previous night to inform him that she would arrive Nigeria on Friday, January 31. He wondered at her sudden change of plan, thinking she probably had run out of money. But she was not broke. Apparently, she only felt homesick. He told her he had a scheduled meeting with his client, Nasco, in Jos but that a driver would be waiting to pick her up on arrival at the airport. He was comforted that she was out of harm's way. His children? God would protect them and he, too, would do his utmost. He quickly gathered the children, took them to a room in the annex of the house and hugged them after which he left a stern instruction: "lock the door and don't open it until I come back to say so." He resolved that he would only go down fighting, so whosoever needed his life would have to kill him first to get it. Wearing a sweat shirt underneath which he had a white vest on top of a pair of jeans, it was clear he was ready for battle. The pump of adrenalin in his gut did not in any way cause him to panic as he began the wait for the unknown enemy.

He did not wait too long. Just before 3.00AM trouble called in full force. From the window of his room upstairs, which directly faced the Opebi main road, Shobanjo counted four marauders but he had the cold comfort of being tucked within the safety of his apartment with darkness as his shield and a rifle as his weapon of defence. Thankfully, he had a licence to carry firearms. For some time, he had been fascinated by reports of the exploits of Nobel Laureate, Professor Wole Soyinka, as a hunter. The stories motivated him to want to be a hunter, too. To actualise his dream, he applied for and secured official approval to acquire a hunting rifle, which he, accompanied by some of his friends, occasionally took to the bush in the Ijebu countryside to fire for the fun of it. The hoodlums shot at his night guard as they tried to force their way into the premises. Shobanjo was outnumbered by the criminals yet he responded defensively by opening fire on them to deny them access to his house. In the thick of the shootings, he still found time to return to the annex to check on the children who were deeply frightened by the staccato of gunshots. The noise of the raging storm was not loud enough to disturb the calm sleep of his youngest child, Dolapo. The exchange of fire resumed and went on for a while. Then it ceased as abruptly as it had started.

A burst of fusillade suddenly began afresh. But a comedy of near-fatal errors had played out during the short break. The aggressors hurriedly left before Policemen in mufti arrived unannounced. Cocooned inside, Shobanjo did not know. On the street, the Police misread the situation and continued to shoot to dislodge the 'enemy' inside the premises. All the while the one-storey building stoically bore the brunt of the furious exchange of gunfire. A few policemen were injured, one seriously. The break of day heralded the resolution of a looming impasse, for when the harmattan haze lifted, both the protector and the protected realised their grave mistakes. An immediate ceasefire was called. Despite having survived an uncommon experience, Shobanjo was quickly herded behind the counter at the Special Investigations & Intelligence Bureau (SIIB) at Panti Street, Lagos. This was his reward for daring to defend his life.

Within hours of her husband being detained by the Police, Joyce arrived home by public transport, having waited in vain at the airport for the driver who never came. She felt uneasy because it was most unlike him to have forgotten to keep his word. The crowd in front of her house and the heavy Police presence further unsettled her as she alighted from the airport taxi. "Where's everybody? What are these holes?" She asked in quick succession, not addressing anyone in particular

She heard so many things that did not make any sense: robbers, shoot-out, Police, detention and children taken away by her friend. None of these added up. She passed out because she believed that the people around had lied to her. She was also convinced that her entire family had been wiped out. Things did not get any better when she was revived. She began a search for the children. The guards at a house located not far away from her residence broke her heart. Thinking she was out of earshot, one of them pointed at her and spoke to his mate about Joyce being the 'Madam' of the man killed in the early morning shoot-out. She heard and quickly turned around to face him before she screamed her lungs out. No one could console her, at least not until she got back home and discovered that her children had taken refuge at the residence of the Editor-in-Chief of Newswatch magazine, Ray Ekpu, on Isaac John Street in Ikeja GRA. Then she made for the Police Station where she got 'too scared' to get close to her detained husband. She was not even sure it was not his ghost that she saw.

The one thing that crossed Shobanjo's mind as he sat behind the counter at the Police station was why the Police personnel did not deem it right to properly announce their presence during the crisis, even if it required the use of a bullhorn. He could not answer his unasked question. Over the years, he tried to downplay the significance of his detention because he had made a conscious decision to forget both the incident and the role that certain individuals played in it. Rather than re-live the occurrence, he preferred to say he had forgotten the sequence of the incidents or that he had forgotten certain names. For one given to proper documentation, this is out of character. Three things are, however, apparent from the incident: he believed that the management of information by the Police is suspect; he believed that society owed it a duty to improve the lot of policemen and he had mixed feelings about policemen: 'some of them are nice; some of them are not.'

He observed that men of the Nigeria Police tended to mangle information to suit their purpose, knowing that their superiors would probably take action that may not necessarily have derived from diligent examination and verification of the content of information put at their disposal: "I think (then) Lagos State Commissioner of Police, Yemi Odubela, got carried away by the event and said some things that were certainly untrue and I thought that as the chief law enforcement officer of the State he owed it a point of duty to go down deep into the case. His men who spoke with me doctored the information he got and he spoke based on this. I would have thought that, given my station in life, it would not have been too much for him to speak with me or send one of his deputies (to do so)."

Considering his experience in the hands of the Assistant Commissioner of Police (ACP) in charge of his case, he believed that law enforcement officers could deliberately exhibit needless mischief in a manner that could, in the end, defeat any search for justice: "I cannot recall the ACP's name. He was instructed to ensure that I was kept in a comfortable place. I remember that the arrangement was for me to be kept in one of the offices, but he would not do that. Instead, he would keep me in the radio room. I don't know why he did it, but I think he wanted to humiliate me. Some policemen could be very mischievous. The first night, about midnight, he phoned that I should be kept in the cell. I was kept there with all sorts of people. As early as 5.00AM, the same ACP phoned that (his men) should quickly get me out of the cell (probably) because he did not want his superior officers to find me there."

Despite everything, he did not lose hope in the Nigeria Police because his brief experience also exposed him to a corps of 'nice' officers who did not necessarily subscribe to the position of their bosses and who worked to do what was right: "They knew that the man was abusing his office. They made sure I was very comfortable; they gave me a very nice cushion, left a blanket on it and ensured that no harm came to me. They even got some of the inmates to fan me. I slept off. I slept very soundly. That was the only time I slept in the cell. I was there for about five hours. I was treated fairly, I think, because they knew one was not a criminal; that I was only trying to protect my life."

Although he avoided romanticising his detention experience by dressing it in the garb of 'one-of-those-things,' one still could feel some degree of psychological bounce in his narration of the experience: "I just cast my mind to the kind of travail that Chief (Obafemi) Awolowo went through. If he could suffer like that, who the heck was I? That gave me strength to withstand the ordeal and the humiliation."

At the time of this incident, speculations were rife in business circles that a contract had probably been out to put Shobanjo out of circulation for handling one 'hot deal' too many. This was because gangland-style killings to settle business scores had become prevalent in Nigeria of that period, with the result that many great and not-so-great lives had been prematurely terminated. The Opebi incident, however, was a needless, isolated occurrence that took place because of the mistaken belief that Shobanjo was awash with money owing to the larger than life image of Insight.

He was released on bail from Police custody on Monday, February 3, 1992 and taken straight to the home of his friend, Engineer Leke Dina and his wonderful wife, Dr (Mrs) Kehinde Dina, who accommodated Shobanjo and his wife for about two weeks. Veteran journalist, Ray Ekpu and his wife, Uyai, also graciously cared for the Shobanjo children for about the same length of time. The passing of years did not diminish Shobanjo's feeling of gratitude to the Dina and Ekpu families for the love and care they lavished on his family at a very difficult time. In the period it took his family to get over the trauma of the shooting incident, their Opebi home also underwent renovation to rid it of the massive bullet marks that had rendered it inhabitable. The injured policeman was transferred to the high brow Eko Hospital for further medical checks, with all expenses borne by Insight. Weeks later, Shobanjo had a thanksgiving service to commemorate his baptism of fire, for he had once more cheated death and was not destined to die young like his father. With hindsight, Joyce rated her husband as 'very, very brave' for taking on the marauders head-on. Many wives would probably have disagreed with her and labelled him an unthinking risk-taker who wanted to consign her to early widowhood. But all are likely to say, like her: "I'd rather have a detained husband than a dead husband."

The midnight encounter later triggered the establishment of Halogen Security, an access control and guards services company, because the management of Troyka became sufficiently alarmed over what appeared to be a co-ordinated plan to hit at the heart of the group. Matters were not helped by the difficult-to-explain role of the Nigerian Police in the series of attacks on key personnel of the group. Since the Police had demonstrated an inability to discharge its responsibility as protectors of life and property, the Group sought to engage private security guards to add another layer of protection to safeguard its human capital and property everywhere. Shockingly, the search revealed that most of the existing security outfits offered no more than glorified 'bouncer' services and were too short of manpower to be effective. Shobanjo felt it was time to resort to self-help within the ambits of the law. Six months after his January ordeal, Troyka incorporated Halogen Security Ltd to provide quality guards' services not just to the group but to as many individuals and corporate organisations as desired to protect their most prized assets in the most technologically advanced manner as was possible. From inception, Halogen lived up to its promise and has since become about the biggest service provider in the assets protection business in Nigeria. By early 2018, Halogen contributed well over 16,000 employees to Troyka Group's pool of about 17,000 direct hires.

Although Halogen's year-on-year financial performance and positive third-party reports have affirmed the company's industry leadership position, Shobanjo's first-hand experience with a guard on duty in one of the company's numerous sites in Lagos gave him a lot of personal satisfaction with the management and staff of the company. On a weekend, he drove himself to visit a friend in an estate manned by Halogen guards. As he approached the gate, the Halogen staff flagged him down and politely requested the visitor get down and open the boot of his SUV to conclude routine security checks. That done, the visitor was asked if he knew the way to his host's residence. Not minding the affirmative answer, the guard still went ahead to give him a graphic description to the destination before he waved him on. On the way out, Shobanjo gave the guard a gift which was not accepted, just as the guard declined to tell him his name, saying he had only done his job. The Halogen Chairman was most impressed with the professional conduct of his staff; the guard did not know he had just had an encounter with his employer. As he is wont to do, Shobanjo related his experience to Halogen's Managing Director who took an administrative note of the excellent performance of the staff.

APCON Fellowship

Shobanjo is quite touchy on matters of professionalism. A few times, too, his mood could determine the vehemence with which he supported his stance. A lot of the time, he would be quite forthcoming; at some other times he could simply dance around a subject. One issue that may, however, require one to read between the lines or interpret his body signs relates to the initial conferment of Fellowships of the Advertising Practitioners Council of Nigeria (APCON). The event was shrouded in some controversy.

APCON is a child of government, mid-wifed by the Association of Advertising Practitioners of Nigeria, AAPN. Its primary role is to regulate the practice of advertising in Nigeria, for which purpose the body also maintains a Register of Practitioners. The four categories of professionals who qualify for inclusion in the Register as stipulated in Section 10 of Decree 55 of 1988, which established the Council, are: Fellows, Full members, Associate Members and Student Members. To be registered, all persons must be above 21 years old; be of good character; have (or be pursuing) appropriate tertiary education and have cognate experience in a 'recognised organisation', the latter of which many had interpreted to mean 'AAAN agency.'

On 8 May, 1992, APCON released its maiden list of Fellows, which comprised Sylvester Moemeke (ex-President, AAPN), Olu Falomo (ex-President, AAPN), Ayo Owoborode (ex-President, AAPN), Chris Doghudje (ex-Honorary Secretary, AAPN), Akin Odunsi (then incumbent President, AAPN) and Joseph Nwabunie (OAAN).

The list raised a lot of dust and the media made a meal of it. Many were surprised that Shobanjo's name was 'conspicuously' missing from the list of six distinguished practitioners despite his stature in the industry. Speculations were rife that his name was deleted at the very last minute or, as one news publication reported, his name 'somehow' appeared and disappeared from the final list. But he was not the only one affected. Olu Adekoya, the man who litigated AAPN into existence, felt insulted by his exclusion from the list because "those who were in school when he was pioneer Media Manager (1960) in Cecil Turner (an expatriate agency) were on the Fellows list and he wasn't."[1]

Shobanjo's displeasure with the list stemmed from the fact that the parameters of selection of the pioneer Fellows of APCON appeared to have been more political than professional. Apart from the membership criteria earlier highlighted, anyone that aspired to the Fellowship of APCON was required to have had 15 years of 'continuous active practice' within or outside a partnership. Were these stipulations to be the criteria used in the maiden exercise, Shobanjo and 61 other applicants would automatically have become Fellows. But the unwieldy number would have made the exercise somewhat meaningless. APCON's Chairman at the time, Moemeke,

---

[1] *Steve Osuji, APCON's First Outing, Media Review, June, 1992 P.7*

would have none of that. He instructed the screening committee to prune down the number, using 'other criteria' to produce an acceptable number. Some of the parameters that were later adopted proved to be quite controversial but not deliberately so.

The screening committee, it would seem, opted to adopt perceived 'significant contribution' to advertising practice as a yardstick to appraise candidates. This parameter, however, did not make a fine distinction between contribution to the growth of sectoral associations and the development of core competencies in advertising practice. It appeared that the Committee fell into the error of assuming that the notion of 'significant contribution' meant active participation in the development of sectoral associations. In addition, sectoral representation was taken into consideration, with the result that the list of six pioneer Fellows consisted of three former Presidents of AAPN, an incumbent President of the Association, a former Honorary Secretary of the Association and a former executive committee member of OAAN.

Was Shobanjo edged out of the list because some people felt uncomfortable with his practice? This position cannot be sustained, as Moemeke eminently argued: "It is absolute nonsense (to link Shobanjo's non-inclusion in the list with spite). There was no question of his name coming on the list and disappearing from it... It was the mixing and searching for a credible number among all the groups (author's emphasis) – AAAN, BON, ADVAN, NPAN, etc – that led to the dropping of many names from the original list. Anybody that links that with (politics), I think, will be unfair to him and I doubt that he would himself make such a comment."

Shobanjo also did not see his exclusion from the list as a slight on his person but he would have been more satisfied if strictly professional criteria of selection had been adopted: "I cannot confer a Fellowship on myself. I was not made a Fellow the first time; I think what happened was that it was felt that past Presidents (of AAAN) should be given the award and I was (at the time) not a past President."

In 1993, he was one of eight distinguished practitioners that were conferred with APCON Fellowships in the second wave of the awards. By the end of 2004, when he bowed out of active advertising practice, this elite group of advertising practitioners had about 57 members on its roll of honour.

Chink in the King's Armour
Insight's success and the emergence of other Troyka companies as leaders in their various fields may lead one to believe all that Shobanjo touched instantly became gold. His vision faltered in a few instances. Over time, the diversification programme that began in 1984 with the founding of outdoor company, Klinsite, suffered series of setbacks that eventually became an important part of the learning curve in the administration of Troyka, the holding company.

The bloodletting in the outdoor business almost killed Optimum Exposures before it was successfully turned around by its immediate past CEO, Lere Alimi. In a similar manner, Captain Deji Bamgbose assumed office as Managing Director of Halogen Security at a time the company badly needed re-engineering. He succeeded in turning around the fortunes of the company and stopped its steady decline. Both Optimum Exposures and Halogen Security are now blue-eyed babies of the group, making very handsome returns for the investors and breaking new grounds in their respective fields.

The Quadrant Company continued to thrive, in part, because of Shobanjo's strong belief that an integrated marketing communications group was incomplete without a public relations consultancy and because of the resolve of staff of the company to regain the confidence of the market and owners of the business. The resurgence of the company under the leadership of its former Chief Executive, Ms Ben Upaa Ayede and her successor, Bolaji Okusaga, and the agency's continuing dominance of the corporate public relations consultancy market in Nigeria culminated in its winning the 'African Consultancy of The Year Award' in the 2012 Superior Achievement in Branding and Reputation (SABRE) Awards that was presented to the company in Brussels.

Other troubled companies like Link Studios; MC& A and MIT Healthcare were not as lucky. They all died.

Each of the companies had its peculiar problem that made asphyxiation inevitable. Link Studios, which offered pre-press services, lost too much money too early in the day and could not meet the objectives of its start up. Troyka shut it down quickly. MIT Healthcare, the country's pioneer healthcare communications company, fared a little better than Link Studios because it made a bit more professional impact. MIT Healthcare's biggest claim to fame was its handling of the launch of Viagra in Nigeria. But the company seemed to have been ahead of its time. It was rested.

The case of MC & A was slightly different from the others because it was a much bigger operation and because it started out with so much promise. The birth of the company was perfect, as Insight found itself turning down good businesses to avoid conflict situations. Shobanjo raised this nagging issue with his partners at Dorlands, where one of its senior business managers suggested the initiative of launching a second line agency. MC & A was not even registered at the time he held series of meetings with Richard

Humphreys and Simon Goode of Saatchi & Saatchi over possible technical affiliation. At these meetings, he confidently reeled off impressive profiles of the 'staff' of MC & A. The success of the meetings could be measured from the fact that MC & A was affiliated to Saatchi & Saatchi before it was born.

The agency kicked off to a roaring start under the leadership of the highly personable Georgie Umunna. Amongst the agency's budding talents were Jimi Bankole, Lanre Adisa and later Steve Babaeko and Paris Agaro. The young and dynamic MC & A did spectacular work for its clients, one of which was the much-talked about 'Good For Everyone' campaign that it launched for Malta Guinness. Another was the immensely popular Story of a Man television commercial for CTMC, a mortgage institution. In just three years after its birth MC & A booked an enviable space in Advertising Age with its sterling performance. Everyone was suitably impressed so much so that the agency's management and owners kept their eyes off the ball whereupon the company began its systematic decline.

Whilst MC & A's rise to the top was meteoric, its irreversible slide to oblivion was no less dramatic. The leadership of the agency, like those of other unit companies, was trusted so completely there was no need to 'micro-manage' the team. But loyalty to the business was no longer total; staff began to moonlight; some became informal car dealers while others ran parallel agencies within the agency. Clients began to cut loose too fast and too soon. In quick succession, the agency lost close to 10 clients. Among these were Nasco; British Airways; Sterling Winthrop; Universal Trust bank and Cadbury's corporate account. Dissatisfaction set in amongst staff, with management and junior employees no longer pulling in the same direction. Staff disengagements became routine, yet systems and processes were not in place to trigger a call to action.

The failure of MC & A was a lesson in the systemic failure of leadership. It was one instance in which Shobanjo did not quickly activate a key learning from Chief Adeyemi Lawson, his former Chairman at Grant Advertising. Chief Lawson believed that a good manager must quickly count and cut his losses from the moment he noticed that things were not going according to plan in an enterprise. Both Shobanjo and Awosika were too engrossed in the running of Insight to notice that MC & A had begun to bleed profusely. Progressively, the symptoms of decay began to manifest in the poor financials posted by the agency, which descended from being a profit-making organisation to a loss leader. By the time Shobanjo's long time friend and associate, Victor Olaotan Johnson, was seconded from Insight to MC & A as Managing Director, with a charge to stem the haemorrhage, it was too late in the day, for the death knell of the agency had been sounded.

Although the recovery road map of the new management team helped to arrest the slide, it did not consistently grow the business and fresh creative hands were reluctant to come on board the agency. Troyka's management appraised the situation and took the painful decision to bite the bullet rather than borrow to continue to run the company. MC & A was shut down in 2002, first by a system of transformation to an events management company, then known as First Kilimanjaro, before it became Sail Events, which handled the successful reveal of Gulder's The Search TV commercial of Nigerian Breweries. It metamorphosed to FK:G2 under the leadership of Dele Anifowose, its then General Manager, who later became the Marketing Director of Cadbury West Africa. FK:G2 thrived for a while but could not keep its head above waters. A last gasp effort to revive the company resulted in its transmutation to Azzagai and its repositioning as a second line full service marketing communications agency under the leadership of an Insight veteran,

Yinka Daramola. The gambit failed to put the company back on its feet. In September, 2012 the management of Troyka pulled the plug off Azzagai's life support machine after every resuscitation effort failed. This firmly closed the chapter on the history of the organisation that started life as MC & A.

Concerning MC & A and the other companies that went under, Shobanjo was quick to admit that: "Leadership failed. Perhaps, we could have arrested the situation a bit earlier but that would have meant our having to micro-manage our business leaders; and that would have defeated one of our reasons for being, which is that we would allow our managers to develop and self-actualise. The lesson in all of this is that a leader must be sure of whom he wants to entrust with responsibility: he must always look beyond professionalism; check character traits and check for trust and reliability. My only regret is that some of our good ideas were not allowed to mature; some of them were clearly ahead of their time."

The need to avoid the mistakes of the past occasioned the inauguration of Troyka Holdings' Quarterly Business Review meetings at which the management teams of unit companies made presentations to Troyka executives. The business review sessions were conceived primarily as 'family meetings' where plans, aspirations and frustrations were frankly presented and dispassionately discussed. The sessions are advisory platforms designed to open the eyes of unit business managers to opportunities they otherwise would have missed because of their closeness to their respective businesses. Broadly, the format of presentations requires the unit heads of subsidiary companies to provide general overview of the direction of their respective businesses, capture the highlight of past performance from an industry perspective and flag potential show stoppers. Thereafter, the Finance Controllers of the companies would lay up the financial health of the businesses for diagnosis, following which Group executives of Troyka would raise questions and make suggestions aimed at improving performance.

These serious business sessions are usually conducted with an admixture of informality and hard-headed strategy appraisals. At these meetings, the contents of presentations and the degree of confidence exhibited by presenters are critically appraised; there is little time for anyone to pussy-foot and definitely no room for anyone to attempt to 'evergreen' the stark reality of any situation on ground. One minute, a business leader could receive a hug for proposing forward-looking, game-changing ideas; the next minute, a sharp reprimand for overlooking or side-stepping critical business imperatives.

Shobanjo always spoke last on any issue so there could be room for robust debates around the table. This also precluded wholesale adoption of whatever position he took. If it, however, became evident that a presentation had derailed completely and there was need to save everyone's time, his intervention was usually short and sharp. He would sum up his understanding of the context and resolutions of any meeting before he lands on a side of the fence. Kudos and knocks are often sign-posted by how he prefaced his remarks. When a presenter repeatedly got called by his second name, there was little doubt that the presentation had derailed. When the presenter had either figured things all wrong or had not listened to or sufficiently respected the perspectives of others, he was told: "No, you're not getting it right"; "I don't agree with you." When, however, the argument was spot-on, Shobanjo would quickly affirm: "absolutely" or "exactly." He always offered a 'because' to justify whatever position he tilted towards; this helps to reinforce his belief that issues must vigorously be debated to arrive at a consensus. For him, no one should leave any meeting feeling railroaded into accepting a position for which he or she was not convinced of the merit or demerit. Aside, the early warning system that the Quarterly Business Review has turned out to be, it has obviated the necessity of micro-managing unit managers in the group. The trust in each manager also meant that Shobanjo has no need to look over the shoulders of his people with the intention of catching a few who might try to beat the system. He focuses on the 'major' and regards the 'minors' as distractions to be dealt with only when they threaten to disrupt the corporate rhythm of loyalty, honesty and transparency. This ability to overlook what some other entrepreneurs might consider 'unforgivable' infractions by line or unit managers is something that Steve Ojo finds even more remarkable in his old friend:

"I once asked him how he recruits his people because all are very smart and he gives them the leeway, the power to operate the companies without looking over their shoulders; I asked how he could trust them all, after all, they are 'Nigerians.' He told me: "how many people's shoulders will I have to look over?"

Over the years, the Quarterly Business Review sessions and trust in subordinates have helped business leaders in the Group to get good counsel in the right places. In turn, it has helped to further consolidate the leadership of Troyka Holdings as West Africa's largest marketing communications group.

In Abacha's Shadow:
1997 began on a high note for Insight and Shobanjo. Early in January, the agency's affiliation with Grey Inc was announced to kickstart a year of multiple industry creative awards; its expansion within the West African sub-region with the founding of Insight Ghana and the

multiple birth of subsidiary companies in the Troyka family. At a personal level, Shobanjo successfully completed his tenure as President of AAAN in April and delivered a thought-provoking yet very well-received paper at an APCON executive retreat in August.

Ironically, 1997 also ended on a sour note for him. In December of that year he ran into a cross-fire occasioned by deadly political power play in Nigeria. Over the years, he had cultivated and carefully nurtured strong relationships that easily cut across geographical, political and socio-economic boundaries in the country. One of his most enduring and very well-known relationships was with the Chief of General Staff and Vice Chairman of the Armed Forces Provisional Ruling Council, Lieutenant General Oladipo Diya, who also was his immediate senior and very close friend at Odogbolu Grammar School. As it turned out, Diya, who then was Nigeria's Number Two citizen, got roped into a highly controversial 20 December, 1997 military coup, which was said to have been hatched to overthrow then Head of State, General Sani Abacha. The incident occurred whilst Shobanjo and his wife were out of the country to attend an event hosted in Lebanon by his long-time friend, Faysal Halabi. The couple had barely stepped into their home in London on their return from Lebanon when Halabi called to inform him of the 'coup' in Abuja: "Your friend is involved," he said.

If Shobanjo thought the news was a practical joke, the notion immediately faded when he caught up with saturated coverage of the alleged coup by the international media. He was speechless. His disbelief soon turned to personal anguish as his phone virtually rang off the hook with calls from friends in Nigeria to tell him that the Abacha regime had begun a nationwide crackdown on friends and associates of all suspects. There was no official confirmation that he was on the administration's list of 'wanted' persons. Nonetheless, many felt it was expedient that he erred on the part of caution by keeping safe well outside Nigeria until the picture became a lot clearer. The note of caution, as Halabi would point out, bordered on the unpredictability of men in uniform: "Under the military, you do not go into the procedure of court and justice but of mood; today, they lock you up, tomorrow they release you."

Although Shobanjo had planned to celebrate Christmas in Lagos, he took heed of the wise counsel he got and remained in London. As he religiously monitored events at home, the hours in London grew into days, then weeks and months. The longer he stayed in London, the more his partners worried about his inability to function professionally. Grey London was sufficiently concerned that it extended an invitation to him to join the company as an Executive Director, New Business. It was a tough call that he discussed with his wife, Joyce. He deeply appreciated the genuine concerns behind the offer. But it also was one act of professional courtesy that came with a heavy moral burden: how would he justify an acceptance of the offer to his colleagues in Nigeria? That question gave him the answer he needed. He politely declined Grey London's well-meaning offer.

Back home in Lagos, Insight held firm, as Awosika admirably took charge of business. The management of the subsidiary companies also ran like clockwork because the administrative systems and processes in place ensured that the businesses were on auto pilot. On the political front, however, things did not go very well for his friend, Diya, who, it became clear, had been set up and neatly caught in an elaborate web of deceit spun by wily characters. He was an unwanted insider in a paranoid regime. The trial of the 'masterminds' of the putsch was hastily conducted by an ad hoc military tribunal and the expected miscarriage of justice culminated in the death sentence pronounced in April 1998 on Diya and some other notable suspects including former Minister of Works, Major

General Abdulkarim Adisa and former Minister of Communications, Major General Tajudeen Olanrewaju.

Marooned in London, Shobanjo hoped against hope. Nothing prepared him for exile and he had never imagined a day he would be unable to freely depart from and re-enter his fatherland. Much of what kept him in London was fear for his personal safety, not that he was a fugitive from justice. He was determined to know the truth of his situation. His friends in government made discreet enquiries, including careful knocks on the inner sanctum of Abacha's regime. The results were the same: the security agencies were aware of his closeness to Diya but there was nothing incriminating against him.

"That one in advertising? We know him; he has not done anything wrong; we know he only does his job," Major Hamza el-Mustapha, the powerful Chief Security Officer to the Head of State, told some of Shobanjo's confidants.

The unofficial clean bill of health issued by the Presidential Villa helped to lift the ominous shadow cast on Shobanjo by happenings under the Abacha regime. He ended his six-month stay in London and returned to Nigeria in June 1998, the same month that Gen. Abacha died in circumstances that are still shrouded in mystery. Abacha's demise saved Lt.-General Diya's life, as the new military administration headed by Gen. Abdulsalam Abubakar stayed action on the death sentences handed down by its predecessors in office. By another unexplained mystery of the universe, Gen. Abubakar's government handed over the reins of power to another Abacha victim, Chief Olusegun Obasanjo, on 29 May, 1999 to usher in Nigeria's fourth attempt at instituting democracy. In 1995, the Abacha regime had convicted Obasanjo and several notable Nigerians for plotting a coup to overthrow his government.

8

The AAPN Presidency

Whoever would be great among you must be your servant.

Mark 10:43

Shobanjo took two shots at the Presidency of the Association of Advertising Practitioners of Nigeria, AAPN (now Association of Advertising Agencies of Nigeria, AAAN). In 1994, he lost by a single vote. When he threw his hat into the fray a second time in 1995, he won, coincidentally, by the same single vote margin. The weight of the initial loss and his subsequent victory coupled with his strong professional antecedents made it appear to observers, especially those outside the advertising industry that he had a 'permanent' ambition to lead AAAN. This, in part, accounted for the erroneous conclusion that his ambition to lead AAAN had been scuttled 'several times in the past.'[1]

In his first attempt, Shobanjo mounted the soapbox against the

---

[1] Steve Osuji, 'Enfant Terrible mounts the Saddle', The Guardian, 7 October, 1995, p.13

incumbent and Chief Executive of Sunrise Advertising, the late May Nzeribe, in what a respected advertising practitioner described as a 'brutal fight'. Nzeribe, at the time, was set for a third consecutive term in office. He had first been elected in 1992 to succeed Rosabel's Odunsi who completed his three-term tenure at the Association's 19th Annual General Meeting (AGM).

Up to this point in the political history of AAAN, only Promoserve's Prince Kehinde Adeosun had served a one-term presidency. All other Presidents were in office for a minimum of three terms (see table below):

President	Agency	Tenure
1. Dotun Okubanjo	Publicity Service	1971 – 1975
2. Sylvester Moemeke	Lintas	1975 – 1982
3. Olu Falomo	OBM	1982 – 1985
4. Kehinde Adeosun	Promoserve	1985 – 1986
5. Ayo Owoborode	PAL	1986 – 1989
6. Akin Odunsi	Rosabel	1989 – 1992
7. May Nzeribe	Sunrise	1992 – 1995

Technically, Shobanjo did not violate the Association's constitution by standing against Nzeribe. The constitution made an office vacant at the end of each AGM, though it also allowed a retiring office holder to seek re-election but not more than twice after the initial election, that is, three terms altogether. By convention, too, an incumbent usually was returned to office unopposed.

The Insight CEO offered himself for election because he had convinced himself that the incumbent had begun to lose steam in terms of giving the Association a clear direction. Although he was eminently qualified to have put himself forward for election into the highest or any other office in the AAAN hierarchy, several of his colleagues felt that his principled challenge of Nzeribe bordered on inordinate ambition to buck AAAN's tradition of three-term presidency. When votes were cast, he lost the election by a lone vote that gave Nzeribe the go-ahead to lead the body for a third, final term. Although Shobanjo lost the battle, he won the war, as he became a part of the move that succeeded in amending AAAN's constitution to peg an incumbent's stay in office at a maximum of two terms of one AAAN calendar year each. Two terms, it was argued, was long enough for any office holder to implement whatever programme he had put together for the Association.

Several reasons have been adduced for Shobanjo's 'problems' with his colleagues, particularly those that an authoritative industry source referred to as 'Bode Thomas Mafia,' which was so-called because of the location of their offices in Mainland Lagos. Among others, his competitive disposition, which some labelled as 'excessive', was said to have taken the fun out of doing business. Proponents of this viewpoint tended to see him more as one who 'cheated' them out of businesses that they believed should, as of right, have been theirs. They felt he was too loud and too brash and had journalists in his pockets, so could do no wrong. There were unspoken fears that he might turn out to be a 'bully' President who might use his exalted office to wage private wars. There also was the major fear that the Presidency would avail him an unassailable position from where he could easily corner a substantial portion of the market.

Were the elections to have been conducted at Troyka, Shobanjo would also probably have lost. But for completely different reasons. For one, he would have had difficulty persuading Awosika to back his aspiration. The latter, at the time, believed that 'the guys at

AAAN were past redemption (in their opposition to Shobanjo).' Another co-director, Ibe, would most likely have abstained since he (Ibe) has tried not to show 'too much' interests in AAAN's activities, because 'these things are not appreciated'. His long-time friend, Johnson, who then headed MC&A, bluntly advised him "not to expose himself to any embarrassment" by seeking elective office in the Association.

Against these strands of well-intentioned counsel, Shobanjo took a second shot at the AAAN Presidency at the Association's 22nd AGM in April, 1995. A host of considerations informed his quest for the Association's top slot. It, indeed, made sense that a practitioner of his standing should be recorded by history as having been a torchbearer of the formidable body. Again, it was commonsensical that he availed his colleagues an opportunity to see, understand and appreciate how he functioned and how his mind worked, even if they did not always agree with the direction in which he was headed.

His co-contestants for office were the fiery late Raymond Adegoke Kester who was CEO of Hunters Publicity and the highly-regarded Oliver Eniola Johnson, the CEO of Intermark Associates. The elections had all the trappings of an epic battle because of the calibre of the candidates and the controversy that attended Shobanjo's nomination. Before the story moves too far afield, it is important that a full picture of AAAN be presented to help readers better appreciate the disagreement that almost made the contest a subject of judicial intervention.

Historically, AAAN is the offshoot of early initiatives by practitioners to give character to advertising. Its progenitor was the ADCLUB of Nigeria formed in 1969 'to project the true image of the advertising profession in Nigeria.'[1] ADCLUB was stillborn, quite unlike the Newspapers Proprietors Association of Nigeria (NPAN) that was established in 1963 to protect the interests of media owners. In the absence of cohesion in the rank of advertising practitioners, NPAN began to legislate on the practice of advertising. Advertising practitioners quickly sensed trouble and resolved to come together to resist external control as embodied by NPAN. They also realised if the industry was to grow, they needed a united front that would engender quick resolution of conflicts in the sector. Against this backdrop, some Nigerian practitioners met in June 1971 to consider the imperative for a body to regulate professional practice. In attendance were Oloye Dotun Okubanjo of Publicity Service Ltd; Biodun Sanwo of Image Makers Ltd and Olu Adekoya, the founder of Olu Adekoya Press Agency Ltd, OAPA. The meeting paved the way for the establishment of AAPN (the precursor of AAAN) on 18 November, 1972.

The Association's first official congress was held on 5 March, 1973 at the Nigerian Institute of International Affairs (NIIA) on Victoria Island, Lagos.[2] 28 delegates from 23 agencies attended. The 'Big Three' agencies, that is, Lintas, OBM and Grant were not represented. Okubanjo was formally elected as pioneer President, with Sam Iyamu as Secretary. Ab initio, membership of the Association was restricted to incorporated limited liability companies rather than individuals.

AAAN, it would seem, was founded to fight battles from within and from without. Even at its formative stage, one of its earliest battles, which was carried over from ADCLUB, was for the inclusion of advertising and public relations in the list of enterprises reserved for Nigerians. The promulgation of the Indigenisation Decree in 1972

[1]Moemeke, op cit. p.22
[2]Laja Akindele, 'The Story of AAPN,' Advertising in Nigeria, March, 1993, p.5

helped to change the face of advertising in the country for good. But NPAN remained a killjoy. On April 1, 1976, it published an announcement on the review of the agency recognition system. Advertising Practitioners initially thought it was a joke in the spirit of the All-Fools Day. Whatever illusions they harboured on the publication was shattered on 30 September, 1976 when NPAN published in the Daily Times a list of 13 agencies recognised by it as follows:

Permanent Grade
1. Lintas
2. OBM
3. Grant

Standard (approved)
1. Overseas & General Advertising
2. Cannon Advertising
3. PAL
4. Image Makers
5. Moses Associated Agency - Enugu
6. Intermark
7. Akrel
8. ROD Publicity
9. Admark
10. Advertising Associates of Nigeria

NPAN did not mask its intention, not even thinly. The recognition of these agencies, it said, was based on 'the need for better regulation for the practice of advertising and the securing of the best advertising practice for advertisers.' The 'recognised' agencies apparently had met a seven-point condition that included having accessible offices; adhering to ethical standards; debt settlement within 30 days; providing indemnity against litigation that might arise from the content of advertisements as well as giving an undertaking not to front for non-recognised agencies. NPAN's President, Lateef Jakande; General Secretary, the late Labanji Bolaji and Chairman of the Advertising Committee, Niyi Alonge, who later established Adwork, an AAAN agency, authorised the publication on behalf of NPAN.

Dr. Jide Oluwajuyitan, a Mass Communication scholar who at the time was an Advert Manager in the Daily Times Group, put NPAN's braggadocio in context: "By the time the advertising profession began to get its bearings, newspapers were already making millions of Naira from advert placements and we helped many of the professionals to set up their agencies by granting them credit facilities."

This, notwithstanding, AAPN went to court. But it did not do so as a body. Its pioneer Secretary, Iyamu, led the fray.[1] He sought an injunction to restrain NPAN from implementing the 'recognition' system. He lost. The court refused to grant an order in nullity because NPAN was not a legally registered body; it was, in the eyes of the law, a phantom that could not be sued.

Olu Adekoya, another founding father of AAPN, picked up the fight from there. In the now famous suit Number LD/1138/76, he sued Jakande, Bolaji and Alonge as private citizens and as officials of NPAN for exceeding their professional jurisdiction and infringing on the rights of practitioners of advertising. Justice Y.A.O Jinadu, who sat at a Lagos High Court on 9 January, 1978 granted Adekoya's prayers that NPAN be stopped from trying to run the practice of advertising by other means. The judge ruled that NPAN wielded power that ab initio it lacked. The judge further held that only AAPN

---

[1]_Moemeke, op cit. p.11_

was competent to legislate advertising codes and standard of practice. The judgment considerably strengthened the hands of AAPN as a body.

The euphoria of the hard-won 'independence' had long worn off by the time Shobanjo made his second bid for the Association's highest office. In its place was deep-rooted distrust that had continually threatened the internal cohesion of the group. Much of the problem bordered on the inability of members to uphold basic ethical standards as outlined in the Code of Standards and Practice for Advertising Agencies. Particularly worrisome was the fact of client poaching, which was a clear breach of Section G, Sub-sections 2, 3, 4 and 5 of the Rules of Practice. There also were widespread allegations of abuse of office by Executive Council members who reportedly promoted their individual agencies at the expense of others that were not privileged to sit in Council. Allied to these were running battles with other sectoral associations, particularly NPAN and the Broadcasting Organisation of Nigeria, BON, over incessant hikes in rates and high industry debts. Beyond these, however, was the real fear of the likely creation of a cartel, which was made manifest by the inconsistent number of members on the Association's register (see table below):

Year	No of Members
1990	72
1991	86
1992	90
1993	89
1994	71
1995	82

Who then was fit and proper to lead AAAN? Kester stepped forward. Johnson, too. Both paraded impeccable credentials of meaningful contribution to the growth of advertising and long, active service in AAAN. Either of them would have made a good President. Weeks to the 1995 AGM, unofficial polls had both running a tight race but a third force was being mustered. Top-level contacts were made to persuade Shobanjo to run but he was reluctant to do so, having vowed after the 1994 experience never again to run for an elective office in AAAN. He was also not unaware of the direction of popular opinion on his person and style of doing business. Nonetheless, colleagues like Dele Adetiba and Akin Odunsi who felt he could compare favourably with the leadership of any Association anywhere in the world drafted him into the race. The 'Shobanjo for President' group clearly believed that AAAN would benefit immensely from his experience and extensive network of contacts in both public and private circles.

His candidacy, however, faced many obstacles, chief of which was that several of his colleagues seemed not to have forgotten the 'sin' of 1994. There also was the fundamental issue of why anyone should vote Shobanjo as President when he appeared to have shown what a few of his fellow practitioners saw as 'proof' that he did not have the interest of AAAN at heart. This latter consideration was warranted by his voluntary exit from the board of the Advertising Practitioners Council of Nigeria (APCON). Since 1991 he had occupied a seat on the board as one of 10 statutory representatives of AAAN. He, however, opted out of the board because he felt that its tenure had been elongated: "(The Board) needed an injection of fresh blood, new people. We had been on it for close to five years (the Decree stipulates three) and I found a lot of repetition going on and I was beginning to see it as a waste of my time. I knew that new people were agitating to get on board. To the extent that I was beginning to feel we were having a 'sit tight' Council, I saw need to excuse myself (because) at a point in a man's life, (he) must begin to take decisions for himself; decisions he believes are in the best interest of what he is doing. I have no regrets that I left when I did."

The first round of voting at the elections, which took place on 20 April, 1995, produced inconclusive results. Kester scored 22 votes, Johnson had 9 votes and Shobanjo recorded 22 votes. A run-off was needed to break the tie. Johnson dropped off to allow for a straight fight between Kester and Shobanjo. Would 1995 be a repeat of 1994? No one was sure. An unnerving silence filled the Function Suite of the Lagos Sheraton Hotels & Towers when the counting of ballots began. Again, it was one of the closest races in the history of AAAN. Kester polled 26 votes against Shobanjo's 27. On the strength of the single vote superiority, Shobanjo became the 8th President of AAAN.

His election raised a lot of dust. An industry elder, Adekoya threatened to go to court because, in his opinion, the new President's nomination breached Section 8(h) of the body's Constitution. Shobanjo's candidacy was reportedly filed outside the 21-day pre-AGM requirement. In truth, not many members knew that Shobanjo was in the race until they arrived at the venue of the AGM. But his nomination, which was filed weeks ahead of the convention, was constitutionally in order. The issue was amicably resolved and Adekoya dropped his earlier threat so as not to allow a 'minor matter' to jeopardise the 'formidable' unity among members.

Opinions on Shobanjo's lone vote victory were as diverse as there are practitioners. Samples: Jimi Awosika: "That tells you how the best usually do not win outright. It is all politics."

Dele Adetiba: "The result of that election was probably not a reflection of (members') perception of (Shobanjo's) competence but maybe of his person which had a lot to do with it."

Kola Ayanwale (Centrespread/one-time AAAN President): "The narrow margin of his election was a measure of the destructive envy that people have of him. Though he won, I thought he should have won (more) convincingly. That really showed the thinking of where most of our members still belonged."

Steve Omojafor (STB-McCANN): "It does not say much about the level of perception of him within the Association. When he lost (in 1994,), there was the issue of why not allow May (Nzeribe) complete his term; which probably was one of the reasons people did not vote for him then. When he was prevailed upon to run, he won narrowly. It goes to show that you have an Association that is not going to pay lip service to anyone."

Allan Olabode (Promoserve): "I think his time (had) come. Whether he won by one vote or not, it (was) time they gave him a chance to prove what he (had) been able to achieve at Insight for the professional body. We agreed we needed the kind of leadership he could provide."

Lolu Akinwumi (Prima Garnet): "The contestants were evenly matched, except there was an attempt to insult (Kester and Johnson) by saying that they were voted for because people did not like Shobanjo. I do not think that is correct. All the contestants were quite influential."

Shobanjo was aware of the undercurrent of issues before, during and after his election. He recognised the quality of leadership that his co-contestants could offer the Association and he appreciated the fact that AAAN had come of age: "I came out after a lot of people thought there were no more candidates. But for the fact that I am highly regarded in the profession, I would not have won at all."

The sequence of events that led to Shobanjo's election raised two quick questions. Was the delayed nomination a clever political ploy to spring the new President at the last possible moment to pre-empt properly co-ordinated opposition? Maybe. Just maybe. If anything, Shobanjo does not fight to run away; he fights to the finish, never for once in doubt that he would be the last man standing. If, of his own volition, he had wanted to stand for election, he would have done so without any prompting.

Was he elected because, as journalist Steve Osuji asked, AAAN had run out of 'politically correct' candidates? Osuji himself had the answer both right and wrong. Right, because the body had a glut of fine materials for President. Wrong, because Shobanjo did not keep at trying to lead AAAN. He killed the idea after the 1994 misadventure. In 1995, he was a 'reluctant candidate'.

Although there is no ideological divide per se within AAAN, Shobanjo can loosely be situated in the far left of whatever centre that there is. If for nothing than for the blunt, perhaps, too direct way he expresses his opinions, particularly in respect of the creative output of competition and the 'dog eat dog' syndrome in the body. Some of his colleagues took strong exception to what they considered his grandstanding because they believed that he stood on tenuous ground on some of these matters. Now that he had the mandate to make the difference, they all waited to see how the 'guerrilla' fighter would transform to a statesman after emerging from the trenches.

Shobanjo assumed office clutching a six-point 'President's Agenda'.

First, he planned to 'refocus' AAAN and win it respect from all quarters. Secondly, he sought to arrest the negative slide in the quality of advertising education and practice. Thirdly, he hoped to improve communication between Council and heads of agencies. Fourthly, he hoped to pick the brains of his predecessors in office to build a better Association. Fifthly, he aspired to achieve better AAAN/Government relations. He also had the objective of co-operating fully with every sectoral body, notably NPAN, Broadcasting Organisation of Nigeria (BON), Advertisers Association of Nigeria (ADVAN)) and Outdoor Advertising Association of Nigeria (OAAN) for 'proper practice of advertising'.

His Presidency was the first under AAAN's new two-term leadership rule. Few, if any, of his colleagues doubted his ability to lead the Association. He did not, as many had feared, wage private wars in office. Rather, he consulted widely and made needful compromises to move AAAN ahead. The 1996 face-off between frontline advertising agency, Adwork Ltd and one of its prime clients, the now defunct Nigeria Airways, provides one of the best illustrations of democracy at work under Shobanjo.

The client, Nigeria Airways, owed its agency, Adwork, an estimated £446,000 in foreign content and N6.7 million in local content on various briefs that were executed between 1990 and 1992. Having failed to persuade the airline's management to amicably honour its debt, Adwork went to court in November 1992 and obtained judgement in May 1993 against the airline, which still did not make any payment to the agency. Adwork consequently 'factorised' the debt by empowering a debt collection agency to professionally and technically handle the issue. This development led to the seizure of a Nigeria Airways DC 10 plane in London in January 1996. The incident was a big political embarrassment to the Federal

Government of Nigeria headed by General Sani Abacha, which, at that time, was also fighting a battle of legitimacy to gain acceptance by the citizenry and the international community. This novel initiative in credit control by an AAAN agency inexorably drew the Association into the fray. The Association needed to take a stand.

As an individual, Shobanjo saw this as a fairly straightforward case. His stance that clients must always pay for work done by agencies had been strengthened by the pronouncement of a competent court to that effect. Based on his conviction and the weight of evidence on ground, he drafted a press statement that he felt should reflect the position of AAAN on the matter. He forwarded the draft to some of his colleagues so he could carry his constituency along. His initial draft was considerably watered-down owing to the sensitive nature of the issue. In the end, AAAN opted to tow a course of least resistance by choosing to work in the background.

The Association sought a 'more friendly way' to resolve the business disagreement between Adwork Ltd and Nigeria Airways and, by extension, the Federal Military Government. Apart from the larger political implications of the issue, AAAN was probably inclined to soft pedal because Adwork had gone to court, in the first instance, without consulting the Association's Professional Practices Committee, which, in the past, had helped other agencies to resolve similar debt-related problems. Shobanjo leveraged the professional clout of AAAN and tapped into his own vast network of personal contacts to dialogue with the Chief Executive of the Nigerian Airports Authority (now Federal Airports Authority of Nigeria, FAAN), who was a top military officer. The personal and professional efforts expended to broker peace ultimately resulted in an amicable settlement of the matter by both parties.

In his first year in office, he helped AAAN secure a parcel of land at the Central Business District, Ikeja, Lagos complete with its Certificate of Occupancy from the Lagos State Government. This landmark achievement was recorded for purposes of building the Association's proposed Advertising Academy and Secretariat. Over the years, AAAN had assumed the role of a guardian angel in matters of worrisome manpower development in the industry. This was because of the near-total absence of quality input in the academic syllabi of major tertiary institutions that produced the crop of new entrants into the advertising profession in Nigeria.

The weight of deficient curricula was felt more by member agencies of AAAN, which employed over 75 per cent of the industry's total work force. The dearth of qualitative and quantitative education meant that the best of local agencies operated below global industry standard. This, in turn, made the agencies less competitive when compared with their foreign counterparts. It also made them less attractive to the advertising savvy and heavy billing multinational clients that would regularly require their services. These constrained the growth of the advertising industry in Nigeria and, when placed on a balance against its potential, made its contribution to Gross Domestic Product abysmally low.

To position themselves against external competition, Nigeria's top 10 agencies expended an estimated N16 million to upgrade the knowledge base of their employees as well as expand their professional horizons.[1] These efforts duly complemented the vision of a former President of AAAN, Moemeke, who in 1979 mooted the idea of establishing an 'educational centre for the study of advertising.'[2] Subsequent leaders of AAAN adopted and fine-tuned the idea. Procuring the piece of land was, therefore, one of the necessary first steps towards this goal.

[1] _Akin Odunsi, Training by Ad Agencies, Advertising in Nigeria, January-March 1997, p.19_
[2] _Ayo Owoborode, The Coming of APCON, Advertising in Nigeria, March, 1993, p.79_

In the immediate, Shobanjo focused on curriculum development. His model was the AAA School of Advertising in South Africa, which had a blend of rich academic curriculum and a good physical infrastructure. He began by changing the focus of the regular AAAN workshops and seminars, which became more sophisticated and up to date in the sense of being anchored on contemporary industry issues that were handled by field experts. His colleagues who appraised the improved form and contents of the courses adjudged them as being more hands-on and, unlike before, less theoretical. More than ever before, too, the programmes were deemed to have been more profitable and better organised in terms of structure, faculty, content and venues. By and large, the revitalised courses became the intellectual raw materials for the blueprint of the curriculum of the proposed Academy.

The physical take-off of the Academy was, however, bogged down by inadequate funding. The projected initial cost of about N40 million ballooned by over 300 per cent to nearly N200 million, which meant that no building block was set on the acquired land before the expiration of Shobanjo's tenure as President. The Secretariat was eventually completed and commissioned for use in 2004.

Could the positively heavy exposure of AAAN in the media rate as one of Shobanjo's achievements while in office? Many of his colleagues think so. His 'very present' personal image in the media makes the question inevitable. Even by his own account, he is 'over-exposed.' For reasons that are not too obvious, a lot of agency owners hesitate to properly manage their individual image in the media. By contrast, Shobanjo is adept at building himself up as a brand in much the same way as his agency builds client brands in the marketplace. His dominant media presence rubbed off positively on the Association, which, by extension, increasingly got more media attention. In two years, he moved AAAN into the domain of public discourse, though in terms of easy recognition by non-professionals, the Association remained miles behind such other professional bodies as the Nigerian Bar Association (NBA) or the Nigerian Medical Association (NMA) or, for that matter, the National Union of Road Transport Workers (NURTW). The Association, it goes without saying, still needs to work hard at projecting its public image.

In truth, not many expected Shobanjo, as President, to under-perform. This, notwithstanding, a few professionally critical grey areas were not wholly and satisfactorily clarified whilst he was in office. Billing, for example, was a major challenge. Before, during and after his presidency, practitioners generally remained tight-lipped on the issue, more so as there was no industry-wide acceptance of the computation of billing or of its component parts. It was not clear whether it should be based on the sum of above-the-line and below-the-line figures or of one to the exclusion of the other. It was also evident that researchers would face substantial difficulty in any diligent effort to determine whether the figures were 'true' or were the result of 'fancy accounting' to impress actual and potential clients or to keep tax authorities at arm's length. Shobanjo had a fairly ambivalent attitude to public disclosure of agency billing. Whilst he often declared himself an 'apostle of making billings public,' he also liked to highlight the fine distinction between being an agency executive and leader of an Association. He maintained that he could not, as President of AAAN, compel the management of his agency, Insight, to go public with these figures, if it chose to exercise the company's prerogative to keep the figures in the closet.

The experience of Akin Adeoya, a journalist, in his search for the elusive figures, put the matter of agency billing in perspective: "Agency people found it **incomprehensible** (emphasis, mine) to discuss their billings on the pages of newspapers, rather preferring to keep the information secret."[1]

When Adeoya interviewed agency heads and sought to know the volume of their annual transactions, everyone, Shobanjo included, reportedly 'had a very good laugh.' He then asked rhetorically: 'what are the agencies hiding? Do not ask Shobanjo. His answer could be either to give a complacent shrug accompanied by a loud clasping of his palms or a long-winded monotone or statistical generalisations. No, he would not publicly rock the boat on the issue of billings; not minding that Insight sits atop the league.

The issue of high industry debt was also not satisfactorily resolved during Shobanjo's tenure as AAAN President. Just before his election as President of AAAN, the advertising industry began to experience relative calm, helped, in part, by the birth of the Advertisers Association of Nigeria (ADVAN) in 1994 to complete the Advertiser-Agency-Media tripod. The industry immediately reaped some of the benefits of this development, chief of which was that media rates enjoyed relative stability because the need for more encompassing consultations in the industry began to act as constraints to incessant price hikes by NPAN. This, however, did not immediately push down the challenge of debts, which continued to mount year-on-year. Media owners screamed that agencies were pushing them out of business; agency owners screamed that clients continued to default and clients screamed that they were being fleeced by agencies and media.

Curiously, all the parties could not establish the quantum of debts owed by whom. But, of the three parties, agencies were the ones

---

[1] *Walking on Billings Way, ThisDay, 5 October, 1996, p.7*

caught between the rock and the hard place. They continued to bear the weight of debts owed to third parties, just as clients desired more in terms of creative output and other services. Although agencies were ill-prepared to do this, they helplessly continued to take up the responsibility of practically subsidising the operations of their obviously more prosperous clients. They did this primarily to keep the clients happy and, by extension, to retain their patronage. Despite Shobanjo's position that no agency or enterprise that hoped to remain in business should by other means finance its client's business, Insight was not immune to the general headache of the industry. By the end of 1996, for example, clients owed Insight more than N94 million, which represented approximately 13.4 per cent of the total N701 million owed 18 members of AAAN.

At various times, APCON intervened to resolve the problem. The regulatory body released a set of credit guidelines that embodied input from all sectoral bodies in the advertising industry. These were intended as solutions to curb mounting industry debts and encourage advertisers to honour debt obligations within 60 days. The impact of the APCON document was hardly felt, as clients continued to default whilst agencies and media owners also continued to groan under crushing debts. Media owners under the aegis of NPAN soon resorted to self-help. They adopted a strategy of applying subtle blackmail in their debt recovery drive. Where they reasoned that some agencies had needlessly piled up debts even after they had been paid by their clients, newspaper owners went directly to ADVAN members to demand payments for media placements made on their behalf by agencies. On this score, Oluwajuyitan exonerated Insight and its management, saying: "Shobanjo is too proud to owe; so, Insight would not owe the media. When others owed millions of Naira and we were fighting, he was not involved. When there was any delay in payment, he made efforts to pay up as at when due."

On his part, Shobanjo led AAAN to fight every inch of the way, as Oluwajuyitan confirmed: "As we (NPAN members) kept increasing our rates, Shobanjo kept fighting for his Association. He would threaten us; he would write letters and he would lead delegations just to get value for AAAN. He once attended a meeting at The Guardian with some of his colleagues at AAAN (during which) he taught me a lesson about preparation because he was prepared for the meeting. He had comparative media rates from around the world which I, as Controller of Marketing, did not even have."

Oluwajuyitan's experience tallied with Kankarofi's at Kano Broadcasting Corporation in the early days of Insight: "Shobanjo's ability to negotiate is amazing; he is a fantastic negotiator and he is always business-like. If he negotiates anything, he would have the best deals whether you like it or not. Even when he speaks, he will never be unprepared; he does not take the risk of going anywhere or doing anything without planning."

Shobanjo also remained steadfast to his position that clients must pay in good time for services rendered by their agencies, which, in turn, must pay the media without undue delays. By 2007, however, he modified his viewpoint because he felt that stakeholders in the industry were 'over-flogging a dead horse' on issues relating to industry debts. At the time, his friend and then President of NPAN, Ray Ekpu, had canvassed the charging of interest on payment default at prevailing bank rates as a panacea for the debt overhang in the industry. Shobanjo disagreed. Instead, he urged a more aggressive approach: "We have been into this for too many years. It is a waste of time for us to be talking about debt here. Where you have a business, you should have trading terms with your clients. Anybody that cannot abide by the terms, do not do business with them."

APCON's ceaseless interventions, years after Shobanjo's exit from the AAAN presidency, have further helped to significantly douse the conflict between media owners and AAAN members. At the core of the dispute was an estimated N8 billion debt that media owners claimed was owed by agency owners. APCON and other stakeholders subsequently conducted a national survey of the debt profile of agencies, which established the debts at less than N1 billion. Much of the disparity resulted from inadequate record keeping on transactions and the absence of transparency in the media. The bulk of what media owners passed to AAAN members were discovered to have been owed by unregistered practitioners and advertisement canvassers. Much of that also resulted from barter arrangements with entities outside of AAAN. The high turnover of Chief Executives of media houses, particularly amongst State-owned broadcast stations did not help matters. The Delta State Government, for example, sacked station managers at will; in Gombe and Plateau States, six Managing Directors and six Permanent Secretaries were appointed in just one year while in other States Chief Executives were appointed and sacked almost every quarter. A senior advertising practitioner explained that the statistics were discomfiting because 'everyone was interested in commercial revenue for the sake of meeting diverse political obligations.' ADVAN, AAAN and NPAN have continued to make concerted efforts that have engendered better relationships by relevant stakeholders in the industry. This has made it much easier to amicably resolve conflicts on the level of debts owed media owners by agencies.

It will be recalled that Shobanjo looked beyond the shores of Nigeria for agency models before the birth of Insight. The attraction was based on his desire to make positive contribution towards redressing the 'messengerial mentality' in client/agency relationships. In his thinking, if a client truly valued the contribution of its agency to the growth of its business, it generally would openly acknowledge the agency's contribution as well as, among other things, respect the worldwide 30-day credit terms of doing business. The warm relationship between Pepsico, owners of the Pepsi brand, and its agency, BBDO, serves as a good reference point for him. By 1996, the relationship between the client and its agency had spanned over 30 years yet the familiarity did not give way to complacency or disrespect on either side. At the launch of the Pepsi 'Going Blue' campaign in the UK that year, BBDO rated highly in Pepsico's acknowledgments at the event. By contrast, most clients in Nigeria hardly respect the terms of credit and almost always forget to give due credit to agencies for jobs well done. Shobanjo's was slightly different because many years after he left the AAAN office he received personal and professional satisfaction when Insight got high commendations from one of its major clients, Nigerian Breweries Plc, for the depth of creativity that gave birth to the Gulder Ultimate Search (GUS) TV reality show and the Legend Extra Stout's Express Yourself campaign. For him, this was a small, yet significant achievement of his dream of agency/client 'partnership.'

Notwithstanding the various views on membership of AAAN, there is an absence of a clear ideological divide in the Association. At best, membership has tended to present a 'liberal' versus 'conservative' dichotomy. Such broad categorisation is only superficial because AAAN is mainly perceived as being just one notch shy of being a cartel. Unofficially, there are more than 300 agencies in practice, of which only 66, at the end of Shobanjo's tenure, were financial members of the Association. Critics say AAAN is anti-liberalisation and that it is more concerned with the financial muscles of its members than their professional output. Available evidence appears to lend credence to this viewpoint, as more agencies have had their memberships terminated for failing to meet their financial obligations than for failing to meet other prescribed criteria of membership.

Shobanjo is not persuaded by the logic of this argument. For him, AAAN, as a voluntary professional organisation, is more concerned with standardisation, not a populist appeal to win respect for the profession. In his view, the stipulated financial and professional requirements of membership are interwoven to engender professionalism without being anti-proliferation. He, however, was no less sympathetic to the cause of non-members of the Association. For that reason, he subscribed to the decision of AAAN to reach out to agencies that were outside the fold but which had good professional track records. This move led to the creation of an 'Associate Member' category to accommodate agencies that could not at once attain the full Corporate Member status. The association's decision was quite pragmatic, considering that the rank of non-members of AAAN continued to swell despite the 'fly-by-night' label pinned on them by members of the Association.

His support of AAAN's extension of the olive branch to non-members clearly recognised a combination of realistic factors that had made practice outside the Association look quite attractive. Officially, a practitioner only needs to be APCON-certified to practice advertising in Nigeria; financially, it is more convenient to practise without the commitments of AAAN membership and membership of AAAN does not confer the monopoly of resourceful creativity on practitioners, most of whom, at any rate, have had the privilege of training in AAAN agencies. Beyond these, most clients do not fuss over sectoral affiliations, particularly in situations where they are able to get good creative services at competitive cost. In the circumstance, AAAN had a choice to either stoop to conquer or unwittingly encourage the formation of rival organisations, as had been the case with several other professional bodies. AAAN chose to reach out, without necessarily compromising its standards. The Association's decision was warmly embraced by several non-member agencies that quickly latched on to the window of opportunity created by the extension of membership categories.

Much as Shobanjo feels an obligation to protect the interest of his sector of the industry, he knew well enough that stakeholders in the sector could only grow apace in a win-win situation. He, therefore, continued to go out of his way to support professionalism in allied professions. After a meeting at The Guardian where he fought and got the concessions he sought for AAAN, he gave his supporting documents that consisted of all the competitive advert rates of newspapers from various parts of the world to the newspaper's Controller of Marketing, Jide Oluwajuyitan, for his 'personal use.' He conspiratorially told him that The Guardian was a good product but that its advertisement rates were 'too low'. Oluwajuyitan picked the hint. The next time he travelled to London he took out time to visit The Observer and other newspapers to learn as much as he could. The advert rates of The Guardian soon went up to being the highest in the market but the newspaper vastly improved its already rich editorial contents to back them up. Oluwajuyitan said: "I reasoned that if this was the way Shobanjo ran his organisations, it would be extremely difficult for anyone to beat him. He is better prepared, he is aggressive and when it comes to business, he does not joke."

The experience was no less different for John Momoh, Chairman and Chief Executive Officer of the award-winning and pace-setting Channels TV, Nigeria's pioneer 24-hour news channel. He had grown accustomed to 'learning moments' each time he interacted with

Shobanjo who often offered quality critique of his station's operation. "He is like a mentor to me. He never hesitated to let me know if something was good or wrong with my operations, which is even more constructive. Although he had watched me grow professionally, he embraced me and brought me into his fold not minding the age gap. People like that are very confident. I looked at his business, his career and success and thought if he could do it and he encourages us to do the same, we should be able to do it as well. He means well not only for his industry but for allied sectors."

Omooba Sam Adebola Ogundogba, Chairman of Emaconprint, vividly remembers Shobanjo's contribution to the growth of his printing press, which was a start-up at the time Insight was also seeking headway: "He helped to nurture our dream for Emaconprint, starting with a calendar job that gave us further exposure to prove that quality printing could be achieved in Nigeria. He was very happy and we were very happy. He knows what he wants and he coordinates everybody. He listens to you calmly and exchanges ideas so you can satisfy him and he, in turn, can satisfy the client he knows but is unknown to you. He is a good payer who does not like to owe anybody. He is somebody everyone is proud to associate with. You don't forget somebody who helped you to grow."

The issue of professional sphere of influence between members of AAAN and Outdoor Advertising Association of Nigeria (OAAN), however, generated substantial controversy during Shobanjo's Presidency at AAAN. Years before the outdoor business became a major industry issue between OAAN and AAAN, the operation of Troyka's outdoor subsidiary, Klinsite, had created mild panic when it ventured into rooftop advertising, a novel initiative pioneered in Ojuelegba, Lagos by Medialink, which was part-owned by Foluso

Babu Akinbobola, Shobanjo's erstwhile junior colleague at Grant. Although the rivalry between Medialink and Klinsite was not too evident, Kankarofi, a mutual friend of the owners of both agencies quickly stepped in to prevent any bad blood. Shobanjo and Akinbobola were receptive to Kankarofi's intervention. The matter was quietly resolved after Awosika and Akinbobola met to douse all flashpoints. As business boomed, however, more AAAN-member agencies began to establish out-of-home organisations to cater to their need for outdoor advertising services. Members of OAAN swiftly moved to resist what they saw as deliberate incursions into their traditional areas of business. Notwithstanding the threats and counter threats of litigation by both sides, the matter was resolved without acrimony particularly because it was evident that OAAN would have encountered substantial difficulty legally stopping AAAN members from floating outdoor companies once they proved they had the professional and financial muscles to sustain such ventures. OAAN, however insisted on the running of the outdoor companies as OAAN affiliates, not as AAAN's outposts.

Outwardly, the relationship between AAAN and Government was cordial, as sign-posted by the presence of then Chief of General Staff, Lt. Gen. Oladipo Diya, at AAAN's 24th Annual General Meeting in 1997. Beyond this, Government did not appear to hold advertising practice in the country in high esteem. Evidence abound that the quality of national and international advertising campaigns executed by foreign advertising agencies on behalf of successive Federal Governments did not justify the faith in them or the huge expenditure incurred by government. The Federal Ministry of Information, too, did not appear to have matured to the point of being perceived as an effective and believable clearing house for government information. More damning in the 1990s was that not one advertising practitioner had a place in the 170-member 'Vision 2010' team that was raised by the Federal Government to draw a blueprint of how to move Nigeria forward in the 21st Century. This was a clear defeat of Shobanjo's goal of making advertising relevant to governance.

As President of AAAN, Shobanjo had a major headache with creative awards. His fascination with creative awards had always been hand in glove with his vision of doing things differently and to perfection. The tall order meant he kept sleepless nights working with staff and service providers, never leaving them to deliver anything less than excellent. Not everyone immediately understood his passion for perfection. Chief Steve Ojo, one of Nigeria's foremost film producers and Founder/President of Galaxy Television, once carried a huge grudge against Shobanjo on this score. Both first met in the late 1970s when Shobanjo was Deputy Managing Director of Grant Advertising and Ojo was Executive Director of Latola Films, which he left to set up his own film production outfit, Interpad Films. They met on several occasions after Insight came on stream. Ojo recalled not leaving with a good feeling after one of his meetings with Shobanjo to request for patronage: "I said "Bibi, congratulations, I'll want to work for you; whatever commercials you have, I'll be happy to work on them." He said to me point blank: "Steve, for us at Insight, 't'ile yi ko,'"[1] meaning he was not ready to settle for Nigerian production. I was furious!"

Ojo did not think Shobanjo was being fair to local producers, especially to him, given his own professional antecedents. He felt the Insight CEO could not pretend not to know that Interpad's show reel boasted of several award-winning TVCs that he had produced for other agencies. He waited to see what 'out-of-this-world' international producers would do for Insight. He thereafter avoided Shobanjo, though they greeted familiarly anytime they met. Omojafor eventually brokered a truce between them, which resulted in Insight and Interpad working together on several

---

[1] *Yoruba, approximating to 'not in this clime'*

projects. Regardless of whatever account they worked on and regardless of wherever they shot their films from Lagos to Jos to Dadin Kowa or whenever they did post-production in London, the results showed excellent productions. Ojo realised that Shobanjo's earlier reference to 'other climes' was just his way of demanding perfection:

"Working with him was good. He does his homework well before implementing anything. Each time we worked together, we always knew it would be an award-winning project. He is an amiable person to work with; a man of perfection, though on some occasions I also felt like telling him to take a walk with his job."

Along the line, Ojo picked a sound piece of financial advice from Shobanjo that, till today, he keeps close to his chest. They argued a lot over cost, which should not surprise anyone, seeing that Shobanjo, an Ijebu man, loves to maximise the value of every Naira and Ojo, an Ondo man, could be quite stubborn and set in his ways. Their disagreement often bordered on the percentage of cost to be pre-paid for work to commence or for the balance to be received. Shobanjo would want lower and later; Ojo, higher now or forget it. Shobanjo quite easily understood the average Ondo man's mindset, after all, Awosika is also Ondo. Ojo recalls Shobanjo telling him after one of their disagreements: "You Ondo people always want money at once; just learn to do like Ijebu people. If someone gives you a cheque or does not pay you in full, collect it, keep it in your pocket, then go back later to pick your balance."

Ojo heeded the wise counsel, which has worked well for him in various business transactions over the years. As he said, "I'll always thank Biodun for this piece of advice." In the long term, the collaboration between Insight and Interpad yielded several awards for both companies in appreciation of their commitment to excellence.

The Nigerian Television Authority (NTA) capitalised heavily on the dearth of reputable industry-based prizes in the 1980s to initiate awards for top-of-mind creative works and their producers. These awards were as widely received as they were widely criticised. Some critics lauded the initiative for helping to sharpen the creativity of practitioners; others excoriated the organisers for masking commercial patronage as creative excellence. The idea caught on nonetheless, as some reputable organisations as ZUS Bureau, an advertising education firm founded by Doghudje, and Diamond Publications, publishers of Media Review and organisers of the Diamond Awards for Media Excellence, D.A.M.E, among many others, soon instituted their versions of these awards. As the years went by, Adworld no longer spoke with one voice on issues that concerned industry awards. This culminated in a directive issued by AAAN in July 1995, which stopped further participation in all awards until clearly defined standards emerged.

Shobanjo signed the order, although, personally, it did not go down too well with him: "I think the reason that AAAN stopped participating in these awards is (because,) one agency was winning more awards than others and a lot of people did not feel comfortable about it. So that Insight should not be accused of being a lone ranger we had to agree to boycott the awards."

His reaction was understandable, for Insight had won more of these awards than any other agency. He, however, agreed that the criteria employed in giving the awards needed to be streamlined for the sake of credibility. His dissatisfaction with many of the awards stemmed from the fact that the criteria of selecting awardees were largely nebulous and did not confer requisite status on winners. His position was supported by APCON, which in June, 1996, enunciated a nine-point guideline for the organisation of awards in the advertising industry. Among others, award organisers were required to be members of relevant sectoral/professional associations. The APCON guidelines also stipulated that every award must be titled; its benefit must be stated and it must promote professionalism. In addition, its frequency must be specified; it must be distinguished by medium; it must adhere to transparent guidelines; its judges must be above board and it must be endorsed by APCON.

Following the release of these guidelines, AAAN in July, 1996 lifted the ban that it placed on various awards a year earlier. This decision thus allowed its members to participate in recognised awards of their choosing. Although the path was cleared for the re-introduction of creative awards, some of the organisers could no longer sustain them. One after the other they began to die naturally thus removing the basis of acrimony amongst advertising practitioners. When the first industry-organised awards, the Lagos Advertising Industry Festival (LAIF), was inaugurated in 2006 the initiative received critical acclaim. In advertising circles in Nigeria, LAIF Awards have assumed the eminence of the 'Oscars' of Hollywood and 'Clio' of global advertising. The awards are trusted, competitive and highly coveted because LAIF is an industry-organised event in which entries are judged on clear industry parameters by a panel that consists of some of the best minds in advertising practice in the country. Though the quality of creative challenge from younger outfits has increased significantly, Insight, too, has continued to garner lots of LAIF and other awards, even with Shobanjo out of its day-to-day administration. Again, this has confirmed Shobanjo's position that no agency had the birthright to excellence and leadership.

His colleagues agreed that he made a great President. At the expiration of his tenure in 1997 and in his 26th year as an advertising practitioner, he relinquished the AAAN Presidency at 'home,' in his native Ijebuland. In the process, he once more activated his favourite buzzword: first. The 24th AGM of AAAN, held in April, 1997 took place in Ijebu-Ode, the first of such outside of Lagos. In attendance was John Shannon, the President of Grey International and Chairman/CEO (Europe, Middle East and Africa). It was his first visit to black Africa and he was the first President of an international affiliate to address an AAAN AGM.

The race for Shobanjo's successor as head of AAAN was, initially, three-way. In contention were his long-time friend, Steve Omojafor (STB-McCann) and his co-contestants in 1995, Kester and Johnson. Johnson withdrew 'suddenly' from the contest to pave the way for Omojafor to defeat Kester by 22 votes to 16 to become the ninth President of the Association. To date, Insight Communications has produced five Presidents of AAAN, namely, Shobanjo plus four members of the Insight alumni association, namely: Udeme Ufot, Enyi Odigbo, Funmi Onabolu and Kayode Oluwasona.

Shobanjo left office satisfied: "For me to have been AAAN President is high honour. I am a Fellow of AAAN. In the past 26 years (in 1997) I have been in Management...I feel we run a successful organisation (Insight) and we have a name out there in the public that quite a lot of people would love to do business with... So what else do I want?"

The answer to his question is not, as one might be led to think, self-evident. It will be very wrong to agree that he desired 'nothing' more.

Honour well deserved and celebrated at the 44th Convocation of Obafemi Awolowo University, Ile Ife on Saturday, 14 December, 2019.

Shobanjo with the University's Chancellor, His Royal Highness Alhaji (Dr) Yahaya Abubakar (the Etsu Nupe) and Pro-Chancellor, Dr Yemi Ogunbiyi.

Biodun Shobanjo, **Doctor of Letters** (D.Litt) Honoris Causa

Together with Joyce

With fellow honoree, Mrs Ibukun Awosika, Chairman of First Bank of Nigeria Plc and former Vice Chancellor, OAU, Prof. Wale Omole

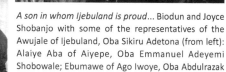

A son in whom Ijebuland is proud... Biodun and Joyce Shobanjo with some of the representatives of the Awujale of Ijebuland, Oba Sikiru Adetona (from left): Alaiye Aba of Aiyepe, Oba Emmanuel Adeyemi Shobowale; Ebumawe of Ago Iwoye, Oba Abdulrazak

Home support

With family, friends and professional associates

Deputy Managing Director,
Grant Advertising, circa 1977

Insight's founding team
From left: Johnson Adebayo (late); Biodun Shobanjo;
Sesan Ogunro (late) and Jimi Awosika.
Not in picture: Richard Ibe and Ibiyemi Amogbe (late)

(backing camera) Sanya 'Soso' Ogunlana; Richard Ibe; Biodun
Shobanjo and James Okesina at an informal review session at the
car park of 1, Calabar Street, Surulere, Lagos

Insight's first ad placement published in
Daily Times, January 11, 1980.

With James Okesina (Centre, Radio Production Manager)
and Jimi Awosika

With Insight's Finance Controller, Ibiyemi Amogbe (late)

Rio De Janeiro, 1982: with Tunde Adelaja (second left); Olu Falomo and David Atilade (late) at the Congress of the International Advertising Association (IAA)

Ahead of Insight Communication's formal affiliation to Bates Worldwide, Chris Sinding (2nd left) and John Hoyne (4th left) of Ted Bates undertook a working visit to Nigeria in 1982. Insight's team at the reception in honour of the Bates' executives (from left): Iyabo Fadojutimi; Biodun Shobanjo; Jimi Awosika; James Okesina and Barth Okigbo.

Signing of the affiliate agreement between Insight Communications and Ted Bates in New York in September 1982: President/CEO of Bates Worldwide, Bob Eakin Jacoby and Biodun Shobanjo

With Paddy Nolan (r) of SQN Productions during the Vaseline Petroleum Jelly film shoot

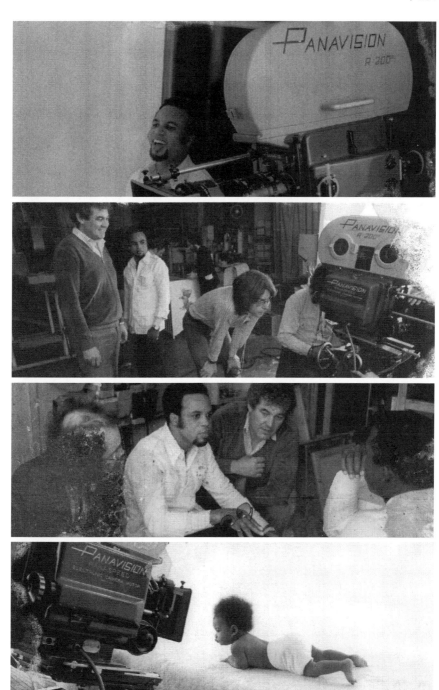

At the Natusan Baby Cream film shoot by David Neil Productions in the UK

From Insight's Ad Archives

From Insight's Ad Archives

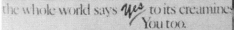

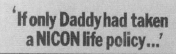

From Insight's Ad Archives

Celebrating Insight @ 10 (1980 – 1990)

Clarifying the Insight dream. Seated: Mr. Chris Doghudje (c) and Chief Akin Odunsi

A toast to the visionary...Standing: former Information Minister, Prince Tony Momoh; Joyce Shobanjo and Chief Akin Odunsi

Custodians of the dream...Richard Ibe, Jimi Awosika and Biodun Shobanjo

The Publisher, Concord newspapers, Chief Moshood Abiola and veteran journalist, Taiwo Alimi

L: former Vice Chairman of the Armed Forces Provisional Ruling Council, General Oladipo Diya and former Information Minister, Prince Tony Momoh.

Shobanjo, leading the road walk to commemorate Insight's 10th anniversary

Client, Chris Ogbechie of Nestle Nigeria with participants at the road walk

Songstress, Onyeka Onwuenu, entertaining guests

...in the groove: Julia Oku and Funmi Onabolu

Early days... Shobanjo, as Executive Chairman, Insight Communications

With former boss at Nigerian Broadcasting Corporation (NBC), Dr. Christopher Kolade

Chairman, Insight Communications, Mr. Goddy Amadi; Prof. Alfred Opubor (late) and former Advert Manager of Daily Times, Mr. Leke Oyekan (late)

Engr. Funso Williams (late); Mrs Sade Ogunbiyi; Editor-in-Chief of Newswatch magazine, Mr. Ray Ekpu and Insight Chairman, Mr Goddy Amadi and wife.

NTA Advertising Awards 1986: **And the winner is…**
Insight Communications. Shobanjo with Richard Ibe (l);
Nasco Foods Sales Manager, Adeagbo and Jimi Awosika

Most Influential Personality in Advertising in
Africa Award, Accra, Ghana, 2014

…Silverbird's Extraordinary Achievements Award, 2018

Every time a winner… with Admiral Jibril Ayinla (rtd);
Joyce and Mac Ovbiagele at the
University of Lagos, Akoka

With the former Managing Director of Sun newspapers,
Tony Onyima; former Governor of Oyo State,
Sen. Abiola Ajimobi and former President, AAAN,
Mrs Bunmi Oke at the Advertising Man of All-Time
award ceremony in 2013

...**Well done, dear...** with Joyce at the Sun's Advertising Man of All-Time award ceremony in 2013

Unending stream of recognitions

When *The Guardian* called Shobanjo with former Managing Director, The Guardian newspapers, the late Dr. Stanley Macebuh (l) and Director of Marketing , Dr. Yemi Ogunbiyi

Richard Ibe; Stanley Macebuh; Biodun Shobanjo

At an AAPN event with Udeme Ufot; Mrs. Bola Thomas and Oliver Johnson (late)

With Daye Oruwari (l); Kehinde Adeosun (late) and Lolu Akinwunmi, all of Promoserve Advertising

At an AAPN educational workshop

When power changed hands: Hand over of AAPN Presidency to Sir Steve Omojafor, CEO of STB-McCann

Done deal: Shobanjo and Maurice Levy, Chairman of Publicis Groupe, after they initialled the Troyka Holdings/Publicis Groupe equity partnership in Paris, France in December 2015

'Baale' and 'Egbs', partnership like no other...Jimi Awosika and Biodun Shobanjo

Fun time:
...Celebrating Troyka Holdings/Publicis Groupe's equity partnership with Insight's founding
member, Sir Richard Ibe and Nobel Laureate, Prof. Wole Soyinka

Commissioning of the Biodun Shobanjo Multi-Media Centre of Excellence ...
with Nigeria's former Head of State, Gen Yakubu Gowon (3rd left), Joyce and former Executive Secretary of the
National Universities Commission, Prof Julius Okojie on June 11, 2014

Wow!
The quality of attendance at the surprise party to celebrate Troyka Holdings/Publicis
Groupe's equity partnership was, well...a big surprise

INNOVATE
OR DIE

Peter Drucker

You win always
when you **think ahead** of your customers
...ALWAYS!

9

Entering The New Millennium

Man cannot discover new oceans
unless he has the courage to lose sight of the shore.

Source Unknown

I n the dying days of the 1990s, Shobanjo began to speak extensively of Insight and, indeed, Troyka Holdings in the new millennium. To this end, there was a significant shift of the group's business focus from its nascent pan-Nigerian beginning to a more broad-based continental direction. The focus on Africa in the 21st century was not borne out of any preoccupation with the size of the group because that point had been proved in the Nigerian market since 1991 when Insight assumed leadership of the advertising industry. 'Relevance' became the new imperative. Shobanjo's concept of relevance was hinged on the desirability of keeping pace with or not lagging too far behind similar agencies in the West. The logic is simple: relevance would enable Insight and other Troyka companies to be at par with the kind of sophisticated clients that he hoped to attract in the new millennium. These were clients that worked smart with the most advanced interactive technology; they were clients that appreciated breakthrough creative thinking; they were clients who demanded the most efficient media mix and they were clients who generally required the services of extremely efficient marketing communications partners. Shobanjo saw relevance within the larger canvas of an efficient and trim organisation that functioned maximally in a deregulated economy. Of course, the scenario was not unlike one of an economic jungle where only the strongest and best positioned survived.

His theory of relevance did not hold in isolation; it operated within the framework of his perception of advertising in the 21st century. He had calculated that, by year 2000, advertising in Nigeria should have matured from the stage of education to the globally accepted stage of presenting choices before consumers. His assumption was a further distillation of the informal industry debate on the 'need to advertise', which was championed by former Lintas boss, Chris Doghudje and the 'right to choose', which was the global theme for advertising championed by the International Advertising Association, IAA.

Proponents of the 'need to advertise' hinged their position on inadequate understanding of advertising and its effectiveness by consumers in Nigeria. The ranking of Nigeria outside the Top 50 big spenders on advertising in the 1990s despite the country's huge market potential provided ample justification for their stance. Whereas countries like the USA, Brazil, South Africa and Malaysia spent $85.6 billion, $2.82 billion, $930 million and $548 million respectively in 1993 to earn respectable positions on the league table, Nigeria spent a mere $68 million.[1] The low ad spend in Nigeria was a direct consequence of political instability and inadequate awareness of the benefits of advertising. The latter factor was also a

---

[1] *Biodun Shobanjo, Managing Technical Affiliations/Partnership, paper delivered at AAAN Strategic Management Course, April, 1997, P.8*

result of near-negative perception of the business by clients, especially between 1982 and 1985, which were the years when virtually all products became 'essential commodities' because they were generally scarce. This was a period when an army of clients entered the market and, quite naturally, failed to imbibe the culture of seeing advertising as an essential part of the marketing process. Whilst the market had changed the same thing could not be said of the people. The low level of understanding of the essence of marketing communications by the generality of consumers in the country thus underscored the desirability of a campaign on the 'need to advertise.'

Proponents of the 'right to choose,' on the other hand, simply wanted more advertising that presented consumers with an array of choices. The thinking was that this made it possible for them to exercise their freedom to choose after thorough examination of the options before them. A clear understanding of the inherent benefits and availability of various brands, products and services, they argued, was needed to build more market confidence because consumers were less likely to suffer post-purchase blues once they were convinced that they had made the right choices out of several.

Shobanjo reasoned that both positions were not mutually exclusive. His middle-of-the-road position was informed by knowledge of clients that appreciated the need to advertise and yet spent little on advertising in an industry that had globally come of age. He maintained that an agency must remain relevant to the needs of its clients for the balance to be tilted in favour of the 'right to choose.' He further argued that all that would be required in Nigeria by year 2000 and beyond would be for businesses to "develop to a level in which most of the raw materials and the finishing are done locally and the standard could compare favourably internationally, assisting in building brand equity and creating distinction for the brands we build." Up until he left active advertising in 2004, however, he maintained that Nigerian agencies were, strictly speaking, not too well positioned to compete internationally.[1] But he also believed that several local agencies had better prospects of breaking into global reckoning by 2010, given the depth and breadth as well as the consistency of their creative output. In his opinion, a relevant agency must 'lead, manage, perform; not follow, respond and conform.' He, therefore, planned that all Troyka companies, especially Insight, must do these and more as they marched into the new millennium.

The focus on prospects of life at the turn of the century led him and his lieutenants to take several crucial decisions. Some of them were hard; others were highly controversial and some more were taken for the basic reason of reorganisation. But all of them, in his view, were 'needful'. Among the hard decisions was the discontinuance of the 14-year old relationship with Bates Worldwide, which had transformed to BSB following the merger with Backer Speilvogel. When Insight's exit from the Bates family occurred, it took about the same long, tortuous road that Insight trod to secure the affiliation in 1982.

Parting ways with Bates, Shobanjo explained, became imperative because: "They had not taken seriously one of the points they needed to address for the relationship to be mutually beneficial. I did not think it was proper for us to operate in the continent in isolation. Put bluntly, Bates did not believe in growth opportunities in Africa because this was a matter I had discussed repeatedly. I discussed it for almost six years. You must look at the competitive environment. We saw what other multinational agencies were doing. I felt very strongly about that, particularly in the opening up of South Africa. I felt there was going to be a lot of co-operation between that part of the continent and this country and that things were going to be rolling out from South Africa. Before now, most of the regional offices in Africa had been in Nairobi; opening South

---

[1] *See Appendix IV*

Africa had resulted in these offices moving there. But Bates was playing games with this."

Perhaps, understandably because Bates' priorities were in other directions of the world. Whilst most other multinationals literally said: 'fine, Africa has her political problems, but we will still invest there,' this was not the situation with Bates. They had their eyes set on Asia and the Far East, particularly China where they developed offices. Shobanjo was thus compelled to say to Bates: "if you are not committed to Africa, then I regret we would have to look in some other directions.' And that was exactly what happened."

The decision to look elsewhere was helped by two key interwoven considerations. In the 14 years that the relationship between both agencies lasted, they shared only one client – British American Tobacco (BAT). Since Insight built its own clientele and with its sparkling performance in the Nigerian market not as a direct result of its affiliation to Bates, it was only natural that it be accorded the second consideration, respect, as a true, equal partner by its American counterpart. Insight initiated the process of disengagement because it believed it was on firm footing and was ready to bear the obvious consequence of resigning the BAT account. Despite Shobanjo's reputation as a clinger to fat accounts, he led his team to sign off both Bates and the cigarette account: "When we served notice to leave, the Chairman/CEO of Bates, Michael Bungey, had discussions with me trying to talk me out of it. Cordiant, the holding company of Bates, tried, too. But I said if I must change my mind, you (Bates) have not given me an alternative. At some point in time, they even suggested that Insight consider an affiliation with Saatchi & Saatchi, which was well represented in Africa. I said no, that MC&A was already affiliated to the agency. Why should we go there? We wanted two totally different networks. Much as they could not give me an answer, they tried desperately to find something. But I said no. Even if Bates had an office in South Africa, it was sold shortly after we left."

As his afrocentric vision of business in the 21st Century fledged, his discussions with Bates headed nowhere. The long-drawn talks with the international agency probably cost Insight the advantage of being Nigeria's first marketing communications organisation to establish a regional outpost in the West African sub-region. It lost the initiative to Omojafor's STB-McCann, which set up offices in Ghana ahead of any of its Nigerian competitors. In September, 1996 Shobanjo formally announced the break with Bates at a meeting of the Insight family. The development put paid to speculations in the grapevine on the true position of the technical partnership between both agencies. But it was carefully kept out of the press. The break with Bates, however, did not undermine the essence of Shobanjo's insistence on international technical cooperation because his business orientation, which manifested in the operations of various Troyka companies, still revolved around conscious development of the work force. This inevitably led to Insight's new affiliation with Grey Advertising, Inc, which, perhaps, was the single most controversial issue in Nigeria's advertising industry.

The new partnership with Grey Inc kicked up a lot of storm in the industry due to debates on whether Insight could legally claim an affiliation with the international agency when, as far as the public knew, Grey had a subsisting agreement with Promoserve, another local agency. At its peak in the 1990s, Promoserve Advertising Limited, which was established in 1974 by Prince Kehinde Adeosun, was unofficially ranked fifth after Insight, Lintas, STB-McCann and Rosabel respectively in the league of the Top 10 agencies in the country. The agency initially enjoyed offshore technical cooperation with Chicagobased Don Tennant & Co., Inc. The relationship ended around 1991. By 1993, Promoserve secured an 'Exclusive' affiliation with Grey International, which was established in 1917. In 1990, Grey billed $2.5 billion and had 200 offices in 40 countries. Advertising Age reported that the agency, in 1993, handled 75 multinational accounts valued at more than $5 million each. Among these were Procter & Gamble, Smithkline Beecham, British Petroleum, Turkish Airlines and a part of the British American Tobacco Company (BATCO) account. The Promoserve/Grey relationship ended in 1996 after just three years. Promoserve blamed Insight for the break of its relationship with Grey by contending that its sister local agency propositioned its international affiliate.

For Shobanjo, the meeting of Insight and Grey was purely coincidental and the resultant affiliation was the by-product of an 'unhappy' relationship between Grey and Promoserve: "Grey, for some time, had not been happy with the affiliate (Promoserve Advertising) they had, just as we were not happy with Bates. They (Grey) did not seem to be making much progress and they had given a whole lot of recommendations (to Promoserve); things that included training, relocation of office; all kinds of things. Also, Grey had tried to help the local affiliate get a slice of their multi-national clients' business here and did not seem to succeed and that was beginning to frustrate Grey because it had implications... Nigeria is such an important market that no one could say 'we do not care about the market.' But it all added up, Grey was looking, Insight was, too. Somehow, we met. That was it."

The Promoserve hierarchy did not share his viewpoint. To drive home this point, the agency initiated legal proceedings at a Lagos High Court to protect its status with Grey. Insight was joined as co-defendants, as was (then) Nigerian Tobacco Company (NTC), which had withdrawn its John Player's Gold Leaf cigarette (a BATCO brand) account from Promoserve and moved same to Insight in the spirit of the new alignment. At a personal level, Shobanjo dragged Promoserve's then Chief Executive, Allan Ola Olabode, to the Police over alleged threats of what a journalist, Akin Adeoya, described as 'spiritual warfare' and 'temporal brimstone'.

The legal tussle was, however, inconclusive, as Promoserve later withdrew the matter from court. Olabode admitted in an interview with this author that Promoserve was suicidal in losing the Grey affiliation. He also believed strongly that Insight's overtures to the international agency accelerated the process. Much later, he left Promoserve in controversial circumstances. The agency, too, went under years after several attempts to restore its initial vibrancy failed. The Insight/Grey partnership that should have come into effect on May 1, 1996, was officially announced by Shobanjo on January 9, 1997.

Incidentally, Shobanjo's enthusiasm about the Grey affiliation was initially constrained by a few personal and professional considerations. One of these concerned Olabode whose mother had died about the time discussions were in top gear between Insight and Grey. The then Promoserve Chief Executive had extended an invitation to Shobanjo to attend his mother's funeral, which, coincidentally, fell on the same weekend that Shobanjo was to travel to the United Kingdom for further talks with Grey officials. Shobanjo honoured Olabode's invitation and he flew to London on the night of the event. He was equally aware of the high probability of a misunderstanding of his agency's aspirations vis-à-vis his leadership of AAAN, which might be interpreted as an abuse of office to snatch his member's technical partner. But he knew there was not one way in which the dilemma could be quietly resolved, given that practically everyone in the business saw him as a hawk. He went ahead because the signing of the new affiliate was a 'business decision' taken by Insight's management in the best interest of the organisation and, in the long haul, for the growth of advertising in Nigeria. He reckoned that the affiliation would underscore the capacity of indigenous agencies to handle big ticket assignments from any corner of the globe.

The reaction of several advertising practitioners confirmed Shobanjo's reservations. They believed that Insight's new affiliation with Grey was too cold, too calculating and extremely provocative. The response of the practitioners was conditioned by the recurrent charge of 'conspicuous consumption' against Shobanjo, who is seen not to be sympathetic to the need for other agencies to grow in the local market.

Historically, the course of the Insight/Grey affiliation was neither new nor unusual. It was pre-dated by a similar union of an international agency, McCann Erickson and a local agency, STB & Associates (now STB-McCann), shortly after the former ended a long relationship with Grant Advertising that, from birth, was affiliated to McCann. As it were, Insight also did not make the first move towards Grey, whose senior executive, the late Ian Shepard of Grey South Africa, nominated the agency for the affiliation. This was on the strength of the quality of work that Insight had executed for some of Grey's traditional clients such as De-United Food, makers of Indomie Noodles. Some of these clients had in the past turned down suggestions to move their accounts from Insight, which then was affiliated to Bates Worldwide, to Promoserve that had a subsisting 'Exclusive Affiliate' relationship with Grey at the time. The decision of these clients to stick with Insight weighed heavily in favour of the agency in its discussions with Grey.

The union, unarguably, was one of strength. Grey brought into it a 1996 worldwide billing of $5.2 billion and 124 offices in 76 countries. From Insight came an estimated 1996 billing of nearly N380 million, staff of 128, the largest in the local industry and a 26-member blue chip clientele, with some of the relationships dating back to the founding of Insight (see table below):

CLIENT	YEAR ACCOUNT WON
CAPL	1984
CPL Industries	1987
Daewoo Automobiles	1992
De-United Foods Industries	1991
Devcom Merchant Bank	1991
Equitorial trust Bank	1991
Femina Hygienical Products	1982
Fountain Trust Merchant Bank	-
Ledrop Exports	1987
Lever Brothers	1987
Middle East Airlines	1996
Nasco Foods	1980
Nasco Management Services	1980
Nestle Foods	1983
NICON	1983
Nigerian Tobacco Company	1994
Nigerian Bag Mfg Co. [BAGCO]	1986
Peugeot Automobiles	1990
Royal United	1996
Seven-UP Bottling Company	1991
SIO Motors	1996
Soft Solutions	1996
Sollatek	1994
Sona Breweries	1982
Texaco	1989
WAMCO	1989

Insight's membership of the Grey Africa Network, yielded early results, the most noticeable being the opening of Insight Ghana early in 1997, which was in tandem with Shobanjo's long-term strategic plan that the partnership should enable Insight to tap into Grey's 'power of rank'. The new relationship also clearly put some of Shobanjo's underlying business assumptions in perspective. When, on leaving office as President of AAAN, he asked rhetorically 'what else do I want?" he left the answer dangling. The 18-word legend that is always conspicuously displayed in all his offices from Akanbi Onitiri Street to Oduduwa Street before he berthed at Troyka's corporate headquarters at Oduduwa Way quite easily demonstrates the answer to the puzzle. It served as a daily reminder of his driving ambition. It is simple, to the point and, reasonably, intended to pre-empt any controversy on the issue: "It is good to be big. It is better to be good. It is best to be both."

It also summed up his position on debates on the place of size in the operation of an agency. The relevance of size, some schools of thought have argued, is exaggerated because the measure of an agency's capacity for ground-breaking creative thinking does not reside in whether the company is big or small. For this group, big size, at best, is a balm to massage inflated egos and, at worst, a bureaucracy that kills the Muse that is the source of inspiration or original thinking. For some others, big is it. However, 'big' is not necessarily only in terms of physical size but of physical infrastructure; the depth of an agency's pocket; the quality of its creative output and the boldness with which it sells ideas, all rolled into one. Shobanjo belongs in this school of thought.

Characteristically, he made no bone of it: "With size comes strength. When you have size, you have collaterals that could be used to further actualise your dream. Today, when Insight speaks, as the Number One marketing communications company in Nigeria, there is hardly any media owner that will not listen. That's because of the sheer size. Besides, the company is better able to negotiate things for its clients, which several competitors cannot do. Thirdly, because you are good, it makes sense that you attract most of the best talents in the industry. Let us be frank about it, there is something in being a part of a winning team and, usually, a winning team is big. There is something about good people gravitating together. It is natural. Do not let anybody deceive you; no one sets out to set up a small agency. No big client goes to a small agency."

His argument is a reinforcement of the early influence of the Saatchis on his business. Like the brothers, Charles and Maurice, Shobanjo is an empire builder imbued, though less glaringly so, with the legendary 'Napoleonic instinct.' He was deeply fascinated by the single-minded determination of the Saatchi brothers to be better than most as they built their empire, which they eventually lost in the boardroom and gradually rebuilt from the ashes of their past mistakes. Indeed, the striking similarities between the Saatchis and Shobanjo and the organisations they founded cannot be missed.

The parallels are outstanding. Whereas Charles Saatchi, with whom Shobanjo had interacted a bit more, reportedly dreamt of building an agency that would last for 100 years,[1] Shobanjo aspired to lead the best outfit in Nigeria and, in the process, conquer the continent. The companies set up by the admen both took off at the beginning of a new decade: Saatchi & Saatchi in 1970, Insight in 1980. At birth, the London agency, not unlike its Lagos counterpart, was considered 'brash, bouncy and noisy.' Within 15 years of their inception, both agencies lost the services of fine support staff that played prominent roles in the growth of their business. At age 10 in 1980, Saatchi & Saatchi was Number One in billing in the UK; Insight, at age 10 in 1990 was Number Two in Nigeria.

These similarities are profound and the energy that went into

---

[1] *Kleinman, P. ix*

scripting and executing the Saatchi model in Nigeria was complemented by single-minded courage and determination to be different. Both qualities played as much crucial roles in the Shobanjo/Insight story as they did in the Saatchis'. In both cases, the men in the success stories created their own 'luck' and watered their own dreams by never letting go of whatever opportunities that came their way. Foremost Bible scholar, John C. Maxwell, described this better: "For the most part, you create your own luck by working hard, practising selfdiscipline, remaining persistent and making personal growth a daily priority. Add to that the blessings of a loving God, and you don't need to talk about luck."

While it is true that the Saatchis' and Shobanjo shared a common ground in their romance with size, they still differed somewhat. Where the Saatchi agency pursued growth through a series of Alice-in-Wonderland acquisitions, Shobanjo's Insight took the route of organic growth through high flying creativity and growing more business out of existing ones. Shobanjo and his team, however, came quite close to growth by acquisition in the early 1990s when he entered preliminary discussions with Kola Ayanwale, the Chief Executive Officer of Centrespread Advertising (later to be known as FCBCentrespread before reverting to its old name). Ayanwale had initiated the move as part of several options he considered to stave off the asphyxiation of his then young agency. The talks were later aborted. Years later, Centrespread became one of Nigeria's 'Top 10' agencies. Ayanwale received some degree of personal guidance from Shobanjo during Centrespread's quest for international technical affiliation that led to the agency's subsequent transformation to FCB-Centrespread.

Six years after the founding of Insight, Shobanjo was brought in direct contact with his professional role models when, in 1986, the Saatchis acquired Insight's offshore technical partners, Ted Bates, for

$450 million, which, for that age, was mind-blowing. Phillip Kleinman, the Saatchis' biographer, noted that the record-purchase, which shot the Saatchis to the Number One position in the world, gave birth to an acronym, S.A.A.T.C.H.I - Single Ad Agency Takes Control of Half the Industry,[1] which was coined by the American advertising industry.

The S.A.A.T.C.H.I tag would have fitted Shobanjo like a glove given his pre-occupation with size and the quality of his operation. Within the context of what Kleinman described as the Saatchis' 'Law of Dominance,' identifying Shobanjo's favourite spot would also have been a no-brainer. According to this 'Law', being First is wonderful; Second is terrific; Third is threatened while Fourth is fatal. Anything else is extinction.

In all the years that Shobanjo led Insight Communications, his perspective of the business – think global, act local – received consistent reinforcement. The sum of his professional worldview is captured by the prime position that the agency occupied (and still occupies) in the business. Insight's trading results between 1991 and 1996, for example, showed that its founders' dream of building the most sought-after marketing communications company had long been fulfilled. In 1995, the agency billed N240 million and nearly N380 million in 1996. Since that time, the results have consistently recorded quantum leap, so much so that by the end of 2003, that is, a full year to Shobanjo's exit as CEO, the agency billed over N2 billion. But for the instability of the local currency in comparison to other major international currencies, Insight's consistently improving financial reports and upper crust clientele would have placed it at par with some of the leading agencies in Europe and America. The impressive financials as well as the agency's record for producing great creative works informed Shobanjo's belief that he had nothing more to prove on the local scene. The emergence of exciting younger

---

[1] *Kleinman. P.88*

agencies that continually demonstrated strength and ambition to significantly reduce the wide creative latitude that Insight used to enjoy, however, made it impossible for the agency to lapse into lethargy. Among these agencies were TBWA/Concept; Prima Garnet; DDB Lagos and Bates Cosse. The birth of these agencies and the quality of their output significantly contributed to building the nation's advertising industry into a creative hotbed in which only the strongest could ever hope to thrive on a long-term basis.

As the 20th Century neared its end, the industry experienced tremors caused by the Federal Government's repeal of the protectionist Nigerian Enterprises Promotion Decree that previously made advertising the exclusive preserve of Nigerians. Expectedly, the deregulation of the business in 1996 created fears of an influx of well-exposed and financially strong expatriate practitioners. This, in turn, created further fears of a high probability of the movement of clients and turnover of agency personnel. The deregulation of the industry also made it appear that mergers and acquisitions would become inevitable. By contrast, the extant business model in which owner-managers seldom ceded failing personal enterprises to better managers made voluntary transfer of ownership seem a remote possibility. The outlook was not totally gloomy. There were expectations that deregulation would improve advertising practice in Nigeria, principally in terms of enhanced quality of creative outputs and agency/client relations. There also was hope that clients would, from that point, be more likely to respect trading terms. In the long term, the anticipation of change compelled agencies to review their business focus and sharpen their competitive edge so that they could be properly positioned to enter the new Millennium.

Quite unlike some of his colleagues, however, Shobanjo was not unduly alarmed by the expected influx of foreigners. From the first day of Insight he had taken a long term, holistic view of the business.

Whilst he considered deregulation to be a welcome development, he was emphatic that the extent of its implications would be felt more by practitioners who paid lipservice to training: "If a man cannot play a piano, he simply cannot play a piano regardless of whether you gave him a grand piano or any other kind. If a company has not invested in its people, I suspect it may have to pay the price."

As events later showed, much of the fears that practitioners entertained concerning deregulation did not come to pass. In particular, the anticipated invasion of Nigeria's communication market by foreigners did not happen. Shobanjo reasoned that the fears did not become real only because the foreigners were held back by Nigeria's relatively low advertising spend that could be attributed to a logical pattern of cause and effects. The low level of advertising spend is caused by extremely low media rates, which, in turn, account for the slow growth of the media. By extension, the slow-growing media cannot justifiably achieve competitive parity by hiking its rates because of low value caused by limited content and obsolete technical input.

Much of the problem can easily be attributed to the challenge of running media institutions as structured businesses in Nigeria. Most media establishments founded by practising journalists have tended to focus more on editorial issues whilst paying scant attention to the economics of production. In the 1970s and early 80s, the daily circulation of newspapers was relatively high, with Sunday Times hitting a record 500,000 copies per edition. From the 90s, however, the combined daily circulation of all newspapers declined considerably, with some of the popular titles producing well below 50,000 copies that were circulated nationwide per day. The reasons are multifarious. Readership declined steadily due to low disposable income as well as the high cost of printing input; obsolete equipment, audience fragmentation and incessant power outages that have all combined to take the bite out of both print and broadcast media. The popularity of the Internet has further compounded the problems. These have all resulted in growing ineffectiveness and high mortality rate of traditional media institutions. This, in turn, has created a new category of influencers found predominantly in the social media.

Apart from these, a host of other challenges have combined to create near absence of value in the media in Nigeria. For one, business owners invest far too little in manpower training such that few journalists can match the knowledge base of their news sources. Remuneration in the profession has remained largely uncompetitive, even if somewhat better at the top. For these reasons, many journalists tend to see their profession as a launch pad to other more financially rewarding professions. Other media platforms such as outdoor have similarly been impacted by systemic failures in the operation of their category of business as well as by poorly or ill-defined policies of government that differed from State to State and often somersaulted from administration to administration within the same State. Over the years, however, noticeable improvements were recorded in the volume of technical and manpower investment in the media. This has resulted in better produced newspapers and magazines and better programming in the broadcast media, most of which now transmit on 24hour basis. The streamlining of the operations of out-of-home agencies by the Outdoor Advertising Association of Nigeria (OAAN) as well as regulations by various advertising and signage agencies established by various State governments, particularly in Lagos State, also helped to restore some sanity in the business.

Shobanjo did not relent in his search for relevance as he made plans to usher in the new Millennium. In one swift movement, he administered 'shock therapy' that resulted in the strategic movement of Insight's top directors. The Creative Director, Ibe, moved over to Strategic Planning, the seat that was vacated by Emokpae who went to Client Service to take the place of Awosika, who became Creative Director. The deckshuffling was informed by three principal reasons: Shobanjo's stance that leaders of the business should have all-round agency management experience; his belief that his men needed to face new challenges having become 'very comfortable' doing the same jobs for years and the need to put other regular staff on their toes. The change was progressively implemented down the corporate ladder in a manner that created a trim and efficient workforce and corrected the unwholesome situation in which less than 60 per cent of the people did 100 per cent of the jobs in the agency. After a few years, Ibe moved out of mainstream advertising with his appointment as General Manager/Executive Director of Halogen Security, which was his last executive duty post before he took an early retirement from the group. For a while thereafter Emokpae doubled as Client Service/Strategic Planning Director.

Aside the lateral movements, Shobanjo outlined several objectives that would be vigorously pursued to ensure that all unit companies remained leaders in their categories and the best partners to all their clients. The roadmap to achieve this was quite simple. Central to this was that the companies must recruit and retain best talents to engender fast turnaround of briefs. This was contingent on training these talents and paying the most competitive salaries in the industry. The companies were also expected to institute efficient credit control systems; respect the terms of payment of third party suppliers; earn respect from clients and non-clients and post good returns on investment for shareholders. These were all non-negotiable conditions.

These objectives were undergirded by the Normative Values of Insight, which were also applied to all unit companies. The values placed emphasis on the workplace being a place of everyday adventure where everyone was expected to subscribe to the vision of never-ending excellence and a collective will to win. The system was intolerant of any sub-culture that did not recognise the client as king; it frowned at attempts to breed prima donnas instead of team players and it did not harbour people who generated or spread negative vibes. Rather than being diminished by the tolls of years of operation or the loss and recruitment of several seasoned practitioners, the Group has continued to wax stronger. This was possible because the form and content of the Normative Values remained consistent with the letter and spirit of the blueprint for the founding of the Group. Troyka is proud of its people - past or present - and it is proud of people who are passionate about the adventure. At Troyka, a leader must be worthy of being so regarded in every sense because the buck effectively stopped at his table. Rule Number One is to keep the vision intact so as to keep the adventure on track. This is in tandem with one of Shobanjo's strongest management beliefs that people in the creative business must consistently be encouraged, not spoilt, to keep raising the bar of performance. As he likes to say, people who help to bake the cake should also eat out of it.

Perhaps the one dark spot in Shobanjo's well-laid out plans for life before the turn of the century was the absence of a definite successor at Insight. All, including him, were agreed that finding the right person to assume the leadership of the agency would pose a big problem. In the past, many had made the mistake of assuming that either of Ibe or Awosika, both being co-founders of the company, would automatically take over the administration of Insight whenever Shobanjo retired. Although both men are widely acknowledged brilliant professionals who could hold their own against anyone in the industry, neither was originally in line for the Number One slot. Stranger still was the attitude of both men to the issue. Ibe did not think of succession in terms of either himself or Awosika but in terms of anyone who could deliver as best as Shobanjo. Although Awosika considered himself as serving a 'life sentence' at Insight, he did not see himself as someday becoming the boss. At the time, Shobanjo, too, was emphatic that neither would succeed to the throne, more so as Ibe and Awosika were well-accommodated in the structure of the holding company, Troyka. Either of the two could easily succeed Shobanjo as Chairman, an office that is more supervisory than gladiatorial.

One key reason for the exclusion of Ibe and Awosika from the original power equation was that neither man got any younger. Shobanjo is a firm believer in young people. The future of advertising, like those of other businesses, he liked to emphasise, belongs to the young who are experienced, bold and restless; who usually worked smarter with the best of technology and who have fiercely competitive mindsets. For him, young professionals usually have style and flair, which are qualities that the old brigade either tend to take for granted or have problems coming to terms with.

Setting up Troyka as a holding company was not a mere 'business decision' taken as part of natural progression in a corporate life. It was a game-changing strategy taken, among other considerations, to manage the multiple streams of income that had been created for the group. It was also informed by a personal resolution. With the birth of Troyka, Shobanjo began a gradual process of 'stepping aside' from the daily chores of running Insight. As the chairman of Troyka, his job was no longer Insight-specific though he was, understandably, attached to the agency. In the new order, he had an enlarged portfolio that required helping all the unit companies attain the objectives for which they had been set up. His transition programme, however, received a rude shock in 1993 when Onabolu, the heir apparent to the throne of Insight, unexpectedly resigned to prepare ground for the establishment of his own business, Cossé Limited, an integrated marketing company.

Onabolu was one of the bright young people that were recruited in the 1980s to join the agency's search for a pathway in the business wilderness. When the former broadcaster, joined Insight in 1982 and rapidly rose through the ranks, Shobanjo could hardly contain his excitement. "Thank God, we found him," he exclaimed to himself. Onabolu, a 1978 graduate of Literature in English from the University of Ife (now Obafemi Awolowo University), like Shobanjo, is a perfectionist; almost a Shobanjo clone. Both men have simple, good taste and they are genuinely warm, extremely neat and very well organised. Quite naturally, Shobanjo took the younger man under his wings and it was clear to all that the Crown Prince had emerged.

He did so well he became Insight's first General Manager. Everyone was shocked when he resigned; Shobanjo the more so. He simply told Onabolu: "please, just don't let's talk about this." Onabolu's decision to leave effectively threw Shobanjo's phased withdrawal from active advertising into reverse gear. He promptly got back in line. For about two years, he and Onabolu did not discuss the latter's disengagement. Much of the time in-between was spent plugging likely disruptions in the system. In 1995, Shobanjo reluctantly let him go, though he still refused to accept his letter of resignation. He still finds Onabolu's resignation quite baffling: "Maybe he was scared, maybe he thought the shoes would be too big for him. I don't know."

He should know. Onabolu was bitten by the same bug that possessed his former boss. He, too, needed to define himself both as a man and as a professional. The younger man chose to throw away so much promise to realise himself, just as Shobanjo did many years before.

Between 1995 and 1999 a host of other young professionals in the house were put through the leadership crucible. Nobody was sure of where Shobanjo would eventually pick his successor, particularly because he was known to be as favourably disposed to making his choice from within as he was from without. The one snag was whether, given the corporate wanderlust that is the hallmark of young, upwardly mobile professionals, the probable successor would stay long enough to justify the confidence. The fear of 'desertion' was, therefore, a critical issue in his succession planning programme: "People being groomed do not even know; they check out before you finish and thus break the rhythm."

Owing to this concern, he began to look a bit more inwards for solution. In October 1999, the company's board approved Shobanjo's appointment as Executive Vice Chairman/CEO, with Awosika as Managing Director. They both officially wore their new ranks in the new Millennium, as their appointments became effective on 3 January, 2000. Awosika, however, assumed full control of the agency in January 2005 when he became Managing Director and Chief Executive Officer. But his elevation was a means, not the 'end,' in Insight's long-term succession plan. One of Shobanjo's commissions to Awosika was that he must replicate himself by producing at least five possible successors to take charge of Insight in the years to come. In the end, a dark horse, Feyi Olubodun, claimed the prize in 2015 when he was announced as Insight's Chief Operating Officer.

In October 2016, he was appointed Managing Director/CEO, by which he became Insight's first non-owner manager in 36 years. In December 2018, the agency appointed Dr. Tendai Mhizha as its first female Managing Director in succession to Olubodun who left the company.

For the other unit companies in the group, Shobanjo did not nurse any fear because they were already being run by some of the most brilliant minds that abound in their diverse fields. The performance of the group, which posted an estimated N17 billion turnover in 2006, bears testimony to the can-do spirit of Troyka executives. Except for one or two companies that were being turned around for better performance, each of the Troyka unit companies is Number One in its sector.

In planning for succession, the possibility of the children of the founders of Insight/Troyka, especially Shobanjo's, joining the group in executive capacity did not feature for strong consideration. As it turned out, too, his children, for diverse reasons, were not keen on pursuing careers in marketing communications. His first child, Babatunde, for instance, was quite mindful of the challenge of following the footsteps of a high-achieving father: "I avoided advertising as much as possible because of who my father is; knowing that people would say 'ah, you're next in line'; knowing the big shoes that must be filled and knowing the comparison that would come with it."

His younger brother, Olufemi, avoided advertising for different reasons that bordered more on personal vision and personality traits: "I just was not interested. From a very young age, I had always wanted to be a business person. You have to be a certain kind of person to go into marketing communications; you have to have the DNA; you have to be an extrovert. I am a more reserved person; more calculating and far more a core business person."

Whatever their individual reasons for not following the professional footsteps of their father, Shobanjo's children are acutely aware that attaining high office in Troyka Holdings would never fall on their lap as a matter of course. Dolapo explained the reason: "He has always made it clear that whatever he had set up he did not create for us. He did not build any of these for us to carry on. He would say: 'This is mine, not yours; so, don't think this is your inheritance. If you want to work in advertising, go work for someone else and if you are so good, we will come and employ you'"

Her viewpoint reinforced the dream of the founders of Insight, who, at the stage of the agency's conception, never defined the company as a family business. And, as the dayto-day administration of Troyka unit companies has shown, Shobanjo would rather entrust the companies to people who are passionate about the business, than to people who would achieve leadership only because they were offspring of the owners, which is mere accident of history. Olufemi, in his younger days, did not understand his father's line of reasoning because in most other Nigerian businesses the career path of the enterprise owner's offspring was quite easily mapped out: school, little work experience, then, executive position in the family business. With age, education, enlightenment and international work exposure, he more clearly understood his father's perspective: "He is a global thinker who operates in a local space; he is always thinking of new ways to do a lot of things. He recognised that the most successful enterprises are usually not run by family members to avoid mixing sentiments with performance and to continually attract and retain best talents. If I have a company, I will adopt the same approach."

Despite carefully laid out plans, it was impossible to completely sidestep bloodlines. The 'Crown Prince', Babatunde, could not escape the pull of marketing communications. His foray into advertising was as accidental as his father's entry into the industry through Grant. Although his educational background was in Business Administration, he chose to cast his net in the advertising industry in the US at a time the world's economy was in a recession in the mid-2000s. He applied to fill a vacant finance position in a

Chicago-based agency, Dimeo & Company, a black agency that closed shop in 2010 but the firm's chief executive who interviewed him had other ideas. The CEO encouraged him to try out core advertising account management for about a month and, if he did not like it, to return to bean counting. Although Babatunde had deliberately avoided the advertising business because of his father's landmark achievements back home, he took to it like fish in water and worked in the agency for two years before relocating to Nigeria. His new-found love of advertising put his father in a dilemma, as he had not planned for any of his children to work at Insight. The elder Shobanjo advised the young man to first seek employment in another reputable advertising agency to gain the kind of experience that he would need to qualify for recruitment by Insight. Awosika disagreed.

He insisted that Shobanjo should allow him to train Babatunde in much the same way that he had understudied his boss since their days at Grant. Even at this, Babatunde still had to demonstrate passion for the business as well as knowledge, skills and experience that he could bring to bear on the company. The younger Shobanjo was not surprised because he already knew that his father would never bend the rules regardless of the international exposure that ordinarily could have justifed his employment by Troyka. At work, being the Group Chairman's son did not confer any special advantage on Babatunde as a staff of Insight. Instead, it made him more vulnerable to the pressure of his professional competence being compared with his father's. He knew this was inescapable: "I welcome the comparison because it sets standards that I have to achieve. It does not bother me to think that I have to do this and that exactly like him. Character-wise, I have assumed my own personality. People see this and they see that I am also learning in the industry. In age, I am still young and I am still young in the industry, so there is still time to start making my own prints and name in the industry."

As we have said, Shobanjo's personal philosophy is hinged on being the best in whatever he did. When this is extended to the corporate level, the meaning is self-evident: Insight and all unit companies in Troyka Holdings must be the Number One frame of reference in their respective fields. The ground for achieving the objective was laid with the dream of entering the Millennium with a roar. Nearly two decades into the new Millennium, Shobanjo's original dream has certainly become bigger, better and bolder. Troyka companies have remained best of class: they post impressive results year-on-year and they are globally recognised. Often, clients, old and new, talked to them first and they have all won creative and enterprise awards within and outside the shores of Nigeria. Best of all, Troyka people, including the Group's former staff, live the dream that propelled Shobanjo into making a career in advertising: they are very well-trained; they make meaningful professional contributions to shaping the direction of growth of the marketing communications industry in Nigeria and, as reward, they live the good life.

Shobanjo discovered these new oceans only because he had the boldness and presence of mind to lose sight of the shore.

10

You Need People With Strong Hearts

No creative organisation...
will produce a great body of work
unless it is led by a formidable individual.

David Ogilvy (1911 - 1999)

Insight has been credited with the fastest growth in the history of advertising in Nigeria. The success of the agency, especially in its first decade, was signposted by the consistent upward thrust of its creative portfolio and the magnetic attraction of quality human capital from within and outside the industry. Year-on-year, the young agency matched its determination to emerge as Nigeria's foremost marketing communications company with impressive financial ratios that underscored its founders' readiness to take on any 'giant' in the market. In its first full financial year ended December 31, 1980 Insight billed N1.5 million, which spiraled to N53.9 million 1990, the agency's 10th year. Even in an industry that is grossly notorious for shrouding vital statistics in great mystery, it is difficult to fault

Shobanjo's description of the agency's accelerated growth at that period as closely resembling 'the sharp scarp of a mountain.'

In its 11th year in 1991, Insight nudged the leading agency, Lintas, off the industry's top spot with a billing of N88 million, compared with the older agency's N85 million and, tellingly, Grant's N10 million, which placed Shobanjo's former agency in a distant seventh position. Much of that success owed to the agency's ability to work with clients to identify or even create new markets as well as deploy the right people to execute ideas that add value to the business of its clients.

The 'magic' of Insight and Shobanjo was not just in working to add value to clients but in helping media platforms to step up to the plate. The agency was always willing to buy ideas that media owners could conceive, develop and diligently execute. Back in the day, Kano Broadcasting Corporation enjoyed very high patronage from Insight and other agencies that it came up with the idea of 24-hour television and AM/FM radio broadcasts to take advantage of the boon. The success of the initiatives resulted in excess airtime that compelled the management of the station to explore various options to turn the challenge into a goldmine. The management turned to Insight to take up the extra volume since, through its transactions with the station, it had demonstrated strong capacity to do so. The agency agreed but the station eventually could not fulfil its part of the bargain owing to difficulty in managing the logistics of round-the-clock transmission.

As Kankarofi testified: "Whereas other agencies were a bit conservative, Insight did things differently; they were daring marketers; if they believed in anything, they went after it. They didn't want to discuss with you from behind a desk; they were not armchair theorists. Their Account Officers visited me regularly and we went through markets to conduct surveys."

Positive testimonials as this in the early days led to unsolicited recommendation of Insight by media managers in various establishments each time prospective clients sought their opinions on the agency they loved to work with. In many ways, this greatly softened ground for client solicitations by the agency, although it often was not aware of who recommended it to business prospects that knocked on its door.

The agency's assumption of industry leadership and, by extension, Shobanjo's path to the top, in no small measure validates the axiom that there is a natural correlation between an agency's performance and its leadership,[1] as postulated by globally renowned advertising guru, David Ogilvy. This view aligns with the big business management notion that colourless individuals almost always lead stuck-in-the-middle enterprises whilst their more successful counterparts are seen to be led by swashbuckling predators. These perspectives are no different from Shobanjo's personal belief that corporate or individual 'leadership' is not passed down as unquestioned inheritance but is earned when aspiration is supported with the investment of the right amount of focus, skills and determination. The sum of these postulations is that an organisation will only be as successful as the quality of the vision of its leader, the attitude and passion that drive the vision and the extent to which everyone in the establishment can internalise the vision and give it life on the field of play.

Understanding the trajectory of his route to the top will help to make the explanation simpler considering that he did not follow the conventional path to the C-Suite. Traditionally, upcoming Chief

---

[1] *Confessions of an Advertising Man*

Executives rise through series of promotions to disparate internal job responsibilities that expose them to key units needed to help their general understanding of the business. This helicopter view then positions them to know something about everything in the organisation. At Grant Advertising, Shobanjo had a one-leap elevation from the relatively junior position of a Senior Account Executive, to which he had risen by 1974, to the position of a member of the Board of the agency in 1976 before he celebrated his 32nd birthday. At 33, he was Deputy Managing Director of the agency.

Although his elevation was fast paced and the gap he needed to cover in the hierarchy was significant, he managed his transition from a supervised executive to a management strategist within five short years by immersing himself in a quest to acquire knowledge as fast as he could. The personal challenge became necessary because he knew there was little time to 'learn on the job,' which meant that success or failure depended more on him than on external factors. He listened to and tapped into the experience of people who had held similar positions, so they could guide him. He also delivered results in the same focused manner with which he had always been known since his days in secondary school. He had the extra boost of being sent to the McCann Erickson London office for hands-on training on how the business was managed.

In many ways, his life exemplified the thesis of management theorist, Horatio Alger, that hard work could facilitate a determined young person's climb to a career peak from a zero base. Without the luxury of university certification, he was propelled by his determination to excel and he stretched himself to be the best in his field by consistently redefining the rules of the game, knowing that competition never went to bed. He was a self-made man who, with a team of brilliant young minds, created his own 'luck'. Like Sir Richard

Branson of the Virgin Group and Sir Alan Sugar, the founder of Amstrad, he started from scratch with little or no start-up capital but with hard work and determination and by envisioning and remaining ruthlessly focused on his creation, he rose to the top.

Babu Akinbobola's first person experience of Shobanjo's consuming passion for excellence graphically illustrates the latter's success at managing people and ideas: "I remember that early in 1978 I worked on one of his accounts, Brytex, a washing powder produced by Nasco. I recollect receiving a memo from him asking me to plan a media campaign for the client. We had started a campaign up North, which the client wanted to extend southward. The memo stated clearly that the client wanted to spend N200,000, which, in 1978, was much. I planned the campaign and gave it to him. He was not impressed. I wondered why that was so. He then asked if I must restrict myself to the client's N200,000. He asked me to plan an ideal campaign for the client. I remember I went back to my office not very pleased with myself. I decided to be mischievous. I re-planned the campaign, this time recommending N800,000. What surprised me was that he said nothing when I gave him the revised plan. Instead of rebuking me, he asked me to defend certain things I had recommended. He then went to Jos, where the client's office was located, came back, opened my door and tossed the schedule with a memo on my desk. I saw a funny glint in his eyes. When I opened the memo, I was surprised...the client approved N600,000!"

By age 35, experience had taught Shobanjo that in the 'natural progression' of things, leadership is best attained and enjoyed when an individual is fully prepared to seamlessly assume a dream position, not when it is thrust on him by circumstances. By this time, too, he had long concluded that complacency was dangerous to leadership, which is not a destination but a never-ending journey. All through his career, he held down various positions of authority and responsibility by mirroring success and working hard at achieving it. His vision of excellence was personified by Dr Christopher Kolade who was his former boss at NBC. It never mattered that he did not have the privilege of working with him at close quarters in Broadcasting House: "He was too far ahead of me (so) there was no basis for (one-on-one) interactions. For me as a young man, he was just an incredible man. I was amazed at the way he conducted meetings and moderated discussions. Although he started out in educational broadcasting, he developed himself in all aspects of the job, rising to become the Director of Programmes; he critiqued every aspect of a programme, from the technical to the practical; his contributions were fantastic. From his tone of voice to the quality of his interventions to his dressing he was a total man. He did not indict but he advised whoever the professional was that handled an assignment under review. When he needed to be firm, he was firm. He proved that a leader must add value and that things must be done in a proper way."

His ability to quickly adapt to the exacting demands of leadership since 1976 can be attributed to what could loosely be described as innate instinct, which no volume of books or training in an academy can adequately teach. This involves an ability to react to things much faster than most people could and it entails an ability to harness the inherent energy and knowledge of every member of his team. It refers to his ability to see farther than most people whilst moving on to seize opportunity where most people were stopped by perceived obstacles. Most important, it refers to the ability to lead oneself by staying the course in every circumstance, particularly during inclement weather when failure to meet set goals could be excused after showing ample evidence of having 'tried' one's best. In his worldview, individuals become nearly prescient by the consistency with which they tap into their inner strengths and the experiences of other people to match their ambition to conquer new frontiers.

As a motivator, Shobanjo believes in making room for his subordinates to feel loved, wanted and appreciated. A young graphic artist, Olumide Ayeni, discovered this side of his employer when he was assigned a 'Chairman's brief' just about a week after he joined Insight in 2006. As he resumed for work, his supervisor, Kayode Tejumola a.k.a 'Tej', called him aside and handed him the assignment, the importance of which he underscored in a light-hearted yet serious manner: "This is your baptism of fire. If you get it right, you stay with us; if not, you might face the gate." A day after Ayeni received the brief, Shobanjo walked into the Finished Arts Unit of the Creative Department. His first words reverberated in the quiet office: "Who's working on my brief sent in yesterday?"

All hands simultaneously pointed in the direction of Ayeni. The Chairman pulled a chair and sat next to the artist who had already thought up a million ways by which he might be skinned alive. Beyond a few suggestions for improvement, Shobanjo okayed the job on-the-spot. The more experienced staff were happy that the new hire scaled through the hurdle. Days after, Ayeni received a 'thank you' message for a job well done and a gift delivered by Shobanjo's Personal Assistant, Gloria Omoregie. The young man never forgot the experience, which not only boosted his confidence to interface with anyone but gave him the courage to be more creatively daring. For Shobanjo, no gesture is too big or too small to serve as a force for motivation. This point, he, again, proved after a AAAN convention in Jos where he disembarked from a flight, just so he could make room for a member of his staff that could not secure a seat on the same flight. The seemingly 'small' act reinforces the perception of Shobanjo as a true leader, not a boss. But then, this is no small thing considering, as erstwhile Saatchi & Saatchi helmsman, Louis Dreyfuss, observed, that the problems with advertising are bloated egos and finding the right people. All else is common sense.

In advertising's knowledge-driven environment, Shobanjo challenges assumptions and questions ideas in the firm belief that adding value to every idea would help achieve the common goal of building brands that win consistently in the marketplace. Although he is primarily a client service person, he authoritatively speaks the language of finance and strategy, just as he is unsparing in his critique of creative concepts. He is never afraid of ruffling feathers in the contest of ideas because of his firm belief that creativity is helped when the playing field is level for the ventilation of all manner of ideas:

"Ego has no place in a creative environment; you must leave your ego at home or at the gate to the office each day so that when your idea is subjected to rigorous debate you do not feel that your person is under attack. It does not matter whether you are the team leader or the subordinate; we challenge assumptions because we always seek the best solutions to every challenge."

Whether at Grant or at Insight, Shobanjo effectively stamped his authority; people who could not conform were free to leave and those who chose to stay were required to adapt to the music that continually changed according to the mood of the times. In his estimation, the critical element of success is that leadership must never be in doubt: "I was hungry for success; I had a piece of job to do; I needed to show leadership in every sense of the word and across all departments. There was no room for sentiments. The corporate environment was conducive but what was also not in doubt was that we were the leaders of the business."

But the downside of leadership hurts. Insight's superlative performance raised quite a lot of eyebrows in the advertising industry, with practically everyone having an opinion on the way the agency operated and on the modus operandi of its vision driver. Some were verbalised; others were passed down as after-dinner stories. The tales were often far too juicy and far too compelling to be kept off the pages of newspapers and there was no short supply of 'credible' sources to feed the media frenzy. A gossip columnist with Lagos Weekend,[1] a once highly-popular Lagos-based racy tabloid, found the tales too irresistible to be kept away from its readers: "The Managing Director of one advertising company, which celebrated its decade of practice in Nigeria, is gradually losing his integrity among his clients. Earpiece (the newspaper's gossip column) gathered that he took some amount of money to the Managing Director of a multinational company also in Nigeria, who walked him out of his office. He lost his face (sic). Earpiece also gathered that he has acquired a (Mercedes Benz) V-Boot and a BMW for his personal use and (Peugeot) 505 for his managers. His company shares the same premises with one of their clients, an Indian concern, which cut their advertisement budget by half because of the company's show of wealth."

Even if the publication did not mention names, it left enough clues to guide its readers to identify the subject of the piece with pinpoint accuracy. At the time, Insight was located at Plot 58 Akanbi Onitiri Close, which also housed the administrative headquarters of the agency's client, Sona Breweries. Shobanjo had also just acquired a Mercedes Benz and a BMW, which were the rave of the time. But the seemingly authoritative tattle led to suit number LD/1279/90 that Shobanjo filed at a Lagos High Court to redeem his reputation that had been sullied by the publication. The Daily Times Group, publishers of Lagos Weekend, offered to settle out of court to head

---

[1] *Earpiece, Lagos Weekend, 27 April, 1990, p.9*

off an expensive libel suit. Settlement was also largely made possible by personal apologies tendered by then Editor of the newspaper, Chinaka Fynecontry.

Rather than be diminished by the negative picture painted of him, Shobanjo reinforced his determination to succeed by never letting any good opportunity to slip by. His tenacity of purpose caused the corporate world to take more interest in his every move as evidenced by the outcome of the 1991 pitch for the First Bank Plc account.

Century-old First Bank is a beautiful bride to be courted by any gutsy creative agency. It is blue chip and its advertising budget is a game changer. Prior to the 1991 pitch, the business had made the rounds of a few agencies. In the early 1980s, it was in the custody of Rocke-Forte Advertising where informed observers credited it with high-voltage creativity that was considerably watered down when the account moved to PAL between 1987 and 1990. The period of account movement from Rocke-Forte to PAL also coincided with the change in the bank's leadership from Samuel Asabia to Oluwole Adeosun. 1990 ushered in a new CEO, Emmanuel Olisambu, who saw need to reform the establishment and stamp his own corporate vision and authority on it. The bank's marketing communications platform was one of the starting blocks for reform, for which reason the account was put in play. The advertising industry went into a wild spin because of the N20 million billing that was at stake.[1]

Fourteen gladiators lined up for a straight fight for the First Bank business. Included in the line up were PAL, the incumbent agency; Lawson Thomas Colleagues (LTC); Lintas; OBM; Insight; Rosabel; Macsell Associates; MC & A; SO & U and Grant. Five of the agencies, Rosabel, Insight, MC & A, PAL and Macsell, made it to Round Two. When the curtain was drawn on the pitch, only three agencies succeeded: MC & A, which was assigned new products; Rosabel, which got old products and Insight, which was to be responsible for corporate advertising.

The combined strength of the Troyka companies, Insight and MC & A, gave the Group a bigger chunk of the First Bank account. Their success, however, gave Shobanjo a king-size headache because the pitch gave rise to some of the juiciest adland gossips concerning him. No sooner had the results become public knowledge than the grapevine went into over-drive with news that 'Insight' (MC & A was not too readily associated with Shobanjo) succeeded on the strength of a sleek Daewoo Racer saloon car that Shobanjo allegedly bought for Olisambu's wife. A host of practitioners could almost swear they saw the vehicle, just so they could prove the story was true. Shobanjo was alerted to the spreading Daewoo Racer rumour when Olisambu raised the issue with him at a public gathering on Lagos Island. His embarrassment was two-fold: it was the first time he heard the story one-on-one and his source was a would-be client.

Sources at First Bank, however, explained that all three winners, MC & A, Insight and Rosabel, merited high scores in terms of the relevance of the business solutions they proffered to the bank's problems as well as their confident professional presentations. This contrasted with the situation in which one of the major agencies that pitched the business dropped valuable points because of awful time keeping owing to the lateness of the agency's team to the venue of the presentation.

In the end, the Troyka companies only nibbled at the First Bank account because the budget for the promotion of treasury products far outstripped that for trumpeting corporate values. This slant aligned with Olisambu's preference for talking more about service offering than the corporate self. In 1994, Rosabel gained an upper hand on the First Bank business with its highly successful handling of the bank's centennial celebrations, which was generally applauded for the skilful execution of its creative idea.

Shobanjo's ability to remain unaffected when making hard-headed decisions probably rates as one of the most easily misunderstood aspects of his life. If he must, he would not hesitate to fire a staff at the point at which he is drinking coffee or beer with the individual because he is especially wary of colleagues who, to use his favourite expression, see themselves as 'the greatest thing God created on earth after sliced bread.' He deals analytically with people and issues and with so much clinical precision that he is deemed to be too ruthless. But the results of his decisions have almost always proved him right, as evidenced by the focused implementation of some of his game plans in early 1991 when all calculations on growth had changed as Insight rapidly climbed the leadership ladder. If the agency was to realise its founders' ambition of being truly different from the others in the market, it was strategically imperative that its management kept faith with the founding philosophy of being big in size, scope and quality. Doing this, however, required that the lessons acquired during 'apprenticeship' working with 'small' clients be reviewed and activated to make room for meeting the challenge of working with 'bigger' ones.

The first casualty was Cocoa Industries Ltd, makers of Vitalo, the brand that gave Insight its break in 1981. Insight reluctantly let go of Vitalo in 1983 to promote Nestle's Milo. This followed the outcome of exploratory discussions with Nestle's management at the instance of the Senior Product Manager, Chris Ogbechie, who had approached the agency in 1983 with an offer to handle its food drink, Milo. The success of the meeting between the managements of Insight and Nestle also culminated in the agency being offered other accounts with which Insight created market leadership paths for two infant formula, Cerelac and Nutrend, as well as Chocomilo and Nescao. As it were, the experience gained working on Vitalo was part of the learning curve that Insight relied upon to perform much better on the bigger accounts that landed on its portfolio. Limca would follow this same path years later.

In the late 1980s, the carbonated drinks market held a lot of prospects that excited Insight, which, at the time was the custodian of the Limca soft drinks account. The bad news was that Limca held little prospects for real growth beyond its lime and lemon and Gold Spot orange brands. Limca suffered the disadvantage of being without a cola brand in a cola-dominated market. In practical terms, this meant that growth for brand Limca and, by extension, Insight, could, at best, only be marginal over an indeterminable number of years. The good news, on the other hand, was that there were bigger and more established players in the market, notably Coca-Cola and Seven-Up Bottling Company (SBC) that were in search of creative and innovative agencies. Of the two, SBC held brighter prospects because it had just obtained the Pepsi-Cola franchise and, consequently, had a bigger marketing canvas that could be utilised to challenge Coca-Cola's market dominance.

SBC's determination to pick market shares off Coca-Cola worked to Insight's strategic advantage. The arrival of Faysal Halabi, a Lebanese advertising practitioner, mid-October 1986 to assume office as SBC's General Manager (Corporate Affairs) was a bonus. Halabi came to Nigeria after working in Dubai for more than ten years with a mindset to work with an agency that could best match SBC's resolve to vigorously push its various brands in the marketplace. As part of his induction programme, he visited several advertising agencies including Insight where, for the first time, he met Jimi Awosika and Shobanjo. For the next five years, 1986 – 1991, and notwithstanding the outcome of Halabi's professional visitations, SBC continued to work with various agencies on ad-hoc basis. Halabi and Shobanjo would again meet at the Nigerian Music Awards (NMA) organised by the Performing Musicians Association of Nigeria (PMAN). By some coincidence, SBC won one of the main awards of the night, which was presented by Shobanjo on behalf of PMAN and was received by Halabi on behalf of SBC.

As the years rolled by, 'good' problems arose that completely swamped SBC's Corporate Affairs Division with work to produce not just year-long creative brand advertising and merchandising but several consumer promotions, dealers' promotions and music concerts just months apart. SBC clearly needed external help. Without throwing up the business for a pitch, SBC turned to Insight for support and appointed it as the agency of records in September 1991. This was in the strong belief that Insight had the capacity to produce creative solutions that could turn the table against competition in the marketplace. Insight, in turn, took on the challenge on the strength of the clarity of SBC's objectives and the promise of bountiful harvest on delivery. SBC and Limca, however, represented conflicting interests that could not co-exist in the agency's portfolio. Insight resultantly resigned its long relationship with Limca and for more than 25 years thereafter has consistently serviced SBC as a key account that has continued to wax stronger year-on-year.

Between 1991 and the dawn of the Millennium, SBC and Insight produced some of the most remarkable marketing campaigns in Nigeria. The agency provided creative support services wherever SBC needed to make compelling statements to push up sales volume and brand recognition. From urban centres to rustic neighbourhoods, the collaboration was borderless. SBC, in conjunction with Insight and a plethora of independent show promoters and marketing consultants, also utilised every platform, from creative advertising to sales promotions and merchandising to sports and to the hosting of music concerts, to take the market by storm. The agency worked with SBC to launch several game-changing campaigns that included 7-Up Hi-Life consumer promo; the Mirinda Orangemen and 7-Up Fido Dido. Publicity for the Pepsi University Football championship and, much later, the Pepsi Football Academy pushed the initiatives to public consciousness just as the programmes contributed immensely to nurturing young football stars that eventually dorned the national colours. In April 1993, SBC played host to 14 international and four Nigerian wrestlers that included some of the most popular matsmen of the time, notably Mighty Igor, Big Tex McKenzie, Dick 'The Bulldog' Brower, Mil Mascara, Argentina Appolo and Power Mike. The campaign that announced the event helped to pack the National Stadium in Lagos full of wrestling fans and further glamourised the game that had gained significant following on television.

Way back in 1989, SBC began to re-define out-of-home entertainment when it signed a three-year contract for the sponsorship of Lekki Sunsplash, a Christmas-time beach party in Lagos. The event then was playround to megastar artistes like afro-beat legend, Fela; reggae icon, Ras Kimono and fuji music maestro, Ayinde Wasiu (KWAM 1, later to be known simply as K1). By the 1990s, Pepsi Music Concerts had become 'must attend' events. At various times the company signed on notable crowd-pulling international and local entertainment stars that included Yvonne Chaka Chaka from South Africa; SNAPP from the US as well as Majek Fashek and Shina Peters from Nigeria, among others to entertain at packed-venues in key cities like Lagos, Port Harcourt and Ibadan. SBC invaded the rural areas and crowded streets with generators, projectors and big screens to show movies and musical performances by renowned artistes like Tina Turner, Lionel Richie, Michael Jackson and several others.

However, plans to work alongside Pepsi International to bring the late King of Pop, Michael Jackson, to Nigeria as part of a nine-city world tour did not materialise because of cost and considerations for the personal safety of the international artiste and other issues of logistics. As Halabi explained: "We thought about how to implement the idea (of bringing Michael Jackson to Nigeria). In the end, we dropped the idea but more because the Naira lost so much against international currencies."

In these efforts, the imprint of Insight and other Troyka companies was hard to miss. Halabi was effusive in his praise of the group's successful handling of the SBC account over the years. He also specially recognised the individual contributions of the vision drivers, Shobanjo and Awosika, in the success of the agency/client relationship: "After trying all the other agencies, if you gave Insight 10:10, the others will be 5:10 or 6:10. That's my experience. I'm not talking of the small boys but of the big boys of advertising. Shobanjo and Jimi (Awosika) are Professors. They not only create ideas; they are masters of implementation."

The ringing endorsement of Insight's handling of the SBC account by Halabi should, however, not suggest that the client/agency relationship was free of slippages. There were occasional flashpoints that bordered on the agency's inability to meet some deadlines for deliverables. Those times brought forth the essential Shobanjo as a General who leads his troops from the front. Halabi recalled: "We once had a campaign for a promotion and Insight delivered late in the evening what they were to have delivered by 2pm. I sparked at the timing and the creative idea. Biodun Shobanjo said: "give me 48 hours to fix it." When they did, it was wow! He knows what to do and he knows how to handle his clients very well, which was good for me."

At the launch of Insight, Shobanjo and his team eyed Nigerian Breweries Plc (NB), a truly bluechip company that had a significant number of Nigeria's leading brands in its stable. Shobanjo's meetings with key members of the company's management including then CEO, Felix Ohiwerei, did not yield any positive result, as the company stuck to its traditional agencies: Lintas, which serviced Star lager beer, Heineken beer and Maltina; OBM, which handled Gulder beer, Nigeria's first premium lager beer and Macsell Associates, which joined the list with the launch of Legend Extra Stout, a product formulated to compete with the market leader, Guinness Extra Stout. Although there were speculations that Insight was kept at bay by Nigerian Breweries because of a standing instruction by a big wig owing to fears that the agency would 'corrupt' managers of the company, concrete evidence could not be obtained to confirm the existence of the order. But some heads of traditional NB agencies appeared to have been aware of the existence of an unwritten rule. One of them boasted repeatedly to his staff that he was certain Insight would never secure a brief from NB Plc. Time proved him wrong.

The reluctance of Nigerian Breweries to do business with Insight did not deter Shobanjo and his team. They went after the lesser known Sona Breweries, brewers of Gold Lager Beer and Wilfort Dark Ale in the strong belief that Insight would need the experience to achieve its longer-term plan of some day working for Nigerian Breweries. It turned out to be the beginning of an apprenticeship programme that would last 20 years after the founding of the agency.

The outlook changed in late 1999 when Nigerian Breweries invited Insight alongside all retained agencies to pitch its business as part of a comprehensive business review to optimise its entire operations. The across-board review, which was undertaken by the company's Cost Optimisation Team (COT), was directed at all service vendors including hospitals, banks, transporters, raw materials/petroleum products suppliers and marketing communications agencies. The goal of the exercise was to retain the services of best-in-class vendors to save money that would further be re-invested into running the business. Through the activities of the Cost Optimisation Team, Nigerian Breweries saved huge sums of money, part of which was expended on the production of the highly successful new bottle of Star Lager beer and the advertising campaign to launch it.

The size of the marketing communications assignment was too tempting for any serious agency to ignore because NB's corporate and product portfolios were all in play. The brief clearly stated that creative interpretation of NB's business, the quality of an agency's workforce as well as the state of its infrastructure would be major parameters of assessment. Insight was ecstatic about being invited to pitch. They were not fazed by the fact that they did not enjoy the historical advantage of working on any NB brand. On the contrary, they banked heavily on prospects of offering fresh perspectives that the incumbent agencies might lack. Deep down, however, Shobanjo and his people were a bit unsettled.

The source of their worry was the debilitating state of the neighbourhood in which the agency was located. Akanbi Onitiri Street, off the popular Eric Moore Road in Surulere, Lagos was a serene business location at the time Insight relocated to the area. But the street had become a jungle of sorts by the time it looked certain that the agency would be invited to pitch the NB account.

Scores of trailers had taken over the street, all lined up to offload several metric tonnes of sugar at Tate Nigeria, a local sugar producing company. Vehicular traffic in and out of the street was severely constrained by broken down trailers or by articulated vehicles entering or backing out of the warehouse that was almost directly opposite Insight. The street had lost the allure of a corporate environment. Instead, it bore the heavy stamp of artisans at work: there was too much noise; there was too much grease, there was too much emission of carbon monoxide by old trailers and there was an assortment of scrap metals everywhere. The agency's woes were compounded by epileptic services offered by the country's then sole National Carrier, NITEL. Fax services were dead, valuable man-hours were lost waiting to get 'dial tone' to make voice calls and index fingers severely ached from working rotary-type telephone boxes.

The agency's management promptly went into a combat mode. They scouted every nook and cranny of Mainland Lagos in search of alternative office accommodation, which they eventually found at 17/19 Oduduwa Street, GRA Ikeja. Whilst Shobanjo wanted the premises to be ready for occupation before the NB pitch; the project architect said no magic would make that happen. He refused to take the architect's 'No' for an answer. Night and day, everyone worked, with him becoming an emergency supervisor of works, visiting the site first thing in the morning and being present as construction progressed in the dead of night. The offices were ready for occupation, but NB did not visit during the pitch to assess the state of the agency's infrastructure. The disappointment at committing so much money at so short a time for a visit that never was turned into a blessing all the same, as Insight got a brand-new corporate headquarters that it still occupies.

The pitch almost became a no-contest, as Insight made mince meat of NB's traditional agencies. It captured the corporate account as well as the Gulder, Amstel Malta and Legend accounts. Lintas retained Star and Maltina. It was an unprecedented and comprehensive routing of incumbents, helped largely by the transparency of the processes instituted by NB. With hindsight, then Corporate Affairs Adviser of NB Plc, Larry Agose, described the performance of Insight at the pitch thus: "The agency demonstrated its capacity and capability to do the job, as it was adjudged by most members of the Cost Optimisation Team as having made the best presentation. More importantly, the advertising projections of Insight Communications convinced most members of the COT that the agency knew where NB's brands stood in the market and how the brands could be further grown."

In 2003, Insight further ate into the pie of Lintas in NB when it captured the Heineken account in a grand style pitch that involved a total makeover of Troyka's headquarters in the corporate colours of Heineken to recreate the look and feel of the Heineken Planet.

Although Insight swam against conventional tide by not firmly clasping sentiments to its chest in order to keep clients that helped it to come of age in a very short time, the agency also inexplicably lost at least two valuable clients that had hitherto helped it to achieve critical mass in the industry. One of these clients, Johnson Wax, fired the agency for what was largely described as 'political' reasons while the other, DHL, opted out of its contract with Insight because the agency reportedly failed to pre-empt competition from former employees who broke ranks with the company (DHL) to float Redstar/Fedex, a rival courier company. Some of the former employees were said to be quite close to Shobanjo.

In 2005, Insight celebrated its Silver Jubilee. The event concept was built on a stylish journey back in time that saw a fusion of themes and schemes of the era that coincided with the agency's story from birth. The event presented a positively overwhelmed Shobanjo a platform to articulate the vision that gave birth to Insight and Troyka Holdings. He could not help but thank staff and clients, past and present, for their contribution to the success of the enterprise. He also seized the opportunity to apologise to companies and individuals that might have felt offended by his organisation's pattern of dropping seemingly minor league clients for big spenders with tall dreams: "I want to make an apology here. There are clients that we worked for as toddlers, who, because of the kind of vision that we had, we had to drop along the line. It was not out of arrogance. We wanted to work for the big boys. When we dropped Cocoa Industries and picked Nestle because we wanted to work on Milo, it was a sensible decision. When we resigned Limca to work for Pepsi and 7-Up, we thought that was a very sensible decision. Who would not want to work for Nigerian Breweries? That was why we dropped Sona Breweries. It is not in our character to be nasty people. Just forgive us."

The sub-text of Shobanjo's submission is that 'sensible decisions' result when enterprise managers realise that 'opportunity' often created conflicting situations that they must resolve by sticking tenaciously to the option that best advanced the original vision that created the business. Fidelity of purpose, however, required, first, an ability to recognise the opportunity and, second, being well positioned to take advantage of it. For him, opportunity spotting is no rocket science; all that is required is to look deeply inwards because the opportunity for business growth is often embedded in existing clients. It also required that professionals be imbued with a strong power of conviction to sell their solutions. Nigerian Breweries, by means of its premier lager beer, Gulder, gave Insight and Shobanjo a chance to prove these points in 2003.

Gulder, since its introduction in the Nigerian market in 1970, had been positioned as a premium brand but never, strictly speaking, as the 'Ultimate' premium product. The new leadership of NB, then headed by the effervescent Managing Director and CEO, Festus Odimegwu, and its cerebral Marketing Director, Bola Akingbade, who was later succeeded by Dan Esiekpe, opted to adopt the positioning of Gulder as the 'Ultimate beer', with an international audience in mind. NB gave Insight a simple brief that required the transformation of the profile and equity of Gulder beyond what had ever been seen in this corner of the world. It was the kind of blank cheque that the agency and its leadership had not received from any client. Insight went to town to keep a date with history.

The result was a big budget two-part historical television commercial, The Search and The Return, shot in Spain, with Shobanjo present, on board the preserved ship with which explorer, Christopher Columbus, discovered America and the New World. The simple storyline was based on the order of an Emperor who commissioned his soldiers to embark on an expedition to discover the mystery of the world's ultimate beer. It was a tortuous journey that only the bravest of men could endure. The Emperor's commission was successfully carried out. Gulder was the headline drink for the celebrations that followed. It was an audacious project that had no precedent in Nigeria's advertising history.

The cost of executing the creative idea was an astonishing £1.5 million British Pounds. Shobanjo drilled his team to be sure that the idea was executable as promised. The Creative Director, John de Villier, assured him that the end-product would truly be great. When the concept and the bill for its execution were presented to Nigerian Breweries, the Marketing Director was staggered. He requested that the budget be presented to the Managing Director, Odimegwu, who in turn told Shobanjo that the company had never spent such a huge amount to produce a single television commercial. Shobanjo personally re-assured Odimegwu that Nigerian Breweries would get more than its money's worth if the company supported the production of the commercial that Insight had proposed. Odimegwu was sold on the idea and, consequently, approved the budget as presented by Insight.

The agency was emboldened to try out the gambit because it enjoyed the support of 'people who had a strong heart,' seeing that the creative idea and its cost of execution were not things that the faint-hearted could have dared to dream about. The management of the parent company of Nigerian Breweries warmly received the commercial when it was premiered in Amsterdam. It also received positive media and public reviews across Nigeria after it was aired locally. The moral: practitioners must clearly think through creative solutions and be bold to sell magic to clients. The underlying principle is that cost is always negotiable but only after the client had removed every vestige of doubts in what he is buying. What the Insight team did with Nigerian Breweries was a clear affirmation of the philosophy of former US Secretary of State, General Colin Powell that 'you never know what you can get away with until you try.'

The accolades that followed the airing of The Search and The Return had hardly reduced when the need arose to introduce Gulder's revamped bottle and labels. Insight returned to the theme of strength and character as twin pillars to conquer adversity. For this purpose, the Gulder Ultimate Search (GUS) was created in 2004. It was Nigeria's first locally produced television reality show. 10 contestants, comprising five male and females each, were selected after rigorous screening at the Sea School in Lagos to embark on a search to find the key to unlock a treasure box that turned out to contain Gulder premium lager beer wearing a new look. For 21 gruelling days, the searchers combed forests, climbed hills and swam in rivers before Emeka Ezugo found the 'key' and emerged as the pioneer 'Ultimate' Man, with N2 million cash and a car to show for his efforts. GUS eventually became a key event in NB's marketing calendar. In 2010, a celebrity edition was added to the primetime TV show that by then had spun a rash of reality shows in Nigeria before it was rested in 2014.

Whilst the communication for Gulder helped to reinforce the perception of the brand as the 'Ultimate', Insight's work on the Legend Extra Stout brand did not immediately help the brand to become a huge commercial success as was envisaged. Despite Insight's change of brand direction, which positioned Legend as 'fun stout' or an 'entry' brand for young achievers to get into the habit of drinking stout, Legend did not succeed in knocking Guinness Extra Stout off its market leadership pedestal. Even with contemporary rap music that is favoured by the target group; even with all the jeans and beach 'rampages' popular with its youth target; even with an appeal to them to 'Express Yourself' and even with the brand's increased visibility, Legend only recorded a whimper rather than a bang in the market that is still dominated by Guinness Extra Stout. Guinness held off Legend's challenge by maintaining its positioning as a 'destination' drink for people who have 'arrived'. The Legend ad itself was considered by many as too irreverent and disrespectful of the old order.

Over the years, however, the consistency of the agency's creative output as well as the improved production and marketing efforts of Nigerian Breweries have combined to shoot up the profile of Legend Extra Stout, which now controls about 25 per cent of the Stout market in Nigeria.

At work or at play, Shobanjo's life is anchored on a simple philosophy: to work hard and play hard. The arrangement of all his offices, from Calabar Street through Insight's then headquarters at 58 Akanbi Onitiri Street, Surulere, to Oduduwa Street in GRA Ikeja and finally Troyka Holdings Headquarters on Oduduwa Way, also in GRA Ikeja aptly captured this attitude. The story of his professional and personal lives is succinctly captured by the design of his office during each phase of transition.

Take, for example, his office at Akanbi Onitiri Street, which was designed by his friend and architect, the late Siji Dosekun. It was probably the most imposing office occupied by a CEO in adland in the 1980s and early 1990s. It was understated in elegance, it was not ego-massagingly large and, with the noticeable absence of a phalange of aides, it was not loud in its proclamation of power. But it was creatively put together to leave no one in doubt as to the character of its occupant. Its work area was dominated by a large, black, glass-topped table, a small size white refrigerator, a unit of desk top computer and a 17-inch colour television set that was perpetually tuned to the Cable Network News (CNN) channel. The lighting of the work area was subdued, and it was deliberately cut off from the 'play zone' by a teak wood panel that held some of the numerous awards won by Insight. The absence of a visitor's chair in front of his desk immediately suggests he does not wish to let anybody in on whatever he was doing. Prying eyes were thus effectively shut out. Since he does not like people coming to disturb him in the work area, the arrangement worked just fine. The structure created an artificial barrier that made it difficult for anyone, his co-directors and staff included, to walk directly to his table.

By contrast, his play area is a brighter, more convivial zone. He virtually forgets about work once here. When he takes his favourite seat by the room divider, he is literally lost in the sea of awards that formed the backdrop of the reception. He faces the door; the guest faces the clock. He is so very much relaxed that a guest would think he had all the time in the world to stay. Wrong. Indeed, a visitor has roughly five minutes to make his point and get him to decide whether to continue to attend to him any further or not. You will never catch him consulting his wristwatch as a polite signal for you to make an exit; he expects you to take your time by the clock that is directly in your line of vision.

Or, presently, his charming and dutiful Personal Assistant, Gloria Omoregie, may pop in to remind him of a scheduled appointment. It is a smooth, pre-arranged 'end conversation' signal. As guests make to leave Shobanjo's office, they will not fail to notice an A4-size legend posted on the wall:

"You need one good idea to be a millionaire;

I have ten wonderful ideas and I'm getting nowhere"

He tells you the search for the 'one good idea' is the reason he has been working hard all his life.

When he moved in 2000 to Insight's current office at Oduduwa Street, he did not alter the setting of his work and play space. The new office was only bigger. For efficient time management, he still did not need to consult his wristwatch or have Omoregie pop in to remind him of a scheduled appointment in order to end a meeting. The split unit air conditioner in his office took care of all that. The visitor's lounge chair was positioned in such a way that its occupant received the fury of freezing cold air from the air conditioner. Only a 'stubborn' visitor would be able to remain seated beyond 10 minutes of cold air hitting at his ribs. From a style point of view, his current office at the Troyka Headquarters is simply out of this world, both in its simplicity and in its elegance. Put simply, it tells the story of a man who is content with his station in life; a man in no hurry; one who is willing to share his time in retirement, even if he still dictates the amount of time he is willing to spare.

Until 1994, when he clocked 50, he resumed in the office by 7.30AM each business day. He resolved to take things easy only after he attained the half-century mark, by which time he shifted his resumption time to 9.00AM. A typical day in the 1990s, for him, began with early morning personal devotion and a light breakfast. Thereafter, by 8.00AM he sets out of his GRA Ikeja home to which he moved after the 1992 Opebi shoot-out. The deliberate delay in leaving home a little later than usual helped him to reduce the length of time spent in early morning bumper-to-rear Lagos traffic jam that was expected to have significantly tailed off by the time he hit the road. He frequently spent the time gained to make early morning calls, if necessary, at the offices of some subsidiaries of Troyka. His love of then favourite jet-black Cherokee 4x4 Jeep was such that he could lecture until sundown on the concept and practicality of four-wheel drive vehicles and the superiority of the Cherokee over other brands of American or Japanese off-roaders.

His presence in the office at Akanbi Onitiri Street about 9.00AM did not necessarily change the tempo of work. The Insight culture holds each officer and his immediate superior responsible for the quality of work that is done and the pace at which assignments are accomplished. The better part of his early mornings was taken up by line and staff functions which entailed interacting with the agency's many clients and dealing with his everyday schedule as CEO. Where no client meetings were slated, he attended to files, replied correspondence, made business calls, wrote speeches, received visitors or sat in at crucial plans or review board meetings.

From 2004 when he clocked 60 and left office as CEO of Insight, he extended his resumption hour by one hour. Rather than come in at 9.00AM, as he did when he was in Surulere, he began to resume at Troyka at 10.00AM, after a commute of about five minutes from his house. His resumption time still did not change after he moved to his new house in Ikoyi on Lagos Island. The content of his day did not change dramatically either. He only dispensed with the chores of being the CEO of an advertising agency. His love of Jeeps also ended with the Cherokee. He found love in the Toyota Land Cruiser off roader that was fashionable amongst the power players of Corporate Nigeria. Even that love faded, as he added the Range Rover 'Autobiography' and a BMW 5 Series to his fleet of 'powerful', jet black automobiles all of which had customised number plates that reflected landmarks in his life. Every other thing about him remained constant.

His desk is always squeaky-clean, never cluttered. No matter is ever left unattended for more than 30 minutes. No document is ever buried deep beneath any pile of paperwork. His rule of a clean table is premised on his belief in empowering subordinates who are competent to run the business as well as he does. A multi-layered reportorial system that gets only extremely knotty problems to his desk keeps him on top of every development in the establishment. Equally significant is that he fine-tuned the habit of maintaining a clean-desk from successful leaders with whom he had interacted and who had varying degrees of influence on his professional life. Among them are Moemeke, Charles Saatchi and the late Chief Adeyemi Lawson. They had the simple style of always keeping their tables so tidy as to make one wonder if they did any job. He readily justified the habit, saying: "Almost invariably, people like (these) have organised lives; they organise themselves well; they organise their business well and they usually are clean people. They have clean heads and, I think, clean hearts."

In a very formal sense, he does not have or subscribe to any high-falutin management creed, even if he reads 'big volumes' on successful people. For him, effective management is all about keeping things moving in the workplace, which does not need to have a tag attached to it. The landmarks of Bates' Carl Spielvogel, Chrysler's Lee Iacocca and Virgin Organisation's Richard Branson enrapture him. He is also sufficiently impressed by the exploits of renowned business giants such as the former CEO of Nestle, Olusegun Osunkeye; one-time CEO of Nigerian Breweries, Felix Ohiwerei and former CEO of Paterson Zochonis, PZ, Kola Jamodu who did not slow down in corporate Nigeria even after they passed age 60. They represent some of his choice business leaders; they were men who were well-grounded in the practice of their professions; who were appropriately well-focused as to always want to succeed; who led their pack from the front and who did not suffer fools gladly. These were men who showed results and made things happen, not men who dwelt on 'process' or harped on how hard they 'tried' to get things done.

If, however, a label needs be attached to his work ethic, it is 'addiction to excellence' largely because of his belief that most employees, especially Nigerians, need to be pushed to achieve maximum productivity. In his view, most employees, given the chance, will almost always seek the lines of least resistance since it is easier to be a part of the crowd and coast along without pushing to break barriers. He likes to push his staff to stretch themselves just a little bit more to match his vision of winning every time. For this reason, he is far more likely to overlook an infraction of policies by junior staffers than by officers. In his experience, the latter group was more likely to rubbish corporate policies. In the early days of Insight, he demonstrated his zero tolerance for imperfection by going around the agency about thrice a day, stopping at every table in different departments to ask questions and offer suggestions. Doing this saved his team the heartache of expensive errors and needless repeat jobs. By his reckoning, however, he did not achieve more than 60 per cent success in realising his dream of always winning.

To move things, he occasionally had cause to howl at rather than hug his staff. A howl could take the form of a verbal reprimand that was expressed by a simple "I'm angry with you." At other times, it could take the form of a 'confidential' memo that was anything but confidential. When Insight got off ground, his Secretary would type the 'confidential' memo; the office assistant would deliver it, open, to the recipient's Secretary who would lay it face up on the table of the offending officer. By the time the staff concerned got to read the memo, the grapevine would have been abuzz with news that 'Mr Show' (to the older generation of Insighters); or 'VC' (Vice Chairman) or plain 'Shobby' had queried the person. It worked because nobody liked to be so embarrassed. But there was nothing personal about it.

Again, watch his face carefully. A fleeting frown tells he is angry. By the time his eyes narrow to two dark slits, he is all worked up, as he was when a soft-sell weekly published a story about how he reportedly danced and 'sprayed' crisp N50 notes at an open party at a recreation club in Lagos. The publication deeply upset him because it was out of character for him to do as the magazine had written. "Lies, damned lies," he wrote on the borderline of the story. "Why do journalists write these?" he queried. It was not a question but a biting indictment of journalists and their penchant for not always observing time-honoured creed of the pursuit of truth or leaving out issues on which they entertained reasonable doubts. He is as critical of journalists as he is in love with them.

In the strictest sense, he runs an open administration, with his door ever rarely closed. He receives practically every visitor, with or without prior appointment. Anyone is at liberty to walk up to him without the strictures of officialdom, but all are aware that he does not romance idle talks. In his domain, it is a known fact that junior or middle level staff are more likely to get sympathetic hearing from him than their more senior colleagues; but he detests any breach of protocol. It is an unwritten law that no superior wilfully pulls rank over a junior, else the 'VC' would step into the fray because there is no justification for attempting to turn any of the group's companies into military camps. He believes that any good organisation must always care about its employees to achieve results. However, a subordinate's case would be made patently bad if rules had been disobeyed. Rules are rules. Simplicita.

Except he is out of town, Shobanjo is always 'in a meeting' between 1.30PM and 2.00PM every weekday. It is a peculiar kind of meeting that dates to sometime about 1984 after Awosika broke out in a rash following a meal of 'amala' and 'ewedu' soup in a local eatery near their former Calabar Street offices. To prevent a recurrence, his wife began to send his lunch from their Surulere home, which then was just a few metres away from Insight. Shobanjo and Ibe loved the idea and before long the practice of communal lunch became a tradition. All three ate together at the same time. Occasionally, other ranking staff of the agency enjoyed the privilege of joining the trio at lunch.

No one ate unless the others were around. Where a partner returned so late that lunch could not be eaten, everyone settled for crunchy groundnuts and the lunch packs were returned home. More than any of his other colleagues, Awosika had a reputation for wasting meals because of his consistent pattern of late arrivals from meetings with clients. More than the others, too, he had a penchant for 'ethnic balancing' at meal times, as he would regularly eat from packs brought by Shobanjo (Yoruba) and Ibe (Igbo). If anything, the idea of having lunch together gained ready acceptance, not particularly because of its convenience but because of the desire to see people in their true colour. Now, distance and occurrences over time have made communal lunch impracticable for the remaining founders of Insight Communications: Ibe is unavailable, owing to his early retirement; Awosika is out because of the distance between his office at Oduduwa Street and Shobanjo's office at Oduduwa Way. But the time remains: Shobanjo eats his lunch at the bar, never in his office, in Troyka Headquarters usually between 1.30PM and 2.00PM.

At work, he does not set great store by allegiance to his person. On the contrary, hard work, eye for quality and love of the job are three threads that would, any day, bind anyone to him. In this scheme of things, it is immaterial whether you liked his person or not; it also does not matter whether he likes your person or not, what counts is your ability to deliver. In his personal life, the rules are not any different. He expects anyone he calls a friend to always give everything to the relationship, just as he would regardless of whether the other person is physically present or not. His measure of friendship is both simple and deep: 'you are my friend not because of how frequently I see you but because of where I place you in my heart.' By this simple logic, it is easy to understand why the median age of his carefully cultivated friendships is about 40 years, for these are people who had known him from the early days and who could be trusted to vouch for him at every turn. Among these could be counted businessman, Dele Fajemirokun; Rosabel's Akin Odunsi; Insight's Chairman, Goddy Amadi; Rev (Engr.) Leke Dina; Lt.-Gen. Oladipo Diya (rtd) and Governor Abiola Ajimobi. In the recent past, though, he has cultivated a crop of young, upright and talented professionals as his 'aburos.'

But friends or no, few are likely to get Shobanjo to attend a function, social or corporate, from start to finish. He is hardly ever likely to turn down an invitation because of his belief that it is an extension of goodwill and a privilege that cements relationships. It is for this reason that anyone is likely to encounter him at the unlikeliest of functions, but his attendance would probably be up to the point at which the host or hostess acknowledges his presence. Thereafter, he would disappear like a ghost and re-appear elsewhere same day, possibly within the hour. In this regard, he has put his fair complexion to good use: since he is easy enough to spot, he does not have to spend any time longer than he deems necessary at any event. It is for this reason that he has been recorded as one of the busiest party goers in the social circuit in Nigeria.

Again, for him, if any business is to be successful, the knowledge base of the professional and his skill at socialising must go hand-in-glove. In his reckoning, any level of success could significantly be improved by a good match of brain power and quality social networking. If, however, it ever became necessary to pick one over the other, he would accord knowledge priority over friendship. He constantly challenges his staff to consciously break barriers to their capacity to network so that the business could always be on the upswing.

"Oga Dotun, I bet you cannot name two night clubs in Lagos," he once said to me.

I certainly did not see the challenge coming at an after-session evening hang-out during the 2007 Troyka Group's corporate strategy retreat for management staff in Ijebu-Ode. Some of my colleagues, who were quietly amused, suspended their glass of beer mid-air, with smug 'God-don-catch-you-today' mischievous smile all over their faces. They could not wait enough for my answer, given my well-known reserve and near pastor-like disposition.
"But, Sir, I know more than two"
"Just give me any two," he insisted.
I did not have to think too hard, as I pulled a straight face and gave him my answer: "Deeper Life and RCCG."

He checked my cup to be sure it contained just wine and that it had not been laced with some unknown chemical substance. He also looked at me more closely to be sure I did not run high fever that could have induced hallucination. He knew he heard me right and that he had asked for social clubs, not churches. But he got the joke.

Not all the challenges he throws at staff are that light-hearted, though. The first day Segun Olaleye reported for work as Insight's Credit Control Officer, he nearly cursed the moment he took the decision to retire from his job in the same capacity at the State-owned Ogun State Broadcasting Corporation (Radio), Abeokuta. For the second time in his career, his path crossed Shobanjo's. On both occasions, he felt badly bruised. The first time, he had chased debt to Grant Advertising where Shobanjo was then Deputy Managing Director. After he had introduced himself as well as his mission to the DMD, he was shocked by Shobanjo's response: "My job is not to pay people; go and see the Accountant." Just as Olaleye could not understand the seeming 'arrogance;' Shobanjo, too, could not understand why he was expected to do other people's jobs. From that moment, Olaleye carefully avoided Shobanjo both at Grant and at Insight when it was founded. This, however, did not stop him from taking a job at Insight when it was offered. He was both shocked and upset as he was introduced to Shobanjo as the new hire. The MD took one look at him and said to the Head of Finance: "How come you went to recruit somebody from the civil service? This guy can't last six months here." He nonetheless welcomed Olaleye to Insight and wished him all the best. A dejected Olaleye raced to his office from where he emerged with a resolve: "When someone says you are not good for him, it is your responsibility to show you are much better. I was at Insight for about two years. The prophecy that I would not last in the agency came to pass but not in the way I had interpreted it."

The story had a very good ending for Olaleye who, over the years and despite his exit from Insight, developed a very close relationship with his former boss. Shobanjo was instrumental to four of the major career moves he made in his professional life. Two of these concerned his two-time return to his old constituency, OGTV, as General Manager. The first was on Shobanjo's recommendation to the Military Administrator in 1997 and the second at Shobanjo's intervention after Olaleye had turned down a request by a civilian Governor for him to make a return to his old seat. The second time was particularly difficult because Olaleye then held the position of Regional Manager of a multinational company based in South Africa, a job for which Shobanjo's opinion had counted when Olaleye was being interviewed. Olaleye was swayed by Shobanjo's subtle appeal to motherland sensibilities that he couched in a Yoruba idiom: "T'a ba n wa owo, t'a pade iyi l'ona; sebi iyi l'ama f'owo ra."[1]

Broadcaster John Momoh provides more insight to Shobanjo's power of persuasion, which is built on implicit trust in the ability of people with whom he has good relationships to deliver: "Whenever there was any good job at a personal level, he would always reach me. He looks after people's interest; he is one who has a total picture of you and he wants to make sure that things pan out well for you in whatever you do."

His testimonial is grounded in experience. As a young broadcaster with Radio Nigeria before he crossed over to television, Momoh did several voice-over assignments on radio and television commercials produced by Insight. In the process, his path crossed Shobanjo's whom he saw as a debonair gentleman who had no airs despite his accomplishments. Years after Momoh set up Channels TV and left doing voice-overs to concentrate on the business side of broadcasting, Shobanjo approached him with an offer to handle an assignment for one of his clients. Momoh could not refuse because 'only a man like Shobanjo could approach me with such an offer and I would listen.' Shobanjo, too, did not take his influence on Momoh

---

[1] *Yoruba, loosely approximating to: 'why chase money when, in the end, it'll be used in pursuit of honour?*

for granted. He ensured a proper contract was drawn up and signed. When the client tried to renege on some terms of the contract, Shobanjo stepped in and ensured that Momoh was fully paid.

When an account matters, Shobanjo has only one ground rule for everyone in all Troyka companies: 'you must win it.' The justification for the admonition is simple. An account must be won, first, because a Troyka company must be perceived as having the best solution to any client's challenge; second, because Troyka's pride is at stake and, of course, because Troyka could always find use for the money. In the beginning, he would himself lead the assault. Now, in retirement, he does not but, he avails his seasoned advice to any unit company that seeks him out. It is common knowledge that Troyka companies do not pitch every account to which they are invited; first, because they pride themselves in the philosophy of Insight at start-up: a 'quality company working for quality clients who manufacture quality products'. Again, the leadership of the group views hunger for new clients as one sure way of losing existing ones, the negative result of which could be gleaned from the bottom line of companies that run after every account. But Troyka's leadership encourages individual companies to go for broke where the prospects of real growth look highly probable. Combined, these perspectives translate to either playing in the big league or not playing at all.

In the past, when a truly big account was targeted, it was routine practice for Shobanjo to ship the creative team to his country home in Aiyepe. This was to ensure that they had minimal distractions that could constrain the creative process; it was also to ensure project confidentiality so that the only people who enjoyed the privilege of knowing what was afoot at that stage were the people who needed to know. The guerrilla-like planning process, perhaps, explains the view in adworld that he ran a cloak and dagger operation. It also fuelled speculations that he often went 'home' to obtain 'jazz' (spiritual reinforcement) to make his companies unbeatable. These retreats have yielded creative business solutions that, in turn, have yielded several plum assignments for Troyka companies, especially Insight. These solutions also ensured that in situations where Insight or any other Troyka company lost any pitch, the quality of their presentation was never described as mediocre. His vision of always winning new business and giving it consistently sparkling performance has naturally flowed down the rank of staff. It also was the basis of Insight's 10th anniversary slogan and subsequent business philosophy: 'Excellence, the will to win.'

His long-time friend, Senator Abiola Ajimobi, a former Managing Director of National Oil and Chemicals Ltd and, later, Governor of Oyo State affirmed Shobanjo's longstanding commitment to excellence when, at a public function in honour of Shobanjo,[1] he recounted their early personal and professional encounters: "After I had compiled the names of agencies and passed everything to the Committee, the Managing Director called and asked if I had friends amongst the people. I said 'No' but that I had acquaintances. Insight won the account. The MD called again to ask why I did not say that I knew any of the competing agencies. I said: 'Sir, if I had told you, you would have told me to choose my friends, but I did not tell you because I know that, based on merit, my friends would win; and, indeed, they won."

The exponential growth of Troyka companies, as had earlier been explained, occasioned broad accusations of inappropriate business ethics against Shobanjo. This is against the backdrop of the fact that few could describe how he managed to get close to powerful people in business without speaking what his friend, Odunsi, liked to mockingly describe as 'vernacular' or plain graft. Although Shobanjo had thrown an open challenge that evidence of wrong-

---

[1] *Testimonial at the conferment of Nigeria's Advertising Man of All Time Award on Shobanjo, 11 October, 2013*

doing by him be presented, there has been no taker. Yet, it is highly unlikely that anyone in the history of the marketing communications industry in Nigeria has received as much knocks as he has. One of the most spectacular knocks he received in his career came because of Insight's handling of Globacom, Nigeria's fourth licensed Global System of Mobile communications (GSM) network and Second National Carrier, owned by the enigmatic entrepreneur, Otunba Mike Adenuga.

Shobanjo's meeting with Adenuga in the early 1990s was fortuitous. His friend, Olu Senbore, who then was a partner in the accounting firm formerly known as Coopers & Lybrand, had introduced him to Femi Ekundayo, then Managing Director of Devcom Bank, which was owned by Adenuga. The introduction paved way for an agency/client relationship between Insight and Devcom Bank and a personal relationship between Shobanjo and the Bank's Chairman, Adenuga, who also owned Equitorial Trust Bank (ETB), which also became Insight's client. Incidentally, too, the younger tycoon and Awosika had known each other in their secondary school days in Ibadan.

In 2001, Adenuga's company, Communications Investment Ltd (CIL), won one of four licences at an international auction supervised by the Nigerian Communications Commission (NCC) to signal the commencement of GSM telephony services in Nigeria. The company, however, lost the licence in controversial circumstances. At the heart of the matter was the dispute over whether CIL met NCC's deadline for the receipt of payments from all licencees. CIL claimed it did; NCC said it did not. In a nutshell, CIL discovered that it had been allocated a contentious and legally encumbered frequency and decided to tread carefully by making qualified payment of the $285 million licence fee to NCC through its bankers, BNP Paribas in Paris, France. NCC responded swiftly by suspending CIL's newly won licence. Appeals by the company to the Commission to change its stance failed to yield results. Left with no choice, CIL took its case to the court of public opinion. Insight joined forces with Adenuga's in-house and retained communications advisers to launch one of the most persuasive, intensive and extensive media campaigns ever seen in the country to reach Nigerians across all sectors to appeal to the conscience of government so that CIL's licence would be revalidated. It was a lost cause. For more than one year, the Federal Government under President Olusegun Obasanjo resolutely refused to openly revisit the issue of CIL's suspended licence.

Adenuga, however, did not relent. In 2002, he got a much bigger bite at the telecommunications pie when he not only got a GSM licence under a new corporate platform, Globacom, but also received a licence for the company as the Second National Carrier. All at a combined cost of $200 million that was considerably cheaper than the fee that was paid for the suspended CIL licence. By the time this happened, Insight was working on the Econet Wireless account, a Grey Worldwide business. The licensing of Globacom necessitated a search by Adenuga for marketing communications agencies to handle the new network's business, a search that he did not discuss with Insight. But, as a friend, he invited Awosika in a personal capacity to sit on the panel to screen agencies that pitched the business. This arrangement would later spark off further controversy in adworld.

Although Adenuga had settled for the appointment of two South Africa-based agencies, JWT and FCB, and by extension, their local affiliates, LTC and Centrespread respectively to handle Globacom, he reversed himself without offering any explanation to anyone. Awosika's professional interventions in the process of appraising the presentations of the agencies, it would seem, caused Adenuga to review his preference for foreign agencies to work on the Globacom business, which he now offered to Insight that did not pitch for it.

Insight accepted the lead agency offer, in part, because of the goodwill extended to it by Adenuga and because the agency's management thought it was better to run with 'kith and kin' than to continue its work for Econet Wireless that was driven by Strive Masiyiwa, a Zimbabwean. Besides, Globacom had prospects of becoming a major player in the telecommunications industry. The reaction to the new Globacom/Insight relationship in advertising circles was largely negative, as Shobanjo was thought to have muscled his way once more into grabbing other people's business.

Globacom, indeed, held a lot of promise. In 2003, Troyka's public relations subsidiary, The Quadrant Company, handled publicity to announce the delivery of the new network's technical equipment. The quality of work done by TQC commanded huge public attention that conditioned subscribers to eagerly expect the yet-to-launch Glo to trigger an earthquake in the evolving GSM telephony market. To the network's credit, Glo re-defined GSM services in Nigeria with its launch of per-second billing platform at a time that the early starters in the market had said it would almost take a lifetime to accomplish. The Quadrant Company, however, declined to work on the Globacom account on a full-time basis even after making two presentations to Adenuga. The agency applied the brakes because none of Adenuga's organisations had a record of working long term with any PR outfit since he had a barn full of media relations advisers. Almost five years later, Adenuga head-hunted TQC's Managing Director, Benedicta Upaa-Ayede, to run the Mike Adenuga Foundation.

On the advertising side, Insight creatively played up the brand promise of Globacom with series of exciting advertisements with the tag line 'People. Power. Possibilities.' Insight invested heavily in the Globacom project. In one year, the agency worked with several South

African agencies, notably JWT, McCann Erickson and Jupiter Drawing Room. Insight seconded about six staff working on the Globacom account to Johannesburg on a near-permanent basis. There was also a plan to dedicate a building to be known as 'Globacom House' within Insight's premises. But all the possibilities went with the wind because Adenuga's thunder struck twice in quick succession.

Without explanations, he fired the South African agencies but left Insight standing. Then, he requested assistance in a fresh search for collaborations with any great UK-based agency. Shobanjo leveraged his vast business network to attract M & C Saatchis, which was signed on by Adenuga who, with Awosika, came to join him in London for a meeting with the agency. Weeks after M & C Saatchis took its first brief from Glo, the agency and Insight had the doors of the GSM network firmly shut against them by Adenuga. Typically, no reasons were given.

The controversial circumstances of the parting of ways between Insight and Glo before the network's rollout were aggravated by the operator's methodical depletion of Insight's workforce to build its internal advertising unit. Before the raid began, Adenuga had formally requested Insight to release the Account Manager on the business, Tunde Kaitell, a former journalist, to be employed by Glo so he could be an intermediary between Glo and Insight. As it later turned out, the release of Kaitell triggered a steady stream of targeted recruitment of Insight's staff, particularly those that worked on the network's account, into Globacom.

Shobanjo was thoroughly displeased: "I thought what he (Adenuga) did was most unethical. All the people he recruited were those he interacted with in the period we used to look after his account. What that tells me is that it is dangerous working for him because if you expose your people to him, he entices them, which is totally unfair."

The basis of his angst is understandable because he is strongly anti-poaching of the staff of service providers by clients. His position is anchored on the fact that this tantamounts to clients killing their vendors whilst trying to grow their own businesses. It stands to reason that a weak service provider cannot be expected to perform at optimal level with a 'second eleven.'

Although the falling out between Adenuga/Glo and Shobanjo/Insight could largely be attributed to a conflict of professional values, it is hard not to see their drift apart as the result of inevitable sparks that often fly at the meeting of two very strong personalities. Shobanjo is dismissive of the notion: "Ego for what? I am not in his kind of business; he is not in mine. I gave him all due courtesies as a client and he reciprocated. He gave us a free-hand; we had a very wonderful relationship while it lasted. Till date, he remains my brother. But to work together, no."

The way he neatly compartmentalised his relationship with Adenuga tallies with the general belief that Shobanjo never burns bridges in his interactions with people. His winning ways are firmly anchored on integrity and honour. His business and personal relationships thrive because they transcend the superficial 'what's in it for me?' Some of his most enduring professional relationships have been solidified beyond the official to the personal and oftentimes to family levels. In this class are friends like the former Managing Director of Bagco, the late Chief Sikiru K. Oluwo; the former Managing Director of Nigerian Breweries, Mr. Festus Odimegwu; the former Marketing Director of MTN Nigeria, Mr. Bola Akingbade and Mr. Faysal Halabi who is the first non-Nigerian to be conferred with the Fellowship of APCON. The relationship with Halabi is especially interesting considering that he is a non-Nigerian. Although both met on the job, their association has become filial. Halabi calls Shobanjo 'father' and Awosika, 'brother'; his children refer to Shobanjo as their 'grandfather.' The relationship has seen Shobanjo travel to Beirut at least six times, including a visit in 2011 to celebrate with Halabi who was conferred with the award of Man of the Year in Advertising in the Middle East and Africa.

Halabi captured the quality of the relationship thus: "I call Shobanjo 'father' because from time to time he has been a real father. I have never, ever hesitated to deal with Jimi and Biodun; they are very credible, very transparent and caring professionals and they teach people how to be honest and credible. I am proud that I made the right selection in my stay in Nigeria to have them in my professional life. I always say to my son: "whenever you want anything, pick up the phone and call Biodun Shobanjo and Jimi before calling anybody else from the Nigerian side."

At a purely professional level, the strength of his leadership both of Insight and the industry transcends both his ever-present image in the media and his very strong personality. It is the result of his capacity to effectively manage followership by strength of character, personal respect and charisma. The net effect, as his friend and fellow advertising practitioner, Adetiba, surmised, is that individuals who like his style have tended to like him immensely while those who do not have also tended to dislike him intensely. Shobanjo is acutely aware of this sharp distinction, which explains his resilience at absorbing the many knocks that he has received in his career. He only would have wished that his critics took the trouble to understand and accept that he had no magic wand beyond the hard work and sheer brilliance that propelled Insight and other Troyka companies to their lofty heights despite the thorns along the way.

His words: "If you do not understand the reason for being of Insight, chances are that you may find it difficult to appraise everything that has come from the agency. My influence has always been (the old) Saatchi & Saatchi. I have never been shy to admit that. That is one company I have looked at over and over. When the idea of Insight was first mooted, we had looked at the Nigerian advertising horizon and one felt there was a gap somewhere, a void that needed to be filled. That, in itself, was the raison d'être for the coming to being of the agency. Advertising or marketing communications needed to be practised in a manner that had never been done. I felt that in terms of creative excellence, quality of service – from account management and planning, media planning and buying to the total quality of a product – something needed to change. I felt if one had the needed human resource, then it became possible that one could actualise this. That, again, was the dream, the cornerstone of the business. I thought we could go out there and do it.

The good thing is that at least two key players in the establishment of Insight are still around. At least some of them are still much focused. For me, I constantly try to whip everybody into line. I say 'listen, you guys are getting out of the reason we are here.' It may be immodest but if you asked my other colleague (Awosika), he will tell you that I am a much-focused person as far as the dream is concerned. When one whips others into line, one is saying: 'do not forget why we are here.' The unfortunate thing is that a lot of the other people who should be helping to propagate this dream have had to move on. Factors responsible have largely been economic, not that they did not share the dream. In a situation where they feel they can make good elsewhere, even if they would be missing something by leaving Insight, they have seen a need to move on.

That has not helped matters, I regret to say. I believe that if as much as 70 per cent of the people who were part of the original building block had remained; Insight would have been way, way ahead of any advertising company in Nigeria. I am talking of way, way ahead, not just being way ahead."

11

The Morning After

I don't want to go the Nigerian way.
Retiring to Troyka opened my mind to look at things differently
and add such value that I have been asking myself: is this real?

Biodun Shobanjo

When Shobanjo announced his decision to stand down as CEO of Insight in December 2004, he shed the last vestige of power in day-to-day, company-specific administration. As a result, protocol instantly became a lively subject within Troyka. Administrative adjustments became inevitable to take care of official designations. The staff of Insight, more than anyone else within the Group, needed to make, perhaps, the most profound turn around in perception. Since 1982, he had been the agency's Vice Chairman, with Goddy Amadi as Chairman. Whilst it was organisationally convenient at Insight to address him simply as VC to reflect his office, the initials, at a deeper level, also made it possible for Insighters to stake a superior claim on the man, after all he, too, had not hidden the fact that he was sentimentally attached to the agency. Now, Insighters needed to lose their 'home' advantage to catch up with the rest of the Group, to whom he had always been 'Chairman.'

Staff of other Troyka unit companies, on the other hand, needed to appreciate the fact that Awosika had also grown in stature. They had become too accustomed to seeing him as 'SD' – 'Supervising Director' (of some of these unit companies). Now, there was need to refer to him by his proper title, Group Vice Chairman. These designations were not at issue; but it was imperative for staff to quickly get used to them because Shobanjo is a stickler for procedure. For him, the devil is always in the details. Group-wide, however, staff knew that the old order had changed when mails were no longer signed by 'Biodun Shobanjo' but by the 'Chairman.' For full effect, he directed that he be de-listed from the official Insight web mailing directory. This way, he could only be reached through his new Troyka web address. The message was clear: he had truly become the father of all.

Retiring to Troyka as Chairman helped him to resolve some underlying challenges of Owner/Manager enterprises, especially those that operate a group structure. As MD/CEO and Vice-Chairman of Insight, he was an executive decision maker of the flagship business unit of Troyka. As Chairman of Troyka Holdings, he had a helicopter view of all the businesses, one that required a distancing from the roots to be able to consolidate the strengths of the Group. In this role, he is the final approving authority on issues that affect all unit companies in the Group. Both roles might appear to be mutually exclusive but, in fact, they are not.

Although his exit from Insight helped make the conflict less pronounced, the extent of the success of the Troyka 'group structure' is only just unravelling in the light of new developments that have helped to achieve more corporate distancing in the day-to-day running of the various companies. The full extent may not be known until he and Awosika fully quit the stage by which time their roles as lead gladiators and mediators would have been completely extinguished. The initial blurring of administrative lines of the staff and line functions of Shobanjo and, particularly, Awosika, inexorably caused some of the business leaders in the Group to lose sight of the essence of the creation of the 'group structure'. Some of the companies started to find it difficult to pull together as Troyka companies. Instead, they began to prefer to work with companies outside of the group whenever they felt that sister organisations offered less competitive services and prices. The gradual loss of group synergy discomfited Shobanjo who also saw the development as a serious impediment to the overriding objective of creating these companies. This notwithstanding, he does not deny being particularly passionate about Insight, as borne out by his statement during an Insight staff retreat in 2000: "My mother is, perhaps, the one person I love most. I have often said it that if she comes between Insight and its success, I will unfortunately have to crush her...If I can crush my mother because of this company, chances are that I will crush anybody without batting an eyelid."

The assertion, though intended to be taken at face value, was meant to underscore the intensity of his vision and passion for the business. Troyka is not a big company; it was envisioned as a compact team to guide and counsel the management of unit companies. Apart from the Chairman, its staff roll comprises a corporate strategist; a lawyer; the Group Finance Director; the Group Human Resource Controller; the Chairman's Personal Assistant and the Group Head of Information Technology, all of whom provide group-wide support to the holding company within the purview of their respective staff roles to complement the work of the Chairman. Troyka functions primarily as a control and an early warning administrative mechanism to avert mistakes of the past that contributed to the failure of some companies in the group. Despite its supervisory role, the management teams of each unit company maintain independent control of the day-to-day operation of their respective businesses. They make their decisions and live by the consequences.

The extent of independence exercised by each company was well demonstrated by The Quadrant Company (TQC) in 2005 when it resigned the public relations consultancy of Virgin Nigeria Airways owing to some differences between the agency and the airline. The airline's business had resided in TQC from the point at which the Federal Government of Nigeria and Virgin Atlantic Airways signed the Memorandum of Mutual Understanding in September 2004 to formally establish Nigeria's now defunct National Flag Carrier. Upon receipt of the agency's letter of the discontinuance of advisory services, a member of the airline's senior management promptly spoke with Shobanjo to persuade TQC to rescind its decision. Shobanjo, in turn, referred the Director to TQC's Supervising Director, Awosika, as the one who probably could try to persuade the agency's management to have a change of heart. Awosika patiently listened to TQC's Managing Director, Benedicta Upaa Ayede's articulation of the issues at stake, including the airline's poaching of one of the agency's staff working on the management of its account. The Supervising Director did not fault the agency's position. He, however, counselled that if there was any possibility of reviewing the agency's stance, the option should not be discountenanced. In the end, the disagreement between TQC and Virgin Nigeria was amicably resolved after a series of meetings. TQC went back to work on its own terms without any prompting from the Group office and thus validated the Troyka Chairman's stance that the independent decisions of his managers must always be respected.

As Chairman, Shobanjo has slowed down considerably. He has developed a tendency to avoid taking decisions in the heat of the moment, perhaps, in the hope that, by staying action, a problem could resolve itself. He no longer feels any compelling need to put out fires because he has people and processes to deal with such situations. He only steps in when business leaders call for help or when he believes there is a compelling need to rescue a situation. Often, he uses a blend of official information management system and the plain old grapevine to assist him in arriving at decisions. Where there is a conflict between the group's larger interest and that of a unit company, he never hesitates to adopt the group's position. In 2006, he had a particularly tough call when the Group's troubled event management company, FK:G2, won the Becks' Beer account. On the face of it, the win appeared to have conflicted with the retainer services provided to NB PLC by Insight and Media Perspectives, a Troyka media independent company.

It was not an issue that could quite easily be resolved to everyone's satisfaction, especially because, from a commercial perspective, FK:G2 needed the business to improve its bottom line and stay afloat. In the circumstance, however, the company was clearly out-gunned by the combination of Insight and Media Perspectives. FK:G2 took its case to the Chairman who admitted the non-existence of a conflict of interest in the day-to-day running of the accounts by the different Troyka companies. Yet, he ruled that FK:G2 should resign the Becks' Beer account, which was a relatively small price to pay compared with the probable high cost of losing the Nigerian Breweries business. The decision did not make him the most popular man with the staff of FK:G2, the more so as the company's boat sank a few years after this incident.

Whereas Shobanjo has slowed down in several areas, he remains unbending on issues of meetings. His rules for meetings are very simple: none must be called for flimsy reasons; there must be prepared agenda and there must be a fixed time. All are interwoven. For him, the seriousness of an issue must compel a results-focused meeting for which the availability of agenda would naturally dictate who got invited. Only people who have the capacity to add value are called to meetings, the notice of which must be served on time and for which lateness or absence are not options.

Despite the successes of his various organisations, Shobanjo prefers to be recognised as a professional, not as a businessman. He was particularly irked by the comments of Doghudje, who once referred to him as a 'business man who made good in advertising.' No matter his preference, it is evident that his professional life exemplified critical lessons in business development and wealth sustenance. He started out early enough; he dreamt big; he stuck to his core competence and he remained the driver of his vision whilst he allowed other people to key into it and run with it. He also recognises that people are the most precious assets of any enterprise and he proved that money will always follow ideas. He affirms that it was all right to respect competition but that no one should be over-awed by the size or age of competition.

His start-up experience affirms the belief that banking institutions are 'reactive' partners who will always not support start ups but relentlessly rush capital to organisations that no longer required them. He reinforces the saying that there are no short cuts to success and he continually preaches diversification as a good strategy to ensure that a professional or a businessman does not get marooned when he hits hard times that would almost always come in the life of a business. Above all, he admonishes all business owners to recognise that God is the source from which all blessings flow.

In retirement, it became imperative for Shobanjo to 'pay back' to society. As of the time he relinquished his position as CEO of Insight, he had not completely figured out how to share his vast professional experience. This book was already in the works, but it was far from being completed. Bit by bit, however, he began to accept, albeit reluctantly, speaking engagements or what he christened 'teaching jobs' that began to eat into his time. Offers came from quarters he hardly could turn down.

In a one week of April 2006, for example, OAAN invited him to chair its Poster Awards event, during which he was also expected to deliver a 30-minute paper. In the same week, one of his favourite senior journalists, Gbenga Adefaye, the former Editor of Vanguard, sought him out to present a paper at the newspaper's management retreat. If he was inclined to finding an excuse to bow out of the assignment, he could not say 'No' to the paper's publisher, 'Uncle Sam' Amuka, who had taken his acceptance of the invitation as a given. Also waiting were requests from APCON and scheduled interviews with Vanguard, TheNEWS magazine and Financial Standard. It was a crowded week. In mock frustration, he responded to one of my many notes, saying: "For a retiree, this is not what I want to be doing, especially as these things carry no financial reward as would have been the situation if this was in the Western world (where) people pay good money to benefit from this sort of experience. You can only pity me."

At the time he wrote the note, he did not know that his life in retirement was about to take on a new turn; one that would launch him back to his roots in broadcasting and bring to the fore the 'show' and 'biz' in his many aliases in professional circuits. But it was a fortuitous development that, again, had the imprint of providence.

Several kilometres away from Shobanjo's mainland Lagos office, Charles Odibo, Head of Corporate Communications of then Bank PHB, an Insight client, was locked in animated discussions with a group of young Nigerian professionals in Diaspora, under the aegis of The Executive Group (TEG). Early in 2007, the bank had begun talks with TEG, which had secured the franchise to air The Apprentice Africa, the continental version of the globally successful business reality television show, The Apprentice. Just a few months earlier the bank had rounded off its sponsorship of Season One of The Intern, a locally developed business reality TV show. The Intern was a hit. But the continental appeal of The Apprentice Africa was a bigger and more compelling platform for the bank, which did not need to be greatly persuaded before it accepted to be the Title Sponsor of the show.

Odibo rationalised this to the media, saying: "Our commitment to inspire brilliance and global standards mean that Nigerians can always rest assured that we will always spare no effort in bringing the world's best to them."

But the challenges of producing The Apprentice Africa were enormous for the simple reason that the show had global standards to meet. TEG and the production company, Storm Productions, had figured out the implementation details of the show that was planned to air in Africa with the notable exception of South Africa. Casting calls had already been scheduled in Nigeria, Ghana and Kenya as well as the United States and the United Kingdom, from where contestants were to be selected. Several sponsors had also been lined up to ensure that funding would not present a headache. Production equipment and personnel did not occasion any hair splitting, as the local and international production crew was truly world class. But who would be the CEO?

From the outset, Mark Burnett Productions, owners of The Apprentice franchise had designed the programme as an aspirational reality show. It was conceived as the 'ultimate job interview' in which the best candidate would have a lifetime opportunity to understudy a world-class CEO who would mentor the winner for one year. For that reason, it was mandatory that the CEO must, in every sense, be a business success, a heavyweight of sorts; one who also must be seen to command so much respect, if not awe, in society. Because the CEO was projected as the 'most important link' in the show, candidates needed to meet a set of universal criteria of achievements. For one thing, he was required to have 'a credible business persona and background.' He must have a 'charismatic character'; live the 'lifestyle of the rich and famous'; be in an industry widely considered as 'sexy' and can offer an 'attractive' job to the winner.

A short list of candidates, including a young, aggressive and envy-of-all bank CEO, was drawn up by the show's producers for consideration by Bank PHB. Eventually, four candidates were given serious consideration by both the producers and the Title Sponsor. Apart from meeting the set standards, each of the candidates commanded considerable measure of media attention arising from their hold-no-hostage attitude to doing business. In the end, Bank PHB and TEG settled for Shobanjo because he was considered as 'one of Nigeria's greatest success stories'; an 'advertising industry legend' and an entrepreneur with 'enviable pedigree and antecedents.' For the team, he had the persona that could match the 'edgy, dramatic and larger-than-life quality' that American maverick billionaire, Donald Trump, had bestowed on the master brand, The Apprentice, since it first aired in 2004 in the United States. All other CEOs of versions of the show had similarly made the programme one to-die-for in all the 23 countries where it had been replicated.

The show went by different names in various countries:[1] 'Traum Job' (Dream Job – Switzerland); Business Baazigar (Business Tycoon – India) or 'el idara jadara' (United Arab Emirates). The long list of CEOs included Amstrad's founder, Sir Alan Sugar (The Apprentice UK); mining magnate, Tokyo Sexwale (South Africa); publisher, Jurg Marquard (Switzerland); real estate billionaire, Mohammed Ali Alabbar (Dubai); businessman, Cyrus Sakuhar (India) and auto industry tycoon, Bill Cullen (Ireland). They were all 'made' people who had seen it all and done it all very well. Many of them were above 60 years, so they had experience to back up the popular perception of them as not being overnight successes. Howsoever the anchor chooses to evict a contestant – by handing out air tickets (India) or saying 'sie sind raus' (Switzerland) – they all pointed their index fingers and said the same thing to majority of participants in the show worldwide: 'You're Fired!'

Shobanjo had already commenced the first leg of his annual vacation in the UK by the time Odibo wrote in August 2007 to inform him of his selection as CEO of The Apprentice Africa. He met the letter waiting for him on his return. He knew that the decision to accept or decline the offer, like several other major decisions he had had to take, would be a collective one by his family. Dolapo, who had read the letter, stirred a mini-United Nations debate on the issue. She immediately faxed it to her brothers abroad because they were not content with her verbal announcement of the offer on phone. Within hours and across different time zones in the world, family members dissected the issue. Different things raced through their minds. Dolapo's fear was whether the production of the show would meet the exacting standards of both her father and the international versions she had seen. His wife, Joyce, could not help but think, 'Oh, this man has again come with his celebrity 'wahala.'

The boys, Tunde, Abimbola and Femi, simply felt it was the right thing to do. Funke was delighted but saw a far greater challenge ahead of the children, for the man had won yet another trophy and raised the bar of performance that they had hoped to match or eclipse some day. The children, however, did not share his view to do the show for free. Funke, especially, could not reconcile her finance training and practice with his decision to play Father Christmas. She felt that a token, at least, should have been paid into a charity of choice. But they all prodded him to have a go at being the anchor of the show because they saw the role as a public extension of the business experience that he liked to share with them after brunch on Sundays. Insight's CEO, Awosika, too, did a major job of selling the idea before Shobanjo finally agreed to host the programme. Dolapo quickly bought him series of The Apprentice DVDs to complement the ones sent to him by Bank PHB to provide insight into the role of the CEO and the format of the programme.

Bank PHB received his acceptance of 'this extremely major challenge' in October, 2007 upon his return to Nigeria. He did not think that any of the conditions stipulated for the CEO presented any problem; his primary concern was the need to produce a programme that everyone would feel proud to associate with. He, however, struggled a bit before he finally picked a female adviser, Mowunmi Fatodu, a Group Account Director and an Insight veteran, to join Troyka's former strategist, Paul Olaleye, to meet the male/female balance required by the show's production manual. In part, he encountered this difficulty because few women occupied senior management positions in Troyka. The highest-ranking female management staff in the Group, Benedicta Upaa Ayede, who attained the position of Managing Director of The Quadrant Company, had bowed out a few months earlier to end a long and successful career in public relations. From 2006, Troyka began to record a high intake of bright female management trainees year-on-year, which significantly improved the odds of having more women occupying key management positions in the Group. This development coheres with Shobanjo's position that 'in the real world, women tend to be wonderful; they think and work smarter than men.'

Shobanjo's unveiling as CEO of The Apprentice Africa in October 2007 was straight out of a movie-making manual. He carried himself the way an accomplished CEO should whilst Bank PHB talked big like a typical big-budget sponsor. The publicity shots showed him in a no-nonsense mood. Radio and television commercials created the hype needed to create a box office stampede. The media, online and print, did the rest: they published news, features, photo news and gossips that heightened viewers' interest in the show. Troyka employees could hardly contain roaring laughter that burst forth when they saw the official photos of the CEO. "Chairman in a killer mood?" No way. Even when he intended to unleash intense venom, he never looked this mean. He always was picture perfect; one got to feel his anger only when he begins to cut a speaker short, saying 'excuse me'. Many wondered at what point, in just three years, they missed the transformation of the 'pensioner' to a stern-looking village headmaster.

Worldwide, anchors of The Apprentice programme are seen mainly from the prism of Donald Trump, who is the face of the show. Practically everyone knows the story of his life by rote: how he came into great wealth; went into great debt and made a great comeback. Against all odds, the businessman decisively beat several established politicians to clinch the ticket to fly the flag of the Republican Party with which he surprisingly, yet roundly defeated former First Lady of the United States and former Secretary of States, Mrs Hillary Clinton, in the November 9, 2016 presidential polls to emerge as President of the United States. Trump lived the lifestyle that many cannot imagine, much less live. He gave the programme a distinct personality, one that shot up its approval ratings everywhere it aired. It became inevitable that Shobanjo be compared with the American billionaire. Both men had quality pedigrees, and, by whatever standard, they are successful; have extra-ordinary media management skills and are men that many would love to hate.

However, whilst Trump's lifestyle is more in-your-face-and-loving-it, Shobanjo's is somewhat understated, even if considered loud by many of his contemporaries. On lifestyle issues, he is especially unapologetic, as exemplified by his 'hot' exchange with Doghudje over the latter's criticism of the lifestyle of advertising practitioners. "I am disturbed," he wrote to Doghudje, "that on some major issues, you seem to have expressed views that are not only incorrect, but such views have been given as if, indeed, they are true." He felt that Doghudje was needlessly apologetic about the constantly improving quality of life of advertising practitioners in Nigeria. He believed that practitioners in the country had put in more than they got and that their peers abroad who had made good were only 'lucky' to be operating in 'more organised environments', not that they were more brilliant or more hardworking. "For you to suggest that we have no right to break this poverty line is what some of us continue to distance ourselves from," he said.

Interestingly, the lifestyle and passion for advertising exhibited by practitioners like Shobanjo, Odunsi, Omojafor and Adelaja were some of the considerations that kick-started the trend of progressive shift in the interest of mass communication students from journalism and public relations to advertising. This was confirmed by Oluwajuyitan, who retired as Executive Director of The Guardian newspapers and currently lectures at the University of Lagos, Akoka:

"When I was studying for my Master's in Mass Communication in the early 80s, very few of my course mates were interested in advertising; it was either Journalism or PR. That changed with people like Shobanjo, Odunsi, Omojafor, Adelaja and co. Without them, advertising would probably have remained where it was. Shobanjo, especially, has a passion for advertising; that is why we see advertising for what it is today. Before him, not many people practised advertising as a profession; he elevated it to a profession and helped to improve its intellectual content so that people suddenly began to see advertising as something worthwhile."

Oluwajuyitan's 'Damascus experience' on the prospects in advertising as a ticket to the good life was made complete when, as Head of the advertising directorate of The Guardian newspapers, he was invited by Insight to an event in honour of some of the agency's clients. The function was hosted by Shobanjo in his home then located at Opebi in Ikeja, Lagos. Oluwajuyitan summed up his experience thus: "It was when I got to Shobanjo's house that I said: 'so there could be money in advertising?' Until I got there, I never thought he had money. The house was impressive; I had not seen that type of house before – the way it was decorated and what he had there. It was clear that some of us had been practising advertising as just 'another job.'"

Regardless of the unavoidable comparison on lifestyle issues,

Shobanjo refused to be drawn into any debate on whether he would be 'another' Donald Trump in his capacity as CEO, saying: "I do not know that one of the criteria for being CEO is that you must be Donald Trump; I am Biodun Shobanjo, CEO of The Apprentice Africa. What you will see is my interpretation of how a CEO should manage crucial challenges for optimal results, having successfully run businesses myself. Take me the way I am."

In accepting to be CEO of The Apprentice Africa, his key objective was to demonstrate to Africa's aspiring entrepreneurs that "It is better to look for the 'open' door rather than cry over the 'closed' door." The show thus became a platform for him to share the secrets of his success over the years. The Apprentice Africa was also an opportunity to align his worldview – that failure is never an option – with the corporate philosophy of Bank PHB that there is no such word as 'impossible'. "I really do not have to celebrate failure in my life; if you are not used to failing, you don't even contemplate failure."

Being CEO of The Apprentice Africa required that Shobanjo took 18 apprentices under his wings for a period of 16 weeks, during which he would subject them to physical and mental exercises to hire the best in class as his 'apprentice' for one year. Nigeria had the highest number of contestants, seven; Ghana, three; Uganda, three; Kenya, three; Guinea, one and Cameroon, one. In this regard, providence played out its very rich sense of humour. 27 years earlier, Shobanjo had launched Nigeria's boldest marketing communications enterprise with 18 real life 'apprentices'. In all those years, he had had cause to directly fire only a handful of employees – from a group workforce that has exceeded 17,000 employees – on grounds of ethical conflicts in the work place. In The Apprentice Africa he would need to rapidly fire 17 apprentices, no matter how good or bad they were, in a space of five months in order to hire just one.

He easily rationalised his low headcount for firing in real life: "I hire people that I do not have to fire; but when I need to fire anyone, I do not think twice about it. A CEO must demonstrate that a right decision had been taken."

None of the 18 contestants had had any close encounter with him before the show but they had read his profile and were sufficiently impressed. Although they eagerly looked forward to meeting him, none of them knew precisely what to expect. When, eventually, they met Shobanjo, their perception of him varied. Many of the contestants declined to discuss the subject of their first impression of the CEO. The few that did requested anonymity. This, understandably, was because none wanted to start out on a 'wrong' footing with the boss so as not to jeopardise their chances of winning the ultimate prize of $200,000 plus one-year employment. The sum of what the contestants said of the CEO was as interesting as they were revealing. Broadly, they saw a man who could not readily be type-cast but who came across as a confident go-getter.

A contestant said: "I expected somebody who was older but very much in touch with the kid in him; (one) that is very serious but at the same time down-to-earth and playful." Another noted that: "He first came across as a no-nonsense person and I felt for sure he was not someone I would love to work with because he seemed stuffy." Another quipped: "He is a humble, knowledgeable businessman with a good soul." Yet another said: "He is a hard-working entrepreneur; a little bit traditional in his thinking." For another: "I initially thought that he was an all-business guy with no-time-to-play."

When the show began to air on February 26, 2008, it became an instant hit and it lived up to its billing as 'Live MBA on TV'. Viewers focused on the content of the programme and paid attention to the performance of the CEO. Task after task, the contestants were exposed to what Shobanjo, whilst resting the Trump/Shobanjo comparison, had earlier described as 'separate and unique circumstances' of doing business in an unstructured economy such as Africa's. He also shared his global perspectives of doing business. The tasks ranged from hawking to presentation skill; from developing financial products to developing special fast food menu and from developing a TV commercial to creating and selling works of art. More than anything else, the tasks that were undertaken by the contestants gave viewers a chance to think through some of the solutions that emerged on the show.

Seeing foreigners and foreign-trained graduates hawk goods in traffic in Lagos was a spectacle for viewers. That first 'street smart' task got a UK-based female Ghanaian contestant evicted because she failed to imbibe the lesson of flexibility in doing business. But as the show progressed, the CEO also landed in hot waters when he stopped short of firing a female project leader because, as he said, she was 'unfamiliar' with Lagos. The contestant who was evicted in her stead, for being 'too aggressive', did not think that the CEO took a right decision. A newspaper contributor took the CEO to the cleaners in a Letter to the Editor of a major Nigerian newspaper, saying in not so many words that the contestant, a Nigerian, was fired for ethnic reasons. His children felt he had some nerve firing their mother's namesake, Joyce (Mbaya, of Kenya), just like that. A girlfriend of one of his sons was not too pleased with him for firing her favourite contestant, Blessing Njoku of Nigeria.

A few other contestants also had cause to disagree with the CEO's reasons for firing them. One felt he did not sufficiently recognise the efforts that she had put into the execution of her assignment. Another felt that he was fired by the CEO because the latter did not like the tang of his cologne. When four 'Project Managers' were fired in quick succession, the surviving contestants tried their utmost to avoid being handed the mantle of leadership because it had become a sure ticket to eviction in the boardroom. A Project Manager chose to sacrifice himself rather than name the 'weak link' in his team.

Contestants forged strange alliances and became manipulative as they spun webs of intrigues to avoid being fired by the CEO. Some chose to 'play safe' in the hope that they would be below the CEO's radar in the boardroom. Some others practically turned themselves into Shobanjo's voice, saying what they believed he wanted to hear to prolong their stay in the programme. Night after night, The Apprentice Africa gave viewers value for their time.

TV critic, Onoshe Nwabuikwu, opined that the show 'made apprentices of all of us (because) there is much you can learn.'[1] True. But the drawing power of The Apprentice Africa was not so much in the 'usual office politics' played by the contestants as it was in the manner in which the CEO resolved the complex interplay of strategy, politics and personalities as well as social and professional skills. The corporate wisdom that oozed forth from Shobanjo's interpretation of the CEO's role in the running of a successful enterprise was legion. As he had promised before the premiere of the show, The Apprentice Africa was both 'educative and entertaining.'

At every point at which he needed to explain a firing in the boardroom, the logic of his argument appropriately justified his position. The core of his position could be summed up as follows:

'Office Politics':
- In every organisation, there will always be politicking. What matters is what you do to rise above it and demonstrate your ability.

---

[1] *Airtime, Thisday, 26 April 2008, page 38.*

'Leadership & responsibility':

- A leader must be daring and cannot be seen to abdicate responsibility; she or he must manifestly lead from the front.
- If the boat is sinking, a leader does not keep quiet and pass the buck.
- A leader must be bold; must own up to his decisions and does not need to sacrifice himself just so he is perceived as a 'nice' leader.
- A leader must clearly define tasks and be very clear and specific about the parameters for measuring results.

'Managing Perception':

- Manage perception religiously in a corporate environment; promptly correct any error, even if it is as minor as being addressed as 'Mr Biodun' instead of as 'Mr Shobanjo'.

'The logic of selling':

- No consumer is waiting to pick information in a cluttered world; when you sell, zero in on one single benefit, not a pot-pourri that will get the prospect confused.
- People talk glibly about 'brand' but it is amazing that a lot of people do not understand what it is. There always must be consideration for 'brand presence'.
- In an African setting, the battle for the consumer is won or lost in the open, not in the 'supermarket', so your labels must be quite legible.
- Your brand name should not necessarily be a 'descriptor' (e.g. Nutty Nut, which is not bad in a body copy).

'The Leader as Guide':

- When things are not going right, ask yourself, as a leader, what guidance or assistance you are giving.

'Seizing Opportunity'

- Never take success for granted; always take advantage of whatever 'advantage' you have.

'Power of Observation':

- Always take into consideration every piece of information in your brief.

'Not Playing the Victim':

- When you are not being heard, you must try your damndest to be heard.
- Those who get blamed the most are those who cannot take decisions.

'Delegation of Authority'

- There is nothing bad in delegation; but when you delegate, you must follow through.

'Buck Passing':

- A leader cannot pass the buck; final decisions rest with the leader, who must always determine the quality of advice she or he is receiving from others.

When Shobanjo signed off the show in July, 2008 at a tension-soaked grand finale, saying, "Isaac (Kwabena Dankyi-Koranteng of Ghana), you're hired!" there was no argument that he had acquitted himself well both from the point of view of being a TV anchor and a top corporate executive. Mid-way into the show, hard-hitting Nwabuikwu scored Shobanjo high on both platforms, arguing that he was neither 'flamboyant' nor 'excessive' and neither 'sentimental' nor 'ingratiating.' "On the show, Shobanjo comes across as shrewd, tough, but fair...willing to give you a chance to defend yourself (and he) does not preach anything he is not willing to practise himself,"[1] she wrote.

---

[1] *Airtime, Thisday, 12 April, 2008, page 38*

Shobanjo twice hosted the contestants. The first at his Ikeja, Lagos residence in honour of the first eight contestants that were fired and a second time at his country home in Aiyepe, Ogun State to formally end Season One of The Apprentice Africa. On both occasions, the contestants saw different sides of his personality. The one that initially found him somewhat 'stuffy' had a turn around experience, though he still had some reservations: "Well, I was glad, after seeing him at an informal level, that he could let go and be relaxed. He is someone I feel I could work with, because, like me, he works while he works and when he plays, he plays. I love the fact that, again, informally, he could serve our drinks and chat one-on-one. He is a perfectionist, though, and he loves to get his way. I think he needs to realise that in-between the 'whites' and 'blacks' of life, there are so many other shades of colour, if only we look hard enough for them."

Another spoke in the same vein: "How humble he is and how highly he spoke of his family. He is not just a great business man but also a wonderful, devoted father of successful children. What a role model!" The only 'Apprentice' who went on record for this book, Oscar Kamukama of Uganda, was unequivocal: "As a person, he is just a business man who can take hostages to achieve his aims. As a professional, he is a tycoon who believes success is everything. He invited us to his house and showed us his good naturedness – social style. He is a nice guy to hang out with."

The appreciative contestants overwhelmed the CEO with a gift of a large hand-crafted and autographed 'Thank You' portrait that loudly proclaimed: 'You're Fired!'

12

The Quest for Immortality

If you must part with portions of your dream, be sure you have genuine partners who would understand your feelings and your pains as a founder.

Biodun Shobanjo

Shobanjo's withdrawal from the hustle and bustle of everyday client interface gave him ample time to re-think the future of Troyka Holdings vis-à-vis the challenge of doing business in an increasingly borderless global economy. If anything, he was certain that Insight and its sister companies that make up the Group were purpose-driven vehicles, not commercial trophies won through successful glory hunting. His belief was buoyed by the recognition of Troyka Holdings as One of Best Enterprises in the Field of Marketing Communications in Nigeria by the Socrates Committee, Oxford, UK in 2015. His colleagues on the board of Troyka naturally shared his confidence that history would further record what they had created for posterity. They knew, too, that something more was needed to consolidate their story of success. As he summed it up: "You can forgive a business owner who died several decades ago whose legacies you cannot find anymore. Is that the route we should pursue? With knowledge and experience over the years and across continents, must we not learn and institute global best practice? We chose not to go the 'Nigerian' way."

Not going the 'Nigerian' way meant settling for immortality. It also meant envisioning an enterprise that would outlast its founders in the same way that global organisations like Leo Burnett, Ogilvy & Mather, Saatchi & Saatchi, Young & Rubicam and Publicis Groupe, amongst many others, had done. The critical question was 'how'?

Whilst planning the future of Insight, Shobanjo and his colleagues gave considerable attention to two critical yet intertwined issues. The first was how to maintain a steady stream of brilliant young business managers to ensure there was no vacuum in the pipeline of succession in the hierarchy. The second was to inaugurate a corporate investment programme to enhance manpower development in the industry. The convergence of both concerns gave rise to the Insight Management Trainee Programme that was instituted in 1989. The programme, which qualitatively answered both needs before it transformed to the group-wide Troyka Management Trainee Programme (TMTP), was launched with a search for candidates not older than 25 years, with either a First-Class degree or a minimum of Second Class Upper division in any discipline. It was not too successful because it flushed out the creative ferment that the leaders of the company desperately wanted. The programme produced highly cerebral people who loved academics, not marketing communications. The selection criteria were further modified to avoid the problems associated with excessive focus on academic brilliance. The scope of the search was thereafter extended to anyone with a minimum of a Second-Class Lower division in any discipline but who was sociable and had an acceptable degree of eccentricities. The age barrier was modified and pegged at 27 years to accommodate victims of the unstable academic calendars of tertiary institutions in Nigeria. Again, there was a problem because the test questions that were administered gave an edge to candidates who were numerate. As a result, the test metrics were re-defined and continually updated to ensure that creative people were not unwittingly weeded out.

Since its inception, the programme has taken on board more than 200 participants. On average, over 4,000 applications are received annually from intending trainees. By 2013, however, the number of applications received for the traineeship programme rose exponentially to about 40,000. Year-on-year, applicants undergo three stages of screening that starts with a general test that is now administered electronically. Successful candidates then undergo oral interview to test their presentation skill as well as assess their comportment and dress sense. Final selection is done by a panel composed of the Managing Directors of unit companies, who, at that stage try to spot talents that could be groomed in relevant professional areas in the Group. The underlying objective is to select thoroughbred candidates by matching the personality traits with the group's vision whilst focusing on the future. The qualities in demand are overt intelligence, confidence, ability to think outside the box (described as 'positively rebellious') and strong middle-class values, especially of integrity, loyalty and stability. These were largely distilled from lessons from past experiences on the factors that led to the collapse of some of the unit companies in the group.

Shobanjo's decision not to take up any 'quota' to place 'highly recommended' candidates of family and friends in Troyka companies routinely pitched him against people who are close to him. His insistence on due process once caused his aunt's daughter to refuse to speak with him for over a year. The young lady just could not understand how, having scaled through three rounds of interviews, her uncle's company still would not employ her. Although he was pained that his niece fell by the wayside, he still maintained his position that if over 30,000 candidates applied for employment in which only 20 would be hired, then it stood to reason that the process must be extremely transparent to ensure that only the best 20 were hired. By making a personal sacrifice of not interfering in the recruitment process, he demonstrated to his colleagues that they would have no excuse to change the rules without inviting sanctions, including possible loss of their own jobs, for their conduct. For him, no punishment was too high to mete out to ensure sanctity and adherence to rules to which everyone had subscribed.

Typically, the Management Trainee programme lasts for one year, during which the trainees undergo in-house attachments at unit companies and, externally, with third party suppliers and clients to understand the expectations of all stakeholders. The trainees are mentally bombarded with a minimum of one lecture every Friday and they write weekly reports that are vetted by the human resource department. At the end of their programme, they write projects that they, in the company of their mentors at the unit companies, must defend during the 'Chairman's Interview' that is conducted by Shobanjo.

The reputation of the Troyka Management Trainee Programme as a finishing school for intensely-focused marketing communications experts has made the programme a favourite hunting ground for poachers. In a particular year, a trainee who got an extension for his inability to scale through the Chairman's interview was snapped up by a major bank that employed him as an Assistant Manager. Even those who passed were lured away with juicy offers made by potential employers, with the result that of every 10 trainees that complete the programme each year, only about six remain in the group. By 2010, Akinola Olanrewaju, of the 1990 set, had risen to become Executive Director (Finance and Account) at Halogen Security. Sam Osunsoko of the Class of '99 became the highest-ranking management trainee in the group, having attained the position of Managing Director of the newly created second agency, Leo Burnett before he bowed out of service. Despite the high rate of turnover of trainees, the Group has continued to invest in the programme in keeping with the goal of maintaining a well-structured scheme that feeds the main human resource management system.

In 2006, Shobanjo quarrelled with managers of the programme for not putting together a 'wholesome' training plan for candidates that were put forward for the Chairman's Interview. He was unhappy because the programme had become too short and too Insight-focused. Worse, it was supervised by staff who, themselves, graduated not too long ago from the programme. He ordered that the lapses be promptly corrected. His concern was far greater than the narrow focus of the programme's content. He sensed that if care was not exercised, there was a real danger that the programme, as it was managed, could end up planting 'a bunch of half-baked executives in the group.' He consequently made up his mind to stop conducting the Chairman's Interview until his instructions were carried out. But he was in for a shocker in 2007.

He did not conduct the annual Chairman's Interview that year. But it was not because the candidates were half-baked. On the contrary, he was deeply impressed. While on a trip abroad, he discovered to his embarrassment that Troyka had no Group website. Apart from Optimum Exposures and The Quadrant Company, no other company in the group had effective online presence. Not even Insight had a useful website. A year before this, the late journalist, Tunmise Adekunle of Thisday newspapers, had written on his discovery that few marketing communications companies in Nigeria had effective online presence. His report generated a lot of furore in the industry. But the noise died down and business returned to the usual. A few trainees in the 2007 class had also made the same discovery whilst preparing to write the test for the traineeship programme. Whatever information they had on Troyka Holdings was sourced from publications and word of mouth. They asked the question 'how come a Troyka website does not exist?' It turned out that it never crossed anyone's mind in the Group. The trainees sought the Chairman's permission to develop a website for the Group. Their request was made about the same time that Shobanjo made his discovery. He promptly approved.

The idea of developing the Troyka website first flashed in the mind of Efe Origbo, an architect trained at the Obafemi Awolowo University, while he was on his way home. After he discussed its possibility with his colleagues, they were convinced that the project could be concluded in about a month. Efe, who, before he left school, had killed the idea of practising architecture, worked on the visuals of the website while his colleagues were divided into sub-groups to collate information, research the online presence of local and international marketing communications companies and write the copy that would be posted on the site. They missed their deadline by a full month because assignments piled up from their respective in-house attachments. They signalled their readiness to make a presentation to the Chairman as soon as they completed an internal review of what they had done.

During the presentation, the trainees unintentionally hit Shobanjo in the guts when they innocently revealed that they navigated the website of BatesCosse during their research and found it to be 'very good'. He jocularly told the team not to rub it in by sticking the young agency in his face. The trainees did not catch the joke. But they screamed with delight when he commended their effort and said that, as reward, he would waive the Chairman's Interview for their set. He kept his word. Troyka got its website. And the trainees were welcome into the Troyka family without individually facing Shobanjo, who, since that time, has also stopped conducting the Chairman's Interview.

Although the Troyka Management Trainee Programme has sufficiently stabilised to produce well-trained middle level managers, the quest to build a legacy institution still required that the Group be made more robust in several other dimensions to compete in the present and face the highly competitive future that beckoned. One route was to list the business on the floor of the Nigerian Stock Exchange (NSE). This was especially attractive because of the high probability of over-subscription if the shares of Insight were floated on the Exchange. Although the Troyka team had earned a right to sit back on easy street to enjoy life after more than three decades of heavy lifting, the possibility of making 'good' money by selling off private equity to the public did not fit their narrative of 'how' to leave a legacy. Shobanjo, especially, was not receptive to the idea of approaching the NSE because, as he said, "listing is not in our DNA."[1] The kind of 'enduring' legacy he had in mind was anchored on long term competitiveness that required matching superior knowledge with the kind of skill, systems and processes that the enterprise needed to survive. In other words, they needed people, more than money, as the 'Oxygen' to guarantee future relevance in business.

---

[1] *http://tribuneonlineng.com/our-creative-industry-has-not-moved-at-par-with-the-rest-of-the-world/(accessed 26 June, 2016)*

As they reflected on these issues, circumstances at home and abroad conspired to shape the direction of their plans. Contrary to conventional wisdom, thunder struck a second time in the same place. The first time was in 1997 when Insight announced its affiliation to Grey Inc after severing its 14-year relationship with Bates Worldwide. The resurgence of international commerce in post-apartheid Africa made the realignment imperative. Grey, which quickly keyed-in to the potential of the new Africa ahead of Bates, however, badly needed strong local partners to complement its strides on the continent. The network, at that time, was quite strong in South Africa; reasonably strong in East Africa but very weak in West Africa. The new InsightGrey partnership used Ghana as its landing base to test its strength in West Africa with the establishment of InsightGrey Advertising in Accra in 1997. Thereafter, the partnership entered Côte d'Ivoire where it signed on with AG-Partners, whose principal, Isabelle Aimonetti, was the indisputable Queen of French-speaking West Africa where she had about eight offices.

The experiment in Ghana was originally an attempt by Troyka Holdings to grow organically on its own steam. The Grey network was persuaded to join the train to make the ride much smoother. Local experience was also infused into the project through a partnership with Great Argon Holdings, one of Ghana's leading integrated marketing communications groups, which was led by Torgbor Mensah. In spite of the quantum of human and material investment that went into it, the boat of InsightGrey in Accra sank owing to a combination of several factors. At home, Troyka could not upscale the quality of attention that it gave to the offshore entity because it also had to manage the challenge of running Insight Nigeria and other subsidiaries. Culturally, it was quite difficult to blend the near-aggressive constant motion of Nigerians with the average Ghanaian's inclination for unhurried living. The dearth of local talents similarly constrained the envisaged scale of operation in Ghana, which had only marginally emerged from her economic crisis that caused marketing communications to be relegated to the back burner. Nigeria's legendary copywriter, Ted Mukoro, was pulled in from retirement to lead the creative process in Accra but this act could not stave off the misadventure. To make matters worse, all the experienced hands, except Emeka Okeke, a media buying specialist, that were seconded to the Accra-based agency from Insight Nigeria were lost to Ghana. The board of Troyka pulled out of Ghana to cut its losses. But the relationship between Insight and Grey Inc subsisted.

History began to repeat itself in 2006 when WPP, then the world's second largest marketing communications network, bought over Grey Inc in much the same way that the old Saatchi & Saatchi bought over Ted Bates in 1986. By this time, however, the global economic meltdown had caused varying degrees of disequilibrium in markets across the world. By 2008, multinational organisations began to seriously review their global corporate strategies as part of programmes of recovery from the recession. Several multinationals looked towards Africa and, by extension, Nigeria because the continent was a relatively virgin territory. This contrasted with the saturation of opportunity for growth in Europe and increasingly limited potentials in Asia.

Whilst others targeted Africa, Grey, under WPP, its new owners, began to progressively de-emphasise its focus on the continent. Noticeably, its support of All-Seasons Mediacom, Troyka's premier media independent company, did not produce the projected professional satisfaction. This contrasted with the fortunes of Media Perspectives, Troyka's second media independent company, which had forged far afield in the market where it enjoyed international partnership with Carat, the world's first independent media planning and buying company. Shobanjo considered Grey's relegation of Africa to the background in its operation a big mistake: "Somebody probably did not read his map right or, perhaps, the readings from the telescope were very blurred. You cannot ever re-draw the map of the world; Africa will always be important and Nigeria will always be an important part of Africa."

His reading of the industry in Africa was predicated on his optimism that the future of marketing communications in Nigeria and the entire continent is bright. Much of this optimism was also based on intuition that was grounded in thorough analysis of global trends. Some forecasts had positioned Nigeria as one of 'Next 11' nations that could define the course of the global economy following progressive shifts in the world's 'economic centre of gravity' from the developed nations of Europe and America to 'emerging' markets. For this to happen, he believed that the local industry must key into global best practice. One of these required developing acute understanding of what he described as the inter-relatedness of 'people, relationships and contexts.' These are at the core of global communities in which people, in the digital age, "directly access media; influence media; influence thinking and are, themselves, media." In this situation, marketers could continually and more effectively 'own' conversations in the market place by using the technique of 'storytelling,' which is not alien to the African culture, to engage consumers. All of this reinforces the notion that brands have capacity to 'deliver the future.' He reckoned that any local agency that desired to be relevant in the long haul must project far ahead into the future; enjoy the advantage of size and be firmly anchored in the digital age.

The picture that formed in his mind subsequently became the fulcrum of the massive industry shake-up that he engineered from retirement. That picture also conformed to his image as 'the man who saw the future,' as veteran broadcaster, Kevin Ejiofor, described him at a 2016 social event to mark the 80th birthday of another old colleague and encyclopedia of music, Benson Idonije. The compliment was an acknowledgement of the height the Troyka Chairman had attained after he took an early decision in 1971 to walk a different path from a promising public service career in broadcasting.

A careful analysis of the market and the direction in which the industry was headed made Shobanjo lean more heavily towards getting institutional investors to take up equity that could give fillip to targeted Troyka companies, particularly the flagship, Insight. Part of the attraction was the growing trend of clients pitching their business on global basis owing to the blurring of geographical and economic borders. Grey had no problem with becoming an equity partner in Insight, but any deal would have to be signed off by WPP's Chairman, Sir Martin Sorrell, with whom Shobanjo continued discussions on the subject in 2010. The WPP Chairman made an offer that required Troyka to cede 51 per cent majority holding to WPP. Shobanjo declined the offer by counter-proposing a 50 – 50 arrangement, which really was no better than listing on the NSE; he was not convinced that the WPP network had anything beyond money to put on the table. His position was premised on the fact that Insight had over the years demonstrated strength to develop and grow its business. "I have never liked the idea of leaning on my multinational partners to give me business because that would weaken my position; it would weaken my hands with them. That is why they respect us."

Equal partnership did not appeal to WPP, which, characteristically, stuck to its well-known global antecedents: a controlling interest in an entity or nothing at all. This position, perhaps, was predicated on a need to further consolidate WPP's books in consonance with the

International Financial Reporting Standards (IFRS). Sorrell dropped hints of a visit to Lagos to further discuss the issue with other Troyka directors in the belief that doing so might significantly soften Shobanjo's stance on equal partnership. Shobanjo, on the other hand, considered the idea a waste of valuable time because Awosika and Ibe, who were also founding directors/shareholders of Troyka, similarly saw WPP's offer as unrealistic. He felt that Sorrell did not sufficiently understand the mindset of an entrepreneur because he appeared to have missed the important point that Shobanjo's attachment to the business was more emotional than commercial. He believed that an entrepreneur in the mould of the former Chairman/CEO of Grey Worldwide, Ed Myer, would, in the same circumstance, probably have shown better appreciation of his position having himself undergone the pains and joy of founding, not acquiring, an enterprise.

On this score, only a very thin line separated Shobanjo's experience with the WPP Chairman from that of the advertising legend, David Ogilvy, and Sorrell. In 1989, WPP splashed an estimated $864 million on Ogilvy & Mather to buy and bring Ogilvy's agency under the WPP umbrella. The sale riled Ogilvy who reportedly lashed out at his fellow Briton, saying "the idea of being taken over by that odious little jerk gives me the creep."[1] Put in proper context, Ogilvy's unconfirmed outburst, according to writer, John Tylee, was indicative of the clash of generational and personal values,[2] one in which Ogilvy was perceived as a 'personification of gentlemen with brains' whilst Sorrell had the reputation of a 'globally consolidated and financially-driven' corporate raider. As it were, this narrative has helped to properly articulate Shobanjo's argument against an entrepreneur surrendering his dream to a partner with diametrically opposed vision and values.

---

[1] John Tylee, *Best of the Bust-ups (David Ogilvy Vs Sir Martin Sorrell), Campaign's pick of Advertising Fights and Standoffs,* May 10, 2002. www.campaignlive.co.uk (accessed 31 July, 2016)
[2] *Cited above*

Even if futuristically he was inclined to ceding majority equity to the WPP network, he did not feel it was right to do so at that point, neither did he believe that it should happen in one fell swoop. Were this to be his key objective, Insight could more easily have been listed on the NSE as earlier explained. Nonetheless, the possibility of equity participation in Insight by Grey was not foreclosed. Instead, key managers of Troyka and WPP were left to discuss and work out various options for future consideration. A three-man Insight team that comprised Shobanjo, Awosika and the Group Finance Director, Kayode Situ, travelled to London to discuss with the WPP team. For 18 months, the talks did not record significant progress. In the intervening period, clouds of game-changing occurrences gathered on both sides of the Atlantic.

As Grey/WPP foot-dragged and focused more resolutely on Europe and Asia, the WPP network got embroiled in a major controversy in Nigeria owing to a business dispute between one of its agency networks, Ogilvy Africa, and its local partner, Prima Garnet. Shobanjo and his colleagues sat back to monitor the unfolding drama, seeing that in light of what was happening, Insight/Troyka could quite easily have been in the shoes of its fellow Nigerian agency.

Way back in 1997, Prima Garnet had established an affiliate relationship with O & M that before then had severed its relationship with the defunct Ogilvy Benson and Mather (OBM) in Nigeria. After several years, the technical affiliation transformed to equity partnership in which Ogilvy Africa took a little less than 15 per cent equity in Prima Garnet, which handled the Nigerian leg of the Bharti Airtel telecommunications account that Ogilvy Africa had won on a continent-wide basis. A full year before Ogilvy Africa won the account across the continent, Prima Garnet had successfully managed the media in Nigeria, and this was one of the factors that contributed to the account being given to Ogilvy Africa across the region. Following the introduction of GSM phone services in Nigeria in 2001, Insight Communications and Prima Garnet were both appointed to work on the corporate and products launch of Econet Wireless Nigeria, the precursor of Airtel. Prima Garnet would later be involved with various stages of Econet's five or six transitions to Airtel. The Prima Garnet/Ogilvy Africa relationship, however, ran into a storm after Ogilvy sought 51 per cent controlling stake in Prima Garnet, which was not ready to sell more than 25 per cent of its equity in the first instance, with a proposal to sell more within a gradual and phased plan covering about five years. WPP/Ogilvy rejected Prima Garnet's proposal, and instead wanted an immediate take over into a majority position of 51%. At some point, WPP also insisted that the deal should cover all Prima Garnet's associate companies, that is, 141 Worldwide, MediaShare and Cutler Ogilvy PR, among others. Prima Garnet flatly rejected the WPP proposal and communicated this in writing to Martin Sorrell, the WPP boss. This was the first of two-successive major turn-down of WPP's bullish attempts at railroading Nigerian agencies in the increasingly attractive African market. Troyka's rejection of WPP's offer became the second.

A twist in the Prima Garnet/Ogilvy Africa story occurred when O & M's parent network, WPP bought into Nairobi, Kenya-based Scangroup, which, in turn, bought 51 per cent equity in Ogilvy Africa network by way of shares swap. Later, the Ogilvy Africa network, in what appeared to be in breach established Scanad advertising in Nigeria to handle the Airtel account after it failed to secure Prima Garnet's co-operation to hands off the account in spite of a $180,000 severance offer that the local agency considered as 'humiliating.'[1] Prima Garnet headed for the courts to contest Ogilvy's right to float a rival agency in Nigeria in spite of a subsisting

---

[1] *Aggregate of various newspaper reports*

contract that clearly said neither party could establish an agency in any market where either of them already existed, without first terminating the master agreement. The matter was eventually settled out of court in December 2017 following 'mutually beneficial discussions' between Prima Garnet and Ogilvy & Mather Africa BV, with both entities hoping to "continue to contribute to the growth of the Nigerian advertising landscape."[1]

Whilst the Prima Garnet Africa Vs O & M dispute played out in court, discussions between Insight and WPP gradually ground to a halt. By then, Shobanjo had begun to have second thoughts on the proposed deal considering the unfolding drama. The Troyka team thereafter decided that it was in their best interest to talk with any of the other global networks at the first opportunity.

Providence once more stepped in the gap late in 2012 when Shobanjo received a mail from the manager of a multinational organisation in Nigeria to request a meeting to discuss matters that could be of mutual benefit. Both men met to hold exploratory discussions that ironically centred on the growing interest of the Publicis Groupe in Nigeria. The interest of the world's third largest advertising network, after WPP and Omnicom, in one of Africa's largest markets was understandable because it was in tandem with the network's focus on emerging markets as one of the drivers of its growth in the business.

Prior to this time, the Chief Executive Officer of Publicis Africa Group, Kevin Tromp, had visited Nigeria several times after his appointment to that role late 2009. At the time, the Publicis brand in the country was represented by Rosabel Advertising, which was affiliated to Leo Burnett and SO & U, which was affiliated to Saatchi & Saatchi. Rosabel's media independent company, Starcom, was also affiliated to Starcom Mediavest, a Publicis company. Tromp's visits were tied to his mandate to restructure the business of Publicis Groupe in sub-

---

[1] *Prima Garnet and Ogilvy & Mather Africa Reach Out of Court Dispute Settlement* (www.brandcrunch.com.ng)

Saharan Africa particularly in terms of bringing affiliate agencies up to the group's global standard. Although the bulk of the group's business in West Africa at the time came out of Ghana, Nigeria was of considerable interest because it was a strategic market in the group's forward plan of connecting the dots in its areas of operation. Publicis needed to get Nigeria right, for which reason there was emphasis on the quality of the brand's representation in the country. The outcome of Tromp's visits to Nigeria may have triggered the correspondence between Shobanjo and the pathfinder who had requested for a meeting.

The Troyka Chairman initially tried to discourage his guest by emphasising that his group was happy with Grey. His antennae, however, distinctly picked the information that Publicis was in search of an equity partner, not an affiliate. This was logical because the network's continental vision had culminated in the launch of the Publicis Africa Group (PAG) in September 2012. The PAG was conceived as a network of Publicis-connected agencies that had considerable influence in various markets in Africa. Key Publicis brands in PAG were Saatchi & Saatchi, Publicis Worldwide, Leo Burnett, Arc, Starcom, Zenith and DigitasLBi to which a host of agencies in Africa were affiliated. PAG consisted of "51 partner agencies in Sub-Saharan Africa, with equity stakes in 20 of the agencies outside of South Africa, and majority ownership in a further 11 agencies in South Africa."[1] Rosabel was the only Nigerian agency listed as a member of PAG at inception.

When Shobanjo met Awosika and Situ to apprise them of his discussions with the Publicis go-between, they persuaded him to hear out his guest. But he was more easily swayed to continue the discussions because of his understanding that Publicis only needed another influential agency group to join Rosabel in PAG. Discussions at the follow-up meeting centred on more concrete issues without

---

[1] *http://www.mslgroup.com/news/2016/publicis-groupe-partners-with-the-troyka-group-in-africa/ (accessed 26 June, 2016)*

side-stepping the 'no-go' areas that Shobanjo had earlier highlighted. One of these involved steering clear of anything that would negatively impact Rosabel Group. This, understandably, was because of his over 40-year old personal relationship with Odunsi and the rest of the Rosabel founding team. Shobanjo's eldest son, Tunde, was the ring bearer at Tunde Adelaja's wedding. He and Odunsi were practically each other's next of kin; they had raised their families about the same time and their children, in turn, had become good friends.

As the meetings progressed, a broad plan was agreed to do a deal with the main Publicis advertising agency, Publicis Worldwide, as well as its media independent, ZenithOptimedia, both of which were not represented in Nigeria. These would then be re-affiliated to both Insight and All-Seasons Mediacom respectively. All other companies in Troyka Group were to maintain their existing affiliate relationships. The arrangement presented win-win scenarios for both parties. For Troyka, the new relationship would give more technical muscle to All-Seasons Mediacom and help it to gain more footholds in its specialised media planning and buying market. Insight, on the other hand, would be assured of technical and human resource upgrade to maintain its industry leadership position long into the future in Nigeria. There was also a high probability of the agency playing bigger continental roles. From all indications, too, the arrangement suited Publicis Groupe, which would have set an unprecedented record of having simultaneous equity relationships in two of Nigeria's biggest marketing communications groups. Coincidentally, Rosabel Leo Burnett had two years earlier recruited an Insight veteran and Executive Director, Kayode Oluwasona, as its Managing Director to strengthen the group's operations and market profile. This, perhaps, was a bonus of sorts as he could be expected to grow to be a 'culture' bridge to link the tripartite entities if the arrangement worked out.

The negotiating parties, however, did not reckon with various twists and turns at both national and international levels that would eventually change the course of their talks as well as the strategic outcomes. One of the unanticipated issues that cropped up before final terms of the agreement were inked was APCON's new Advertising Practice Reforms that came into effect in January, 2013. One of its principal clauses was that "any shareholding of 74.9 percent and above (up to 100 percent) by Nigerians qualifies an agency as a national agency while 25.1 percent and above (up to 100 percent) by foreigners qualify an agency as a foreign agency. A foreign agency shall practise advertising business targeted at a market outside the shores of Nigeria." In plain terms, this meant that no foreign partner could take up more than 25 per cent stake in any local enterprise but it could set up wholly-owned agencies that would prospect business outside of Nigeria. This regulation effectively killed off the request of the WPP/Ogilvy Africa/Scanad Group for 51 per cent equity in Prima Garnet Africa; it precluded the possibility of Publicis asking for any higher stake in Insight and it took the bottom out of WPP's insistence on 51 per cent equity that had stalled its discussions with Insight.

Grey/WPP woke up too late to press for 25 per cent equity in Insight after it became clear that it could neither circumscribe local regulations nor ignore rumours that Insight had begun serious dialogue with a rival global network. Grey's missed opportunity became more evident when its Worldwide Chairman/Chief Executive Officer, Jim Heekin, met Awosika in Europe at a Grey network conference in 2013.

"Where's Bibi?" he asked Awosika whilst introducing him to one of Grey's top executives.

Although Awosika confidently replied that Shobanjo was in Lagos, both men knew quite well that the question was not intended to elicit information on the physical location of the Troyka Chairman but on where he stood in relation to all issues under discussion. It also fished for information on whether there was any truth in the rumblings that Insight was actively shopping for a replacement global agency network.

As Publicis and Troyka inched closer to sealing their deal in Nigeria, tremors of a colossal magnitude shook the global advertising industry in July 2013 with the announcement of the mega merger of New York-based Omnicom and Paris-based Publicis Groupe, the world's numbers Two and Three largest marketing communications networks. The emergent behemoth, Publicis Omnicom Group registered in The Netherlands, had $23 billion in revenue and half of the global industry's networks under one roof.[1] These networks included BBDO, TBWA and DDB from Omnicom and Publicis Worldwide, Leo Burnett, BBH, Saatchi & Saatchi, Starcom and ZenithOptimedia from Publicis Groupe. Nearly all the agencies in one form or the other had affiliates in Nigeria. The new entity, which at its announcement upstaged WPP from its global Number One position, also had a market capitalisation of $35.1 billion and more than 130,000 employees worldwide.[2] An ecstatic Publicis Chairman, Maurice Lévy, described the development as "a historical opportunity to reshape and establish a new industry standard" considering the challenge posed by the new media.[3]

Not everyone was as excited by the scale of the merger or its implications for global business. David Jones, the former Global CEO of Havas Group, the world's No. 5 largest network, sarcastically dismissed the Publicis/Omnicom union as "an industrial merger in the digital age."[4] His position was anchored on "the industry's obsession with mergers and acquisitions in a world where digital and technology have made scale irrelevant." Sir Martin Sorrell, whose network, WPP, was the key target of displacement from the top slot,

[1] AdWeek: Leaders Unveil Publicis Omnicom Group, July 28, 2013
[2] AdWeek: op. cit
[3] AdWeek: op. cit
[4] New York Times: Merger Is Set To Create World's No. 1 Ad Company, July 28, 2013

simply waved off the merger as "strategically puzzling and structurally clunky."[1] He did not think it would succeed because, in his view, its scale was based too much on 'ego' rather than strictly business considerations.

Later events proved Sorrell right. After nearly one year of extensive discussions, the Publicis/Omnicom merger plan was shelved in May 2014 owing to "difficulties in completing the transaction within a reasonable time frame."[2] The league of 'Big 5' global marketing communications networks promptly reverted to status quo ante, that is, WPP, Omnicom, Publicis Groupe, InterPublic and Dentsu Carat. Without disruptions occasioned by developments on digital and data platforms, this table may remain the same far into the foreseeable future.

The ripples of the Publicis/Omnicom mega-merger, prior to its collapse, changed the planned partnership equation between Publicis Worldwide and the targeted Nigerian agencies. Based on the economy of scale, it was no longer realistic to negotiate equity partnership at unit agency levels but at an all-encompassing holding company level that left no room for cherry-picking. Everything was offered as a standard package. The collapse of the global merger talk made the new strategy road map even more attractive to Publicis, which clearly spelt out to both Rosabel and Troyka groups the exigency of flying with just one group to the exclusion of the other because doing so was tidier and less complex.

Head-to-head, Troyka and Rosabel offered basically the same bouquet of services under the same roof. On the digital platform, Rosabel had Bytesize, which was slightly ahead of the younger Hot Sauce in Troyka's stable. In PR, Troyka's TQC was a clear leader in the market where Rosabel's Edison Ross had long ceased to exist.

---

[1] *In conversation with Donna Imperato, CEO of Cohn & Wolfe, at the 2013 Global PR Summit*
[2] *Public statement by Omnicom to announce the de-merger*

Rosabel's Starcom Media was in strong contention with Troyka's Media Perspective and All-Seasons Mediacom in the media independent's market where Rosabel's second agency, Momentum Media, still sought relevance. In creative advertising, Troyka's flagship, Insight Communications, was stronger than Rosabel Leo Burnett, which was being strategically re-positioned by Oluwasona. Troyka's second creative agency, The ThiinkShop, was also growing to be a powerhouse in the market. Although both groups appeared to have been evenly matched, the combined strength of Troyka companies presented the group as being much closer than Rosabel to matching Publicis' picture of a strong, world-class marketing communications organisation. From a relationship perspective, however, Rosabel played on home ground having been in a 16-year relationship with the Publicis Groupe. Neither Troyka nor Rosabel was sure of where the Publicis pendulum would swing when the global network began to conduct due diligence on the fit of both agencies.

By late-2013, however, it began to emerge that Troyka had surged ahead of Rosabel.[1] Perhaps, this was to be expected because the reality in the market place was that the equity of Troyka companies, even if based on the sole parameter of blue-chip clientele, had more strength, more spread and more clout than Rosabel's. One of the earliest giveaways of the flow of the tide was the parting of ways between Media Perspectives, one of Troyka's media independent companies, and its international partner, Carat, which had pitched its tent with Dentsu, the Japanese worldwide agency network and global No. 5. With the business re-alignment in the horizon and the intensity of competition amongst global networks, it stood to reason that the relationship between Media Perspectives/Troyka and Carat/Dentsu was no longer tenable. The fall-back option was for Media Perspectives and All-Seasons Mediacom to find

---

[1] *Brandcrunch, "Rosabel parts ways with Leo-Burnett, Insight may be next home to global network," 21 November, 2013*

accommodation with either Starcom Mediavest or ZenithOptimedia respectively in the Publicis network if the transaction was successful. The Quadrant Company, Troyka's public relations subsidiary, faced similar cross-over situation, especially considering its affiliation to Fleishman-Hillard, an Omnicom company.

On 22 April 2014 Brandcrunch, an authoritative Nigerian marketing communications online platform, reconfirmed its earlier story that Publicis had settled for Troyka.[1] Neither Shobanjo nor the Group CEO of Rosabel, Ayo Oluwatosin, commented on the development. Behind the scene, the decision, hard as it was for Publicis to take, was already known to key executives of Troyka and Rosabel, as Shobanjo confirmed to this writer in a 2016 interview:

"What people didn't understand was that every inch of the way, I gave my friends feedback on what was going on; there was nothing to hide. We probably had a slight edge over Rosabel; it wasn't anything that anybody influenced. I had a responsibility to carry the Rosabel people through everything that was going on. Not only did I tell Akin (Odunsi), I took my time to tell his two partners, Steve (Omojafor) and Tunde (Adelaja). The things that bind us are much stronger than business. The outcome has not affected our friendship in any way."

Shobanjo and the Chairman of Publicis Groupe, Maurice Levy, met before the commencement of due diligence by both sides. Each took to the other from that very first meeting. They were easily connected by an entrepreneurial spirit that complemented the positive personal chemistry that brought them much closer. Coincidentally, Levy, two years older than Shobanjo, joined Publicis as IT Director in 1971,[2] the same year that the Troyka Chairman began his career in advertising. In a career that has spanned more than four decades with Publicis, the Moroccan-French man had

---

[1] *http://www.brandcrunch.com.ng/bnrch/index.php/news/agency-top-stories/1476-publicis-groupe-to-strike-it-big-in-nigeria how-troyka-was-picked-over-rosabel (accessed 26 June, 2016)*
[2] *https://en.m.wikipedia.org (accessed 11 August, 2016)*

grown to clearly understand the vision of the founder, Marcel Bleustein-Blanchet, and had experienced the pains, anxiety and joy of an entrepreneur ever before he assumed leadership and part ownership of the network in 1987. This contrasted with Sorrell's acquirer's disposition that, perhaps, accounted for the quick collapse of discussions on possible partnership between Troyka and Grey/WPP. There were also institutional similarities between Troyka and Publicis. Like the 90-year old Publicis, Troyka's flagship, Insight, in about 36 years, had only had two Chief Executive Officers, Shobanjo and Awosika. In both organisations, the first leadership transition was made from the founders to legacy-driven subordinates in what appeared to be a deliberate policy to implant evergreen institutional values of people and quality service. Levy was to Blanchet what Awosika was to Shobanjo, the difference being that Levy joined the Publicis train midway whilst Awosika was on board Insight's from the stage of conception.

Whilst Levy was impressed by the positive reports he had heard and read concerning his opposite number as the go-to person in Nigeria's marketing communications sector, Shobanjo did not have any difficulty engaging the French man because the chemistry was right: both thought in terms of preserving the long-term institutional interests of their respective organisations. Levy also did not speak like a behemoth that was intent on swallowing a minion as a matter of favour. These impressions convinced Shobanjo that the French global network would make an ideal partner to crown his age-long dream of not just building the biggest communications agency in Nigeria but also in being a significant part of a global network.

"We did not want to partner with a group that would, because of the bottom line, treat those who work for organisations in a way that is alien to us. There will always be problems and disconnect with partners that place money ahead of anything else," Shobanjo explained.

'Reasonableness' dictated the direction of negotiations between Troyka and Publicis during the due diligence and subsequent negotiations. Both sides engaged various external business and accounting consultants like PriceWaterhouseCoopers (PWC), KPMG and Ernst & Young as well as a battery of legal consultants that included Banwo & Ighodalo; Jackson, Eti & Edu and Lewis Silken Solicitors, who all worked round the clock in Lagos, London and Paris to deliver on target.

For starters, Troyka Holdings was unbundled into two core assets: communications and non-communications. Whilst the former was available to Publicis for investment, the latter, which consisted of four companies – Halogen (security); Promoworld (airports advertising); Optimum Exposures (out-of-home) and Black Onyx (real estate) – retained its original structure of ownership. To engender proper valuation, the shares of every investor in Troyka's marketing communications companies – Insight; All Seasons Mediacom; Media Perspectives; The Quadrant Company and Hot Sauce – were warehoused in a special purpose vehicle (SPV). These companies operated in four core professional areas – creative advertising, media independents, public relations and digital marketing – where their respective strengths could be complemented by business relationship with key Publicis agencies, notably Publicis Worldwide; Leo Burnett; Saatchi & Saatchi; Starcom Media; Zenith Optimedia; MSLGroup and Nurun. The SPV, in turn, acted as the custodian of the Publicis multinational brands. This arrangement now truly brought all the Troyka communications brands under one umbrella. This was a departure from the earlier practice of affiliating agencies in the Troyka group to different international partners regardless of the network to which they belonged.

The agreement for Publicis' purchase of 25 per cent equity in the SPV was signed in Paris in December 2015 by Shobanjo and Levy for Troyka Holdings and Publicis Groupe respectively. Again, this was a departure from previous international agreements that Shobanjo had signed. In September 1982, he and Bates' Chairman, Bob Jacoby, co-signed Insight's first ever affiliation with Ted Bates. But this was only circumstantial because the ceremonial signing of the agreement took place in the New York head office of Bates. The lead up discussions took place largely between Insight and Bates' President of International Operations, Stephen Rose. The 1996 agreement between Insight and Grey Advertising was signed by Shobanjo and John Shannon, Grey's President in charge of Europe, Middle East & Africa (EMEA). Since Bates and Grey were composite companies of larger networks, it followed that the endorsement of affiliate relationships could only be conveyed by the highest-ranking executives in charge of Insight's area of operation. The same scenario would have played out if discussions between Troyka and Grey/WPP had not fizzled out. The multiplicity of agencies under WPP's umbrella would at best have yielded a composite company-to-Group arrangement owing to the near-impossibility of warehousing all WPP agencies in one Nigerian agency as was done in the arrangement with Publicis Groupe. On 26 February, 2016, Publicis Groupe fully paid for its 25 percent holding in the new corporate entity that was born.

MSLGroup, the public relations arm of Publicis Groupe, formally broke the news of the group's "equity partnership with the communications arm of Troyka Group, the first wholly integrated marketing communications service provider in West Africa, including a total of 6 agencies"[1] via a press release issued in Paris on 16 March, 2016. The statement was emphatic that the partnership would be a launchpad to create "a powerful communications entity that will allow for competitive advantage across all areas of operation in the West African landscape." The CEO of Publicis Africa Group, Kevin Tromp, was effusive in his praise of Troyka Group companies, which he described as "the gold standard in Nigeria." He was optimistic that "the combination of Publicis Groupe's global expertise (and) Troyka Group's local strength will provide an unbeatable partnership in (West Africa's) challenging and fast developing market." An equally elated Shobanjo remarked that the partnership would "avail us access to global tools, process and platforms while helping to redefine route to market for the brands we work for, the ultimate consequence being better outcomes in terms of market expansion and growth." Neither party mentioned the total cost of the transaction.

Shobanjo resolutely maintained a position not to be drawn into any debate to disclose how much Publicis paid in exchange for its allotted shares, disclosing only that the transaction was denominated in the local currency, Naira, not in dollars. He was also emphatic that money was not the driving force:[2] "It's not about money because we are in a people's business, a talent industry. I know what I was paid as a shareholder, but I don't know what the others were paid. It's not the value of the shares that were sold that's of importance."

His reluctance to discuss money could be rationalised in the context of his belief that Troyka shareholders practically discounted the value of their equity holding as sacrifice for business continuity. He reckoned that full value was difficult to negotiate because of low appropriations for marketing in a relatively unstructured market like

---

[1] *Publicis Groupe Partners with the Troyka Group in Africa. http://www.mslgroup.com/news/2016/publicis-groupe-partners-with-the-troyka-group-in-africa/*

[2] *http://tribuneonlineng.com/our-creative-industry-has-not-moved-at-par-with-the-rest-of-the-world/(accessed 26 June, 2016)*

Nigeria's. In the calculations of the shareholders, going public would, at best, have guaranteed the availability of financial resources to buy technology to run the company. Getting a global power like Publicis to invest in Troyka as it did, on the other hand, was a sure-fire strategy to sustain the business in the long haul, particularly in terms of implanting tested systems and processes as well as guaranteeing hands-on manpower development that all came as standard with the agreement.

He explained: "If the principles for calculating the value of an advertising agency were used, there wasn't much to the transaction. The shareholders made a sacrifice for the future of the business because of the urge to want to turn it to an institution so that if the current owners were to die tomorrow, it doesn't become the kind of business we've seen in this environment and in Africa where the investor works so hard, adds something to build the enterprise, dies and the business dies."

Quite unlike what happened in 1997 when advertising practitioners were quick to slam Shobanjo and his team in the wake of Promoserve's loss of its Grey affiliation to Insight, the announcement of the Troyka/Publicis Groupe partnership hardly elicited any disquiet. This could have been because the transaction was different from anything the advertising industry in Nigeria had ever recorded; or because retirement had softened the interest of Shobanjo's highly competitive contemporaries in the advertising industry or because current leaders of the industry are far more preoccupied with doing their 'own thing' to be bothered with the veteran's characteristic roll of thunder. Nonetheless, a few voices still called for caution: "Too early to make any comment. Let's all be careful and watchful as business without conscience is meaningless."[1]

---

[1] *Odun Fadoju Snr, Founding CEO and Executive Director at DP Partnership+FCB. http://www.brandcrunch.com.ng/bnrch/index.php/news/agency-top-stories/1476-publicis-groupe-to strike-it-big-in-nigeria-how-troyka-was-picked-over-rosabel (accessed 26 June, 2016)*

Much of the success of the Troyka/Publicis transaction could be traced to the respect that both parties accorded each other from the outset. This manifested in the kind of things that were said and the way they were said. The proper understanding of all issues also made it easy to quickly conclude serious negotiations in about two years, which, considering the complexity of the deal was a record of sorts. For Shobanjo, who was involved in all aspects of the negotiations from start to finish, the deal was 'not difficult at all' because the 'willingness, co-operation and support' of Publicis were never in doubt. "I can make comparisons because I've met some other groups before and I could see the difference. Some come to you feeling superior; they may even talk down at you sometimes as if they were doing you a favour. Nobody comes here and talks down at our people; we'll show them the door. It's as simple as that. This was not our experience with the Publicis executives who will also confirm that the guys at Troyka were not easy to crack."

Industry-wide, the Troyka/Publicis Groupe equity partnership invariably had more far reaching implications for some of the major players in Nigeria. Perhaps, the most obvious was that it ended all previous Publicis Groupe's local technical partnerships in the country. Inevitably, the integrated deal affected the businesses of Shobanjo's close friends in ways that were not contemplated when discussions on the partnership began. Most affected was Rosabel Group, which had to end its relationships with Leo Burnett and Starcom Mediavest. Udeme Ufot's SO & U had already shed its relationship with Saatchi & Saatchi before the formal announcement of the Troyka/Publicis Groupe partnership. In the case of Saatchi & Saatchi, berthing in Troyka was a second home-coming for the network, which had first entered Nigeria when the defunct MC & A was affiliated to Saatchi & Saatchi. Although one or two local companies had yet to drop their attachment to the Publicis brand, Shobanjo believes time would take care of such issues:[1] "If someone says he is your child without being a relation, you do not drag him to court; you just say: but you know I am not your father."

On the face of it, the Troyka/Publicis partnership appeared only to have re-drawn the commercial map of marketing communications in Nigeria. At a deeper level, however, it has helped to put in perspective the imperative for professionalism and relevance in an increasingly shrinking, digital and technology-driven global market. The implication is that local agencies would need to re-strategise if they ever hope to play significant roles in the 'one world' that clients have created for their brands and products, as manifested in the growing practice of pitching businesses on global or continental platforms. The exponential growth in global media spend, especially on data and click platforms, has also made it imperative that agencies be properly positioned in terms of the quality of their human capital, size and technology platforms. The sum of these considerations is that the re-alignment of local and international networks has presented, perhaps, the best opportunity yet for communications agencies in Nigeria to explore merger options to be stronger, more competitive and more attractive to international partners and multi-national clients. It is yet uncertain how these permutations would play out in future.

Shobanjo felt good that he accomplished his primary task of doing a major global partnership. Yet, he was mindful of the learning points from his experience of conducting an international mega-deal at a time there was no precedent from which he could draw in his industry:
"I found that those who do not practise this profession very well, who run the business as a 'typical' Nigerian business may not be able to pass the rigorous test...I found that multinational organisations do

---

[1] *Late 2017, Rosabel Group's Starcom Media officially became Media Seal, an affiliate of Worldwide Partners Inc (WPI)*

not have to like your face; there is a job to do and they will just go by the facts that are available to them...I found that in this kind of global negotiation, multinationals are looking for people they can trust and they will keep checking on your reputation...I found that there were minimum standards that are acceptable to multinationals in terms of professionalism, structure and even physical presence...they look at your environment, they look at your processes and they talk to your people to find out how deep they are...Once you are able to win their trust, they will open up to you and make you feel comfortable."

Ironically, the personal and professional satisfaction that he ought to have derived from the long-drawn, though successful completion of the Troyka/Publicis deal was muffled by its emotional after-taste: "On one side of my brain, I am still struggling with it because my friends are involved one way or the other. I feel personally pained that my friends are affected. The gentleman who led the partnership deal at Publicis also feels the same way as I do because he had an emotional relationship with some of the owners of Rosabel. I suppose we were all caught in the international mega deal."

Whilst his script for a 'new direction' in the marketing communications industry in Nigeria is easy enough to read, only time will tell how the narrative itself would end long after the master storyteller is gone.

13

Now That Tomorrow's Here

"I believe very strongly that the future of this business
is in the hands of young people,
but we need to prepare them first"

Biodun Shobanjo

The business of marketing communications in the 21st century is far different from what it used to be in earlier times. Much of the global change was brought on by the convergence of technology and an emergent mass of millennial consumers whose world has been drastically re-defined by companies like Google, Facebook and Uber. In the new world, technology has successfully blurred time and space across geographical frontiers. Consumers, too, have become adept at randomly creating 'reasons to buy' without waiting for information from producers before they make buying decisions. They routinely leverage technology to get information at the snap of a finger and, consequently, have weaned themselves of the pervasive influence of radio and television commercials that hitherto were the primary channels for demonstrating product benefits. The new thinking that emerged in the digital age has made it possible for consumers worldwide to behave in much the same way regardless of age, socio-econonomic status or locations on the world map. In the circumstance, it has become more evident that marketing communications requires new mindsets and skills to effectively reach new-age consumers in every market regardless of its level of saturation.

As it turned out, global business consultancies caught on much faster than their communications counterparts to the rapidly evolving psychographics of consumers and the 'new paradigms in marketing.' Not surprisingly, clients began to gravitate towards consultancies for solutions to marketing challenges because of the quality of their insights to contemporary consumers. Agencies, too, needed no telling to realise that the face of competition had changed and, with it, the imperative to speak the language of consumers and, by extension, work to regain the confidence of their clients.

Publicis Groupe, Troyka's new partner, was one of the major global networks that quickly keyed in to the new thinking. In February, 2015, the group completed an estimated $3.7 billion buy-over of Sapient Nitro, the 24-year old US based digital, technology and marketing consulting company, in a deal that was touted as 'the largest and most strategic of its kind in the industry' and 'a truly transformative acquisition for Publicis Groupe.'[1] The primary objective of the acquisition was to make Publicis 'best positioned' to help its clients 'transform their businesses and navigate the new world.'

These 'new age' realities, which were at the core of the business transformation that Shobanjo had envisaged, made it strategically imperative that the new Troyka/Publicis Groupe partnership emplaced a structure of nimble and knowledge-driven organisations

---

[1] *https://www.sapientglobalmarkets.com/press_release/publicis-groupe-completes-acquisition-of-sapient/*

in an increasingly competitive global industry. For this to happen, a process of business restructuring was needed to create a synergy that would guarantee that the companies were well-grounded in the local environment and are able to excel in a global field.

The imperative to restructure was also informed by the fact that all founding members of Troyka Holdings, including Richard Ibe, were now effectively out of everyday administration of the Group. The implication was that Shobanjo could not hope to quietly walk into the sunset of life in retirement on the conclusion of the deal with Publicis. He and his team were still needed to stabilise the new entity and put it on auto pilot.

The process virtually started from scratch with Troyka Holdings retaining its name after the transaction. It, however, shed significant weight occasioned by the movement of its communications outfits to a new holding entity. In its present form, Troyka Holdings comprised the four non-core communications companies – Halogen Security; Promoworld; Optimum Exposures and Black Onyx – all of which are still owned 100 per cent by their founders and are independent of the arrangement with Publicis.

On the other hand, the shares of the communications agencies that were hived off the old Troyka were relinquished into a new holding company that was christened 'Insight Redefini.' All the Troyka companies retained their registered corporate names, except All Seasons Mediacom, which dropped 'Mediacom,' which was inherited from its previous affiliation. The company now trades as All Seasons Zenith. The relationship between the Troyka companies and the Publicis Groupe brands were correspondingly streamlined to reflect their business orientation within the context of the new partnership. The flagship, Insight Communications, had access to trade with Publicis' creative agency, Publicis Worldwide. In public relations, The Quadrant Company is in partnership with MSLGroup. In media buying, Media Perspectives was aligned to Starcom while All Seasons Media had Zenith Optimedia. On the digital platform, Hot Sauce is in league with Nurun. Publicis also gave approval for Leo Burnett to be properly incorporated as a local agency in Nigeria. The agency has now taken over the business of The Thiinkshop, a Troyka company, which was previously associated with Leo Burnett. The new company will also service Saatchi & Saatchi clients. With the realignments, Insight Redefini became the lead Publicis Groupe office in West Africa. Its jurisdiction also extended to parts of Central Africa, notably the Democratic Republic of Congo. The octopoidal reach notwithstanding, Insight Redefini was structured to operate from Nigeria without satellite offices outside the country. This development once more rekindled Shobanjo's aborted dream of servicing clients across geographies and, in particular, playing a major role in the West African sub-region.

In line with global operating standards, Insight Redefini adopted a model that enabled it to cut the cost of its operation by outsourcing strategic 'backroom' services that included, legal, administration, finance, technology platforms and human resource management. These were made to reside administratively in the new Troyka, which offered the services on arms-length basis. Operationally, the tight ship of trimmer, fitter and more efficient business units has made it possible for the unit companies to focus on their core competencies to deliver first class creative services at competitive cost to clients who had become increasingly price-sensitive.

The new structure, which matched the Japanese Keiretsu enterprise model that gave birth to Troyka in the first place, still effectively ensured that money flowed in a cyclical manner within the 'family' and guaranteed high return on investment to every shareholder. Operationally, Insight Redefini embodies the 'Power of One,' the strategic concept that is driven by 'a common purpose, a powerful spirit, shared behaviour, great character and a relentless focus on clients' within the global Publicis Groupe.

Although Insight Redefini, in terms of physical presence, is still evolving, its administrative reporting system is clearly defined. The four-member board of directors comprises the Chairman, Shobanjo; the Group Managing Director (GMD), Awosika; the Group Chief Finance Director and a representative of Publicis Groupe. All Managing Directors, General Managers and Chief Operating Officers of unit companies in the group report to the GMD who, in turn, reports to the board of the company. The holding company also has a Group Chief Operating Officer, Dr. Ken Onyeali-Ikpe, who combines the function with his primary position of Managing Director of All Seasons Zenith.

Even before discussions began with Publicis Groupe, the management of Troyka Group had reasoned that a mix of youth and heavy investment in capacity building would be preconditions for keeping the quest for immortality on track in a digital age. The Group's human resource policy, which ab initio recognised youth and experience as key considerations in succession planning within the group's hierarchy, made it unnecessary to effect any immediate change in the leadership of the six operating units of Insight Redefini. With a median age of 40, all the principal executives had been in executive management positions within or outside the group for no less than five years. Dr. Ken Onyeali-Ikpe, Managing Director of All Seasons Zenith, who is in his 50s, is the oldest in the team. Bolaji Okusaga, the immediate past Managing Director of The Quadrant Company, was in his mid-40s before he exited. Sam Osunsoko, the former Managing Director of Leo Burnett, was also in his 40s and was in the group, which he joined as a Management Trainee, for more than 18 years. The former Managing Director of Insight Publicis, Feyi

Olubodun; the Managing Director of Media Perspectives, Dr. Tayo Oyedeji (and his successor-in-office, Jude Odia) and the Managing Director of Hot Sauce, Dayo Adefila, are all in their 30s. All are very well trained and experienced on the job. The emphasis on youth is deliberate and in keeping with the global trend of entrusting the management of businesses to young people mainly in their 30s because they understand and are able to speak the language of youth.

Shobanjo's belief in the power of experienced young people, however, did not come about overnight or just for its own sake; it is rooted in his personal history. At 32, he was Deputy Managing Director/Chief Operating Officer of a major Nigerian agency; at 35, he co-founded Insight and he concluded his first successful global affiliation at 38. Drawing a parallel from national leadership, Nigeria's second military leader, Gen. Yakubu Gowon, became Head of State at nearly 32 while the bulk of the young military leaders who fought the nation's war of unity from 1967 – 1970 were under 30. All were well trained in the best military academies in the world. The key learning is that anyone that aspires to leadership must be properly prepared to assume the responsibility that comes with it.

Shobanjo sums up his position on youth and leadership as follows: "If you are a young person in business and have not been prepared for a role, you are going to fall on your face. If, today, you make a 32-year old the President of Nigeria without intellectual, practical and political preparation, he is going to struggle. In my view, a lot of the young people who say they want to run things today are not well prepared. When you find young agencies that are doing well, you will find that some of their key people have served a lot of apprenticeship."

Paradoxically, Shobanjo's landmark professional legacies, Insight

Communications and Insight Redefini, were born at periods when the cycle of Nigeria's economic development was in decline. Between 1980 and 1983 when the fledgling Insight Communications was just gathering momentum, Nigeria was in the throes of an economic downturn. By 2016 when Insight Redefini came on stream, Nigeria was, again, in the thick of what government initially described as a 'technical' recession. Not much has changed since then. But the present time has made it possible for preparation to meet opportunity in a manner that in the long haul would cause a separation of men from boys.

Much of the 'combat-readiness' of Insight Redefini is geared towards helping clients ride the massive waves that continually threaten to drown ill-prepared brands in increasingly competitive local and global markets. Shobanjo's 'survival guide' in times of recession requires that agencies become more creative to help their clients survive and, in turn, be closer to their clients to also survive. Being 'closer' to clients, to him, means a whole lot of things including seeing them everyday with new ideas and suggestions. The primary objective is to ensure that an agency's client gets a piece of every Naira that a consumer spends, regardless of whatever the client manufactures or sells. Anything to the contrary, for him, detracts from the reason for being in business: "The days of puffiness and flowery communication are gone; you need to hit at the heart of the consumer, so he can take a buying decision. Insofar as your client can manage to produce a brand or service and put it in the market place, you have to ensure that your client's brand is picked in preference to competition's."

Considering his view that the future of advertising does not lie in attempting to make a ball roll uphill, it is no surprise he advocates storytelling as a brand-building and creative award-winning tool. For this to work, he enjoins clients and agencies to forge proper partnerships that would secure the future of the brand and the agency. Whilst both must 'share knowledge and expertise,' they also must recognise core areas of responsibility as well as the mutual goal of brand-building. For him, it is the responsibility of the client to ensure that the truth of its brand is unquestionable and that the assets perform as promised. Combined, these make the brand 'authentic' and mean 'something specific to the consumer.' Where these conditions are met, it then becomes the responsibility of agencies to 'weave stories and narratives' about the brand in ways that command rational and emotive attention that make impact on consumers and get them to continually talk about the brand. For him, therefore, effective storytelling, the kind that gets people to 'talk about your brand, is the most powerful strategy of all.'[1] "It is more about who you are, what you are and what you say you are. It is not what you call me, but the name I answer to."

Soon after the formal announcement of the Troyka/Publicis partnership in May 2016, the investment gave more bite to Shobanjo's worldview. It began with a group-wide programme of total 'immersion' in global best operating standard designed to provide more access to world class systems and processes and, ultimately, to enhance manpower development. The programme largely involved integrating the 'energetic' Troyka/Nigerian and 'gentlemanly' Publicis/French perspectives through staff training programmes to build hands-on professional capacity across cultures. An early indication of the success of the process of acculturation was the centre-stage presentation by Insight Publicis at the 2016 edition of the Cannes Lions Festival in France. It was a first by any Nigerian agency at a global stage.

The presentation, which was headlined "Let my Enemy Live Long: How Brands Can Aim for the Heart of The African," focused on highlighting 'the nuances of marketing to the African consumer, from

---

[1] *Distillation of Challenges of Marketing in Nigeria, a lecture delivered by Biodun Shobanjo at the investiture of the President of the National Institute of Marketing of Nigeria on 17 March, 2017*

the sub-Saharan African perspective'. It sign-posted the fact that the future had, indeed, arrived Nigeria and the gameplan of the business had truly changed!

Several very important appointments were made as fallouts of the true partnership that Troyka and Publicis Groupe had created. The Executive Creative Director of Insight Communications, Chima Okenimkpe, was appointed as Chief Creative Officer (West and Central Africa) of Publicis Groupe, with office in Accra, Ghana. The Managing Director of Media Perspectives, Dr. Tayo Oyedeji, also moved to Johannesburg, South Africa to hold office as Managing Director, Starcom South Africa and CEO, Starcom Africa. The appointments, which became effective on January 1, 2017, were landmarks in the fulfilment of Shobanjo's dream of putting his people on the global map. They also vindicated the decision that both partners made to jointly take on the world. At a personal level, the development was Shobanjo's crowning glory. This much, he also has acknowledged.

John Momoh's apt summary of the essence of Troyka Holdings affirms Shobanjo's professional legacy built from scratch on excellence and nurtured to being an institution that continues to set standards in the practice of marketing communications and, indeed, business in Nigeria and beyond: "Troyka is a brand that has been built; the work ethic is prim and proper in the sense that there is nothing out of place. It is near-perfect. Everything is structured and to time and the staff hold their heads high in the industry. You could see the camaraderie among staff; it is like a family. Shobanjo has brought up a lot of people. The alumni of Insight and Troyka will carry the flag forward."

14

All Said...

Don't wait for the Last Judgment. It takes place every day.

Albert Camus (1913 - 1960)

The quality of Shobanjo's vision as a marketing communications professional with nearly half a century experience has never been in doubt. Neither is it a secret that he would never accept being second best when he lives his personal life in a manner that amplifies his belief that "Winning is the only thing." The sum of his vision is best explained in his words: "I like to dream big; I like to go out there and fight all the time."

As an individual, he is unapologetic on his stance that individuals must script their destiny and never grant power to third parties to derail their plans. This very well clarifies his decision to jettison Public Relations for core advertising early in his career to avoid having his professional success determined by the action or inaction of journalists. Whilst in active professional practice, he engaged in the biggest prize fights in his industry because he never stopped believing his team had probably the best solutions that could help clients win in the market place. In turn, the quantum of big-ticket business gains by Troyka companies, particularly Insight, helped to demonstrate that he truly walks his talk. The success of Insight, as he admitted, was 'fairly fast' and this, perhaps, unwittingly opened his flanks to controversy, more so as several of his professional colleagues believed he tended to grandstand:

"We got called all sorts of names. Some of our competitors accused us of giving wonderful gifts to people to secure business. There is nobody, NOBODY that can say that either Insight or I have ever given one kobo to get a job. NEVER. EVER. I find these things painful, but we decided not to lose track because we felt it was just a question of time before people knew the source of our success."

The late doyen of the advertising business in Nigeria, Sylvester Moemeke, former Chairman, Lowe Lintas, appeared to have clearly understood the pain the Insight founder felt in a business environment where everyone played hardball whilst subscribing to rules that were neither hardly different nor diametrically opposed. Said Moemeke: "I remember that (a former) Commercial Manager of Daily Times told me many years ago that many people in advertising did not have a good word for Biodun Shobanjo. I told him such people probably do not know what a good word is. This is a country where people who do not perform accept that grapes are sour only in their mouths. I have the highest regard for him; he is a good influence on the advertising scene. He is very much misunderstood probably because of peers who did not think he should get where he has got. Admittedly, not everything he has done will be done by everyone else."

The multiplicity of opinions on Shobanjo across personal, professional and gender boundaries affirm the view that the history of advertising in Nigeria cannot be written without a chapter being devoted to his role as a pathfinder. Often, the words or contexts used to describe his personality or work ethic differ only slightly. Yet, when taken together, they reinforce some of the key attributes of brand 'Biodun Shobanjo,' as identified in earlier chapters, leaving one in no doubt about the ingredients of his success. Let us take, for example, his personality and way of doing business.

Some of his colleagues obviously had reservations about his methods and tactics but none disputed that he is a purpose-driven individual who did not dabble into the business of establishing a sound marketing communications network. Former Managing Director of Promoserve, Allan Olabode, articulated this position quite well: "Shobanjo set out to be an industry leader; (but) he has a serious image problem, part of which could be attributed to petty jealousy and envy and part of which could also be attributed to the way he has related to his colleagues. He has to adopt a strategy of humility. He has a very likeable personality; it is only when you get into a business context that you begin to wonder why he (did) certain things. I do not think he can talk positively of others. As far as he is concerned, he is the only one doing the best thing around. I like him as a person. I like his vision of forming Insight (but) I see him as an advertising practitioner whose method I do not condone; the desire to win at all cost seems too cold-blooded. It does not mean I am right."

Festus Akinlade, former Managing Director of Grant Advertising concurred and further shed light on the strides of his former deputy, which he ascribed to providence, his energy, creativity and consistency: "I knew him when he closed his chapter on being a broadcaster and opened another as a professional in advertising. He joined Grant Advertising as a young man, very likeable, very hardworking and (he possessed) a lot of intelligence. Today, he is at the peak of his career. With Insight, he brought creativity into advertising and gave everybody a shake in the industry. At Grant, I think he did certain things under pressure from certain people. I pray for him; I will ask him to give his life to Christ. With that, he would see life in its true perspective."

It could reasonably be said that Shobanjo's 'sharp personality' may be responsible for much of the way his personality is measured, as canvassed by his friend and former Managing Director of Lowe Lintas, Dele Adetiba: "He is a man who loves to win. There are few people in other disciplines that can point to higher achievements than he has accomplished in advertising. I think he has not been able to get all the credit due him because he has a fairly sharp personality. Some like him immensely, others do not. There are many people in history like that. If he knows that sometimes being right and being correct is not the only answer to life; he would be an all-round fantastic person."

The views expressed by many more people who shared their experiences of the Troyka Chairman with the author, it also could be said without equivocation, reinforced the portrayal of a no-nonsense gladiator who would neither ask for nor yield a quarter in the battle for anything to which he sets his mind:

"He is nice, kind and very fair. He gets emotional and he gets deeply and easily hurt, that is why he puts out a strong exterior. He is a clear-headed thinker (whose) most outstanding quality is the ability to see things through. If he says to you 'this is where we are going,' you can be sure no matter what happens he is going to get there with you. If he decides to support you, thank your stars; if he decides to be on the other side, you had better watch it. He sometimes gets so fixed in his focus that it is difficult to unlock the focus and you can get bruised along the line. If, for instance, he believes we should go after an account, he would do so with everything he has got and if you are not seen to be moving as fast as he expects you to, he would not understand you. But if he rubs you the wrong way and he gets to know of it, he is man enough to always come back and say he is sorry."

Jimi Awosika, Group Managing Director, Troyka Holdings.

"He has irresistible charisma that draws people to him. He started a revolution he could not stop. He is not a casual person; he is an exceptionally brilliant human being with ability to give attention to details and he is tough. Biodun Shobanjo has excellent relationship with a lot of people. He is a rare breed: a good man with a good heart. He makes people think, even if they do not like him. After I. S. Moemeke, Shobanjo represents a new chapter in advertising in Nigeria."

Alhaji Garba Bello Kankarofi,
Former Registrar/Chief Executive, Advertising Practitioners Council of Nigeria (APCON)

"He is a perfectly honourable man. His cheque will not bounce, that is something you cannot say of many Nigerians. He does not like to apologise, at least not directly. Women tend to like him (though) I will not call him a womaniser, but he is not a saint either. He respects professionalism. He is very tight with money; there have been times I have felt like throwing his files at him. By and large, he pays well. He has the trappings of wealth and he believes only poor people flex muscles with money. I will say deal with him. I really can vouch for him and will always vouch for him."

Chief (Mrs.) Biola Ayimonche,
Principal, Biola Ayimonche & Co (Solicitors)

"He is quite a nice person, good at his job and an astute businessman. He is jovial and down to earth. He does not mince words. If he does not like you, he will tell you immediately why he just does not like you and that is it as far as he is concerned. If you look at him as an individual and Insight as an entity, I think it is his driving force that has taken the company to its present height."

Mrs. Nike Alabi,
Former Managing Director, Universal McCann

"He respects people, regardless of your age; he is not arrogant; he does not look down on anybody. He takes things as they come. He is not difficult, but he is a man of high principles who is happier coming to you than you coming to him. He singles people out in a crowd. I learned from him that whoever you are, there is somebody who knows what you do not know. His name signals positive thinking. I call him an icon because, as a professional, he knows his onions. In his industry, you don't have to add his surname after you mention Biodun, which means, he has made a name that is quite high."

Omo'ba Sam Adebola Ogundogba,
Chairman, Emaconprint Ltd

"At a personal level, he is a 'cool guy,' as they say in today's parlance; a great example of who a real gentleman should be; a great family man and a very friendly man. As a professional, he is passionate about his job; he is knowledgeable on the industry; he is well versed; he is hard working and he is a go-getter. He has a voracious appetite for success, to do things differently and that is the result of what we are seeing today. He is a great asset to the Nigerian economy and a man who has left his footprints in the sands of time whilst he is still living. He is a living legend."

John Momoh,
Chairman, Channels TV

"He is clean; his mind and life are uncluttered. He has very good memory; he always remembers what he said, wrote or passed out. 90% of the time, he is right; and he admits the 10% when he has made mistakes. He is fair-minded, and he likes people to be fairly treated because he hates injustice around him. He has a good sense of humour; he laughs a lot. He is not too demanding; he just asks that things be done properly and promptly. He expresses his opinions and respects the opinions of other people. With him, there are no sacred cows."
Gloria Omoregie,
Personal Assistant

"He is a nice man, but he is too blunt. I believe this (the lack of tact) is his major weakness."
Sina Ogundipe,
Shobanjo's long-standing driver, Troyka Holdings

Shobanjo's position that business and friendship be kept at arms-length came to the fore during background interviews to assemble materials for this book. Some of his friends who are positioned to do him great favour by unilaterally placing their business in his care easily spoke of his attitude to keeping things in tight compartments, as confirmed by Chief Oladele Fajemirokun, an industrialist: "He is a forthright person; he is well-focused and he is a principled achiever. He is a reliable friend. It is not easy to use the word 'reliable' for just any person. He has been my friend longer than anyone else in the (advertising) industry, but he never came to me to say, for example, that he wanted the Xerox job, which several years ago was high billing. If he had wanted it, of course, I could have influenced the company to give him the business because he has the advantage of being close to me. I often tell his children 'you will be doing your father a world of good if you look at the way he works and follow his steps.' It is not easy to start a business from scratch and reach the top."

The former Governor of Oyo State, Senator Abiola Ajimobi, spoke in a similar vein: "In Biodun Shobanjo you have all the ingredients of success. We went through different stages of life together, from being acquaintances to being very good friends till we migrated to being brothers. We were always comparing our various levels of achievements with his. If there is anything that has been established over the years, it is that Biodun Shobanjo, like a goldfish, has no hiding place. Any day, anywhere and in any profession, he is a goldfish. He is a man I consider to be synonymous with excellence."

On the job, his panache, vision, inspirational leadership, uncompromising attention to details, empathic listening skill, single-mindedness and uncommon ability to effectively communicate his ideas featured prominently in the description of his prodigious work ethic by business partners and other associates, many of whom literally swear by him:

"He is a dreamer. He has a quest for excellence; to go out there and do what has not been done before. He will get whatever he wants. He has the sixth sense to recognise talent from a mile off. There are rumours flying all over the place about how he bribes people to win accounts. I do not think Mr Shobanjo would bribe anyone. A lot of people do not know him; they have a wrong perception of him. He is someone I can stake my money on and go to bed. He is well put together; he is a good person."
Sesan Ogunro (late),
Chief Executive Officer, Eminent Communications

"He has some style the way he does his things. He does not believe in half-measures; he does not care one bit what anybody thinks about him. He cuts his own image, he nurtured it to maturity and you either take it or leave it. He does not apologise to anyone. He is a practical example of someone who believes that hard work does not kill. He seizes advantage when he sees one; he does not miss an opportunity. He has taught the industry that laziness is not how to get returns. It is just that because of his string of successes people are bound to wonder: is he the only one there? How come he grabs, grabs, grabs? I have heard rumours of his unorthodoxy, but I do not believe them. He is simply an aggressive, dynamic, hardcore professional advertising person."

Steve Omojafor,
Chairman, STB-McCann

"It was on him I started noticing three-piece suits, looking smart all over the place. The one thing I have always noted about him is his zest for work. I used to see him as an overbearing, standoffish fellow. But when you come closer, you discover he is a very amiable person. In our society where we tend to be tribalistic, anybody who delivered as best as he wanted is his kinsman. Left to him, he would have been a totalitarian boss (who) knows what he wants and wants to whip everybody into line. But at some point, maybe with age, he began to accept that things are better done democratically. You have to present superior argument for him to accept your point of view. Once he is convinced, you will get all the support. He is wonderful."

Richard Ibe,
Co-founder/Director, Insight Communications.

"Biodun Shobanjo is a visionary who knows how to be successful, how to manage and grow his business and, ultimately, how to protect that success. He is a credible and caring professional who knows the world of advertising and knows how to do things to international standard. His way of communicating is his greatest strength; he is very calm and to the point all the time. He is blessed with Jimi Awosika, just as Awosika is blessed with him and I am blessed with the two. They were very well brought up by their ancestors. The advertising industry in Nigeria will talk for many generations about the roles of Shobanjo and Awosika. Maybe someday students will be taught on who they are."

Faysal Halabi,
PromoWorld Ltd, Former General Manager (Corporate Affairs),
Seven Up Bottling Company Plc

"He is an absolutely hardworking man, very focused, very fiercely committed, very professional, very determined and very loyal. He can be blunt to a fault; he never shies away from a fight. He comes on strong, which sometimes detracts from the degree of value of whom he is or what he has achieved. But I believe he does not mean to hurt anyone."

Funmi Onabolu,
Managing Director, Cossé Limited

"He is full of ideas. He has always been a pioneer; he is always showing direction. In advertising, public relations, outdoor, media buying and even assets protection, he created niches because he knew and still knows the direction from which change would come in his industry. There is nothing to which he put his hands that does not turn to gold not because he 'wants' them to but because of the hard work and efforts put into them. He does his homework before implementing anything he sets his mind on. He would have sleepless nights working with his people, never leaving them to do the work alone. Once he believes in something, he would get it; he does not go to pitches to play games; he plays to win because he wants to be the best working for business owners who want to be the best. He is still professionally relevant today as he was when he started."

Chief Steve Ojo,
Founder/President, Galaxy TV

"He is a fantastic manager of men, money and material. You cannot take that away from him. He is a hard-nosed businessman who has a vision of what he wants to achieve and he goes for it. He would hire the best hands wherever they are in the world and he would put these hands to the hardest tasks. If he must borrow to make an idea work, he will. That is why he wins most of his pitches. He is not a loud person; you hardly can know what he is worth. Beneath the hard business façade, he is one of the kindest human beings you can ever meet."

Segun Olaleye,
Former Credit Control Officer, Insight

"I see him as someone who transcended just being the boss. But he is a leader, truly inspirational and he is the kind of person who would give you a task and call you to take ownership of that task and handle it beyond expectation. He is an inspirational leader and a great motivator (who) has a way of knowing clearly the strength and the weakness of his key people all the way down the agency and knows exactly where to apply each person for the best, optimum result."

Udeme Ufot,
Group Managing Director, SO & U,
(TheNEWS, February 8, 2010)

"He pays unbelievable attention to details. He drives you to perfection and he sets an example, so you can see clearly that he is calling you to where he himself is ready to go. I have maintained a good relationship with him because we had a great friendship in the

first place. He did not hold back in teaching me everything I needed to know about marketing and PR. He took me as a son and I have tried to reciprocate by treating him as a father."
Dr. Phil Osagie,
Head Strategist, JSP Communications,
(TheNEWS, February 8, 2010)

"Biodun Shobanjo is daring in conduct, deep in content, methodical in approach, efficient in delivery and peerless! He undeniably belongs to the exclusive class of those whose reputation stems from ascertained accomplishments. His success, like those of other great achievers, derives from a systematic acquisition of unique skills and the meticulous application of those skills for the improvement of society."
Chuddy Oduenyi,
Managing Director, Compact Communications Ltd,
(TheNEWS, February 8, 2010)

Professional colleagues readily credit Shobanjo with having made significant contribution to the growth of the marketing communications industry in Nigeria by running what could be considered a capacity 'demonstration shop' at Troyka; by encouraging sectoral group collaborations and by improving the professional image of practitioners amongst various stakeholders:

"He is a pure professional who put the interest of the advertising profession even before his own personal interest. As President of AAPN, the way he fought for things that concerned the profession, you would think that his life depended on these. He still fights very hard for anything that concerns advertising. He is industrious, and I think he has a magic touch to have recorded a lot of achievements. He is a very brilliant man and he strikes me as an honest person; very

simple, very generous, kind-hearted and without airs around him. He is always prepared and does not joke with business."
Dr. Jide Oluwajuyitan,
Lecturer, University of Lagos, Akoka, Retired Executive Director (Editorial & Advertising), Guardian Newspapers Ltd

"He is purposeful and confident, and he knows what he wants. I have heard one or two things about him; maybe these are people's excuses for losing a pitch. Whether you like him or not is irrelevant. What is important is his contribution; he has been able to put something into the profession. As (a former) President of the Association of Advertising Practitioners of Nigeria, AAPN (now Association of Advertising Agencies of Nigeria - AAAN,), he added some dash to the Association and profession's image in the media and in the public's eyes."
'Lolu Akinwunmi,
Managing Director, Prima Garnet Africa

"With Insight, he made a point that advertising is both a profession and a business. For me, that is the greatest contribution I have seen from him. He is an intellectual giant, though he did not have the benefit of a university education. He is an articulate man, a go-getter who needs to re-assess himself and come down a bit on his ego because that could be his greatest undoing."
Kola Ayanwale,
Chairman, Centrespread Advertising

On matters of reputation, Shobanjo is quite touchy because of his belief that an individual is worthless without a good image. As much as possible, he tries to listen to every party to an issue before forming an opinion so as not to take precipitate actions that could forever ruin a person's reputation. Where he can help it, he solves all reputational challenges within 24 hours. He also tries to always speedily clear up the basis of whatever doubts he harbours on any issue, so they do not fester and spread uncontrollably to third parties. Given the many tales that abound on his exploits in the industry, it took a long while for him to receive the same benefits of doubt in professional circles. Some notable voices in the industry voices, however, strongly conducted his defence in interviews with the author:

"As a practitioner, he is one of the best things that ever happened to the advertising profession in Nigeria. His getting in galvanised the profession. Most accusations against his agency are results of (1) envy, (2) the Pull Him Down (PhD) Syndrome and (3) practitioners being very competent in the ignoble art of the pot accusing the kettle of its blackness."
Chris Doghudje
(Former MD, Lintas:Lagos) Chief Executive, Zus Bureau

"Some of the negative things people say (of him) are exaggerated, some of us are equally guilty of these things. When you have summed up all the pluses and minuses, I think his name must have a very visible place when the history of advertising in Nigeria is written"
Allan Olabode
Managing Director, 21st Century Communications
(Former MD, Promoserve)

"There is no basis for anyone to single him out in the industry as being unethical; it is the general thing. If he bribes and he is incompetent, there is no way he would keep his accounts. He is successful because of his energy and because he was destined to succeed."
Festus Akinlade,
Managing Director, Ad-Inter Team
(former Managing Director, Grant Advertising)

"I heard unprintable things said about him. I have stopped trying to defend him because many of his accusers are not even ready to listen. They have made up their minds that he is crooked, that he employs unethical methods. There is nothing like that. He is pretty constant, he stays the course, he sees an opportunity and he goes after it. He is good; he is dedicated, finicky, punctilious, hardnosed but very fair. He has honed his vision and his strategy. That has raised a lot dust here."

Victor Johnson,
Long-time friend/ former Managing Director, MC & A
and, later, Sail Events.

Shobanjo maintains a simple creed of 'family first,' the depth of which members of his immediate family revealed as they spoke glowingly of overwhelming love and with pride in the personal and professional accomplishments of the head of the family:

"He kind of swept me off my feet with his humour. He is a very sweet person, a very strict father (who is) very committed to his children. He is very impulsive, but once he blows his top it is over the next minute. He tends to leave official matters in the office. He left Grant with nothing, but he had confidence in his ability, he had God on his side and the support of his family and colleagues. And we have cause to thank God today."

Mrs. Joyce Shobanjo,
Wife

"His life is like an open book; what you see at home is the same thing you see professionally. He is a no-nonsense guy, straight laced, to the point and not one to dilly-dally. For him, business is business, friendship is friendship; there is nothing personal about getting work done and in a timely fashion. All these things I learned growing up as his son. He has managed parenting the best way he could. Over the years, he has proved, first, to be a great friend and, second, a good father. He is loving to his immediate family and he has made the extended family so 'small' and so tight. It is fantastic being a Shobanjo because the man has achieved so much and laid the foundation that has made it easier for me to take on the role of his first child. He keeps guiding me. If I had a tenth of his qualities, I think I will be great; I will rule the world."

Babatunde Shobanjo,
Son

"His greatest impact on us, his children, is that he makes us recognise that there are no limits; no boundaries. He is very open; he makes you figure out all the angles. 'Where is the expertise? What makes you think you are the right person to do what you want to do?' he would always ask. It is a motivational drive for the whole family. We all sit to play the devil's advocate to one another, so we help each person figure out many possibilities that many other people would consider impossible."

Funke Shobanjo,
Daughter

"Biodun Shobanjo is a guy with character. He is a dogged fighter, someone who is not afraid when he must take a course of action, even at the risk of death. In a nation that is short of role models, he is a good role model in the way he conducts himself both privately and in public. He places a premium on teaching and mentoring younger people; he is always using every experience to teach life's lessons. He always had time for us, his children. If there was any issue he wanted us to take learning from and he did not have all the facts, he would always reach out and introduce us to people who know a lot more or who are experts on the subject. I have learned to trust his instincts because I do not have any regrets over most of the things he had encouraged me to do. I know he always has our best interest at heart. The one word I can use to summarise Biodun Shobanjo is 'great'."

Olufemi Shobanjo,
Son

"He never treated one child better than the other one; if you did wrong he would discipline you. He hardly ever gets physical; but he would talk with you in a way that you would not want to make the same mistakes. He has taught us never to take things for granted; never to rely on anyone to do things for us and that if anything unpleasant happens, we should simply move on without dwelling on it."

Abimbola Shobanjo.
Son

"I recognise that he has done great things in his business. People tell us he has money, but we never grew up thinking we had money. A few of the people we grew up with are now directors in family businesses, but he is very much against people who go ahead to employ their children without their earning it. It's kind of cool and I respect him for that because I would not want things to be that easy. I want to fight and win my own battles. Maybe if I had studied advertising things might have been different but I am a scientist and he does not have a clue about what I do. I think this is good for me because people cannot say, 'Oh, her dad did that for her."

Dolapo Obuaya (nee Shobanjo),
Daughter

Even if Shobanjo had had to abandon Public Relations, a profession that requires constant media interface, he never let go of his friendship with newsmen. His media-friendly disposition, indeed, made it easy for mainstream journalists to reach independent conclusions on the quality of his contribution to the advertising profession. His crowning as Nigeria's 'Advertising Man of All Time' can, therefore, be considered the sum of media perspectives on Shobanjo's enterprise:

"To become a success in life for Shobanjo... is like luggage he has had to lug perpetually without respite...look out, he may be blasé and like a true adman, he is very smooth. But this honcho is no run of the mill... he has proved to be a terrifying self-motivated and dynamic personality."
Steve Osuji,
Journalist (The Guardian, October 7, 1995)

"Stories that are told about him could make a good plot for a television serial... (He) has become a giant not only in the world of advertising but (also) in Nigerian business in general. Perhaps (the) ability to take a dispassionate stand on issues is the secret of Shobanjo's success."
Claudia Binitie,
Journalist (Tell, August 22, 1994)

"The advertising terrain is certainly a slippery one, which demands dexterity and shrewdness of mind to tread. The intricacies involved can only be surmounted by a man like Abiodun Olusina Shobanjo."
Ejiro Onabrakpeya,
Journalist (Sunday Times, March 21, 1995)

"Custodians of a fulfilled dream have long memories. Abiodun Shobanjo falls within this category."
National Concord, January 28, 1990
[Citation on Shobanjo on his nomination as one of '50 Most Fascinating Business People in 1989']

"First impressions matter to Shobanjo. Somehow, everything about him, his home and office attempts at nearing perfection. He is a man after ideals, the ultimate, a form of pre-eminence, set and determined by himself... In years to come, his name will be among those that advertisers and marketers and communications experts will swear by."
Onuora Chuzzy Udenwa,
Journalist (Crown Prince, December, 1991)

"He needs no introduction in the advertising industry in Nigeria. Chief (sic) Abiodun Shobanjo, Managing Director, Insight Communications Limited, remains one of the nation's best brains in the industry."
ThisDay, May 25, 1997

"The coming of people like Insight Communications' Biodun Shobanjo gave advertising a business-like stature."
The Source, May 9, 1997

"The guardian of the new advertising order. He is constantly in tune with happenings in the industry globally and constantly shares his experience, too."
Vanguard, February 26, 1993

"The Trustees of DAME acknowledge (Shobanjo's) lifelong devotion to advancing the frontiers of knowledge and strengthening the media as a market place of ideas for free and commercial speech to thrive. You have earned the reputation of a consummate professional. Indeed, many of today's leading names in Nigeria's Marketing Communications world have been positively shaped by you. DAME holds that such recognition (as the DAME Lifetime

Achievement Award) will help younger professionals to live out the beauty of their professional calling."
Ambassador Moses Ihonde,
Chairman, Board of Trustees, DAME

"Biodun Shobanjo, the Chairman of Nigeria's largest marketing communications conglomerate, Troyka Holdings, is a man of value, hard work and focus. We are thrilled to honour him as the receiver of our MarketingWorld's Lifetime Achievements Award."
Akin Naphtal,
Group Publisher, MarketingWorld

"It was a decisive decision to bestow the 'Advertising Man of All Time' honour on Mr. Biodun Shobanjo because of his indelible footprints on the sands of advertising in Nigeria and, indeed, Africa. From the turnout of the leading professionals in the industry, it is plain to see that he is worth the honour."
Tony Onyima,
Former Managing Director, The Sun Publishing Limited

Very little, if any, of all the things said concerning Shobanjo surprised his childhood friends. If anything, they maintained that these viewpoints have only reinforced his persona because, with him, 'what-you-see-is-what-you-really-get':

"He has been advertising himself ever since he was in school; he was a keen debater and a showman on the rostrum, quite disciplined and very, very neat."
Omoba Oluwole Kehinde,
(Chartered Accountant), Shobanjo's junior at Odogbolu Grammar School)

"He is still the same, except in age. He is a very funny man, well loved by others and very, very hardworking. He is highly principled: if he had an opinion, it is difficult to change it. He is always willing to assist, he donates very generously, and he would listen to you, if you have a just cause. But he does not have time for trivialities and all that."

Segun Onayemi,
Classmate/childhood friend

In conventional wisdom, a man is often acquitted by his own testimony; by the evidence of other witnesses and by the judgment of God. Arising from Shobanjo's sense of worth and the preponderance of third-party evidence more in support of his strength than his weaknesses, it is safe to assert that he has done his duty by man. The rest is up to God.

Epilogue

When you were born, you cried and the world laughed;
Live your life so that when you die you will laugh
and the world will cry

Middle East Saying

S hobanjo primarily sought glamour when he ventured into advertising practice in 1971. By December 2004 when he announced his decision to 'stand down' from the everyday chore of running an advertising agency, he had unarguably become the most successful practitioner, dead or living, in Nigeria. But the passing of time has not diminished the passion with which he began his journey into the profession. All through his professional life, he saw beyond the narrow, yet comfortable zone of his peers. With Insight and, later, the subsidiary companies that make up Troyka Holdings and now Insight Redefini, he has delivered the future in his industry. His vision of doing things excellently well has received undeniable validation with the plethora of his personal successes in the industry; the successful brands his companies have helped to build and a replication of these successes by several former employees of Troyka Group. In the long run, his gains have made the pains of his walk through thorns a worthwhile adventure. These gains have also affirmed the popular notion that "for the tenacious, no road is impassable."[1]

---

[1] *Motto of Spyker Car NV (Nulla tenaci invia est ia) introduced in 1915*

It is instructive that it took the stirring of an old war horse like Shobanjo to ignite a bit more passion in the industry with the market excitement created by news of the Troyka/Publicis partnership. Prior to this, the local advertising industry could be said to have steadily become dull and routine. Gone were robust public discourse of people, issues and clients. Indeed, the early exit of a generation of experienced advertising practitioners made it quite evident that the industry had lost significant bite and shine. The retirement of Kehinde Adeosun (Promoserve), Olu Falomo (Forum Advertising) and Niyi Alonge (Adwork) marked the end of an era. Activism in the industry lost momentum after Olu Adekoya (Olu Adekoya Press Agency) and Raymond Adegoke Kester (Hunters Publicity) died. Intellectualism dipped with the withdrawal of Chris Doghudje (Lintas:Lagos) from mainstream advertising and the passing of May Nzeribe (Sunrise Advertising/former President of AAAN). The killing of Sesan Ogunro (Eminent Communications) drained creative ferment and the death of Sylvester Moemeke (Lintas:Lagos) robbed the industry of institutional memory.

The light of 'friendly fires' was put out when Shobanjo joined the rank of Ayo Owoborode (PAL); Mac Ovbiagele (Macsell Associates); Akin Odunsi (Rosabel); Tunde Adelaja (Rosabel); Steve Omojafor (STB-McCann); Dele Adetiba (Lintas:Lagos); Bola Thomas (LTC/JWT) and Billy Lawson (LTC/JWT) to take a back seat in day-to-day agency administration. Over several decades, these colourful personalities sparred in tough business terrains as they collectively and individually shaped the course of professional advertising practice without compromising the essence of friendship. Each easily stood out in a crowd and each could more readily be aligned to one cause or the other.

The depleted league of versatile strikers and playmakers in the industry thus created a void that their successors did not seem to be in any hurry to fill. Noticeable lethargy naturally crept into the profession with the result that it became increasingly difficult to identify single industry-defining issues or pinpoint individuals who could set performance agenda in the way that the old brigade did. Senior practitioners like Lolu Akinwunmi (Prima Garnet Africa); Funmi Onabolu (Cosse Ltd.) and Udeme Ufot (SO & U) quietly and efficiently got the job done though they largely prefer to fly below radar except when it becomes expedient to do otherwise. Although creative sparks from exciting contemporary gladiators like Steve Baba-Eko (X3M Ideas); Lanre Adisa (Noah's Ark); Kayode Oluwasona (1201Brandsway) and Tunji Olugbodi (Verdant Zeal) sporadically light up the industry, the jury is still out on how well or how fast they have fitted into their new roles as industry leaders.

From a media perspective, the 'retirement' of veteran newshound, Akin Adeoya; 'on duty, off duty' Azuka Onwuka and the untimely loss of Tunmise Adekunle placed the heavy burden of effective reportage of brand communications on the shoulders of John Ajayi (publisher of Marketing Edge); Lekan Babatunde (publisher of the online Brandcrunch) and Wale Alabi (publisher of Brandwise), who lead the few veterans left on the field. Combined, the steady diminution of big time newsmakers, the near absence of 'exclusives' on jaw dropping pitches and campaigns coupled with the diminishing quality and number of hard-nosed reporters have caused significant dip in the quality of media coverage of the marketing communications sector. Much of the major news stories on issues and personalities are still pegged on the old brigade whilst the media independents sub-sector has managed to provide some editorial content relief with news of account movements that are due mainly to international agency network re-alignments. The news drought inexorably compelled several newspapers and magazines to reduce the number of pages that had hitherto been generously devoted to the reportage of marketing communications.

It will be recalled that as President of AAAN Shobanjo made a commitment to redressing the dearth of knowledge among advertising practitioners one of the pillars of his administration. Under his leadership, AAAN bought a parcel of land in the Central Business District in Ikeja, Lagos for purposes of building a Secretariat and an Advertising Academy. Whilst the Secretariat is now fully functional, the pace of success achieved for the Academy has not been at par. Successive Presidents of AAAN notably Lolu Akinwumi and his successor in office, Funmi Onabolu, however, succeeded in pushing the issue of the Academy back to the front burner to bridge the gap in the education of members. An immediate fall out of this was the appointment of Shobanjo as the Chairman of the Academy's Governing Council. Work on the academy's curriculum and its structure took a large chunk of his life, post-retirement until he stood down from the office in 2014. Whereas the Academy aims at reinforcing the intellectual quotients of individual practitioners, the real challenge is embedded in professional practice where agencies and, indeed, the industry, tend to struggle rather badly.

Prior to the 43rd Annual General Meeting of the AAAN in 2016, about 12 agencies were delisted from the Association owing to their inability to meet various membership obligations. This was a logical consequence of unmet yet cyclical challenges across all platforms of the marketing communications business. With the increasing failure of agencies and their owners to keep pace with global trends, clients were left with no choice but to look in the direction of specialist boutiques to deliver traditional agency services. Logically, too, the loss of clients' confidence translated to a steady loss of revenue stream, made worse by accelerated developments in digital marketing, media planning and buying as well as creative services. It did not come as a surprise that AAAN gradually began to lose its voice and bite. The reality of the situation dawned in 2014 when the

Federal Government appointed a non-advertising practitioner, Prince Ngozi Emioma, to succeed Lolu Akinwunmi as Chairman of APCON. The decision was not reversed until after 18 months when the combined efforts of industry stakeholders, notably, AAAN, ADVAN, OAAN, BON and MIPAN culminated in the appointment of Udeme Ufot, a former AAAN President, in February, 2015.

Like several other elders in the advertising profession, Shobanjo is discomfited by the declining influence of AAAN. Much of his concern stemmed from fears that a less vibrant AAAN could inadvertently create room for a dearth of talents and cause further complacency: "We seem to be losing steam very fast. Who is training those who are in the industry? If you do not have talents, nothing will happen. Even if a company has all the talents, it still does not say much without competition to fire you up. Complacency will set in."

His concern about the diminishing stature of AAAN was not enough for him to convince Awosika to run for the Association's presidency at a time the industry was in search of direction. A caucus within AAAN discreetly approached Shobanjo to speak with Awosika because he had the right credentials to lead the Association: he is charismatic and an intellectual powerhouse as well as a very influential networker who could win AAAN much respect and credibility. The problem was how to get him to accept to serve. The idea fizzled out when Awosika was non-commital and there was no time before the AAAN elections to exert maximum pressure on him. Besides, some members of the Association had begun to warn that he might be too hot to handle. In the end, the caucus settled for the former Managing Director of STB-McCann, Rufai Ladipo, as a compromise candidate who was eventually elected as AAAN President.

Close to the end of the first decade of his retirement from active practice, Shobanjo received a major acknowledgement of his contribution to the development of mass communication in Nigeria from an unexpected quarter. As he quietly continued to keep busy at Troyka with 'very little to do than to strategise,' his life was also being quietly reviewed by the Office of Advancement of the University of Lagos, which had stepped up its endowment drive. The University was, however, not searching for just any rich or influential donor; it was out to get men and women of integrity who were true achievers that had made positive impact in society. The Advancement Board had a huge basket of needs that included physical expansion of the Department of Mass Communication, which since its establishment in 1966, had produced graduates who had become some of the most successful executives in journalism, broadcasting, advertising and public relations in Nigeria.

The primary objective of the project was to add one more floor to the Department's existing one-storey building to accommodate the rapidly increasing population of staff and students as well as make room for audio-visual studios to aid the teaching of diverse professional courses. The university was not short of accomplished alumni who had the wherewithal to execute the project and had made significant impact on the practice of mass communication from a private sector perspective. Yet, the Office of Advancement approached Shobanjo who was neither an alumnus of the University of Lagos nor an alumnus of any university. On impulse, he declined the university's request to handle the project when his old friend and Chairman of the Advancement Board, Mac Ovbiagele, discussed the subject with him. Both men had known each other since their days at NBC. Ovbiagele refused to take Shobanjo's refusal as final.

"Orisa," he hailed Shobanjo by the peculiar nickname he calls him, "You just have to do this."

"Okay, give me time; let me think about it some more."

Shobanjo's reluctance to commit to the project was due, in part, to his involvement in several other social investment projects at the time, which made him think he probably would not have enough resources to carry the new request through. Yet, he felt uneasy about turning down a friend, just as he thought it improper and impolite to turn down a well-intentioned honour that a world-class academic institution had bestowed on him. Weeks after his initial discussions with Ovbiagele, he called to accept the university's proposition. He, however, did not reckon with some unforeseen developments that would drastically affect his decision.

The team of structural engineers and other building specialists that he sent to appraise the state of the building to which he had agreed to add one more floor came back with unexpected news: the existing structure could not support an additional floor without crashing! The only option was to pull down the structure. The report tore his original financial projections to shreds, yet he could not back out of his commitment because honour had been put on the line. The university's engineering team confirmed the findings. Approval was given for him to demolish the building. Unit companies in Troyka Holdings chipped in their widow's mite to the construction of a new structure that was supervised by Black Onyx, the real estate subsidiary of Troyka.

Tragedy struck as work on the project progressed when the university's Vice-Chancellor, Prof. Tokunbo Shofoluwe, suddenly passed on. He had shown deep interest in the project and had availed the university's benefactor every encouragement he needed to complete the task. During Shobanjo's condolence visit to Shofoluwe's home in the company of the new Vice Chancellor, Prof. Rahmon Bello, and Prof. Ralph Akinfeleye of the Mass Communication Department, he was pleasantly surprised to

discover that the late Professor's widow, Funmi, was his junior colleague at NBC. Even in her grief, she gently told Shobanjo:
"Please remember that Tokunbo's mind was on this project; I'll very much appreciate if you can complete it."

The soft-spoken widow fired Shobanjo's resolve to speedily complete the project, which was also quietly monitored by the university's new helmsman, Prof. Bello, whom Shobanjo described as a 'fine gentleman.' The imposing, well-landscaped edifice that emerged from the rubles of the old structure was appropriately named after its donor in appreciation of his contribution to the development of mass communication in Nigeria. The Biodun Shobanjo Multi-Media Centre of Excellence was formally commissioned on June 11, 2014 by Nigeria's former Head of State, General Yakubu Gowon in the company of the University's Pro-Chancellor, Prof. Jerry Gana. The Centre was thereafter handed over to the university by its deeply overwhelmed donor: "I can't express the depth of my gratitude to the university for giving me the opportunity to do this and for them acknowledging the little that one has been able to do for the mass communication industry in Nigeria. No words can express my feeling."

Although his industry strides have continued to be recognised by major players across various professional groups, the Biodun Shobanjo Multi-Media Centre of Excellence cemented his place in history both in theory and in practice. In his 42nd year in the marketing communications business and on the 40th anniversary of the birth of the Association of Advertising Agencies of Nigeria, AAAN, the Sun Newspapers crowned him in 2013 as Nigeria's Advertising Man of All Time. This was barely two weeks after he received the 2013 Lifetime Achievements Award conferred on him by MarketingWorld Magazine. In 2014, he was conferred with the D.A.M.E Lifetime Achievement Award "as worthy testament to a life of enterprise, commitment and achievement in the marketing communications sector." Indeed, with the passing of time superlatives became so much fewer that award organisers were compelled to find newer combinations to lavish praise on him. Early in 2018, two major news outlets, Silverbird Group and Daar Communications conferred on him the Extraordinary Achievements Award and Lifetime Achievements Award respectively. The Zik Prize in Professional Leadership that was conferred on him in 2016 by the Public Policy Research and Analysis Centre (PPRAC), however, came as a big surprise because it was unlike any award he had ever received. It was not about advertising or marketing communications, but it was everything about leadership across several boundaries of human endeavour.

The extent of Shobanjo's success as a career advertising practitioner is well-articulated by the late Moemeke, the man that everyone in the advertising business deferentially called 'The Source': "You just have to look around the man and what he has achieved and you cannot but recognise that he came and offered damn good service and got damn good reward for it."

Much more than the professional accolades, Shobanjo derives a lot more personal and emotional satisfaction from mirroring his journey through life from the lense of his mother, Morinatu. Many years after he got into executive management position at Grant Advertising, his mother could not get over the picture in her mind of a young man who felt terribly pained by his inability to travel overseas for further studies. Out of curiosity at the frequency of his foreign travels, she asked him if this was the same 'Ilu Oyinbo'[1] that he so desperately missed out on in the early years. Mother and son laughed heartily when he answered 'yes, it's still the same place only that it is much nearer now.' Such is the sound of success!

---

[1] *Foreign land*

This, for him, has made the sacrifices of past years well worth it. Madam Morin Shobanjo, at age 100, passed on in September, 2018, as this book was set for press.

With hard work, firm focus on goals, unrelenting acquisition of knowledge and the grace of God, Shobanjo has ticked most boxes in his life: "I kept developing myself as I made various sacrifices because if I did not, I would have been handicapped about helping people. If I had not, maybe my mother would not have lived for as long as she did. I had been her husband for nearly 60 years and she told anyone that cared to listen that 'Biodun is my husband.' That says a lot and, in itself, is good news for me. My siblings have done well. Like most Nigerian parents, we continue to make sacrifices for our children. What more can one ask for? People should never give up on doing good; there are rewards for these things, even if some people never reciprocate the gestures."

48 years into Shobanjo's journey in marketing communications and ten days to his 75th birthday, the Governing Council and the Senate of the Obafemi Awolowo University (OAU), Ile Ife, one of Nigeria's first-generation tertiary institutions, surprised him with an award of Doctor of Letters (D.Litt) Honoris Causa, which, perhaps, was the first of such honorary awards to be conferred on any Nigerian adman, dead or living, by any Nigerian university. The award, which was conferred on him at OAU's 44th Convocation ceremonies on 14 December, 2019, was 'in recognition of his outstanding corporate achievements, unique contributions to the media and communications industry, humane social activism and promotion of the ideals, vision and mission of Obafemi Awolowo University.'

He was especially humbled by the university's gesture, which he also saw as worthy recognition of the collective contributions of staff to the success of Troyka Group as an enterprise and, by extension, his personal and professional success.

Barely 24 hours after OAU, Ile Ife conferred the degree of Doctor of Letters (D.Litt) Honoris Causa on him, Shobanjo again mounted the dais to receive high honours from one of his primary constituencies, the media. On 15 December, 2019, the administrators and Board of Trustees of the Nigeria Media Merit Awards (NMMA) honoured him at the 27th NMMA grand presentation ceremony with its highest accolade of 'Distinguished Leadership Award for Outstanding Service to the Media and National Development.' This was a befitting acknowledgement of the quality of Shobanjo's personal and professional relationship with the media, which has spanned 55 years after he began his career in broadcast management as a Studio Manager (Trainee) in 1964.

By and large, the sum of the opinions of the 'Apprentices' in the rested television serial, The Apprentice Africa, has helped to succinctly capture the universality of views on Shobanjo. These all point in the direction of a committed individual who saw far into the future of his profession and properly positioned himself, personally and professionally, to lead the charge into that bright future despite all distractions along the path. The man himself fully understands this, particularly in light of the road he had travelled to achieve the level of success he had made of his life since his days of humble beginning in Jebba, Kwara State. It is for this reason that it is appropriate that the 'final word' on the remarkable Abiodun Olusina Shobanjo be pronounced by the man himself:[1]

"When you find a man who is self-confident, whether that self-confidence is based on his knowledge, his experience and other positive factors, those who do not understand where he is coming from see that as pride...I walk with my head straight because I understand the business in which I am. For goodness sake, when a man has spent (more than 40) years in a profession, he needs to walk straight...I am a very self-confident person; I have no apologies for that and that is the truth."

Exactly.

[1]*The Return of the Magi, Brands & Products, December 2003/January 2004, Page 48*

Shobanjo's Work Rules

1. Have a mission:
The dominant goal is the success of an enterprise before the fulfilment of social responsibility

2. Go for result:
Have a disciplined approach to diagnosing the problems of a brand; clients are willing to pay more for value-added

3. Know what you sell:
Product usage is rarely ever different; nobody uses Vaseline as jam on bread in Nigeria and Coke is never used to wash dishes

4. Look for opportunities:
Refuse to let them pass you by

5. Be persistent:
If there is a will to win, you can achieve excellence; excellence is being the best

6. Be consistent:
An agency that shows flashes of creativity, sound accounting, media planning, good quality production can never win, can never be the best

7. Be bold:
Never feel incomplete before anyone. You only make a good impression once; dress well and have the required dose of confidence

8. Employ the best:
Clients judge services partly by the calibre of staff that deliver them rather than by the reputation of an organisation; the quality of people can only generate quality work that will build quality brands

9. Keep your clients:
The single biggest determinant of customer retention is the retention of associates. Higher associates' retention, therefore, equals lower cost and loyal customers

10. Grow by design:
The hungriest people out there for new clients are the ones losing the ones they have and you can measure it directly in their profitability

11. Develop manpower base:
We, as CEOs, should not begin to comb other agencies with a view to luring away staff... TRAIN your people

12. Think 'breakthrough':
Help your client promote deliverables, not dreams

13. Be the best:
In today's terms, winning is not everything, it is the ONLY thing.

Leadership in Action...

(Excerpts from memos by the Chairman to CEOs
of Troyka companies)

On Building Great Institutions...

There really isn't any rocket science about building great institutions – be they countries or organisations. At the heart of the significant difference is ATTITUDE. That is why we constantly preach that developing a right attitude is critical to our making a difference. That is why we always counsel that the values which we hold dear should not be subsumed, to enable a culture of excellence emerge and be sustained.

On the relevance of an integrated network...

It is clear to me that some of our CEOs have lost touch with why Troyka started the various companies in the group. While some of you go mouthing the need for integrated communications to your clients, I am at pains to find that you and your staff pay no allegiance to companies within the group who have the collateral to offer such services. Rather, you would find pleasure and justification for recommending competitive companies who have no understanding of your client's brand proposition. Of course, you would usually find allies in those client contacts, who, strangely, pay lip service to the brand health of the brands in their custody.

While not making excuses for any of our companies who fall below par, in terms of their service delivery standards, the point should be made that we deliberately invested in these specialist companies so they can offer certain collaterals to clients so that their brands can grow, offer employment and, hopefully, make some returns to the providers of capital. By denying these companies the oxygen they deserve, it is only a matter of time that the raison d'etre for the establishment of these companies will be made nonsense of.

On what drives Troyka Group...

I always say: "If you don't know and understand the dream, you cannot live and act the dream." Our group was founded on a dream – to build a world class marketing communications group... we have always anchored our existence on people – our people. People that we trust totally, never mind that in some instances, some of these people have let us down. But this has never stopped our resolve to continue to place our trust and confidence in our people. One other point that needs to be made and very clearly, too, is that everybody in our group has the potential of becoming our leader. A leader whose opinion we would seek, and when found to be superior, we would buy. There is no mystery in the way we run our businesses...We think of the idea, flesh it and give it to our people to make it come alive. It's always our people, our people and our people. In other words: YOU!

On Sharing Experiences...

I have in the recent past been sharing my thoughts on leadership with some of the drivers of our businesses. This is so because as we continue to build our various enterprises, the need to correct misconceptions about true and enduring leadership becomes critical. It is in continuation of this exercise that I am expanding the recipients of this mail to include those, who, in my view, represent both the current and future leaders of our group.

On Leadership...

Our working definition of leadership is "the energetic process of getting other people FULLY and WILLINGLY committed to a new course of action to meet commonly agreed objectives, whilst having commonly held VALUES. So, leadership is not just about style or charisma or forcefulness. The leader, at every opportunity, must constantly articulate the vision and mission of the company so that his colleagues can fully understand it and willingly buy into it...We set out to build a company with a difference. To build such a company, we knew we had to do things differently, work extra hard and enjoy ourselves in the process. Without our people, we could not have succeeded. And because we did, our leaders were regarded as good leaders. And I think they are still seen in that light today by all stakeholders – clients, ex-staff, etc. Leadership is about understanding people and about the process of getting people all pointing and acting in the same direction. It depends on having a unique vision, making strategic choices and designing and enabling an organisation to get the job done.

On the Troyka Management Trainee Programme...
The future of our enterprise will have to be dependent on a sustained recruitment of, training and retention of the brightest and best of Nigerian university graduates from various disciplines of learning...If senior managers do not understand the importance of the MT programme, then such managers don't deserve to be in our employment. Period.

On the Secret of Business Success...
At the heart of our success will be what our most important asset (our staff) are able to achieve. The quality and quantum of their success (with our clients) will be directly proportional to how much interest we show in their lives. No staff is ever passionate about a business where the boss constantly harasses, hounds and is unsupportive of that individual. And before we forget, no boss ever succeeds if his staff do not.

On Bullying...

I cannot pretend not to have heard of bullying by senior colleagues in some of our organisations...There is no basis for turning any of our companies into military camps. There is no basis for threatening your junior colleagues as if they were some secondary school students. And worse, there is no basis for invoking silly sanctions against these people for minor offences or mistakes that could be talked over. And guess what, some of the sanctions being invoked are usually illegal, for which the employee can sue the company...When you are in a service business you need well motivated and happy people. (Bullying) is something we abhor as a group and it will never get the approval of the owners of the business.

New Year Message...

I cannot sufficiently make the point that ours is a service business. Resultantly, you must remember that you, our people, remain our most precious asset. You, as an individual, must be willing and committed to mentor, train, encourage and give opportunities for self-actualisation to your junior colleagues. Let your juniors make their mistakes – in so far as they are not mistakes of the head – they should be able to learn therefrom.

Let us banish the mentality of master/servant relationships. Rather, we should embrace the leader/junior colleague model. Because, in truth, a company is only as good as its people make it. It is the sum total of this that reflects what people see as 'the company.' We need to build friendly, warm and caring organisations; not companies where fear and bullying are the order of the day. We need to encourage our people to develop self-confidence, because it is the only way they can excel and soar away like the eagles that they are.

Finally, we must never lose sight of who our paymasters are, our clients, and must constantly make them winners. Because it is only when they win that we win also. Let us always remember that yesterday's standards belong to the past and will never be good enough. Let us always remember to challenge ourselves; it's the only way to stay at the top, it is the only way to be winners.

Hall of Fame: Shobanjo/Insight

1. PERSONAL

A) Membership of Professional Associations:
Past President, Association of Advertising Practitioners of Nigeria (AAAN)
Fellow, Advertising Practitioners Council of Nigeria (APCON)
Fellow, Commonwealth Journalists Association (CJA)
Member, International Advertising Association (IAA)
Member, Chartered Institute of Marketing, England (CIM)
Member, Institute of Public Relations, London (IPR)

B) HONOURS:

Award	Organisers	Year
50 Most Fascinating BusinessPeople	National Concord	1990
Star of Achievements	Classique Magazine	1991
Men of Achievement	Corporate Press Service	1992
Top 50 Influential Men	Poise Magazine	1993
Advertising Man of the 20th Century	Weekend Concord	1999
100 People in The News (1899 – 1999)	TheNEWS	2000
Entrepreneur of the Decade	Success Digest	2003
150 Heroes of Modern Nigeria	Daily Times	2003
Marketing Professional of the Year	BMA	2004
100 Nigerians that Ever Lived	Encomium	2004
One of beacons of National Development	Vanguard	2004
Top 25 Leaders of Professional Integrity	Daily Independent	2004
Heritage & Honours	AAAN	2005
50 Notable leaders in Corporate Nigeria	Newswatch	2005
Architect of Economic Fortunes in Nigeria	Vanguard	2005
50 Drivers of Change in Corporate Nigeria	Financial Standard	2005
30 Most Inspiring Nigerians	TheNEWS	2006
True Icons of Nigeria	TheNEWS	2008
Heroes of the Economy	Financial Standard	2008
Outstanding Role Models	The Guardian	2009
50 Yoruba Men/Women of Integrity	TheNEWS	2009
50 Notable leaders in Corporate Nigeria	Newswatch	2009
Ambassador, Mass Medical Mission	NCPP	2010
CEO of the Year	City People	2010

Award	Organisers	Year
20 Outstanding Enterpreneurs (2000-2010)	The Guardian	2010
Lifetime Achievement	NIMN	2010
Brand Personality of the Year	Marketing Edge	2011
BrandPower Award for Distinction	BrandPower	2012
Great Nigerian Entrepreneur	BusinessWorld	2012
Certificate of Excellence	Excellerate	2012
Lifetime Achievements Award	MarketingWorld	2013
Advertising Man of All Time	The Sun Newspapers	2013
Champion of Brand Trust Award	BrandHealth	2013
Lifetime Achievement Award	D. A. M. E.	2014
Most Influential Personality in Advertising in Africa	African Dev Magazine, Ghana	2014
One of Managers of the Year	Socrates Committee, UK	2015
Zik Prize in Professional Leadership	PPRAC	2016
Extraordinary Achievements Award	Silverbird Group	2018
Lifetime Achievements Award	Daar Communications	2018
Living Legends Industry Award	Red Media	-

2. INSIGHT (Circa: 1990 -2004)

A) PRINT:

Award	Organisers	Year
Most Supportive Ad Agency	National Concord	1990
Best Annual Report Design (ETB)	Adworld	1991
Golden Crown Award ('Icheoku')	Adworld	1992
Certificate of Merit ('Ponds')	Adworld	1992
Certificate of Distinction (NRC)	Adworld	1992
TV COMMERCIAL (Consumer Goods)	D.A.M.E	1993
TV Commercial (Devcom: Chief Koko)	Adworld	1993
Certificate of Distinction: (Vaseline Hair Tonic)	Adworld	1993
3rd Prize: Press Ad: (British Airways 'Oliver')	Adworld	1993
Certificate of Distinction:('NUTREND': Radio)	Adworld	1993
3rd Position: Annual Report Design (New Africa Merchant Bank '91)	Adworld	1993

TV Commercial:

Award	Organisers	Year
(Consumer Goods: 7-Up Hi-life)	D.A.M.E	1994
Best Radio Commercial		
(Consumer Goods: Indomie Noodles)	D.A.M.E	1994
Press Advertising: (British Airways 'Oliver')	D.A.M.E	1994
1st Position: Annual Report Design (ETB '92)	Adworld	1994
2nd Position: Annual Report Design		
(Devcom '92)	Adworld	1994
1st Position: Annual Report Design (ETB '93)	Adworld	1995
1st Position: TV Commercial		
(Bagco 'Business Woman')	Adworld	1996
3rd Position: TV Commercial		
(Peak Milk Fantasy Island)	Adworld	1996
1st Position: Press Advert (Services)	D.A.M.E	1997
1st Position: TV Commercial (Services)	D.A.M.E	1997
1st Position: Radio Commercial (Services)	D.A.M.E	1997
2nd Position: TV Commercial (Services)	D.A.M.E	1997
2nd Position: Radio Commercial		
(Consumer Goods: Mirinda)	D.A.M.E	1997
TV Commercial (Consumer Goods)	D.A.M.E	1998
TV Commercial (Services)	D.A.M.E	1998
Radio Commercial (Consumer Goods: Gulder)	D.A.M.E	2001
TV Commercial (Consumer Goods: Pepsi Star Wars)	D.A.M.E	2001
Press Advert (Consumer Goods: Gulder)	D.A.M.E	2001
Press Advert (Services: Soft Solution)	D.A.M.E	2001
Press Advert (Services: Econet Wireless Libertie)	D.A.M.E	2002
Agency of the Year	NPAN	2003

B) ELECTRONIC:

Award	Organisers	Year
Advert of the Year	NTA	1985
Advert of the Year (1st)	NTA	1986
Advert of the Year (2nd)	NTA	1986
Advert of the Year (Food & Beverages)	NTA	1987
Advert of the Year (2nd: Corporate Services)	NTA	1987
Client of the Year	FRCN	1988
Agency of the Year	NTA	1991

| Agency of the Year | NTA | 1992 |
| Best Copy (ETB: 'Mat') | NTA | 1992 |

CERTIFICATE OF MENTION:

Award	**Organisers**	**Year**
Best Copy (Bagco)	NTA	1992
Best Ad: General Interest		
(Nigerian: Bagco Supersack I)	NTA	1992
Certificate of Mention		
(Best Ad: General Interest)	NTA	1992
Appreciation Award	FRCN	1992
Agency of the Year	NTA	1993
Best Ad: Drugs & Cosmetics (Vaseline)	NTA	1993
Best Ad: General (Bagco 'Pick Up')	NTA	1993
Most Outstanding Ad Agency	FRCN	1995

C) General:

Positive Contribution (Ad)	Nasco Group	1991
Print Production Planning	Soatone	N/A
Grand Poster (Espero)	OAAN	1997

Point of View...

[*Reproduced below are excerpts from what may yet be the most down-to-earth contemporary appraisal of the state of advertising practice in Nigeria. The paper was presented at the APCON Executive Retreat on Advertising Policy and Strategic Planning held in August, 1997*]

INTERNATIONAL COMPETITION: CAN NIGERIA ADVERTISING MAKE AN IMPACT?
(By Biodun Shobanjo)

One can always argue whether Nigeria's attainment of Independence in 1960 was not premature just as well as the promulgation of the indigenisation decree was not a bit hasty. I wonder what advertising would have been like had the indigenisation decree not been promulgated until 2010. You only have to look at Hong Kong today opposite mainland China or compare advertising in that same country to what we have here now. Of course, the other side of the coin is to say that we would not have been able to produce so many Presidents or Heads of State and as many indigenous Managing Directors and Executive Directors of Nigerian-owned agencies. But the issue is, is it a question of quantity or quality? My honest view is that there are only very few Nigerian practitioners who can hold their own against international competition in our business. And this explains why we continually seek the intervention of foreign agencies as affiliates or partners.

AFFILIATIONS
I must be quick to add that affiliations are a third world or developing nations' phenomenon. There is a subtle acceptance that these countries are either on a learning curve, or that the economies in those countries cannot justify the establishment of fully-owned multinational agencies. For example, of the 55 countries where

Bates (Worldwide) has 178 offices, 120 are wholly owned in 35 countries. The same applies to Grey. It has 352 offices in 84 countries, where 300 are wholly owned. In the whole of Africa, Bates only had part equity in South Africa, and used to have an affiliate in Nigeria. Grey has a wholly owned agency in South Africa and six affiliates in other countries. It is the same story with Saatchi & Saatchi; Lintas; McCann-Erickson and Ogilvy & Mather. J. Walter Thompson; DDB&M; Young and Rubicam; Foote Cone & Belding (FCB); Leo Burnett and other multinational giants are yet to make an impact. If you consider that advertising spend in Africa is very small, you can begin to understand why Central Europe and Asean countries hold more attraction to these multinationals.

Today, it is true to say that only 6 agencies enjoy real affiliation status - Insight with Grey, STB with McCann, and MC&A with Saatchi & Saatchi (MC&A is now defunct, while SO&U is now the local affiliate of Saatchi & Saatchi*). Others are Sunrise, with DDB&M, LTC with J. Walter Thompson, and Lintas with Lintas Worldwide (now LOWE Lintas) and Prima Garnet with Ogilvy & Mather. (Centrespread with FCB; Novell Potta with Young & Rubicam, among many others).

I took a look at worldwide advertising expenditure amongst the first 40 advertising nations as at the end of 1993. Advertising spend excluding direct marketing was put at $218.7 billion. The United States with a spend of $85.6 billion controls 39.2% of total spend; Japan with 15.8%, came second with a spend of $34.43 billion; Germany ranked third, spending 7.7% or $16.83 billion, while UK with a $12.39 billion spend and controlling 5.7% of worldwide advertising expenditure, came fourth. Among the developing nations, Brazil came l2th with 1.4% of worldwide advertising spend. South Africa in the 25th position, spent $930 million i.e. 0.4% of worldwide spend, while Malaysia ranked 36th with 0.3% or $548 million advertising spend. Not surprisingly, Nigeria, being a non-advertising literate market was not listed. These facts, presented by me in a paper over a year ago, have been quoted copiously by many intellectuals.

I am aware that a lot of agencies have made enquiries from multinational agencies. I am also aware that some multinational agencies have made enquiries locally seeking potential partners. In a lot of cases, these multinationals have not been highly impressed with what they found on ground. Except in one or two cases, they felt that most of us belong to the third division.

AFFILIATION: OPERATION AND MANNING

My experience is that where you are able to find an affiliate and where the affiliate is genuinely committed to the relationship, you will find that certain things will be insisted upon. First, will be the structure of the agency. The company will be expected to be well structured, with a CEO who is accountable to the affiliate's regional or head office. The affiliate is not usually interested in a one-man agency but a team. The foreign partner is usually interested in seasoned practitioners. Second is accountability. The company's books must be open for scrutiny. So, you need qualified accountants as part of your team. Thirdly, where you handle any account that is a traditional client of the affiliate (and make no mistake, this is not a right), you will be expected to give a monthly status report on the local business to a worldwide Director who will usually give advice on how the business is to be managed, what international materials are being used and where. The CEO will be required to give either a monthly or quarterly report of the agency's operations - billings (estimate versus actual), reasons for differences, clients' status, staff status, financial report etc. Account receivable, payable, monthly trading report must be supplied. At the beginning or end of the year, a detailed report of the business is usually requested.

You will find that with an affiliate, a discipline of accountability is a sine qua non. Of course, if you do not have the right quality of men, these requirements may be difficult to meet. Of course, one of the things that most multinational agencies insist upon is the need for the local agency to be in an ideal location, and must also be accessible by telecommunication, notably: phone, fax, E-mail or the Internet.

NIGERIAN-OWNED AGENCIES ABROAD: WHAT IMPACT?

There has been a recent effort by one or two Nigerian agencies to fully or partly own agencies in other countries. I am aware that Ghana offered the springboard for this effort. Such efforts have either been informed by the opportunities and challenges in these countries or have been client-driven. With specific reference to the Ghanaian market, you will recall that that country went through a period of recession. For almost ten years, there was almost zero advertising. What this meant was that the advertising industry was almost paralysed; (there was) no investment in the key resource (talent). In fact, there was a massive brain drain since most professionals sought their livelihood from outside (the country). With the current upswing in Ghana's economy, the need to offer people the right to choose has become a front burner issue. Regrettably, the quality of advertising is about ten years back.

The desire to address this shortcoming necessitated the establishment of STB Ghana and Insight Advertising Accra. As in Nigeria, there are all sorts of advertising agencies - from Lintas to Media Magique (and from) Media Whizz Kid to the one-man-and-his-dog agency. Very few of these agencies parade experts. Of course, as in Nigeria, Lintas is the oldest agency, but perhaps the most tired. STB McCann is about two or three years old while Insight Advertising is seven months old. These two agencies have made so much impact within such a relatively short time. The two agencies, in my view, are the best structured agencies in Ghana today and are run on professional lines. I think STB is, perhaps, the second largest agency, and Insight must be in the 'First Five' category in terms of billings. I see this position changing rapidly in the next 12 months. As far as creativity is concerned, I suspect Insight is perhaps the most creative. The agency's creative, client service and finance departments are headed by Nigerians. Within three months of opening offices, the agency is known by 90% of client companies in Ghana. Of course, the agency has Grey Advertising as its affiliate and follows the reporting lines that all affiliates must follow.

FOREIGN AND NIGERIAN AGENCIES: A COMPARISON

I do not see major differences between well-run Nigerian agencies and their foreign counterparts, especially when the sizes are about the same.

Where you begin to notice the differences is if you were to look at agencies in terms of size. I doubt if the largest agencies in Nigeria employ more that 150 people. I also know that no agency in Nigeria bills up to N500 million i.e. less than £4 million. If you compare this with Saatchi & Saatchi London, J. Walter Thompson, Ogilvy & Mather, Grey London with billings of over £300 million and staff strength of 400, then you will begin to see the need for a different type of structure.

The very large agencies tend to have a Chairman who is usually the Chief Executive Officer. They also do have a Managing Director who runs the agency on a day-to-day basis; he is the Chief Operating Officer. There is also the tendency to have a medium to large Board of Directors who are not necessarily Executive Directors. These are usually key managers who are responsible for a set of businesses and will cut across account management, account planning, creative, media, new business, and research.

The heart of the agency in the West is usually the creative

department. The creative department of Saatchis has about 90 people. It is headed by an Executive Creative Director. It has two joint Creative Directors, and the members of the team are broken into four groups, each headed by a Head of Creative. Each group is further broken into twos - a writer and an Art Director. Each team is rewarded on chemistry, quality and speed of 'product' delivery.

Age is not usually a determinant of successful teams. For example, Nikolas Studzinki (25) and Jason Fretwell (28) are such a successful team at Saatchis. They both met in 1990 at school studying advertising and copywriting. So are Alex Paton (28) and Tim Brookes (27), a wonderful team at Collette Dickinson Pearce (CDP).

If the agency is the lead agency for a multinational business, it will also have a worldwide Board Director on the business with a whole staff complement to look after the business all over the world. Such clients as BAT, Smithkline Beecham, Mars, Nestle, Levers, Procter & Gamble, Pepsi, Coca-Cola, to mention a few, offer this challenge. Sometimes these look like mini-agencies within the agency. Running multinational accounts require a specialized skill and this explains why clients tend to stay with their agencies for a long time, and if they need to move, they usually will give the business to an agency that has this expertise.

Of course, because of the level of talents available in the West as well as their sense of responsibility and knowledge, I notice that running a foreign agency is much easier than doing same here. First, there is very little need for constant supervision as is the case here. Because you can rely on the judgement of key managers, they are encouraged to see a job through and have authority to speak for the agency before clients. In the period when Michael Bungey was Chairman of Bates London, hardly ever did he get to see BAT ads before exposure. Before he left for New York, he had only met Jimmi

Rembiszewski, the Marketing Director of BAT, twice in a period of three years. The point is: Bates has more than enough senior management people to interact with Jimmi to allow Michael rub minds with the CEO of BAT. The systems for developing great advertising, for ensuring that clients receive flawless account service, media planning and buying are followed meticulously. Everybody sees himself as a quality control point.

And because the environment is so competitive, any agency that fails to deliver on these criteria is bound to lose its clients. And with this comes automatic retrenchment. There are no sacred cows. Only a few weeks ago, the Creative Director of Bates, Tim Ashton, was relieved of his job for failing to deliver. It is not unusual to fire a whole team, including Board Directors and the top creatives on a piece of business.

Every week, Campaign carries a page on accounts under review. This clearly shows a list of dissatisfied clients who seek to find new partners. No secrets are made of this effort. The incumbent agency, the value of the account and the agencies invited to pitch are clearly stated.

Because of the competitiveness of the marketing environment in the West, the need has arisen for the establishment of specialist organizations, which hitherto had been serviced by conventional advertising agencies. Amongst these are Media Independents, Direct Mail organizations (where the communication is seen as one-on-one), compugraphic companies, Public Relations, Sales Promotion and Events Marketing. Bates' 141 is an example and they handle all BAT events marketing including the popular Golden Tones.

Today, the biggest media independents are owned by either advertising agencies or top shot media executives, and their role is to offer such media products that advertising agencies may not necessarily be able to offer.

The foreign agency parades quality experience - men who have been in the business for over 35 years - from Bob Jacoby to Nigel Grandfield to David Ogilvy, Maurice Saatchi, John Shannon, Michael Bungey, Carl Spielvogel, Bill Baker, John Periss, David Abbot, John Hegarty, John Salmon, Frank Cockman, Ed Meyer, Roger Edwards, Mike Ferrier and David Hemsley, to mention a few. Some of these men are well past their 60s or close to it. When they talk, clients listen because they know. Clients respect them; seek their views and seek their partnership and friendship. This calibre of men cut across departments - from management, to creative, to client service to media. They make the difference between excellence and mediocrity.

Operating a Nigerian agency can be a nightmare. From managing half-baked managers who parade themselves as stars, to dealing with clients who haven't the least regard for their advertising agencies, to agencies who go touting for clients' business (sometimes with unsolicited creative proposals) resulting in utter disregard for advertising practitioners by clients. The list is endless. Sometimes I am ashamed about how some of our practitioners prostitute for business, to the extent that I wonder if they've heard of 'canalization' in the advertising business. Most major agencies in the West have New Business Directors. Their task is to solicit new business in a decent manner. That is what we should be doing and not selling ourselves cheap.

The situation is exacerbated by suppliers who break delivery deadlines recklessly and printers whose knowledge of the trade is suspect. Any wonder most practitioners do not encourage their offspring to show an interest in the business? How many Moemekes, Onikoyis, Falomos, Sanwos, Okubanjos, Adekoyas, Aroloyes are in advertising practice today? The opposite is the case in the Western world; indeed, the opposite is the case in some other Nigerian professional businesses: the younger Folawiyos, Ojoras, Subomi Baloguns, Daisis, Olashores and Adegbites, are playing enviable roles in businesses where their parents have interests.

FOREIGN AND NIGERIAN CLIENTS: A COMPARISON

When I was learning the ropes in this business over two decades ago, most of my teachers were my expatriate client contacts - from the then Managing Director of Beecham to Brian Brockes, the Marketing Director of what was then Burroughs Wellcome to Peter Lang, the Managing Director of Merck Sharpe & Dhome. They were my teachers and friends. These were people old enough to be my father. They were always patient with me; they rebuked me nicely if I was stupid, but they never ceased to encourage me. We talked about their brands and how, working together in true partnership, we could make those brands winners. These men typify the foreign client.

In 1977, I was a guest of A.B. Volvo in Gotheburg, Sweden, the home of Volvo cars. At the insistence of that client, I was to spend one week in that Swedish city learning all I could about the manufacture of Volvo cars. Their view was that I could not possibly understand the brand if I did not see what was involved in its production. Of course, it made me understand why the Volvo is called the 'safety cage'. And I have since owned two Volvo cars in my life, based on my conviction of the safety of the Volvo. In 1982, I was at Stamford, Connecticut, the home of Singer Sewing Machine. In that same year, I was a guest of Champion Sparking Company in Maryland, USA - both at the invitation of these clients wanting me to learn more about their products. In 1986, British Airways took me on a tour of Heathrow Airport, where I did not only go through some simulation exercises, but physically entered most of their aircraft types including, for the first time, the Concord. BA's view (and to a large extent Saatchi's) was that to do a good job of advertising the airline in Nigeria, I needed to understand their business. I must not forget the various meetings on BAT and Smithkline Beecham in the UK and Indomie Noodles in Republic of South Africa. When you are part of a multinational agency working for a multinational client, the client insists that all his agencies worldwide must meet at least once or twice a year at the lead agency's offices to discuss his business. Of course, the client is also in attendance to give further insights into his business. It is a partnership that can never be compromised.

Only very few Nigerian clients match up to their foreign counterparts. Count yourself lucky if you find a local client who gives you a written brief. Count yourself extremely lucky if he gives you any brief at all. You must be the luckiest agency if he gives you time to think through the problem. Sometimes the foreign client gives you six to twelve weeks to develop a campaign for him. My agency recently worked for a client who expected creative campaigns for five new products in one week! When my colleagues turned up two hours late trying to meet this impossible deadline, all they received was a tirade for coming late and a lecture on how three other agencies were on the queue soliciting for his business.

A foreign client will give you product samples so you could interrogate the brands to find the unique selling proposition of these brands. In the days in which Bates used to handle Rover cars, the agency team would be given 3 samples of any new model to be advertised for three months' use. How do you write an ad on a product you have not experienced? When we do car ads in my agency, my creatives write an admixture of fiction and what they see in the car's brochure. It's a joke - from Oroyo to Milo to Nasco Cornflakes. The last time the CEO of Nasco told his marketing chaps to send the agency some product samples it took three months for the products to arrive, and this after three complaints from the agency to the client's CEO. For all you care, we were being done such a big favour. The truth is: most Nigerian clients do not appreciate the role their agencies play. If it was possible they would rather do without the 'burden'. Once upon a time in this country, clients made it a point of duty to attend agency meetings - I am talking of the most senior people in the marketing departments. Occasionally, the client company's CEO also found time to attend. The venue of such meetings was rotated between the client's office and the agency. Not any more. You'll be shocked to know that 95% of bank CEO's do not know where their agencies are located. The same is true of the Executive Directors directly responsible for the bank's advertising. Even when the agencies go to attend meetings on the client's premises, these Directors are too busy to get involved in their bank's advertising. This is the direct opposite of what you find in the West. Today, clients see account allocation to agencies as jobs for the boys. It's a question of who do you know? Where are my friends, or in which agency do I own shares?

A foreign or international client rewards his agency for work done and does so promptly. As far back as 1976, UK advertising agencies had been encouraged to raise invoices on a fortnightly basis. I understand that weekly invoices are even raised now. All sorts of modalities are constantly considered for remunerating agencies - from commissions, to fees, to bonuses. In the West, clients pay huge sums for creative work. These payments are made as at when due. This invariably enables the agencies to pay media owners and suppliers promptly. This empowers agencies to also negotiate better with these partners for the benefit of the client. Most importantly, because media owners are paid promptly, it facilitates the investment of these media owners in modern technology and research.

When I started my career in this business, one thing you didn't have to do was chase clients for payments. Don't forget, you dealt mainly with expatriates who had no need for a token before releasing your cheque. Many years post-indigenisation, most clients here put settlement of advertising bills as the last in their priority list. Excuses for this unkind act go from need to purchase foreign exchange to raw materials and spares and the need for working capital. The list goes on and on. A client once owed my company for over 12 months; when we exerted pressure on him, he proposed a 24-month repayment period. There is a bank that now owes us over N3million dating back to 10 months. The debt is not in doubt, but no concrete plan for payment has yet emerged. There is yet another who wants a 6-month campaign but would rather have a 12-month payment for the advertising. It just puts the whole client/agency relationship in perspective. Bunmi Oni of Cadbury will want quick response time from his agencies and so many alternatives, for which little or nothing should be charged.

When I recently advised all our clients that we would charge for 'intellectual property', otherwise creative work, some clients had the nerve to say they will not pay - as if this was an unknown phenomenon. There is constant friction between clients and agencies. My impression is that clients in Nigeria want something for nothing. My consolation is that we have the Felix Ohiwereis and Bola Akingbades (the new ADVAN President) of this world who say: 'don't advertise if you don't have the money to do so'. This is what it should be. Today, a lot of clients make no cashflow projections for their advertising. If we sell, we'll pay. Even when they do on a cash and carry basis, they still don't pay. APCON's involvement in the matter yielded no dividends. It is to my knowledge that when some agencies wrote their clients recently advising them of their level of indebtedness as well as requesting for account reconciliation, (this at APCON's behest), most agencies did not as much as have their letters acknowledged.

In the meantime, there is so much suspicion between media owners, agencies and other suppliers. Agencies are weakened so badly to the extent that, given their debtor position, they are unable to negotiate better for clients. Invariably, the same debtor clients go to the media directly, pay upfront or promptly and get discounts which should go to the agencies. The agency is left stranded all the time - called names by media owners and suppliers and treated as errand boys by the client. I wasn't surprised when about a week ago, a junior colleague from an agency came to me to ask, 'is there any future in this business?' I actually told him I wasn't sure. Not except most clients hearken to the voice of reason - Bola Akingbade's voice. This business is a partnership; it must be a partnership that works - apologies to Equitorial Trust Bank.

Right before our very eyes, we can literally see the media dying. They are dying because agencies owe them; they cannot invest in new technologies, in basic research, in manpower development. Same goes for the agencies. This trend must be reversed now. Clients must learn to fulfil their financial obligations so that the whole circuit can be completed. In the meantime, I can only hope that the media will stop shooting itself in the foot by dealing with clients directly.

Perhaps we played into the hands of these clients. What quality of manpower do we parade? Half baked, ill-experienced men and women who think smart suits and Beverly Hill designer frocks and fine faces will cover up for ineptitude. Where are our own equivalents of David Ogilvy, David Abbot and Ed Meyer? They've all gone into early retirement - the Moemekes, Solarus, Adeosuns, Adeoyes, Onikoyis. This is the bane of our profession. Today, we are despised by clients who hardly see our relevance in their businesses, who have little regard for our profession. Once a man turns fifty in our profession, he is thinking of retirement, because he thinks he is too old. In the West, at 70, the game has just begun.

FOREIGN VERSUS NIGERIAN MEDIA

As for the media in the West, no space or airtime is offered for sale without adequate information on why you need to buy. In Nigeria, what is uppermost is the rate, not a scientific justification for the rate. Such information as circulation figures, readership, listenership or viewership figures, audience profile, potency are taken for granted. In the West, the media saturate you with data. With the information, you can pre-determine your reach and strike levels. And such information is research-authenticated. Any wonder why clients these days are shifting from commercial media to below-the-line. They see media as a rip-off.

Advanced technology guarantees flawless reproduction and signal reception on both radio and television. The opposite is the case in Nigeria. I suppose Eddie Iroh's parallel of the trip to Mars and the queue for kerosene and petrol is still very germane here. Maybe to a large extent, the Nigerian media must have contributed to the lack of respect and suspicion between client and agencies. In any case, it was the media's constant default that gave birth to ADVAN - since advertisers felt that agencies must be in collusion with media owners for these defaults. While most newspapers print in colour in the West, we are still grappling with problems of poor black and white reproduction, running ink, poor quality newsprint in 1997, when America is about putting somebody on the moon. There just is no basis for comparison.

Whereas USA TODAY, a paper which was started in 1982 as a full colour national daily, currently has a circulation put at about 3 million daily, reaching 3.4 million on Fridays, with readership at about six million per day, Nigeria's oldest surviving newspaper the Daily Times, has a circulation currently put at 100,000 (which I doubt), with readership at 300,000 per day. TELL, the largest circulating magazine, does not do more than 27,000 weekly. How do you compare that to Time or Newsweek's American edition which runs into millions per week? In any case, didn't RMS recently tell us that readership of newspapers declined from 68% in 1994 to 22% in 1997? Conversely, literacy level developed at almost the same pace during the same period. You can see the irony of advertising practice in Nigeria.

While the electronic media in the West keeps getting more and more exciting from its programming and technological advancement, and, therefore, is able to deliver on its audience, the opposite is the case in Nigeria. The influx of private radio and television stations has resulted in massive audience fragmentation. You now need to spend five times as much as previously to reach the same target via a hit or miss approach.

INTERNATIONAL CREATIVE QUALITY

In 1977, I was a participant at a management training programme at McCann-Erickson's London office. One of the tasks we were given was to write campaigns for both Fanta and Sprite for the year 2000. This task was given to us 23 years ago! I thought that was madness, but when I recently heard the 'Welcome to the World' campaign for Fanta, I said to myself, the plans laid some 23 years ago have started coming to fruition. The Fanta commercial talks to today's kids and not yesterday's. If you followed the way the 'New Generation' campaign for Pepsi has progressed, you probably will notice that were man to inhabit the moon tomorrow, he would most likely include 50cl cans or bottles of 'Big Blue' as part of his luggage. The campaign is indeed for the new generation. It left Michael Jackson way behind and talks to those who constantly seek information from the Internet. Today's

Pepsi drinker is not necessarily a follower of a 'moon-walker' dancer whose marital life is unstable.

I have, over the years, watched keenly the quality and content of creative work from the West opposite what we do here. It will be an understatement to say that we are poles apart. Such factors as environment, level of education, experience, sophistication, production values and technology are clearly to the advantage of the international advertising agency. Because there is also plenty of time to think about the problem, I find that creative solutions from the West are usually so simple and extremely imaginative. Tony Cox, the Creative Director of BMP-DBB, says that the levels of cinematography and craft are critical for excellent creative work.

A writer like David Abbot, who personally writes most of Volvo and Sainsbury's advertisements, has been a writer for over 27 years. His art director has been in the same business for about the same time. These are great minds that enjoy what they do and are rewarded adequately. David Abbot, as Chairman of Abbot Mead Vickers BBDO, sees himself first and foremost as a copywriter. That's the title you'll find on his door. But his salary is in seven figure digits. One of the finest art directors I've met is Andrew Cracknell. As Creative Director of Bates, he brought about a change in that agency's creative profile, resulting in stunning work for Halifax, Benson & Hedges and Rover cars, to name a few. Today, Andrew Cracknell is Chairman of Ammirati Purit Lintas where his creative reputation continues to soar as well as his pay cheque. Of course, my favourite agency remains Saatchi & Saatchi London, where I have a couple of friends. Saatchi's creative reputation remains first class. This has to be so, given the manner in which the agency operates - creative freedom is the norm. There is almost a house style to Saatchi's ads and yet no two ads must look alike. The Executive Creative Director signs off all campaigns with the CEO. It also encourages a mish-mash of the young with the not-too-young. Saatchi's advertisements must always be built around the SMP - the Single-Minded Proposition or what Bates calls the USP - the Unique Selling Proposition. There must always be a hook somewhere.

To create great advertisements, most Western agencies find a central idea, and turn it into an ad that is relevant, clear and doesn't take itself seriously. When great scripts have been written, the throughput from some of the world's greatest production companies can only result in stunning, award winning and successful commercials. Such great producers as Tony Kaye and Paul Wieland are examples of those who add excellent production values.

Here at home, we take off from a disadvantaged position: a poor brief from the client, inexperienced personnel who parade themselves as star writers and artists. Based on the inadequacies which I referred to earlier on, we end up writing scripts that are unfocused - usually leaving so many messages in one commercial. Sometimes you have to try very hard to find the message. At some other time, because we cannot find the solution, we do some technological razzmatazz to cover our deficiencies. Have you noticed how many commercials will employ muffs and digital effects to deceive the client and invariably ourselves? About 30% of Nigerian television commercials must have dance sequences in them. Of course, we also forget that television is a visual medium; we over-write the audio section and turn them into mini-documentaries. Almost all commercials must 'educate'. If we must remember that all we need do is give the consumer the right to choose, then the least we can do is identify what is different in our client's brand and do this excitingly with music, a smile, a tear or a symbol.

I've heard this time and time again, that the Nigerian consumer is dumb. Yet we forget he/she is our wife, son, girlfriend, or mother.

They are not dumb. There is a lot we can plug into, being Africans, which will endear our creative work to the international community. Our culture, music, unique locations and work of art can find a place in our commercial communication. What we need are ideas-based commercials, the kind of commercial that talks to you in a human voice and is easily understood. Something I call 'story-telling' from an African perspective.

One of the exercises that multinational agencies carry out quarterly is to request current creative work from all their offices round the world. Usually you are requested to send not more than three commercials at a time. These commercials, running into hundreds, are viewed and between 15 and 20 are then selected, these representing the best work from the group. The Chairman talks about his creative vision for the group and the commercials are then dubbed and sent to each office. Insight has been a part of this exercise since 1982 when we signed on with Bates, and lately with Grey. In this 15-year period, only 4 of our commercials have so far made the grade. And we were so excited because a lot of other countries were yet to make it. Believe it or not, Bagco Supersack, shot in pidgin English was one of the successful commercials. Our recent introductory commercial for Pepsi Big Blue and Naira Lottery were the others.

Maybe the picture is not as gloomy as I have painted it. I was to read in one of our national dailies that MC&A recorded some successes within Saatchis' African network recently. That's a right way to start. If you must know a successful TV commercial, turn off the sound on your TV set. If the picture conveys a meaningful story, then you've got one.

I am aware that we have a couple of individuals whose creative talents are comparable to some of the best in the world - Banjo

Solaru, Kehinde Adeosun, Akin Odunsi, Sesan Ogunro, Jimi Awosika, Lere Awokoya, Julia Oku and Jimi Bankole, to mention a few. There might be a few that I have left out – no offence meant. What I find mainly are people writing descriptive ads or 'smart' ads that offer nothing. These are then embellished with fine drawings. Did I forget: every agency now talks of having hi-tech as a major collateral. I say foul. Your computers will never do the thinking for you. I find that we are all gravitating and ignorantly deceiving ourselves that once we are fully computerised, then we can play Saatchi & Saatchi, AMV-BBDO, or Hunt Lascaris TBWA. Didn't IBM say 'machines alone are enough'?

I believe that those who are supposed to give the throughput into enhancing our own efforts e.g. voice-over artistes, models, photographers, film production companies, producers, cine-cameramen and lighting technicians still need a lot of catching up to do. Once I saw a simple script for British Airways from Saatchis. By the time I saw the commercial produced therefrom, I had to ask myself if what was shot was from the script. The script only contains the big idea. Translating that big idea on celluloid is a different ball game. I once saw a BA commercial shot on 3 locations - the US, Australia and Spain. The result was outstanding. Here in Nigeria, you tend to get your script replicated if you are lucky, or turned upside down. The latter tends to be the case. Ask yourself: when was the last commercial shot outside Lagos? No recce, no location shots are ever presented before a shoot. TV production here is a joke.

My agency recently shot a food commercial. Not only was the food presented in a most unappetising manner, one of the models, whose role was so important, just couldn't show the facial expression desired. The mastertape kept going to and coming from the UK for post-production and we missed campaign break date by about two weeks. You ask any of our film production directors how many served their apprenticeship in reputable 'commercial production companies'. A successful career in TV broadcasting is no guarantee of success as a TV commercial producer. Whereas in the former, you tell stories in 30 minutes or one hour; in the latter, you only have 30 seconds or 60 seconds to tell your story. I have an English film producer friend who has been in the business for 32 years. In his office are two framed letters. The first was his letter of employment in 1965 as an office boy. The other was that of his appointment as an Executive Director in 1976 in the same company. He is one of the best producers of TV commercials in the UK today. Whether we like it or not, with experience comes knowledge and expertise.

Except we all serve adequate apprenticeship, we can never be professionals. That is the bane of this industry. People who have been in the business for as little as three years are suddenly becoming Creative Directors, Presidents and Managing Directors simply because they have read Mass Communication and have inadvertently been registered as Advertising Practitioners. Sometimes the law can be an ass. I read in the papers the other day how a young man (obviously a registered practitioner) who only recently worked in the PR department of an insurance company, was moved to set up an advertising agency because he found that a lot of warehouses were stocked with unsold products. He also claims that he responds to a client's brief within 24 hours. This sounds to me like an eaglet doctor who decides to open a clinic because he hears there are usually lots of patients at LUTH. He also says that any patient who comes to his clinic will be cured in 24 hours, no matter his ailment - cancer, AIDS and all.

Great advertising is rarely produced in 24 hours as our young man would want us to believe. In any case, I have seen some of the ads that this man's agency produces - I can only feel sorry for his equally ignorant clients. This is my 26th year in this profession and I can tell you that great advertising is planned and carefully thought out. It is never rushed, and there are procedures and disciplines for arriving at it. You just don't take things from the top of your head. I hope our young advertising practitioners are listening.

CONCLUSION

Can Nigerian advertising make an impact? Perhaps. Some years ago, Lintas claimed it won an award in New York with its Star Beer commercial. If we leave the awards out for a second, and you know there are lots of them - D&AD, Clio, Cannes Festival, New York Arts Festival - in South Africa, there's also an equivalent, I believe it is not impossible for Nigerian advertising to make an impact. We may have to start from the continent. I know that with the opening up of South Africa, post-apartheid, multinational clients are going to maximize their resources by developing pan-African campaigns. In fact, this has started - Lux, Pampers, Malta Guinness. This could form a basis for assessing the creative ingenuity of Nigerian agencies, especially those that are a part of multinational agencies.

I also hold the view that given the fact that the world is becoming a global village, if we discharge ourselves creditably, we may even find a situation where Nigerian or African concepts can become global. For example, if Insight is able to come out with breakthrough advertising for Indomie Noodles, the concept could be adapted in other Indomie markets. I am aware of discussions in this regard. But be not deceived, the quality of work from South Africa is as good as what you get from Europe and America.

One sure way in which Nigerian agencies can accelerate the learning process could be the involvement of international agencies. I do not see these multinationals coming to float their agencies. Firstly, the political and economic climate does not justify the investment. Secondly, billing levels are abysmally low to warrant the trouble. However, through affiliations or part ownership, this could be possible. From this kind of relationship will come shared knowledge, accelerated training both locally and overseas (if you can pay for it), and the possibility of shared multinational clients. Please note that this is not necessarily automatic and should never be the reason why you want a partnership.

I suspect that the interaction of the West and Nigerian agencies can only result in the enhancement of our creative product. I was watching one of the cable channels the other day, and was astonished at developments amongst the Asean states. They represent a great chunk of what is referred to as areas of advertising boom. Why would the West abandon these politically and economically stable, viable and vibrant markets for ours? To those who are losing sleep over the possibility of multinational agencies invading this market because of some decree, I say, please take a good dose of sleeping tablets because it's not going to happen. Maybe with some luck we may get a few more affiliations.

If you also look at the multinational brands in this market (they happen to receive the most marketing support appropriation), you will find that they pale into insignificance compared to the top 100 UK brands. Why aren't those mega brands here? The truth is, if they are not, we would not have mega advertising budgets.

I believe that the interaction of the West and Nigerian agencies can only result in the enhancement of our creative product, and maybe by the magical year 2010, we can begin to make an impact internationally.

Index

Index

Printed in Great Britain
by Amazon